LANGUAGE APTITUDE

Language Aptitude: Advancing Theory, Testing, Research and Practice brings together cutting-edge global perspectives on foreign language aptitude. Drawing from educational psychology, cognitive science, and neuroscience, the editors have assembled interdisciplinary authors writing for an applied linguistics and education audience. The book is broken into five major themes: revisiting and updating current language aptitude theories and models; emerging insights from contemporary research into language aptitude and the age factor or the critical period hypothesis; redefining constructs and broadening territories of foreign language aptitude; exploring language aptitude from a neurocognitive perspective; and exploring future directions of foreign language aptitude research. Focused on critical issues in foreign language aptitude and second language learning and teaching, this book will be an important research resource and supplemental reading in both applied linguistics and cognitive psychology.

Zhisheng (Edward) Wen (PhD, Chinese University of Hong Kong) is currently an Associate Professor in the School of Languages and Translation at Macao Polytechnic Institute, Macao, China, having previously taught at universities in Hong Kong and mainland China for over 15 years.

Peter Skehan (PhD, Birkbeck College, University of London) has worked as a Professor at St Mary's University College, Twickenham, London; the University of Auckland; Chinese University of Hong Kong; King's College London; and Thames Valley University.

Adriana Biedroń (PhD, School of English, Poznań) is currently Professor of English at the Faculty of Philology, Pomeranian University in Słupsk, Poland.

Shaofeng Li (PhD, Michigan State University) is Associate Professor of Foreign and Second Language Education at Florida State University and previously worked as a Senior Lecturer in Applied Language Studies at the University of Auckland.

Richard L. Sparks (EdD, University of Cincinnati) is a Professor Emeritus in the Mount St Joseph University's Department of Graduate Education, USA.

Second Language Acquisition Research Series
Susan M. Gass and Alison Mackey, Series Editors

The *Second Language Acquisition Research* series presents and explores issues bearing directly on theory construction and/or research methods in the study of second language acquisition. Its titles (both authored and edited volumes) provide thorough and timely overviews of high-interest topics and include key discussions of existing research findings and their implications. A special emphasis of the series is reflected in the volumes dealing with specific data collection methods or instruments. Each of these volumes addresses the kinds of research questions for which the method/instrument is best suited, offers extended description of its use, and outlines the problems associated with its use. The volumes in this series will be invaluable to students and scholars alike and perfect for use in courses on research methodology and in individual research.

Language Aptitude
Advancing Theory, Testing, Research and Practice
Edited by Zhisheng (Edward) Wen, Peter Skehan, Adriana Biedroń, Shaofeng Li and Richard L. Sparks

Of related interest:

Second Language Acquisition
An Introductory Course, Fourth Edition
Susan M. Gass with Jennifer Behney and Luke Plonsky

Second Language Research
Methodology and Design, Second Edition
Alison Mackey and Susan M. Gass

For more information about this series, please visit:
www.routledge.com/Second-Language-Acquisition-Research-Series/book-series/
LEASLARS

LANGUAGE APTITUDE

Advancing Theory, Testing, Research and Practice

Edited by Zhisheng (Edward) Wen, Peter Skehan, Adriana Biedroń, Shaofeng Li and Richard L. Sparks

Routledge
Taylor & Francis Group

NEW YORK AND LONDON

First published 2019
by Routledge
52 Vanderbilt Avenue, New York, NY 10017

and by Routledge
2 Park Square, Milton Park, Abingdon, Oxon, OX14 4RN

Routledge is an imprint of the Taylor & Francis Group, an informa business

© 2019 Taylor & Francis

Library of Congress Cataloging-in-Publication Data
A catalog record for this book has been requested

ISBN: 978-1-138-56386-5 (hbk)
ISBN: 978-1-138-56387-2 (pbk)
ISBN: 978-1-315-12202-1 (ebk)

Typeset in Bembo
by Apex CoVantage, LLC

MIX
Paper from
responsible sources
FSC
www.fsc.org   FSC® C013056

Printed and bound in Great Britain by
TJ International Ltd, Padstow, Cornwall

CONTENTS

CONTRIBUTORS

Raphael Berthele (PhD) is Professor in Multilingualism at the University of Fribourg. He directs the MA programmes in multilingualism studies and in foreign language didactics, and he co-founded the Fribourg Institute of Multilingualism in 2008. His research interests cover different areas from cognitive to social aspects of language use. His main interest currently lie on the empirical investigation of multilingual language learning and using, focusing on topics such as literacy development, receptive multilingualism, and convergence phenomena in the semantic and syntactic patterns in linguistic reference to space. His recent books include *Age and Foreign Language Learning in School* (Springer, 2015) and *Heritage and School Language Literacy Development in Migrant Children: Interdependence or Independence?* (Multilingual Matters, 2018)

Adriana Biedroń (PhD, University of Adam Mickiewicz, Poznań, Poland) is Professor of English at the Faculty of Philology, Pomeranian University, in Słupsk, Poland. Her main areas of interest are SLA theory and research and individual differences in SLA, in particular, foreign language aptitude, working memory, intelligence, personality factors, and linguistic giftedness. Her recent publications include *Foreign Language Aptitude: Yesterday, Today and Tomorrow* (co-authored with Zhisheng (Edward) Wen and Peter Skehan, 2017, *Language Teaching*), *New Conceptualizations of Linguistic Giftedness* (co-authored with Mirosław Pawlak, 2016, *Language Teaching*) and *Polish Listening Span: A New Tool for Measuring Verbal Working Memory* (co-authored with Mirosław Pawlak and Katarzyna Zychowicz, *Studies in Second Language Learning and Teaching*, 2017).

Joshua Buffington is currently a graduate student in Psychology at the University of Illinois at Chicago (UIC). His research interests include the contributions of long-term memory systems to second language acquisition. Prior to coming to UIC, Josh completed an MA in Linguistics at Cornell University and a BA in English with minors in Psychology and Spanish at Texas A&M University.

Robert DeKeyser (PhD, Stanford University) is Professor of Second Language Acquisition at the University of Maryland. His research focuses on topics such as implicit vs. explicit learning, automatization of rule knowledge, individual differences, and study abroad. He has published in a variety of journals, including *Studies in Second Language Acquisition, Language Learning, Applied Linguistics*, and *Applied Psycholinguistics*; he has also contributed chapters to several highly regarded handbooks. In 2007 he published an edited volume with Cambridge University Press entitled *Practice in a Second Language: Perspectives from Applied Linguistics and Cognitive Psychology*. He served as editor of *Language Learning* from 2005 to 2010.

Rod Ellis (PhD, University of London) is currently a Research Professor in the School of Education, Curtin University, in Perth, Australia. He is also a professor at Anaheim University, a visiting professor at Shanghai International Studies University as part of China's Chang Jiang Scholars Program, and an Emeritus Professor of the University of Auckland. He has recently been elected as a fellow of the Royal Society of New Zealand. His published work includes articles and books on second language acquisition, language teaching, and teacher education. His latest book is *Becoming and Being an Applied Linguist* in 2016 (John Benjamins). Other recent publications include *Language Teaching Research and Language Pedagogy* in 2012 (Wiley-Blackwell with Natsuko Shintani), *Exploring Language Pedagogy and Second Language Acquisition Research* in 2014 (Routledge) and *Understanding Second Language Acquisition, Second Edition* in 2015 (Oxford University Press). He has also published several English language textbooks, including *Impact Grammar* in 1998 (Pearson: Longman). He has held university positions in six different countries and has conducted numerous consultancies and seminars throughout the world.

Michael Erard (PhD, University of Texas at Austin) is currently writer in residence at the Max Planck Institute for Psycholinguistics in Nijmegen, Netherlands. Trained as a linguist, he has spent two decades writing for *Science, The Atlantic, The New York Times, New Scientist, Aeon,* and other publications about language and linguistics topics. He is the author of two books, *Um . . . : Slips, Stumbles, and Verbal Blunders, and What They Mean* (Pantheon, 2007) and *Babel No More: The Search for the World's Most Extraordinary Language Learners* (Free Press, 2012), which has been translated into six languages. From 2008 to 2013, he was senior researcher at the MacArthur award–winning FrameWorks Institute. In 2016, the Linguistic Society of America awarded him its Language, Linguistics, and the Public award.

Gisela Granena (PhD, University of Maryland) is an Associate Professor in the School of Languages of the Universitat Oberta de Catalunya. She has published research on the role of cognitive aptitudes in both instructed and naturalistic learning contexts, aptitude–treatment interactions, task-based language teaching (TBLT), measures of implicit and explicit language knowledge, and the effects of early and late bilingualism on long-term L2 achievement. Recent publications include *Sensitive Periods, Language Aptitude, and Ultimate L2 Attainment* (John Benjamins, 2013) and *Cognitive Individual Differences in Second Language Processing and Acquisition* (John Benjamins, 2016).

Amelia Lambelet (PhD). At the time of writing the chapter, Amelia Lambelet was a Senior Researcher at the University of Fribourg, Switzerland. She is now a Visiting Scholar at the University of Maryland (USA), working on a longitudinal research project on age effect and foreign language aptitude outside the classroom. Her research expertise includes individual differences in foreign language learning, receptive multilingualism and heritage speakers' language development. Her recent books include *Age and Foreign Language Learning in School* (Springer, 2015, with Raphael Berthele) and *Heritage and School Language Literacy Development in Migrant Children: Interdependence or Independence?"* (Multilingual Matters, 2018, with Raphael Berthele).

Lanrong Li (PhD, Beijing Normal University) is currently pursuing her second doctoral degree in Educational Measurement and Statistics at Florida State University. Her research interests include foreign language aptitude, individual differences in second language acquisition, the Rasch model, and issues in educational statistics.

Shaofeng Li (PhD, Michigan State University) is an Associate Professor of Foreign and Second Language Education at Florida State University. He is also a Yunshan Chair Professor at Guangdong University of Foreign Studies. He has worked in China, New Zealand, and the United States and has extensive teaching experience in various instructional and cultural settings. His main research interests include language aptitude, working memory, form-focused instruction, task-based language teaching, corrective feedback, and research methods. His publications have appeared in *Applied Linguistics, International Review of Applied Linguistics, Language Learning, Language Teaching Research, Modern Language Journal,* and *Studies in Second Language Acquisition,* among many others.

Minhua Liu (PhD, University of Texas at Austin) is Professor in the Translation Programme of Hong Kong Baptist University, having previously taught in Taiwan and the United States. She is co-editor of the international journal *Interpreting* and sits on the advisory board of several peer-reviewed journals. Her research focuses on cognition of interpreting, testing in interpreting, and language policy. One of her research projects led to Taiwan's first certification examination for translators and interpreters.

Julie Luebbers (PhD) currently teaches at Thomas More College in Crestview Hills, Kentucky. She has teaching and research interests in foreign language acquisition and pedagogy (also teaches undergraduate Spanish) and pre-service teacher identity development. Her recent publications can be read in *Foreign Language Annals, Journal of Learning Disabilities*, and *CTSCFL Report 2017*.

Shaoqian (Sheila) Luo (PhD, Chinese University of Hong Kong) is currently a Professor in the School of Foreign Languages and Literature, Beijing Normal University, China. Her research interests include task-based language teaching and learning, language testing and assessment, Chinese as a second language teaching and learning, and foreign language teacher development.

Kara Morgan-Short (PhD, Georgetown University) is an Associate Professor at the University of Illinois at Chicago (UIC) with a joint appointment in the Department of Hispanic and Italian Studies and the Department of Psychology, where she directs the Cognition of Second Language Acquisition Laboratory. Kara is also affiliated with the Laboratory of Integrative Neuroscience at UIC, is currently an Associate Editor for *Language Learning*, and serves on editorial boards. Her research is informed by the fields of linguistics, cognitive psychology, and neuroscience and aims to elucidate the neurocognitive processes underlying adult-learned language acquisition and use. Results of her work have been published in such journals as *Language Learning*, *Studies in Second Language Acquisition*, *Bilingualism: Language and Cognition*, and *Journal of Cognitive Neuroscience*.

Jon Patton (PhD) is a Senior Research Computing Specialist and an Adjunct Assistant Professor in Computer Science and Engineering at Miami University in Oxford, Ohio. His research interests include applied statistics, translation studies, and optimization. He has co-authored (with Richard L. Sparks and Leonore Ganschow) several articles in language learning. Also he (along with Fazli Can) has contributed a chapter 'Determining Translation Invariant Characteristics of James Joyce's *Dubliners*' in the monograph *Quantitative Methods in Corpus-Based Translation Studies* (2012).

Daniel J. Reed (PhD, Indiana University) has served as Head of Testing for the English Language Center (ELC) at Michigan State University (MSU) since 2005. He oversees test administration as well as research and test development in support of MSU's English exams for incoming international students. Under Dr. Reed's direction, the ELC provides exams that are used for the following purposes: determining whether international students have met MSU's English proficiency requirement for admission, placing students into English language classes, and evaluating the spoken English proficiency of graduate students who are non-native speakers of English and candidates for teaching assistant positions. Dr. Reed has played major roles in the development of proficiency tests in more than half a dozen languages and has conducted research on language aptitude and the learning of less commonly taught languages. He also serves on the board of directors for the Language Learning and Testing Foundation. In addition, Dr. Reed, along with ELC Director Dr. Susan Gass, has led the development of a large-scale English language testing program in Greece in collaboration with Anatolia College and the American College of Greece.

Susanne Maria Reiterer (PhD, University of Vienna) is currently Associate Professor at the Linguistics Department and Centre for Teacher Education at the University of Vienna. She has research interests in cognitive neuroscience of multilingualism and second language acquisition, aiming to contribute to improvements in language learning/teaching methodology. Despite a general interest in the "neurobiology of language" and brain imaging (fMRI and EEG), one of her main interests centers around hyperpolyglottism and individual differences in language talent (native and foreign language aptitude) and how this relates to linguistic theory. Dr. Reiterer has published widely in top-notch journals in linguistics, psychology, and neuroscience, such as *Cortex, Frontiers in Psychology, Brain and Language, Bilingualism,* etc. Her books include *Language Talent and Brain Activity* (Mouton de Gruyter, 2009) and *Exploring Language Aptitude: Views from Psychology, the Language Sciences, and Cognitive Neuroscience* (2018, Springer).

Peter Skehan (PhD, University of London) is currently a Professorial Research Fellow at St Mary's University College, London, having previously worked at Auckland University, The Chinese University of Hong Kong, King's College London, and Thames Valley University. Professor Skehan's research interests and numerous publications lie in major areas of applied linguistics and SLA such as L2 task-based language teaching, learning and testing, and individual differences (especially foreign language aptitude). His early influential books included *Individual Differences in Second Language Learning* (1989, Edward Arnold), *A Cognitive Approach to Language Learning* (1998, Oxford University Press), and *Researching Pedagogical Tasks* (Routledge, 2001, with Martin Bygate and Merrill Swain). His more recent volumes are *Processing Perspectives on Task Performance* (John Benjamins, 2014) and *Second Language Task-Based Performance* (Routledge, 2018). Professor Skehan is a recipient of the International Association of Task-based Language Teaching Distinguished Achievement award.

Richard L. Sparks (EdD, University of Cincinnati) is Professor Emeritus at Mt. St Joseph University in Cincinnati, Ohio, where he taught courses in reading science, learning disabilities, educational assessment, and research/statistics. His research interests are reading and reading disabilities (dyslexia), foreign (second) language learning, second language aptitude, individual differences in language learning, and postsecondary learning disabilities. He has published extensively in the native language (L1), second language (L2), and learning disabilities (LD) literature in venues such as *Modern Language Journal, Language Learning, Journal of Learning Disabilities, Journal of Educational Psychology, Language Teaching*, and *Foreign Language Annals* and has published several book chapters in second language volumes. He serves as Consulting Editor for the *Journal of Learning Disabilities*. Dr. Sparks also has a private practice in which he conducts psychoeducational evaluations and serves as a disability consultant for professional testing agencies and licensing boards.

Charles W. Stansfield (PhD, Florida State University) is president and founder of the Language Learning and Testing Foundation (LLTF). Since its founding in 2003, LLTF is the publisher of the MLAT and other language aptitude tests. In 1994, he founded and served as president of Second Language Testing, Inc. (SLTI), which was acquired by Berlitz Languages, Inc., in 2011. SLTI develops second language proficiency instruments and practical approaches to the testing of non-native English speakers. Dr. Stansfield has published and lectured on the testing of all four language skills and on the testing of translation and interpretation performance. In 1992 Dr. Stansfield became the founding president of the International Language Testing Association (ILTA). From 1986 to 1994, he served as Director of the ERIC Clearinghouse for Languages and Linguistics and the Division of Foreign Language Education and Testing at the Center for Applied Linguistics (CAL) in Washington, DC. From 1981 to 1986, he was an associate director of the TOEFL program at Educational Testing Service (ETS). From 1970 to 1981, he was a professor of Spanish and applied linguistics at the University of Colorado. Dr. Stansfield is widely respected as a teacher and trainer. He is author, co-author, or editor of a dozen books and monographs, as well as 60 articles, mostly on language testing.

Loan C. Vuong (PhD, Rice University). Her research focuses on sources of individual differences in language learning and processing, including the role of executive functions in semantic and syntactic interpretation among healthy and aphasic individuals. Her current projects include examining bilingual language development in Vietnamese children who learn English in an immersed context in the United States and those who learn English in instructed contexts in Vietnam.

Zhisheng (Edward) Wen (PhD, Chinese University of Hong Kong) is currently an Associate Professor at Macao Polytechnic Institute, Macau SAR, China. He has teaching and research interests in second language acquisition, psycholinguistics, cognitive sciences, and translation studies, with a particular focus on the roles of foreign language aptitude and working memory in first and second language learning. Besides this current edited volume, his other books include *Working Memory in Second Language Acquisition and Processing* (2015, Multilingual Matters), *Working Memory and Second Language Learning* (2016, Multilingual Matters), and two forthcoming volumes on *Researching L2 Task Performance and Pedagogy: In Honor of Peter Skehan* (John Benjamins, 2019) and *Cognitive Individual Differences in Second Language Acquisition: Theories, Assessment and Pedagogy* (Mouton de Gruyter, 2019).

Patrick C. M. Wong (PhD, University of Texas at Austin) is the Stanley Ho Chair in Cognitive Neuroscience and Professor of Linguistics at The Chinese University of Hong Kong (CUHK). He is also the Founding Director of the Brain and Mind Institute at CUHK. His research, supported continuously by the National Insitutes of Health (NIH) for more than a decade, examines the neural basis and disorders of language and music, covering topics such as neural predictors of language learning success, speech perceptual learning, cochlear implants, and amusia. He was on the faculty at Northwestern University before moving to Hong Kong, and is a licensed speech-language pathologist in Illinois. He is a two-time recipient of the Faculty of Arts Outstanding Teaching Award at CUHK.

Yucel Yilmaz is an Assistant Professor of Second Language Studies at Indiana University. His research focuses on second language interaction and corrective feedback, computer-mediated communication, task-based language teaching, individual differences in second language acquisition, and explicit and implicit learning processes. His recent publications include *Cognitive Individual Differences in Second Language Processing and Acquisition* (John Benjamins, 2016).

Jinxing Yue (PhD, IDEALAB programme at the University of Groningen and University of Newcastle upon Tyne) is currently an Associate Professor in the English Department at Harbin Institute of Technology, China. Dr. Yue's research interests include neuro/psycholinguistics and second language acquisition. His research focuses on the neurocognitive bases of linguistic knowledge and language learning by applying behavioural and electrophysiological methods. His recent publications include the papers 'Early access to lexical-level phonological representations of Mandarin word-forms' (with K. Alter, D. Howard, and R. Bastiaanse) in *Language, Cognition and Neuroscience* (2017) and 'Cortical plasticity induced by rapid Hebbian learning of novel tonal word-forms' (with R. Bastiaanse and K. Alter) in *Brain and Language* (2014).

FOREWORD

Rod Ellis

The study of language aptitude (LA) is a major strand in second language acquisition (SLA) research. But it did not start off as such. John Carroll's seminal work in developing the Modern Language Aptitude Test (MLAT) was not motivated by any wish to explain how second language (L2) acquisition happens, but by the need to be able to identify those language learners most likely to benefit from language instruction. That is, it had a practical goal. Nor did early work in SLA, as reflected in the theories of Corder and Selinker in the 1960s, pay much attention to LA. In my book on early SLA research (Ellis, 1985), LA warranted just two pages in a chapter entitled "Individual Learner Differences". It was not until much later that LA was viewed as a construct that could help explain how an L2 is acquired. In the second edition of my book (Ellis, 2015), LA warranted seven pages in a chapter I labeled "Psychological Factors and Second Language Acquisition". There were also numerous references to it in other chapters. In the 30 years that separated the publication of these two books, LA had metamorphosed from a test for measuring learners' potential for learning to an explanatory factor relevant to just about all the central issues in SLA.

My discussion in the 1985 book was, in fact, quite critical of the LA construct. I noted that it was not really clear what cognitive abilities were subsumed under it and that the tests used to measure it were inadequate because L2 acquisition involved not just the ability to master the sound and grammatical systems of a language but also the ability to use these systems to communicate meanings. I also noted that it was not clear to what extent general intelligence and LA were separate constructs. I pointed out that LA might only be relevant to the conscious processes involved in 'learning', not the implicit processes involved in 'acquisition', as Krashen (1981) argued. In other words, aptitude tests perhaps only provided measures of the academic abilities required for the formal study of languages, not of the abilities involved in the learning of languages naturalistically. Finally, I speculated that while LA predicted the rate and success of language learning, it was of no relevance to explaining the universal route of acquisition, which was the focus of much early SLA research.

The second edition of my book presented a much more favourable account of LA. I commented that LA and general intelligence were related but also distinct constructs. I acknowledged the robustness of Carroll's MLAT as a measure of LA and that LA was "probably the single best predictor of achievement in a second language" (Gardner & McIntyre, 1992). I pointed to research that had shown that because tests such as the MLAT provide measures of different abilities, they can help differentiate learners not just in terms of their overall aptitude but also in terms of the particular abilities they possess. In other words, LA allowed for more than one route to success in learning an L2. I discussed the key issue of whether LA is fixed and immutable or modifiable through training and experience and suggested that the answer might depend on specific abilities—for example, phonological sensitivities could change over time. I also addressed whether LA served as a factor that could explain implicit as well as explicit learning and whether the importance of different cognitive abilities (e.g. memory and language analytical ability) differed according to the learners' age (e.g. young children vs. adolescents or adults). Finally, I referred to research that had investigated the interaction between type of instruction (e.g. implicit and explicit) and type of abilities. I concluded by examining proposals (e.g. Skehan, 2002) for incorporating working memory into a model of LA and of building a theory of LA that explained how the different abilities that comprise LA relate to different L2 processes. In short, the second edition of my book positioned LA as a key construct in SLA. It could explain not just the rate and success of L2 learners but also the processes involved in both explicit and implicit L2 learning. It was implicated in the effectiveness of different kinds of instruction. So where LA was peripheral in SLA in 1985, it had become central in 2015. Today no account of SLA is complete without considering LA. For this reason alone, the current collection of chapters on LA is most welcome.

The current volume reflects the issues I raised in the 2015 edition of my book. A key issue continues to be how best to assess LA. Articles in Part I of the book describe developments in the MLAT and the design of completely new tests. Then the question of the role that LA plays in learners of different ages is addressed in Part II, with chapters reporting studies with primary-level and high school learners. The aptitudes involved in different kinds of learning and the importance of different types of memory are considered in Part III and Part IV.

Like all good books, this book does more than just reflect the current state of research into LA. It offers some new lines of enquiry. Li and Luo, for example, describe the development and validation of a test for Chinese EFL learners. Liu asks what kinds of abilities are required for skilled interpreting. Two studies (Biedroń; Erard) consider the abilities of exceptional language learners. Another two studies (Yue; Reiterer) investigate the neural correlates of aptitude abilities. This is especially interesting, as this approach may provide evidence that will help to distinguish the different abilities involved in different aspects of language learning more definitively.

There is now a wealth of empirical studies that have investigated LA. This is an area ripe for meta-analysis. Li draws conclusions from three meta-analyses that he has recently published. His chapter helps to bring theory, research findings, and applications together. DeKeyser, and Vuong and Wong too, offer a synoptic account of aptitude research—both chapters also consider future directions. One such direction is the need for more and better-designed aptitude–treatment interaction (ATI) studies to help optimize instruction for learners with different abilities. Here, however, I see the need for caution. Many factors, affective as well as cognitive, that interact in complex ways go into what makes instruction effective for particular learners. It is doubtful whether isolating specific aptitude abilities for treatment in ATI studies will tell us much about what kinds of instruction are the most effective for particular learners. And even if this does prove possible, it is difficult to see how aptitude–instruction matching is logistically manageable in the large classes where most of world's language learners learn a language. LA research is of obvious importance for theory testing and theory building in SLA—as the chapters in this book demonstrate—but more thought is needed about how to make the best use of this research in language instruction.

References

Ellis, R. (1985, 2015). *Understanding second language acquisition*. Oxford: Oxford University Press.

Gardner, R., & McIntyre, P. (1992). A student's contributions to second language learning. Part 1: Cognitive variables. *Language Teaching, 25*, 211–220.

Krashen, S. (1981). *Second language acquisition and second language learning*. Oxford: Pergamon.

Skehan, P. (2002). Theorizing and updating language aptitude. In P. Robinson (Ed.), *Individual differences and instructed language learning* (pp. 69–95). Amsterdam, The Netherlands: John Benjamins Publishing Company.

ACKNOWLEDGMENTS

The successful completion of this volume would not have been possible without the generous support and the amazing help from many organizations and individuals, to whom we wish to express our sincere gratitude. To begin with, as the book has grown largely from major papers that had been presented at the 2017 Macao International Round Table Forum on "Language Aptitude" (6–9 June 2017, Macao), the editors wish to gratefully acknowledge the financial commitments and the logistics support provided by the host, Macao Polytechnic Institute (MPI), which enabled the successful organization of the round table as part of the 6th International Conference on English, Discourse and Intercultural Communication (EDIC). In particular, our heartfelt thanks are due to the following administrative and academic units as well as the many faculty and staff at MPI: the board of management (Prof. Lei Heong Iok, former President; Prof. Im Sio Kei, Marcus, current President; Dr. Cheang Mio Han, Hester, Secretary-General); School of Languages and Translation (Prof. Luciano Rodrigues de Almeida, former Director; Dr. Lili Han, current Director; Dr. Lily Lim, coordinator of the Chinese-English Translation and Interpretation Program; the staff at the general office Manuela and Carmen); MPI-Bell Center and the EDIC conference committee (Prof. Lin Ziyu, David Sansom, Joanna Radwanska-Williams, Linda Lam, Isabel Ma); and the Public Relations Office (Ms. Dina Ferreira Martins). Our former MPI colleague and initiator cum founder of EDIC, Chairman Mao Sihui, Executive Director of the International Association of Intercultural Communication Studies (IAICS) and Dean of the Faculty of Arts of Shantou University, also deserves our special thanks for his great support and endorsement to the Aptitude Round Table from the very beginning.

We also wish to place on record our sincere gratitude to the incredible help from our sponsors of the Round Table. These have included, first and foremost, the Faculty of Arts and Humanities (FAH) of the University of Macau (UM) and, in particular, the Dean of FAH, Chair Professor Honggang Jin, for the generous and timely financial support and for her impeccable academic leadership (as our co-convener of the Round Table) in gracefully steering the second phase of the forum held on the UM campus. Our appreciation also goes to the incredible help (especially in logistics) from the professional and efficient team at UM (Xiaoming Hou and Iny Chan in particular). Our three other sponsors also deserve our sincere thanks for their great support to the Round Table: ShenZhen Polytechnic Institute (in particular, Prof. Kesheng Tang, Dean of School of Applied Foreign Languages, and his team: Prof. Yanyu Li, Meryl Zhao Minyi, Fiona Jiang Ying in particular); and the Asia Pacific Association of English for International Communication (in particular, Prof. Gengshen Hu and Xiaohua Jiang).

Most important of all, the editors wish to thank all the authors of the book chapters for their commitments (in terms of time, energy, and money) towards completion of this book project, by first traveling all the way to attend our Round Table in Macau and then by contributing their chapters to our volume. With respect to the reviewing of chapters, some of our chapter authors deserve another round of thanks for having not just written their own chapters but also helped in reviewing other chapters (Robert DeKeyser, Charles W. Stansfield, and Kara Morgan-Short in particular). Related to this, we also acknowledge our sincere thanks to the external reviewers for their professional and prompt reviews of major chapters in the book. These have included (in alphabetical order) Alan Juffs (University of Pittsburgh), Richardo Munoz Martin (Universidad de Las Palmas de Gran Canaria), Jing Yang (Guangdong University of Foreign Studies), and Hui Zhang (Nanjing Normal University). Their professional commitments have ensured both the quality and the smooth progress of this volume towards its completion. Last but not least, the editors wish to extend our special thanks to Rod Ellis and Loan C. Vuong and Patrick C. M. Wong for agreeing to write the Foreword (Ellis) and the Epilogue (Vuong and Wong) to our book at such short notice.

Needless to say, the successful publication of this book would not be possible without the endorsement and support from Susan Gass and Alison Mackey (Series Editors of the 'Second Language Acquisition Research' series) and the Taylor & Francis Routledge editorial team (first Kathrene Binag, Judith Newlin, and then Elysse Preposi, and finally Helena Parkinson and Ze'ev Sudry). A big "thank-you" to you all for your great support to our language aptitude endeavors!

Zhisheng (Edward) Wen
Peter Skehan
Adriana Biedroń
Shaofeng Li
Richard L. Sparks

1

INTRODUCTION AND OVERVIEW

Zhisheng (Edward) Wen, Peter Skehan, Adriana Biedroń, Shaofeng Li, and Richard L. Sparks

Researching Language Aptitude: From Prediction to Explanation

In its broadest sense, the concept of foreign language aptitude refers to the special talent that allows one to learn a foreign or second language (L2) faster and more effectively than others (Carroll, 1962, 1981, 1990). Since its inception in the late 1950s and 1960s, foreign language aptitude underwent a period of relative marginalization that lasted for several decades (Skehan, 1998, 2012; Wen, Biedroń, & Skehan, 2017). Since the early 2000s, however, there has been a renewed enthusiasm for language aptitude research (as shown visually in Figure 17.1 from Vuong & Wong, this volume). When contemporary foreign language aptitude is interpreted from the framework of developmental paths and essential constituents of an aptitude theory (e.g., as conceived by Snow, 1992), the half-century period (from the 1950s to the 2000s) could be considered the first phase of aptitude research. This period was dominated by John Carroll's early work, especially his Modern Language Aptitude Test (MLAT, Carroll & Sapon, 1959/2002), and characterized by a strong focus on psychometric testing and Carroll's four-factor aptitude model, which has provided a strong foundation for ensuing language aptitude research. These four factors comprised phonetic coding ability, inductive language learning ability, grammatical sensitivity, and rote memory (Carroll, 1981, 1990, 1993). Most other aptitude tests developed in this period or later and either were benchmarked against or were variants of the MLAT (see also Stansfield & Reed, this volume).

Indeed, when it comes to predicting ultimate foreign language learning success, the predictive power of the MLAT has been unparalleled, even until today (Li, 2015, 2016; Skehan, 2002, 2012). In subsequent validations and evaluations of the MLAT, Carroll (1981, 1990) tended to believe that there might not be much room for further improving the predictive power of the MLAT. He was also confident of the four essential language aptitude components that had been derived from his factor analyses and were assessed by the MLAT. Despite its impressive predictive validity, both the MLAT and the concept of foreign language aptitude have been criticized (for example, see Neufeld, 1979; Krashen, 1981). One criticism was that the construct of language aptitude still needed to be fully specified (Li, 2016; McLaughlin, 1995; Miyake & Friedman, 1998; Skehan, 1998, 2002). That is, Carroll's MLAT, *predictive* as it is of final learning outcomes, nevertheless has been seen as falling short of offering an overarching framework for *explaining* L2 learning, processing, and development. This criticism translated into the impetus for the second phase of language aptitude research, towards the theory-constructing phase (Wen, 2016; Wen et al., 2017; cf. Snow, 1992).

Currently, language aptitude research has entered a new era, or as it has been called elsewhere, the 'Theory-Construction' phase (Snow, 1992; Wen, 2016; Wen et al., 2017). Entering this new era, aptitude research has witnessed not just an expansion in research scope but also a slight change in research focus. On the one hand, continued efforts are being made to develop new aptitude test batteries with a view to complementing the MLAT. For example, the Cognitive Ability of Novelty in the Acquisition of Language-Foreign (i.e., the CANAL-F test) attempts to tap into learners' cognitive ability to handle 'novelty' in linguistic materials (Grigorenko, Sternberg, & Ehrman, 2000), and a high-level language aptitude battery (i.e., Hi-LAB) aims to be particularly effective in predicting success at high levels of accomplishment (Doughty, 2014; Linck et al., 2014).

In addition to the development of new test batteries, more emphasis has been placed on the 'explanatory' power of foreign language aptitude as a central construct of individual differences to account for L2 acquisition and processing (Ellis, 2004; Robinson, 2005, 2012; Skehan, 2012, 2016; Wen, 2016). Currently, concerted efforts are being mobilized from multiple disciplines, including applied linguistics, educational psychology, cognitive science, and neuroscience, towards this ambitious goal (Wen, 2016; Wen et al., 2017). As demonstrated in some recent volumes on language aptitude (e.g., Granena, Jackson, & Yilmaz, 2016; Granena & Long, 2013; Hyltenstam, Bartning, & Fant, 2018; Reiterer, 2018), the contemporary research agenda endeavors to both disentangle and elucidate potential cognitive and neuropsychological aptitude constructs underlying and facilitating L2 acquisition, real-time language processing, and long-term linguistic development from multidisciplinary perspectives (Wen et al., 2017). As part of the joint research efforts, the current volume aims to both reflect current progress in language aptitude research and, more importantly, to foster further development in theory, testing, research, and practice.

Rationale and Motivations for This Volume

The direct motivation for compiling this volume originated from a recent state-of-the-art review article published by three of the editors in *Language Teaching* (Wen et al., 2017). Following that article, they agreed that the concept of foreign language aptitude should be revisited and needed to be reconceptualized from multiple perspectives that subsumed contemporary and emerging insights from applied linguistics, educational psychology, cognitive science, and neuroscience. Therefore, they decided to organize an international roundtable forum on language aptitude and then edit a volume with contributions from the forum. (For the edited volume, two additional editors, Shaofeng Li and Richard L. Sparks, joined the editorial team.)

The International Roundtable Forum on 'Language Aptitude' was successfully held at the Macao Polytechnic Institute and the University of Macau between 6 and 9 June 2017. During the forum, most contributing authors to the current volume (except for a few who could not attend) presented their individual chapters and participated actively in the roundtable discussions of relevant issues. The edited volume is based on the major papers presented at the aptitude roundtable, plus those of the authors who were unable to attend the forum. The editors identified five major themes that emerged from the papers: (1) updating current language aptitude theories and testing instruments; (2) emerging issues and insights from more contemporary research into the long-standing relationships between language aptitude, age, and ultimate attainment; (3) redefining cognitive constructs and models; (4) perspectives from cognitive neuroscience; and (5) providing final commentaries reflecting on current practices, identifying future directions and research agendas. In the next section, we briefly highlight the key issues discussed in each chapter under these major themes.

An Outline of the Book

Theme I: Updating Aptitude Tests and Theories

The first section of the volume contains four chapters that revisit and update aptitude tests and aptitude theories. The first chapter, co-authored by Charles W. Stansfield and Daniel J. Reed, is entitled, "The MLAT at 60 Years". As the title clearly indicates, this chapter tracks the historical development of the most important language aptitude test by all standards, the Modern Language Aptitude Test (MLAT), over its 60-years history. After a brief background of John Carroll's early work, the authors briefly review different versions of the MLAT that have been developed in several languages, including French, Arabic, Braille, Mandarin, and so on. As indicated by the authors, the adaptation of the MLAT and Carroll's four language aptitude components to a different language has been a fundamental challenge to the test developer in each case. The chapter also describes the various end-user groups for the MLAT, including governments of many English-speaking countries and consulting psychologists who work with students. The chapter ends with a brief description of some criticisms leveled against the MLAT, the potential challenges it is currently facing, and future initiatives to make the battery available online.

The second chapter, entitled "Development and Preliminary Validation of a Foreign Language Aptitude Test for Chinese Learners of Foreign Languages", contributed by Lanrong Li and Shaoqian (Sheila) Luo, continues with the running theme of aptitude testing. Since there has not been a valid tool for measuring the foreign language aptitude of Chinese EFL learners, these authors developed an aptitude test for this purpose (targeting learners aged over 16) and used Rasch modeling to examine its validity. A test battery with six subtests was constructed and administered to 158 Chinese high school and college students. Rasch analyses showed that the test had high reliability, the vast majority of the items in each subtest exhibited good fit to the Rasch model, and all subtests showed good unidimensionality, except for the subtests of auditory associative memory and inductive language learning ability. However, a small number of items in some subtests were found to be too easy for the students. The subtests correlated significantly with each other, except for one subtest measuring phonetic coding ability and vocabulary in Chinese. In terms of external validity, the two groups' aptitude scores showed significant correlation with their English achievement scores. Overall, the chapter concludes that the test has satisfactory validity and reliability, though some subtests will need further revision and improvement in the future.

The third chapter, written by Peter Skehan and titled "Language Aptitude Implicates Language and Cognitive Skills", discusses broader theoretical issues of language aptitude. In his chapter, Skehan calls for a more balanced view on the language aspect of the foreign language aptitude construct, that is, how linguistic skills contribute to foreign language aptitude in tandem with general cognitive skills. Such an issue is both relevant and timely, given that most current conceptualizations of the construct of foreign language aptitude seem to emphasize general cognitive capacities (such as the memory systems). The chapter begins with a clear thesis statement that equivocally argues for a place for linguistic abilities in conceptualizing foreign language aptitude. This is followed by a broad description of a series of putative acquisitional processes that give rise to aptitude constructs that can be further conceptualized and measured in future research. In this macro-SLA aptitude model, processes at early stages are mainly concerned with handling sound materials and pattern identification, while later stages are characterized by automatization or proceduralization of such sounds and patterns. The chapter's position is that even at these later stages, language abilities are still relevant, and these abilities should be fully incorporated into theoretical conceptions and assessment of aptitude in the future.

The last chapter in the first section, by Shaofeng Li, is entitled "Six decades of Language Aptitude Research: A Comprehensive and Critical Review". This chapter is a synthetic review based on the results of three meta-analytical studies conducted by the author that have explored the associations of language aptitude with other individual difference (ID) variables and learning outcomes. Overall, the synthesis shows that aptitude is (a) a domain-specific cognitive device for language learning that should be distinguished from other cognitive and affective variables; (b) more important at initial rather than advanced stages of L2 learning; (c) essential for adult language learning rather than child language learning; and (d) more correlated with the effects of explicit instruction than those of implicit instruction. The chapter concludes with a discussion of methodological issues such as inconsistency in the measurement of aptitude and learning gains and the implementation of instructional treatments. The chapter also proposes future research directions towards matching instruction with aptitude profiles, adopting an eclectic approach, and using instruction that does not implicate aptitude.

Theme II: Language Aptitude, Age, and Ultimate Attainment

The second section contains four chapters that revisit the long-standing issues of the age factor and L2 ultimate attainment as these relate to language aptitude. The first chapter in this section, written by Amelia Lambelet and Raphael Berthele, is entitled, "Difficulty and Ease in Learning Foreign Languages at the Primary School Level: General Learning Ability, Language Aptitude or Working Memory?" On the basis that most language aptitude tests were developed to assess adults and young adults, this chapter aims to fill the lacuna by focusing on testing language aptitude at the primary school level. The author first reviews the literature on language aptitude in a school context and then discusses data from a pilot study drawn from a larger empirical research project on aptitude and foreign language learning at the primary school level in German-speaking Switzerland (involving children aged between 8 and 11). In this research project, aptitude tests as well as working memory tests and general learning ability tests were used, whose results shed light on a better understanding of children's difficulty in learning foreign languages in a primary school setting.

In the second chapter in this theme, Richard L. Sparks, Jon Patton, and Julie Luebbers contribute an investigation entitled "Language aptitude: Insights From US High School Students". In the empirical study reported in the chapter, monolingual US high school students were followed through Spanish courses at three levels (I, II, and III). At the beginning of Spanish I, they were administered a large test battery consisting of measures of L1 reading and writing achievements, L1 oral language and vocabulary, phonological and working memory, metacognition, and L2 aptitude (i.e., MLAT). They were then followed through three years of Spanish courses and administered standardized measures of Spanish, including word decoding, spelling, reading comprehension, writing, listening comprehension, and vocabulary, at the end of each year. Factor analyses of the test battery yielded four factors that explained 64% of the variance in Spanish achievement and could be labeled Language Analysis, Phonological/Orthographic, Phonological and Working Memory, and Rote Memory. These four factors then were used as predictor variables to explain the students' achievements in the six Spanish skills. Results from regression analyses showed that different factors explained the largest amount of variance in different Spanish skills. For example, Spanish word decoding and Spanish spelling skills were explained largely by the Phonological/Orthographic factor; Spanish reading comprehension by both the Language Analysis and Phonological/Orthographic factors; and Spanish listening comprehension and Spanish vocabulary by the Language Analysis, Phonological/Orthographic, and Phonological and Working Memory factors. The results are discussed with reference to studying an L2 in a monolingual context, when students are learning to speak and comprehend the L2 while at the same time learning to read and write the L2.

The third chapter in this section, authored by Michael Erard, is entitled, "Language Aptitude: Insights From Hyperpolyglots". The chapter provides an overview of contemporary and historical cases of very gifted foreign language learners, polyglots, and savants and how they can inform research on language aptitude. Given the exceptional abilities or talents to build and maintain high proficiency in a large number and wide variety of languages, one might expect these hyperpolyglots to consider language learning aptitude relevant to their pursuits. However, as the author demonstrates in the chapter, this was actually not the case. The author also reports on results from an online survey with 390 individuals to unveil the reasons behind the low prevalence of hyperpolyglottism and the higher prevalence of certain types of multilingualism. Finally, the author discusses the challenges to studying the genetic basis of hyperpolyglottism and language aptitude and suggests directions for future language aptitude research falling into this line of inquiry.

The last chapter under this theme is by Adriana Biedroń. It is entitled "Language Aptitude: Insights From L2 Adult Exceptional Learners". The chapter begins with basic terms such as foreign language aptitude, linguistic giftedness, and talent, which is followed by a more in-depth discussion of the age factor and its impacts on near-native-like proficiency and the dynamic nature of foreign language aptitude. The chapter ends with an outline for the various cognitive, personality, and neurological characteristics of different populations of exceptional learners, as well as similarities and differences between them.

Theme III: Redefining Cognitive Constructs and Models

The first chapter in this section, by Zhisheng (Edward) Wen, is entitled "Working Memory as Language Aptitude: The Phonological/Executive Model". Building on multidisciplinary insights from cognitive sciences and applied linguistics, this chapter first highlights unifying characterizations of the working memory (WM) system as they relate to language acquisition, online processing, and long-term development, culminating in the central proposal of 'WM as a language acquisition device'. Following this general overview, two key components of WM, i.e., the phonological component (PWM) and the executive component (EWM), are pinned down as key constructs of language aptitude, and their respective roles in specific SLA domains and skills are hypothesized. Such WM–SLA juxtapositions give rise to the overarching framework (i.e., the Phonological/Executive Model; Wen, 2015, 2016) for conceptualizing and implementing WM in SLA research. Specifically, it is postulated that the sound-based PWM component is a 'language learning device' that underlies the chunking process of L2 phonological sounds and linguistic sequences, which in turn lead to the acquisition and development of L2 lexis, phrases, and grammatical structures. On the other hand, EWM is conceived as a 'language processing device' that plays an essential role in serving selective cognitive processes (especially cognitively demanding processes) implicated in L2 comprehension and production activities such as L2 subskills learning. It is believed that such a thorough analysis of the strengths, weaknesses, opportunities, and threats of the proposal of WM as language aptitude is both relevant and timely and will have significant implications for future research in both theory and methodology.

The second chapter, entitled "Declarative and Procedural Memory as Individual Differences in Second Language Aptitude", is by Joshua Buffington and Kara Morgan-Short. In this chapter, the authors mainly consider the role of two long-term memory systems, i.e., declarative and procedural memory, as a source of individual differences in SLA. After defining the two memory systems, the authors review three theoretical perspectives regarding how both memory systems contribute to SLA. With a view to testing the hypotheses laid out in the three models, the authors summarize empirical evidence from behavioral and neuroimaging research. Towards the end, the authors highlight the need for future research to be directed towards a deeper understanding of procedural memory, as well as unresolved theoretical questions on the role of declarative and procedural memory.

In the last chapter of this section by Gisela Granena and Yucel Yilmaz on "Cognitive Aptitudes for Explicit and Implicit Learning", the authors argue that previous aptitude research in SLA has mostly focused on cognitive aptitudes that belong to the domain of explicit, attention-driven cognitive processes but overlooked aptitudes in the domain of implicit cognitive processes, such as implicit inductive learning ability. To fill up the gap, the authors focus on a widely researched area of instructed SLA: negative feedback. As such, the authors discuss new aptitude constructs in the domain of implicit learning processes and argue that individual differences (IDs) in implicit aptitude might be related to L2 learning in negative feedback conditions where feedback is relatively less obtrusive. The chapter ends with an outline of a research program that investigates the predictive validity of implicit language aptitude for learning under implicit negative feedback conditions.

Theme IV: Perspectives From Cognitive Neuroscience

Part IV of the book explores language aptitude from a neurocognitive perspective. In the first chapter under this theme, Jinxing Yue recognizes that although most models of language aptitude have taken the form, meaning, and structure of languages into account, the exact predictability of these components, i.e., linguistic aspects of language aptitude, on the outcome of language learning remains unclear. To address this issue, the author examines the neurophysiology of language as a potential solution to quantify the linguistic components of language aptitude. First, five pre-requisite conditions are identified, which are followed by an evaluation of three neurophysiological responses: N400, P600, and mismatch negativity (MMN). The literature review in the chapter suggests that while N400 and P600 responses have relatively clear functional associations with semantic- and syntactic-related processes, respectively, the MMN is a versatile response that approximates various types of linguistic processes under different experimental conditions. Furthermore, the MMN may reflect more automatic linguistic processes, whereas the N400 and P600 responses may be related to more controlled processes. Interestingly, N400 and P600 responses in the L1 appear to predict one's achievement in learning an L2, while the MMN is sensitive to the potential for learning the language by which the MMN is elicited, i.e., L2 elicitation predicts L2 learning.

The next chapter under this section's theme of cognitive neuroscience is written by Susanne Maria Reiterer. The chapter explores the neural, psychological, cognitive, and phonetic markers for pronunciation/speech imitation as language aptitude. According to the author, previous research has suggested that higher speech imitation aptitude in adults and children is accompanied by (a) a higher singing ability; (b) a higher general musicality and auditory WM; (c) increased openness to new experiences and empathy as personality markers; and (d) differences between the sexes, with males showing elevated speech imitation skills and females showing superiority in grammar and vocabulary learning aptitude. As a case in point, a phonetic marker of pronunciation aptitude for English as a second language is the ability to isolate the initial schwa sound, which rather accurately predicts overall pronunciation ability in the L2. In addition, the author reports very low to zero correlations between L2 phonetic imitation aptitude and general nonverbal IQ, reading speed, and executive functions.

The last chapter under this theme, "In Search of a Cognitive Model for Interpreting Expertise", is from Minhua Liu, who discusses the search for a neurocognitive aptitude model for interpreting expertise. Interpreters are often considered a special group of bilinguals who not only enjoy the benefits of bilingualism but also possess abilities acquired through their training or experience in interpreting.

But how much interpreters' expertise derives from their domain-general bilingual abilities and how much is attributable to their domain-specific aptitude for interpreting language remains unknown. As such, the author sets out to answer these questions by first creating a cognitive profile of expert interpreters based on previous research. The interpreters' cognitive profile thus portrayed involves attributes from both domain-general and domain-specific abilities that are specific to the skill of interpreting.

Theme V: Research Agenda and Future Directions

In this final section, there are two commentary chapters that deal with future directions and agendas for language aptitude research. The first is by Robert DeKeyser entitled "The Future of Language Aptitude Research". This chapter offers suggestions as to possible directions for aptitude research, such as to develop aptitude tests that measure different components of aptitude (or different aptitudes) for different domains of language, different stages of language development, and implicit and explicit learning. He also calls for research with different populations (such as those L2 learners who have little schooling). At the same time, DeKeyser indicates that the field needs further research to understand better what aptitudes do, such as how aptitudes interact with age, treatments, and structures. It is argued that such an understanding could lead to more theoretically motivated hypotheses about expected interactions, leading to further research important from both a practical and a theoretical point of view. The author also highlights a few caveats and cautionary notes about potentially premature applications of existing or new tests based on very limited aptitude–treatment interaction research. Finally, the author cautions that a learner's previous experience with learning languages may also constitute an aptitude (or rather a whole set of aptitudes) that is rooted in experience with language learning strategies, communication strategies, and metacognition.

In the last chapter by Loan C. Vuong and Patrick C. M. Wong, "From Individual Differences in Language Aptitude to Personalized Learning", the authors explain how findings on individual differences (IDs) in language aptitude can be implemented in an overarching theoretical framework they have developed, namely, the paradigm of "Personalized Learning". The overall objective of their paradigm is to identify powerful predictors of language learning so as to inform optimal teaching paradigms. Evidence from behavioral as well as neural and genetic studies is also reviewed in the chapter that provides initial support for the applicability of personalized learning as a viable framework for guiding future empirical studies and achieving learning effectiveness for individual learners. That said, the authors also acknowledge the need to carry out more extensive testing in the laboratory and in the classroom before the framework can be put into teaching practice. Potential challenges involved in these endeavors are also discussed.

Final Remarks

In sum, it is hoped that the current volume will inject new dynamics into the resurging research on the significant role of language aptitude in *predicting, explaining,* and *mediating* ultimate learning outcomes (Wen et al., 2017), as well as its significant implications for diagnosis, recruitment, and selection purposes in language education and personnel training. These insights hopefully will benefit not just the academic community (teaching as well as research) but also the business and industry sectors, as well as governments and the community at large. It is the editors' strong conviction that such an in-depth understanding of the latest research findings on foreign language aptitude will be of great importance to a wide range of stakeholders, including linguistics researchers, language learners/ students, language teachers, and parents of students, as well as government policy-makers and other educational practitioners.

Thus, we hope that this volume has addressed critical issues in foreign language aptitude and second language learning and teaching and will inform and benefit not just the field of applied linguistics but also educational psychology and cognitive science, with the ultimate goals of advancing theory, testing, research, and practice in relevant areas in a timely manner. As such, it is the editors' hope that this book will provide state-of-the-art reviews of critical issues in the research of foreign language aptitude for upper-level undergraduates; postgraduates in their course-required reading (in programs of applied linguistics, second language acquisition/education, TESOL, psychology and language, cognitive science, and educational psychology, etc.); offer insights and practical guidance for language teachers and language policymakers; and provide worthwhile recommendations for experienced researchers in the diverse fields of language, education, psychology, and neuroscience. We expect that the updated and in-depth analyses in this volume will usher in additional knowledge and enthusiasm into the investigation of this key construct in second language learning and teaching. That constitutes the rationale and the ultimate reward and joy of editing this volume!

References

Carroll, J. B. (1962). The prediction of success in intensive Foreign language training. In R. Glaser (Ed.), *Training research and education* (pp. 87–136). Pittsburgh, PA: University of Pittsburgh Press.
Carroll, J. B. (1981). Twenty-five years of research on Foreign language aptitude. In K. C. Diller (Ed.), *Individual differences and universals in language learning aptitude* (pp. 83–118). Rowley, MA: Newbury House.
Carroll, J. B. (1990). Cognitive abilities in Foreign language aptitude: Then and now. In T. Parry & C. W. Stansfield (Eds.), *Language aptitude reconsidered* (pp. 11–29). Englewood Cliffs, NJ: Prentice-Hall.
Carroll, J. B. (1993). *Human cognitive abilities: A survey of factor-analytic studies.* Cambridge: Cambridge University Press.

Carroll, J. B., & Sapon, S. M. (1959/2002). *Modern Language Aptitude Test (MLAT)*. New York, NY: The Psychological Corporation.

Carroll, J. B., & Sapon, S. M. (1959, 2002). *Modern Language Aptitude Test (MLAT)*. New York, NY: The Psychological Corporation. (Reprinted in 2002)

Doughty, C. (2014). Assessing aptitude. In A. Kunnan (Ed.), *The companion to language assessment* (pp. 25–46). Oxford, UK: Wiley-Blackwell.

Ellis, R. (2004). Individual differences in second language learning. In A. Davies & C. Elder (Eds.), *The handbook of applied linguistics* (pp. 525–551). Oxford: Blackwell Publishing.

Granena, G., Jackson, D., & Yilmaz, Y. (Eds.). (2016). *Cognitive individual differences in L2 processing and acquisition*. Amsterdam, The Netherlands: John Benjamins Publishing Company.

Granena, G., & Long, M. (Eds.). (2013), *Sensitive periods, language aptitude, and ultimate L2 attainment*. Amsterdam and Philadelphia: John Benjamins Publishing Company.

Grigorenko, E. L., Sternberg, R. J., & Ehrman, M. (2000). A theory-based approach to the measurement of Foreign language aptitude: The CANAL-F theory and test. *Modern Language Journal, 84*, 390–405.

Hyltenstam, K., Bartning, I., & Fant, L. (2018). *High-level language proficiency in second language and multilingual contexts*. Cambridge: Cambridge University Press.

Krashen, S. (1981). Aptitude and attitude in relation to second language acquisition and learning. In K. C. Diller (Ed.), *Individual differences and universals in language learning aptitude* (pp. 155–175). Rowley, MA: Newbury House.

Li, S. (2015). The associations between language aptitude and second language grammar acquisition: A meta-analytic review of five decades of research. *Applied Linguistics, 36*(3), 385–408.

Li, S. (2016). The construct validity of language aptitude. *Studies in Second Language Acquisition, 38*(4), 801–842. doi:10.1017/S027226311500042X

Linck, J. A., Hughes, M. M., Campbell, S. G., Silbert, N. H., Tare, M., Jackson, S. R., . . . Doughty, C. J. (2014). Hi-LAB: A new measure of aptitude for high-level language proficiency. *Language Learning, 63*(3), 530–566.

McLaughlin, B. (1995). Aptitude from an information processing perspective. *Language Testing, 11*, 364–381.

Miyake, A., & Friedman, N. P. (1998). Individual differences in second language proficiency: Working memory as language aptitude. In A. F. Healey & L. J. Bourne (Eds.), *Foreign language learning: Psycholinguistic studies on training and retention* (pp. 339–364). Mahwah, NJ: Lawrence Erlbaum Associates, Inc.

Neufeld, G. (1979). Towards a theory of language learning aptitude. *Language Learning, 29*, 227–241.

Reiterer, S. M. (2018). *Exploring language aptitude: Views from psychology, the language sciences, and cognitive neuroscience*. Heidelberg: Springer-Nature.

Robinson, P. (2005). Aptitude and second language acquisition. *Annual Review of Applied Linguistics, 25*, 46–73.

Robinson, P. (2012). Individual differences, aptitude complexes, SLA processes, and aptitude test development. In M. Pawlak (Ed.), *New perspectives on individual differences in language learning and teaching* (pp. 57–75). Berlin and Heidelberg: Springer-Verlag.

Skehan, P. (1998). *A cognitive approach to language learning*. Oxford: Oxford University Press.

Skehan, P. (2002). Theorising and updating aptitude. In P. Robinson (Ed.), *Individual differences and instructed language learning* (pp. 69–94). Amsterdam, The Netherlands: John Benjamins Publishing Company.

Skehan, P. (2012). Language aptitude. In S. Gass & A. Mackey (Eds.), *Routledge handbook of second language acquisition* (pp. 381–395). New York, NY: Routledge.

Skehan, P. (2016). Foreign language aptitude, acquisitional sequences, and psycholinguistic processes. In G. Granena, D. O. Jackson, & Y. Yilmaz (Eds.), *Cognitive individual differences in L2 processing and acquisition*. Amsterdam, The Netherlands: John Benjamins Publishing Company.

Snow, R. E. (1992). Aptitude theory: Yesterday, today, and tomorrow. *Educational Psychologist, 27*, 5–32.

Wen, Z. (2015). Working memory in second language acquisition and processing: The Phonological/Executive model. In Z. Wen, M. B. Mota, & A. McNeill (Eds.). *Working memory in second language acquisition and processing* (pp. 41–62). Bristol: Multilingual Matters.

Wen, Z. (2016). *Working memory and second language learning: Towards an integrated approach.* Bristol: Multilingual Matters.

Wen, Z., Biedroń, A., & Skehan, P. (2017). Foreign language aptitude theory: Yesterday, today and tomorrow. *Language Teaching, 50*(1), 1–31. doi:10.1017/S0261444816000276

PART I

Revisiting and Updating Tests and Theories

2

THE MLAT AT 60 YEARS

Charles W. Stansfield and Daniel J. Reed

Introduction

The emergence of second language acquisition as a serious field of study has resulted in a strong interest in what factors lead to success in the learning of additional languages. The process of acquiring bilingualism informally had become pretty well understood by 1990. As a result, many language learning researchers turned their attention to the factors that explain success or failure in formal language instruction. These include learner attributes such as language aptitude, learning strategies and styles, cognition, strength of motivation, etc., as well as program or school attributes such as quality of instruction and time provided for learning (Carroll, 1963; Spolsky, 1989). From 1990 forward, there has been increasing interest in language aptitude by SLA specialists, as is evident in the meta-analytic reviews conducted by Li (2015, 2016, and this volume). Naturally, in order to study the effect of aptitude on learning, we must first have a way to measure aptitude. Thus, tests of aptitude are a necessary component of any good study of the role of aptitude in language learning. There are currently only a few published tests of foreign language aptitude. Among them, the Modern Language Aptitude Test (MLAT) is the oldest. Because of its longevity, it is useful to review the development and history of the MLAT over the past 60 years. We will start by reviewing Carroll's four components and how they are tested on the five parts of the MLAT. This serves as a frame of reference for describing and discussing the adaptations of the MLAT that have been developed for native speakers of other languages. We conclude with remarks on the various uses of the MLAT from its inception to the present time.

The Modern Language Aptitude Test (Carroll & Sapon, 1959) was developed between 1953 and 1958. It was published by the Psychological Corporation, which continued to publish it until 1995. In 2003, it was republished by the Second Language Testing Foundation, whose name was changed to the Language Learning and Testing Foundation (LLTF) in 2011.[1] Carroll, a distinguished psychologist and psychometrician, had a particular interest in foreign language learning and in linguistics. His natural interest in languages was further stimulated at age 13 when he attended a lecture at his local public library by linguistic anthropologist Benjamin Lee Whorf on his studies of the indigenous languages of Mexico. In a conversation after the lecture, Carroll told Whorf that he was already studying Latin and Greek and convinced Whorf to let him be his research assistant. Carroll went on to major in classical languages in college, studying Roman and Greek literature in the original. Right after graduating in 1937, he attended the LSA summer institute, where he studied Sanskrit, descriptive linguistics and field methods in anthropological linguistics with Edward Sapir. He devoured Whorf's typewritten papers while in high school and ultimately published them as a book, *Language Thought and Reality* (Carroll, 1956). So although Carroll did his doctorate degree in psychology, he had a strong interest in languages and linguistics, which he cultivated from the time he was in seventh grade through graduate school and throughout his career.

Carroll was also a distinguished statistician and made many contributions to psychometrics, particularly in the area of factor analysis. He was an outstanding educational psychologist; his *Model of School Learning* (Carroll, 1963) is still fundamental reading for anyone interested in education and instruction. So given his strong background in the psychology of learning, cognition, factor analysis and psychometrics, it was natural for Carroll to investigate aspects of cognition as they relate to the learning of additional languages and the measurement of language skills in general.

Components of Language Aptitude—Carroll's dissertation in psychology, defended in 1941 at the University of Minnesota, was a factor analysis of verbal abilities. Thus, he was well prepared to study the factor structure of language aptitude when the Carnegie Foundation offered him a series of grants for this purpose in the early 1950s. Through factor analyses, he concluded that there were four basic components of language aptitude. When he began to develop the MLAT, he collected data on 30 different item types. From these, he included five on the MLAT that provided some unique variance while still being predictive of the global construct of language aptitude. The four subconstructs identified by Carroll are presented next, essentially as he defined them originally and in subsequent publications. Note that two of the four components (grammatical sensitivity and inductive learning ability) deal with learning the grammar of a foreign language (FL).

Phonetic coding ability—the ability to identify distinct sounds, to form associations between those sounds and symbols representing them and to retain these associations. The learner must consistently and correctly perceive sounds. Learners with good phonetic coding ability hold these sounds in short-term, intermediate and eventually long-term memory. Perceiving and holding sounds in the memory requires phonological awareness, which is knowing that words consist of individual phonological units that are not meaningful in themselves. Phonological awareness is important in learning to read in alphabetic languages. Carroll has noted the phonetic coding ability is like spelling, but is broader than spelling, since it may involve the ability to notice relationships between the sound of letters in an incorrectly spelled word and the probable word it represents (e.g. tox—talks; hpy—happy). Carroll notes that phonetic coding may be a reflection of individual differences in the learning of phoneme–grapheme correspondences. Skehan (1999) has argued that phonetic coding ability comes into play in the early stages of learning a FL, and it determines the degree to which learners can make use of both oral and written input. Carroll (1981) also noted that phonetic coding can involve the association of certain sounds with meaning. In addition, Carroll (1990) says that phonetic coding is closely related to certain types of dyslexia. Thus, if a child doesn't know that words can be decomposed into smaller phonological units, he or she can't match them to graphemes. Ultimately, children with dyslexia can have good speaking skills but poor spelling and writing skills.

Grammatical sensitivity—the ability to recognize the grammatical functions of words (or other linguistic entities) in sentence structures.

Rote learning ability for foreign language materials—the ability to learn associations between sounds (or words) and meanings rapidly and efficiently and to recall and retain these associations.

Inductive learning ability—the ability to infer or induce the rules governing a set of language materials, given samples of language materials that permit such inferences.

In the five parts of the MLAT, these four components of language aptitude are tested as follows.

Part I. *Number Learning.* This part involves learning numbers in an artificial language made up of nonsense words formed from English sounds. It seems to measure several components of foreign language aptitude. This part also has a fairly large specific variance (strength and uniqueness), which one might guess to be a special "auditory alertness" factor that would play a role in auditory comprehension of a foreign language.

Note that Number Learning then is a measure of Rote Learning ability and Inductive Learning ability, but includes auditory alertness, and thus may also involve Phonetic Coding ability. Thus, a strength of Number Learning may be that it taps, although weakly, three components of Carroll's model.

Part II. *Phonetic Script.* This part requires the examinee to learn phonetic symbols for English sounds and to retain those associations throughout a syllable-recognition task (selecting the choice that represents the phonetic transcription of a spoken stimulus from a set of four options). This part appears to measure what Carroll called sound–symbol association ability, that is, the ability to learn the correspondences between speech sounds and orthographic symbols.

Note that Phonetic Script is a direct measure of Phonetic Coding ability. It also measures memory for sounds, and it correlates with the ability to mimic them, which is the starting point for good pronunciation.[2]

Part III. *Spelling Clues.* This part involves selecting a partial definition of a stimulus word that has an incomplete and/or phonetic spelling. It also measures the same kind of sound–symbol association ability measured by Part II, Phonetic Script, but to a lesser extent. Scores on this part depend to some extent on the student's English vocabulary knowledge. It is highly speeded. That is because Carroll wanted this task to require rapid recognition of the meaning of the stimulus.

Spelling Clues measures sound–symbol association ability, plus English vocabulary. It measures the ability to recognize correspondences between symbols and speech sounds but in a different way than Part II does, i.e., the examinee has to look for symbols in the stimulus, imagine how they would be pronounced and then relate them to the meaning of the options.

Part IV. *Words in Sentences.* Part IV requires an examinee to select an underlined word or group of words in a sentence that matches the grammatical role played by a designated word or group of words in a stimulus sentence. This part measures sensitivity to grammatical structure, and may be expected to have particular relevance to the student's ability to handle the grammatical aspects of a foreign language. No grammatical terminology is involved in this part. Instead, the examinee must recognize the grammatical function of the word or words in the stimulus. All sentences are in English.[3]

Carroll (1981, p. 108) says his own research found this part is related to knowledge of grammar; however, it is not clearly related to formal training in grammar. He cites Politzer (1965), who found the same result. However, clearly Part IV measures grammatical sensitivity. This is a topic worth investigating, since it could mean that formal instruction in grammar increases one component of language aptitude. If that is the case, then this part may also tap into deductive reasoning.

Part V. *Paired Associates.* Part V requires the examinee to learn a small set of vocabulary items in a new language. This part measures the rote memory ability of the foreign language learner when tackling foreign language vocabulary leaning.[4]

This means that as a group the five parts tap all four components.

Component 1 (phonetic coding ability) is measured by Part II, Phonetic Script, and partially by Part III, Spelling Cues, and perhaps partially by Part I, Number Learning.

Component 2 (grammatical sensitivity) is measured by Part IV, Words in Sentences.

Component 3 (rote learning ability) is measured by Part IV, Paired Associates, and partially by Part I, Number Learning.

Component 4 (inductive learning ability) is partially measured by Part I, Number Learning.

Table 2.1 displays the MLAT sections that tap each of the four components. Some of the sections are only weakly associated with a particular component and are so specified. Table 2.2 simply reverses the display to show which components are targeted by each MLAT part.

It is evident from the information in Table 2.1 and Table 2.2 that the MLAT parts were not designed to tap the four components in a one-to-one fashion. The parts of the MLAT were designed to work together. Use of any one part in isolation constitutes an incomplete and relatively weak measure of language aptitude. On the other hand, since the 1960s use of one or two MLAT parts has been common in research studies, where it is used as a control or moderator variable to ensure the comparability of two groups in terms of language aptitude, or to be able to adjust for differences in the language aptitude across the groups.

Other Versions: Adaptations, Not Translations

We turn now to a review of adaptions of the MLAT to other languages. In reviewing versions of the MLAT for speakers of languages other than English, it is crucial to emphasize two points. First, the MLAT was not, and could not be, simply

TABLE 2.1 How Carroll's four language aptitude components are tapped by the five MLAT parts

Phonetic Coding Ability	Grammatical Sensitivity	Rote Language Learning Ability	Inductive Language Learning Ability
MLAT II, Phonetic Script		MLAT V, Paired Associates	
MLAT III, Spelling Cues★ (weakly)	MLAT IV, Words in Sentences★		MLAT I, Number Learning (weakly)
MLAT I, Number Learning (weakly)		MLAT I, Number Learning (weakly)	

★ These parts are primarily English based.

TABLE 2.2 How the five MLAT Parts tap Carroll's four language aptitude components

Part I Number Learning	Part II Phonetic Script	Part III Spelling Cues	Part IV Words in Sentences	Part V Paired Associates
Phonetic coding ability (weakly) Rote learning ability (weakly) Inductive learning (weekly)	Phonetic coding ability	Phonetic coding ability	Grammatical sensitivity	Rote learning ability

translated into other languages in a straightforward manner. For example, three of the five MLAT parts make use of the subtleties of the English language, which may be theoretically interesting, and may also make the test more accessible to individuals who have never studied a foreign language. However, the English items cannot simply be translated. A clear example is the use of consonants only in most of the stems for the "Spelling Cues" part of the MLAT, an item type that is obviously not possible for languages that do not use phonetically based writing systems (e.g., Chinese), or languages whose writing system focuses primarily on consonants (e.g., Arabic, Hebrew, Persian, etc.). When adapting the MLAT to a language that uses a consonantal writing system, this part might have to be changed, since examinees would already be accustomed to guessing the word by the consonants seen on paper.

Another example is the "Words in Sentences" part. Each component of English grammar may be expressed quite differently in another language. For instance, some languages have "zero anaphora" (essentially a gap in a sentence where English would use a pronoun), while others allow free word order (e.g., objects before or after verbs). Thus, a mere translation of the stem and the options of the original MLAT items may not produce appropriate items for speakers of other languages. Finally, the adaptations have to be sensitive to age and cultural differences and to cognitive maturity.

Second, each adaptation is itself a serious and formidable test development project. Creating an adapted LA test entails attaining a good understanding of Carroll's components of language aptitude, deciding how to measure them given the native language of the examinee; developing specifications; and then writing, reviewing and revising items. One must also conduct field testing to determine the usefulness of each item, the reliability of each part and total test reliability. One should also design and execute a validity study (ideally with reliable and valid criterion measures) and, if possible, create some initial norms for the target population. We now turn to a description of several of the adaptations.

UK English

A version of the MLAT using a speaker of British English was created in 2007. The test book was also modified to include spelling modifications appropriate to British orthographic conventions. This version is appropriate for test users in the UK and other countries, and for any examinee who is more familiar with British than with North American English. A computer-delivered version was created also and was available to users in the UK until recently.

French

Perhaps the best-known adaptation is the Test d'aptitude aux langues vivantes (TALV), developed between 1974 and 1978 (Wells, Wesche, & Sarrazin, G. (1980).

It should be noted that Carroll was a consultant to the Canadian government agency that developed the test. Carroll made several trips to Canada in this capacity during the test development process. The TALV closely followed the MLAT's development in terms of including five main parts modeled on the original MLAT sections. It was field-tested and normed on more than 1600 examinees—550 adults and 1100 secondary-level students. The manual also reports norms (in stanines) for these populations for each section of the test and the total (for both the short version and the full-length version). In addition, validity coefficients are reported in the form of correlations with criterion measures such as scores and final grades. These correlations range from .40 to .53 for the short form and .29 to .69 for the full-length version. The KR 20 reliability coefficient was (.91), which is comparable to the odd-even reliability coefficients reported in the MLAT manual. TALV test-retest reliability for a group of 77 adults was .89.

The correlation between the full-length and short form of the TALV was .94 for adults and .88 for students at the secondary school level. All parts showed high correlations with the total score. The highest correlation with total score was for Part I (.84), while Part II correlated the lowest (.70). However, Part II showed the highest KR 20 reliability, while Part II showed the lowest for several groups, indicating that reliability of the parts played a significant role in the pattern of part–total correlations. The variation in reliability of part scores was almost identical to the reliabilities of part scores on the English version of the MLAT where Part I had the highest reliability and Part II had the lowest for nearly all groups.

Innovative Uses of MLAT and TALV

Uses of these parallel language aptitude tests in Canada have included streaming (placing students into a course that moves through a curriculum at a pace that aligns with their rate of ability to learn), matching (placing students into classes that have instructional approaches compatible with particular learner types) and guidance (such as counseling students on how best to attack a curriculum).

Wesche (1981) examined the use of language aptitude test profiles in conjuction with counselor observations in the Public Service Commission of Canada's system of matching students with instructional approaches and concluded that this practice "encourages positive attitudes and enhances achievement among highly analytical students" (Wesche, 1981, p. 137). She also reported anecdotal evidence to support the same finding for students placed into classes that employed the "Analytical Approach," as well as positive outcomes for students placed into classes with a "Functional Approach" (ibid). This use of the MLAT/TALV evolved over time to include only one curriculum, but one which was flexible and within which individuals were counseled to draw on its resources in a way that best suited their learning styles. Wesche also provides useful information on how the individual components of language aptitude, measured by the MLAT/TALV and the Pimsleur Language Aptitude Battery (PLAB), become manifest in student performance, difficulties, attitudes and behavior in the classroom. It is noteworthy that Ehrman (1996, 1998) discusses the use of the MLAT at the US Foreign Service Institute and reaches similar conclusions on the relationship between part scores and student success in speaking and reading and in student anxiety.

Both the MLAT and TALV are reportedly still used in Canada by the Public Service Commission, *not* to select employees for training, but to obtain diagnostic information and to decide on duration of training for each student to reach the required level of proficiency. At the Canadian Centre for Foreign Languages and Intercultural Learning, and at several other Canadian government agencies, teachers use aptitude scores and subscores to better understand students' language learning abilities and preferences.

Japanese

Murakami (1974) developed an aptitude test for native speakers of Japanese. While it was in good part based on Carroll's theories, the task types were different from the MLAT. We do not know if the test is still available.

In 1991, Miyuki Sasaki developed the Language Aptitude Battery for the Japanese (LABJ) using parts of the MLAT and parts of the PLAB. The test was developed along with measures of English skills to investigate the relationships between second language proficiency and cognitive abilities in Japanese learners of English. This was a dissertation project completed at UCLA in 1991. The study was later published as a book (Sasaki, 1996). The LABJ was modeled on the short version of the MLAT Parts III, IV and V, which do not involve the audio recording. The parts of the LABJ involved paired associates, language analysis and sound–symbol association. Sasaki used MLAT Part V (paired associates), PLAB Part IV (language analysis in a foreign language) and MLAT Part III (sound–symbol associations) as LABJ Part III.[5] She adapted English on the test to Japanese (Katakana). While the LABJ only used two of the five parts of the MLAT, its structure was based on Carroll's research and the MLAT short form. The LABJ is well known among SLA researchers in Japan and has been used by a considerable number of them with the permission of Sasaki and LLTE.

Braille

The MLAT-Braille was developed by Maria Eugenia Santana Rollán in 2012 as a part of her dissertation, which investigated foreign language aptitude in visually impaired students. The MLAT-Braille addresses a requirement of the Individuals with Disabilities Education Act (1990) and the Americans with Disabilities Act (1990), which require appropriately accommodated standardized tests.

Time was a significant factor in adapting the MLAT for readers of braille. Research has shown that braille reading requires more time and more attentional resources than visual reading. Therefore, the testing time was extended from 60 minutes to about 90 minutes. Time was doubled for each task within Parts III (Spelling Clues) and V (Paired Associates), and time was added into Part I (Number Learning) in between each utterance of a number. This ensures that examinees have enough time to record their answers. Lastly, since Part IV of the MLAT (Words in Sentences) has a heavy reading load, it was omitted from the braille version to conform to this study of language aptitude in visually impaired people. Its omission affects the scoring of the test, dropping the number of items from 192 to 142. (Percentile ranks raw scores published in the MLAT Manual for grades 9, 10, 11 and college were transformed to compare the results from the norm group in the manual and the participants in this study).

Another accommodation was the inclusion of a familiarization list in Part II (Phonetic Script). The list is included since accent marks and phonetic symbols are not common in braille, and unfamiliarity with the symbols may affect performance. The list provides examples of accent marks and phonetic symbols, their spelling broken down into braille and their use in a sentence. Examinees are given two minutes to read over the list before starting the section.

In her study, Santana Rollán administered the MLAT-Braille to 53 visually impaired students between the ages of 12 and 25 from the United States, Canada and the United Kingdom. Thirty-four were blind and 19 had a severe visual impairment. All participants were visually impaired at the time of birth or in infancy and did not have any other disability that could affect their performance on the MLAT. These subjects' MLAT scores were compared to the adjusted MLAT scores obtained by the 971 sighted individuals (in grades 9, 10, 11 and college) who participated in the norming of the MLAT as indicated in Tables 12 and 13 of the MLAT Manual. Results reveal that the blind sample showed higher quartiles on all MLAT parts administered, regardless of grade or sex, except for males in grade 9. However, the differences in total score were statistically significant only for grade 10 and 11 (both sexes), where the blind sample showed a significantly higher language aptitude than the sighted individuals who participated in the original norming study. Results also indicate that on Part I of the MLAT (Number Learning) visually impaired students behave in a more homogeneous way (regardless of sex, age or reading modality), obtaining significantly higher scores than the sighted population. This section measures the subject's memory as well as an "auditory alertness" factor, which would affect the subject's auditory comprehension of a foreign language. This exceptional performance of the blind sample in establishing sound–meaning associations without written input in order to retrieve the information quickly, as well as the ability to learn inductively, confirms higher skills in memorization and attention tasks in the blind population.

In light of the results, Santana Rollán concluded that blind students could be above-average foreign language learners if adequate pedagogical accommodations are provided as early as possible in the learning process. Santana Rollán gifted the MLAT-Braille to LLTF for use with visually impaired braille readers in the future.

Arabic

Recently, an adaption of the MLAT was developed for Arabic (Moskovsky, Alshahrani, Ratcheva, & Paolini, 2015) in Saudi Arabia. As with the LABJ, the MLAT-Arabic is based on the MLAT short form, which includes Parts III, IV, and V. The MLAT-Arabic includes a 20-item part called Vocabulary and Written Coding (equivalent to Spelling Clues), a 20-item part called Grammar Sensitivity (equivalent to Words in Sentences) and a 24-item part called Memory (equivalent to Paired Associates). The latter uses the same items on the MLAT, but the options are translated into Arabic.

The MLAT-Arabic and shortened TOEFL (50 items) were given to 56 first-year college students of English at the beginning and end of a seven-month intensive course. There were significant but moderate correlations between the measures; .29 at the start of the course and .34 at the end. There was essentially no gain in scores on the MLAT-Arabic on the second administration. The reliability of these shortened tests (MLAT and TOEFL) was not reported. The authors concluded that language aptitude is a stable construct that is generally unaffected by L2 learning or training. They also concluded that MLAT adaptations like theirs and others can be a useful selection and diagnostic tool for language teaching institutions.

Polish

An adaptation of the MLAT for Polish native speakers was created by Rysiewicz (2008). The effort included adaptation of the test and initial piloting, concurrent validation with measures of English and then further field testing and validation on a larger sample of secondary and tertiary students in Poland (Rysiewicz, 2011). This Polish adaptation is referred to as the *Test Uzdolnień do Nauki Języków Obcych* (Polish Language Aptitude Test), or TUNJO.

The TUNJO sought to represent all four subcomponents of Carroll's language aptitude construct: phonemic coding, grammatical sensitivity, inductive language learning and rote learning. In doing so, the test developer elected to drop the Number Learning task (MLAT 1), and a new Artificial Language task was added to directly target the inductive language learning subcomponent that the MLAT does not directly measure. The Artificial Language task presents a list of contrived words and Polish equivalents and several phrases with translations to illustrate morphosyntactic constructions. The Artificial Language task consists of 20 multiple-choice items requiring examinees to translate from Polish to the fictional language or vice versa.

The other four TUNJO tasks more closely reflect the original MLAT tasks. The Phonetic Script task is a straightforward adaptation of the MLAT II task, though slightly more speeded and with some additional orthographic obfuscation. The Spelling Clues task was adapted for Polish and shortened, which involved inducing greater orthographic opacity and includes 20 fewer items than the MLAT III task. The Words in Sentences and Paired Associates tasks remain relatively unchanged from corresponding MLAT tasks (Parts IV and V, respectively), though the Words in Sentences task (in Polish) was shortened due to practical concerns (22 fewer items than MLAT IV). The TUNJO contained 123 items, whereas the MLAT contains 192. Also, the number of options was reduced from five to four on the TUNJO. Normally, reducing the number of options decreases reliability among tests with an equal number of items.

During field testing, each TUNJO part was piloted with Polish secondary students (students piloted one part only; in all, 147 students were involved). Then, in the validation study, 250 secondary students in Poznań took the entire test. Later, 650 students in Poznan (62 secondary and 588 tertiary) took the TUNJO (Rysiewicz, 2011). The tertiary students represented three different academic fields (English $n = 447$, linguistics $n = 89$ and economics $n = 52$).

The split-half reliability based on 245 students was .89. The reliability of each part was also estimated with Cronbach's alpha. Part score reliabilities ranged from .41 (Artificial Language) to .85 (Paired Associates). All parts showed reliabilities of .66 or higher, except for the new task (Artificial Language), which showed a reliability of .41.

Some evidence for the construct validity of TUNJO scores was obtained. The correlations between part scores were in the .2 to .3 range, which is lower than the correlations between a given part and the TUNJO total score, which indicated that the tasks are measuring partially independent facets of a unifying broader aptitude construct. A similar pattern exists for the MLAT.

Additionally, some evidence was found for the predictive validity of the TUNJO. The correlation between the teacher-made tests of vocabulary, grammar, reading and listening comprehension in English and the TUNJO was .31. The correlation is somewhat lower than those normally reported for the MLAT. Rysiewicz felt that this outcome was partly due to the unsuitability of the teacher-made tests and the similarity of the students. Because the researcher did not receive item-level response data from the teacher-scored tests, no reliabilities for the tests were calculated.

Based on the intercorrelations among tasks, Ryseiwicz concluded that the TUNJO does measure the aptitude construct in a fashion similar to the MLAT. However, the new Artificial Language task introduced by the TUNJO appears to be less closely related to the aptitude construct. In terms of predictive validity, TUNJO obtained lower coefficients than the MLAT, but they were nonetheless positive and significant.

Hungarian

During the 1990s, István Ottó created the language aptitude test for Hungarian learners of English, called the MENYÉT (Magyar Egyetemes Nyelvérzékmérő Teszt [Hungarian Standardized Test of the Gift for Languages]; Otto, 1996). The purpose of the MENYÉT was to assess the language aptitude of Hungarian language learners of the English language.

Similar to the design of the MLAT, the MENYÉT consists of four subtests targeting similar constructs based upon Carroll's four-component model of language aptitude. Indeed, he made an attempt to target the components more directly.

Descriptive statistics on the test are found in Otto and Nikolov (2003). The test was administered to 130 adults. Their scores produced a range from 25 to 78, with a mean score of 56 (out of 80 possible points). Women composed about 75% of the sample. Each of the four parts had a total of 20 possible points, and scores ranged from 0 to a perfect score of 20. (Note that this test was about one half the length of the MLAT.) The MENYÉT score was compared to a score on a language test presented by each subject. A correlation of .45 was found between the MENYÉT and the language test score. Otto also found a negative correlation between the MENYÉT score and examinee age, which he attributed to a loss of language aptitude with age within the group.

As for future directions for the MENYÉT, Ottó (1996) proposed a deeper investigation into how language aptitude interacts with the dynamic construct of creativity, increases in metacognitive linguistic awareness, general learning abilities and language learning strategies.

Other Languages

We are aware that adaptations of the MLAT have been done for several other languages. These include Italian (Ferencich, 1964), Dutch (de Graaff, 1997), Swedish and Hebrew. However, only the MLAT French adaptation has been published and is readily available to institutions and examinees through a commercial publisher. While some of the MLAT adaptations are still available from their author, most are not available, and the older ones seem to have completely disappeared. Where we have been able to find a published reference to their work, we have included it here. However, most translations eventually become lost. A number of researchers have developed translations or adaptations of one or two parts of the MLAT to another language as a moderator variable in order to control for group differences in studies of success in learning English or another second language. Similarly, researchers have done the same in studies of individual differences in cognition, aptitude, learning styles, etc. Generally, these tests employ fewer items than the corresponding part of the MLAT in order to save testing time. Again, they generally disappear, since they were created by and for a single researcher.

Predictive Validity of the MLAT for Communicative Methods of Instruction

Occasionally, one hears it said that the MLAT was made and validated at the time of the grammar-translation method. Therefore, it is not valid with today's students in today's communicatively oriented classrooms. This is slightly erroneous thinking about validity. Normally, once a test is shown to be valid for a given purpose, it remains valid until it is shown that it is not valid in a specific context or for a specific group.

Moreover, the claim that the MLAT was validated on students studying under noncommunication-oriented methods is hard to substantiate. Certainly most secondary and college students who participated in the validation and norming of the MLAT in the 1950s must have received grammar-oriented instruction, since the grammar-translation method was dominant at that time. However, others were enrolled in US government intensive programs that emphasize oral skills and language proficiency (rather than knowledge or achievement). A dissertation by Winke (2005, 2013) and several other studies have shown that the MLAT continues to predict success at the US Defense Language Institute, which definitely uses a task-based communicative approach and has done so since the 1980s. Ehrman's (1998) study at the US Foreign Service Institute had approximately 1000 cases covering all language categories and found respectable correlations (.33 to .55) with end-of-course language proficiency ratings in speaking and reading on the ILR scale, which is the predecessor of the CEFR. These correlations are particularly notewor- thy when one considers the lack of variation in such ratings, since students in these programs are normally focused on attaining the same designated level of proficiency.

That is not to say that no other test is needed. Certainly other aptitude tests can and should be developed; then, researchers can carry out studies comparing the validity of the test for a given type of student. Unfortunately, we do not often see controlled, large-scale research on language aptitude tests today, and few com- parative studies exist. Generally, when studies comparing the DLAB, the PLAB and the MLAT have been done, they have been shown to have similar predictive validity, even though there are differences in the approach that each uses. This suggests that carefully constructed language aptitude tests have similar validities and that for most students language aptitude does not vary much under different instructional methodologies.

More Forms Needed

Only one form of the MLAT has ever been developed. This is due to several reasons: the cost involved combined with the low probability of recuperating the investment, the need to equate subsequent forms to a common scale, the difficulty of recruiting examinees who would take two multiple forms, the need for a fairly large sample, etc. Because we only have one form, we have to be very conscious of test security. That is the main reason why the sale of the test to potential users is restricted. If several forms were available, it would be possible to have degrees of security for different forms, with the most recent forms being the most secure. Multiple forms would also permit retesting examinees, which can be useful for a testing program and in a number of research projects where the goal is to examine

[margin annotations, handwritten: Interagency Language Roundtable; Common European Framework of Reference]

the effects of a treatment on test scores. Carroll (1990, p. 12) himself noted the need for additional forms over 25 years ago.

Once the MLAT becomes available online, if it is well received by current users, it may become possible to develop, field test and equate a second form of the MLAT. Field testing and equating would require the cooperation of test score users, but that may be possible if the availability of additional forms is viewed as important by the users.

Conclusions

Given that no one has developed a language aptitude test with better predictive validity than the MLAT for its intended uses, notwithstanding the excellent work reported in this volume and elsewhere, it is likely that the test will remain in use for several more years. The question then becomes what uses should be supported. The rationale for various uses requires us to reflect on the construct definition, on the nature of language aptitude and on backing data for uses to date. Carroll treated language aptitude as *probable ability to learn* a language to a level where one is fluent, but not highly proficient, under particular conditions of formal instruction (thereby excluding use of the test to predict who will learn a language to an extremely high level of proficiency under "natural" conditions). More importantly, for Carroll, language learning was situated in a school context, and he went on to develop a Model of School Learning (Carroll, 1963) in general. Spolsky (1989) further enumerated the conditions for language learning.

Carroll also presented data and arguments that clearly distinguished language aptitude (a relatively stable trait that remains essentially unchanged throughout one's lifetime) from other constructs relevant for language learning, such as attitudes, study habits, motivation (an unstable trait that may change even from moment to moment), intelligence and even verbal intelligence (Carroll, 1993). The Model of School learning incorporates these other constructs independently. Carroll pointed out that intelligence tests typically have predicted success in other school subjects better than success at foreign language learning. He further stated that because intelligence is complex, tests to measure it often target multiple abilities, not all of which are relevant to language learning per se, and thus dampen the correlation coefficients with measures of language learning success (Carroll, Sapon, Reed, & Stansfield, 2010, p. 22). A table directly comparing the predictive validity of MLAT and intelligence and other tests is contained in the MLAT Manual (ibid, p. 23).

The rationale for the most common uses of the MLAT have been consistent with the considerations just discussed. Historically, the test was designed to predict FL learning in adults and to identify and select rapid language learners where learning opportunities were limited. More recently, as described earlier, the MLAT has been used innovatively in Canada to determine duration of training rather than for making selection/exclusion decisions. Both of these applications are consistent with the notion "time needed to learn," with time being fixed in the former case (length of one available course) but more flexible in the latter case. In other contexts, the MLAT has been used for diagnostic purposes. This is an increasing trend. Language aptitude tests be can used by schools for selection, placement and guidance purposes. The use of aptitude tests enables teachers to know their students in advance. Subscores can be combined with information provided by psychoeducational test batteries, background information on record, interviews, etc., to diagnose potential foreign language learning problems and disabilities. A diagnostic profile of a student's cognitive abilities can be constructed from subscores, which counselors can refer to when guiding a student toward curricular options that are best suited to the student's strengths and weaknesses (e.g., classes that require more auditory skills than analytic skills). For example, Ehrman (1996) has found that the occurrence of high scores on MLAT Parts III and IV in conjunction with lower scores on other parts indicates an analytic learner. Similarly, a high score on Part II co-occurring with lower scores on Parts III and IV indicates an experiential or global learner. Pimsleur, who was particularly interested in students who had difficulty with language learning, noted that PLAB subscores could be used to predict which students would do better under an analytic approach, which would fare better given a more global approach and which would perform better or worse with regard to spoken versus written language. He also observed that auditory ability was frequently associated with foreign language learning problems.

A more controversial use of the MLAT has been to identify individuals with a "foreign language learning disability" (FLLD). Reed and Stansfield (2004) considered this issue in depth and concluded

> although research and validation efforts should be ongoing, if the individual diagnosis is comprehensive and discerning, and if all of the safeguards we recommend are in place, then use of the MLAT along with other measures to aid in determining if a student has a FLLD is both ethical and appropriate.
> *(Reed & Stansfield, 2004, p. 175)*

This case highlights the point that an individual test should never be used in isolation from other available information and emphasizes the more general principle that each new use of a test must be validated, even in the case of a well-established test.

Since LLTF took over MLAT sales and operations in 2003, there have been substantial improvements in the program. The MLAT was removed from the catalog of the previous publisher in the early 1990s due to declining sales. Carroll was not happy about this, but accepted it as their decision. Once LLTF took over and made its availability known through the Internet, inquiries and sales began to come in slowly but at a steadily increasing rate. The updating of the MLAT Manual and the updating and reprinting of the test booklet and other test materials also helped. The creation of a scannable answer sheet for the MLAT and then a computer-based MLAT, along with a UK version of both tests, meant that we were able to satisfy the needs of more users. Still, the MLAT is not a profit-maker for LLTF. Indeed, the cost of maintaining a website, reprinting or replacing test materials, handling orders and answering questions and inquiries from the public generate annual losses, which the organization absorbs. Although Carroll died in 2003 and Sapon in 2010, we believe they would both be pleased to know that people are still benefitting from their test 60 years after it was developed.

> The fact that over the 53 years of its life the MLAT has maintained high predictive validity for these multiple settings involving a range of language and teaching methods is evidence that the test is a robust measure of important and fundamental aspects of language aptitude.

This evaluation by Sasaki (2012) several years ago in another historical overview still seems to be valid.

Notes

1 The authors are on the board of directors of LLTF, which owns the copyright to the MLAT.
2 The sounds in the syllables on Part II are all English sounds, even if the spelling patterns representing those sounds are not. So here also, Carroll chose to avoid a foreign or artificial language learning exercise. The symbols he used are based on the Trager and Smith version of the IPA.
3 Carroll chose to not use a foreign language or artificial language for this section because he didn't want to bias the test in favor of those with language study experience. Indeed, he wanted to develop a test that would identify talent in someone who had never studied a foreign language. Carroll probably used English because he felt that an FL task would be too direct and simple. Short FL immersion courses in Chinese, Russian and other languages had been used to screen applicants for foreign language learning ability. Carroll rightfully thought that this approach was expensive and cumbersome, and he believed that it would be possible to develop a test of the mental abilities underlying language aptitude and that such a measure would ideally rely on English to the greatest degree possible. Carroll also thought that a test of the abilities underlying language aptitude was more theoretically interesting than a short course, even if the latter was predictive. Carroll recognized that a number of things could be predictive (attitudes, motivation, work habits, etc.), even if they have no or little relation to aptitude.
4 In an interview with Carroll, he told us that the MLAT's original publisher changed the directions, telling examinees that the 24 words were from Kurdish. Carroll said they felt that this would make the paired associate learning task more interesting for examinees. However, the words used here are nonsense words.
5 It is interesting to note that by including PLAB Part 4 (Language Analysis) instead of MLAT Part IV (Words in Sentences), Sasaki (and Pimsleur) were able to more directly assess inductive foreign language learning ability along with grammatical sensitivity. Carroll could have done this but opted not to for various reasons discussed in previous footnotes.

References

Carroll, J. B. (Ed.). (1956). *Language, thought, and reality: Selected writings of Benjamin Lee Whorf.* Boston: MIT Press.

Carroll, J. B. (1963). A model of school learning. *Teachers College Record, 64,* 723–733.

Carroll, J. B. (1981). Twenty-five years of research on Foreign language aptitude. In K. Diller (Ed.), *Individual differences and universals in language learning aptitude,* pp. 83–118. Rowley, MA: Newbury House.

Carroll, J. B. (1990). Cognitive abilities in Foreign language aptitude: Then and now. In T. S. Parry & C. W. Stansfield (Eds.), *Language aptitude reconsidered* (pp. 11–29). Washington, DC: Center for Applied Linguistics.

Carroll, J. B. (1993). *Human cognitive abilities: A survey of factor-analytic studies.* Cambridge: Cambridge University Press.

Carroll, J. B., & Sapon, S. M. (1959). *Modern language aptitude test.* New York, NY: Psychological Corporation. Republished in 2002 at Rockville, MD: Language Learning and Testing Foundation.

Carroll, J. B., Sapon, S. M., Reed, D. J., & Stansfield, C. W. (2010). *Modern Language Aptitude Test-Manual.* Rockville, MD: Language Learning and Testing Foundation.

de Graaff, R. (1997). The eXperanto experiment: Effects of explicit instruction on second language acquisition. *Studies in Second Language Acquisition, 19*(2), 249–275.

Ehrman, M. E. (1996). *Understanding second language learning difficulties.* Thousand Oaks, CA: Sage Publications.

Ehrman, M. E. (1998). The modern language aptitude test for predicting learning success and advising students. *Applied Language Learning, 9*(1), 33–70.

Ferencich, M. (1964). *Modern Language Aptitude Test—MLAT (Reattivo di attitudine linguistica): Adattamento italiano.* Florence: Organizzazioni Speciali.

Li, S. (2015). The associations between language aptitude and second language grammar acquisition: A meta-analytic review of five decades of research. *Applied Linguistics, 36*(3), 385–408.

Li, S. (2016). The construct validity of language aptitude: A meta-analysis. *Studies in Second Language Acquisition, 38,* 801–842.

Moskovsky, C., Alshahrani, M., Ratcheva, S., & Paolini, S. (2015). Aptitude as a predictor of second language achievement: An investigation in the Saudi Arabian context. *Arab World English Journal, 6*(1), 3–21.

Murakami, K. (1974). A language aptitude test for the Japanese. *System, 2*(3), 31–47.

Ottó, I. (1996). *Magyar Egyetemi Nyelvérzékmérő-Teszt.* Angol Alkalmazott Nyelvészeti Tanszék. Budapest, Hungary: Eötvös Loránd Tudományegyetem.

Ottó, I., & Nikolov, M. (2003). Magyar felsőoktatási intézmények elsőéves hallgatóinak nyelvérzéke. *Iskolakultura, 6–7,* 32–44.

Politzer, R. L. (1965). Some reflections on transfer of training in foreign language learning. *International Review of Applied Linguistics, 3,* 171–177,

Reed, D. J., & Stansfield, C. W. (2004). Using the modern language aptitude test to identify a Foreign language learning disability: Is it ethical? *Language Assessment Quarterly, 1*(2–3).

Rysiewicz, J. (2008). Measuring Foreign language learning aptitude: Polish adaptation of the modern language aptitude test. *Poznan Studies in Contemporary Linguistics, 44*(4), 569–595.

Rysiewicz, J. (2011). *Test Uzdolnień do Nauki Języków Obcych—TUNJO* [Polish Language Aptitude Test—PLAT]: *Analysis and statistics.* Poznań, Poland: Author.

Santana Rollán, M. E. (2012). *La aptitud lingüística en estudiantes ciegos* (Unpublished doctoral dissertation). Madrid: Universidad Complutense. Retrieved from http://eprints.ucm.es/22395/1/T34661.pdf

Sasaki, M. (1996). *Second language proficiency, Foreign language aptitude, and intelligence: Quantitative and qualitative analyses.* New York, NY: Peter Lang Publishing.

Sasaki, M. (2012). Review of the modern language aptitude test. *Language Testing, 29*(2), 315–321.

Skehan, P. (1999, March). *Aptitude.* Paper presented at the conference on Individual differences in foreign language learning: Effects of aptitude, intelligence and motivation, Tokyo, Japan.

Spolsky, B. (1989). *Conditions for second language learning.* Oxford: Oxford University Press.

Wells, W., Wesche, M., & Sarrazin, G. (1980). *Test d'aptitude aux langues vivantes.* Montreal: Institute for Psychological Research.

Wesche, M. B. (1981). Language aptitude measures in streaming, matching students with methods, and diagnosis of learning problems. In K. Diller (Ed.), *Individual differences and universals in language learning aptitude* (pp. 119–154). Rowley, MA: Newbury House.

Winke, P. (2005). *Individual differences in adult Chinese second language acquisition: The relationships among aptitude, memory, and strategies for learning* (Unpublished doctoral dissertation). Georgetown University, Washington, DC.

Winke, P. (2013). An investigation into second language aptitude for advanced Chinese language learning. *Modern Language Journal, 97*(1), 109–130.

3

DEVELOPMENT AND PRELIMINARY VALIDATION OF A FOREIGN LANGUAGE APTITUDE TEST FOR CHINESE LEARNERS OF FOREIGN LANGUAGES

Lanrong Li and Shaoqian (Sheila) Luo

Of the various individual factors in foreign language (FL) learning, FL aptitude is considered one of the most important individual differences (Skehan, 1998; Stansfield & Winke, 2008; Wen, 2012). Among tools for measuring FL aptitude, the Modern Language Aptitude Test (MLAT) developed by Carroll and Sapon (2002) is probably the most well-known. A great amount of research (see reviews by Carroll, 1981; Sawyer & Ranta, 2001; Skehan, 1998; Sparks & Ganschow, 2001) has shown that FL learners' performance on the MLAT correlated significantly with their FL attainment. Consequently, the MLAT has been used for a wide range of purposes such as selection and placement (Carroll, 1965; Wesche, 1981), diagnosing and treating L2 learners' problems (Gajar, 1987), informing curriculum design (Sawyer & Ranta, 2001) and research (DeKeyser, 2000). Though more than half a century has passed, the MLAT has stood the test of time and has been found to be predictive of FL learning outcomes in both formal and informal contexts (Harley & Hart, 1997; Horwitz, 1987; S. Li, 2015; Ranta, 2002; Stansfield & Reed, in press).

In China, a relatively small number of studies on FL aptitude have been conducted. One reason might be the lack of a valid and reliable tool for measuring FL aptitude of Chinese speakers. Most studies on FL aptitude in China have been confined to literature reviews (e.g., Dai & Cai, 2008; Fan & Du, 2001; Wen, 2005). A small number of empirical studies of Chinese FL learners (Dai, 2006; Wu, Liu, & Jeffrey, 1993; Ma & Wang, 2011) have shown that aptitude plays an important role in FL learning. However, all studies used the MLAT to measure the aptitude of Chinese FL learners. Since the MLAT is designed for native English speakers, there is a validity issue associated with using the MLAT to measure the FL aptitude of speakers of other languages. That is, the English language proficiency of test-takers can affect the validity of the test results and their interpretation.

Additionally, a closer look at the MLAT reveals that it is partly based on the measurement of the test-takers' native language proficiency. For example, MLAT-II Phonetic Script is based on the English sound system, and MLAT-IV Words in Sentences measures one's grammatical sensitivity in the English language. Moreover, though the MLAT has been shown to be highly reliable and valid and has become the benchmark for developing new FL aptitude tests (Grigorenko, Sternberg, & Ehrman, 2000, p. 397), it does not have a subtest specifically measuring inductive language learning ability, an FL aptitude component well represented in the Pimsleur Language Aptitude Battery (PLAB; Pimsleur, 1966). However, the PLAB, originally designed for English-speaking students in 7th to 12th grades, has been found to be too easy for Chinese college students (L. Li, 2015). Given the significant role FL aptitude plays in second language acquisition, this study aims to develop a tool for measuring the FL aptitude of adult Chinese speakers (over 16 years of age).

Theories in FL Aptitude

FL aptitude refers to "the individual's initial state and readiness and capacity for learning a foreign language, and probable degree of facility in doing so" (Carroll, 1981, p. 86). Carroll (1965) noted that FL aptitude does not determine whether or not one can learn an FL. Instead, FL aptitude can predict the speed and ease of learning an FL given the presence of motivation and opportunities for doing so. Based on the findings of his empirical research, Carroll (1981, p. 105) proposed that FL aptitude is not a monolithic construct but is composed of four components: 1) phonetic coding ability (the ability to identify sounds and establish associations between sounds and their symbols); 2) grammatical sensitivity (the ability to recognize grammatical functions of words in sentences); 3) rote learning ability (the ability to form associations between words and their meanings rapidly); and 4) inductive language learning ability (the ability to infer the rules underlying a set of grammatical materials).

The four aptitude components are held to be independent, yet correlated. For example, Carroll (1965) hypothesized that rote memory ability involves some phonetic coding ability, and inductive language learning ability may entail some rote memory ability. Carroll's FL aptitude theory laid the foundation for subsequent research in FL aptitude. Though many researchers have proposed their own FL aptitude theories (e.g., Robinson, 2005, 2007; Skehan, 1998, 2002), their theories either develop or complement Carroll's classical aptitude theory and have yet to be fully supported by research. Therefore, this study used Carroll's FL aptitude theory as the theoretical framework for developing the FL aptitude test.

Research in FL Aptitude Test Development

Since the introduction of the MLAT, a large number of researchers have developed new aptitude tests for different populations of FL learners or to test new theories.

For example, Petersen and Al-Haik (1976) developed the Defense Language Aptitude Battery (DLAB), Parry and Child (1990) developed VORD and Grigorenko et al. (2000) developed the Cognitive Ability for Novelty in Acquisition of Language – Foreign (CANAL-F). Aptitude tests have also been developed for speakers of other languages (see Stansfield & Reed, this volume). Recently, researchers at the University of Maryland developed a new test to predict advanced FL proficiency (Doughty et al., 2010; Linck et al., 2013).

Researchers in China have also attempted to develop an FL aptitude test for Chinese FL learners. For example, Liu, Liu and Deng (2005) developed a test to measure the grammatical sensitivity of Chinese college students. They designed eight different tasks and selected 15 students with the highest and lowest English achievement scores, respectively, to take the test. The results showed that the students' performance on the tasks using English as the test language was significantly correlated with their English achievement scores. However, their performance on the tasks using Chinese was not correlated with their English achievement scores. They interpreted these as being caused by the typological differences between Chinese and English and concluded that grammatical sensitivity to the Chinese language could not predict students' English achievement. However, this conclusion contradicted one of Carroll's (1965) research findings: one's grammatical sensitivity in one's native language could predict one's success in learning any FL. In addition, since the tasks on which students' performance showed correlation with students' English achievement were in English, the correlation could be due to students' English proficiency rather than FL aptitude, which calls the validity of the test into question.

Liu and Jiang (2006) also attempted to develop a test modeled after the MLAT and PLAB to measure Chinese college and middle school students' FL aptitude. They administered the test to 301 first-year English majors. Though their study showed that the students' overall aptitude scores correlated with their English achievement scores (with coefficients ranging from .154 to .306), the correlations were not strong compared to those of similar studies on FL aptitude tests. Furthermore, data on the psychometric properties of the test were not provided.

Xia (2011) made a similar attempt to develop an aptitude test for Chinese FL learners. She designed two tests: one was based on French and the other on Korean. Her study showed that students' performance on the French-based aptitude test could explain 31.6% of the variance in their English final examination scores, but their performance on the Korean-based aptitude test failed to reach significance in the regression model. Based on this result, Xia concluded that the Korean-based aptitude test was not able to measure students' FL aptitude. However, the study did not provide data on the reliability of the tests or the correlations between different aptitude subtests and English achievement. Additionally, using an existing FL as the test language of an FL aptitude test may limit the scope of the use of the test, as the test may not be able to validly measure the aptitude of test-takers who have some amount of proficiency in the test language.

To summarize, though researchers in China have made some explorations in developing an FL aptitude test for Chinese speakers, a valid and reliable FL aptitude measure has yet to be developed. In addition, most research in FL aptitude testing, both abroad and domestically, has been conducted in the framework of Classical Test Theory (CTT). However, there are fundamental limitations with CTT. For example, the raw scores are not interval data, item properties and person ability are sample dependent and errors are erroneously assumed to be equal (Alagumalai & Curtis, 2005). These drawbacks could be overcome by using the Rasch model (Rasch, 1960). The model converts raw scores into interval data, the item and person parameters are sample independent and each item and each test-taker have their own associated errors (Bond & Fox, 2015). These characteristics provide an advantage for the Rasch model over CTT in developing and validating tests. The objective of this study is to develop an FL aptitude test for Chinese FL learners who are at least 16 years old by drawing upon Carroll's FL aptitude theory, current cognitive psychology and second language acquisition theory and to provide preliminary evidence for the validity of the interpretation of the test by applying the Rasch model.

Research Method

Development of the Test

The test was developed by modeling the content after the MLAT and the PLAB. In terms of the test language, Chinese and artificial languages were used. The Chinese language was chosen because some aptitude components reflect knowledge and ability in one's native language. For example, MLAT-III Spelling Clues and MLAT-IV Grammatical Sensitivity both measure one's native language ability. Therefore, the Chinese language was used to measure test-takers' grammatical sensitivity. Artificial languages were used to ensure that 1) all test-takers have an equal chance of being exposed to a new language, which makes it possible to measure aptitude more objectively and reduce the threat to its internal validity; and 2) irregular language phenomena are better controlled. Because the test development was in its early stage, only a paper-and-pencil test was developed.

Six subtests were designed to measure the four aptitude components in Carroll's (1981) aptitude framework. The subtests were 1) Number Learning, 2) Spelling Clues, 3) Phonetic Script, 4) Paired Associates, 5) Words in Sentences, and 6) Language Analysis. Each subtest is described here.

Subtest 1–Number Learning corresponds to MLAT Subtest 1 and was designed to measure the auditory associative memory ability of language materials. Given the potential influence of familiar Chinese sounds on students' auditory memory, we selected consonants and vowels in Mandarin Chinese and other Chinese dialects and combined them to form meaningless syllables. However, each syllable still followed the structure of a typical Chinese syllable (a consonant + a simple or compound vowel). Each digit was indicated by one syllable, and place values of digits were indicated by additional syllables.

Subtest 2-Spelling Clues corresponds to MLAT Subtest 3 and was designed to measure phonetic coding ability. On the MLAT, this part uses pseudowords. The test-taker must be familiar with English word spelling and pronunciation rules and have strong English vocabulary knowledge to perform well in this subtest. For example, in order to find a synonym for the pseudo-word "simbl", the test-taker must be able to pronounce the new word and associate it with the English "symbol". The test-taker must also know the meaning of "symbol" in order to choose the right pseudonym. To develop a similar task in Chinese is a challenge, as the Chinese language has two separate writing systems to represent words: Chinese characters and Pinyin. Though some Chinese characters have phonetic radicals to indicate their pronunciations, the pronunciations of most Chinese characters cannot be inferred from their written forms. Moreover, one Pinyin syllable can represent a range of Chinese characters with totally different meanings. For example, "ge" with the first tone can be used to represent the pronunciation of "哥", "歌", and "割", which mean "brother", "song", and "cut", respectively. Therefore, contextual clues are typically needed to distinguish between different Chinese characters represented by the same syllable. To ensure the reliability of this subtest and in view of the characteristics of the Chinese language, we decided to use four-character set phrases as the basic test materials. Each set phrase has one fixed meaning, and the pronunciation of each character is also determined by the set phrase. To examine students' ability in dealing with Chinese sounds, we used different characters with similar pronunciations to those in a set phrase. For example, for a set phrase "马到成功" (meaning: win immediate success) with four characters pronounced as "mǎdàochénggōng", we used the combination of four characters totally unrelated in meaning "麻导秤巩" (the meanings of the four characters are numbness, guide, weigh and consolidate, respectively), which were pronounced as "mádǎochènggǒng". The test-taker's task was to identify the set phrase from the four characters with the same pronunciation but different tones.

Subtest 3-Phonetic Script corresponds to MLAT Subtest 2 and was designed to measure phonetic coding ability. All phonemes were from the Chinese language. However, syllables combined by these sounds had no corresponding Chinese words, so that the effect of familiar sounds on memory could be reduced to a minimum and students could focus on the association between the sounds they heard and their written symbols. In selecting symbols, we used symbols resembling Roman letters and Chinese Pinyin symbols.

Subtest 4-Paired Associates corresponds to MLAT Subtest 5 and was designed to measure associative memory of visually presented language materials. We analyzed the vocabulary of several rare natural languages and made adaptations to their spelling forms and used them as the basic testing materials for this subtest. To decrease the burden on students' visual memory, this part used lowercase Roman letters only. Combinations of these letters were readable but did not have tones.

Ellis and Beaton (1993) found that word class is a major factor affecting the difficulty in memorizing foreign words. To vary the difficulty of items, we measured words from various word classes, including nouns, verbs, adjectives and adverbs.

Subtest 5-Words in Sentences corresponds to MLAT Subtest 4 and was designed to measure grammatical sensitivity. A wide range of Chinese grammatical features was measured, including subjects, objects, predicates, complements and some features specific to the Chinese language.

Subtest 6-Language Analysis corresponds to PLAB Subtest 4 and was designed to measure inductive language learning ability. We used an artificial language based on an examination of the structure of several languages of different families (e.g., Indo-European, Sino-Tibetan). The words in the new language could be pronounced but were meaningless in both Chinese and English. Based on Skehan's (personal communication, 12 June 2012) suggestion, we applied Pienemann's (1998, 2005) Processability Theory in designing this part. The theory states that learners follow developmental stages in acquiring the grammatical features of second languages. The first stage is meanings of words/lemma. The second is the grammatical category of words, followed by grammatical information exchange (e.g., using inflections) within phrases and then within simple sentences (e.g., subject–verb agreement). The last stage is the exchange of grammar information within complex sentences. Higher stages are hypothesized to be based on the lower stages and involve more cognitive processing resources. Guided by this theory, we examined basic sentence structure and verb rules first, followed by noun formation rules and compound sentences.

Participants

To maximize the variability in the foreign language aptitude of test-takers, we selected students from two high schools and one university in Beijing. The two groups of high school students were from 12th grade of an elite high school and 10th grade of a nonelite high school, respectively. The college students varied in years of study in college and majors. In total, 160 students took the aptitude test but 2 failed to complete the test. The remaining 158 students had a mean age of 17.96 with a standard deviation of 2.95 years. There were 61 males and 97 females. On average, the college students and the high school students had studied English for 9.82 and 10.41 years, respectively, at the time they took the test.

Instrument

Due to practical constraints in administering the test to the high school students and in view of the potential difference in FL aptitude between high school and college students, we prepared two versions of the test: Test A (the complete version) for college students and Test B (a shortened version) for high school students. Test B was not only shorter than Test A, it was also expected to be easier as it was formed by removing some items considered to be more difficult in each subtest of Test A. Following is a description of each subtest.

Subtest 1-Number Learning had two testing phases. In Phase 1, the students learned numbers (e.g., 13, 561) represented by meaningless syllables by listening to the recordings of these numbers in a novel language, followed by some practice. In Phase 2, they were asked to write the numeric forms of the numbers they derived. The recording was played only once.

Subtest 2-Spelling Clues had 20 pseudo-Chinese set phrases composed of four Chinese characters. Each character was a homophone (differing only in tones) of the original character of the set phrase. Students needed to identify the set phrase from the combination of the four homophones. To avoid having the students fail simply because they didn't know how to write a character, we reminded them that they could use Pinyin if necessary.

The items in Subtest 3-Phonetic Script were divided into several blocks. In each block, test-takers heard the recordings of some meaningless syllables while looking at their corresponding written symbols in the answer sheet to establish the associations between the sounds and their symbols. After each block, they were tested on their memory of the associations. For each item, they would hear one syllable, and their task was to select its corresponding symbol.

Subtest 4-Paired Associates first asked students to memorize the meanings of some foreign words in a short time. Each word was given its Chinese equivalent. Then, they were given two minutes of practice to write the Chinese equivalent of each word. In the testing phase, students needed to select the correct Chinese equivalent from four options.

Subtest 5-Words in Sentences presented students with a pair of sentences in each item. The first sentence, also called the key sentence, had one word highlighted using bold font and a rectangle frame. In the second sentence, four words were highlighted. The test-taker needed to select the word that had a similar grammatical function as the highlighted word in the key sentence from the four options. Following is a sample item:

北京是中国的首都。 (**Beijing** is the capital of China)
第一次手术的成功极大地增强了我们的信心。
A B C D
The success of the first operation greatly enhanced our confidence.
B A C D

Subtest 6-Language Analysis presented words and sentences from the artificial language developed for the test along with their Chinese equivalents. They needed to infer the grammatical rules governing the sentences. Each item had a sentence in either Chinese or the novel language, and the students were asked to select the correct corresponding sentence expressed in the novel language or Chinese. Following is an example (with options omitted):

下面给出了两个外语单词和一个外语句子以及它们相对应的汉语意思 *(Below are two foreign words, one foreign sentence, and their Chinese meanings)*:

aijo: 妈妈 (mother)
la ponra: 那只狗 (that dog)
aijo la ponram ne: 妈妈喜欢那只狗 (Mother likes that dog.)

现在请你根据上面给出的内容，想想下面的中文句子该如何用这种新的语言来表达 *(now please think about how the following sentence should be expressed in the new language)*:
那只狗喜欢妈妈.(That dog likes mother.)

In this subtest, there were also items that asked the students to choose the correct Chinese equivalents of a foreign sentence from four options.

Table 3.1 shows the components measured, formats, number of items and the test length of each subtest for the two test forms.

All items were objective test items and were dichotomously scored. There were 182 items in Test A and 113 items in Test B. The testing time for the two forms were around 60 and 45 minutes, respectively. The first page of the answer sheet was a short questionnaire, which was designed to collect demographic information about the test-takers. To examine the external validity of the test, we collected the midterm English examination scores of the two groups of high school students.

Procedures

The test was administered to the students in September 2012. The college students took the test in a quiet classroom in the university, and the high school

TABLE 3.1 Components of the FL aptitude test for Chinese FL learners

Task	Aptitude component	Format	Number of items (A/B)	Time (A/B)
1NL	Associative memory	Fill in the blank	42/28	7/6 min
2SC	Phonetic coding	Fill in the blank	30/18	4/ 2.5 min
3PS	Phonetic coding	Multiple choice	30/20	10/7 min
4PA	Associative memory	Multiple choice	24/24	7/7 min
5WS	Grammatical sensitivity	Multiple choice	31/20	10/7 min
6LA	Inductive language learning ability	Multiple choice	15/9	20/15 min

Note: NL = Number Learning, SC = Spelling Clues, PS = Phonetic Script, PA = Paired Associates, WS = Words in Sentences, LA = Language Analysis.

students took the test during normal class periods. The students volunteered to take the test, and each was offered a gift as compensation for their time.

Data Analysis

We used Winsteps 3.74 (Linacre, 2012a) to conduct the Rasch analysis of the test items and to examine the internal validity of the test. We investigated item fit statistics, unidimensionality, item reliability, person reliability and item targeting.

Item fit indicates the extent to which data fit the Rasch model. There are two fit statistics in the Rasch model: infit and outfit. Infit is more sensitive to unexpected responses by persons on items that are roughly targeted on them. The outfit is more sensitive to anomalous responses by persons on items that are off the target of their abilities (e.g., a high-ability examinee answers an easy item incorrectly or a low-ability examinee answers a hard item correctly) (Linacre, 2002). When data fit the expectation of the Rasch model, both infit and outfit approach the value of 1. For low-stake tests, values between 0.7 and 1.3 and their t values between -2 and 2 are considered as showing good fit (Bond & Fox, 2015). When the value is greater than 1.3 and its t values exceed 2, it is called underfit, indicating that there is some random behavior unexplained by the Rasch model. When the value is less than 0.7, it indicates overfit. Overfit suggests that there might be some redundant items. As large infit values are a greater threat to validity, we chose an infit value greater than 1.3 and a t value greater than 2 as the criteria for identifying misfitting items.

Besides infit statistics, the principal component analysis of residuals after removing the Rasch measure also provides evidence for the unidimensionality of the data. When the eigenvalue of the first component of the residuals is greater than 3 (Linacre, 2012b), a test is generally considered to be unidimensional.

In the Rasch model, reliability is the replicability of a person/item parameter when similar items are administered to the same test-takers or another similar group of test-takers take the same test (Bond & Fox, 2015). Additionally, the Rasch model provides person/item separation index. The separation index shows the number of different levels persons/items could be divided into.

Winsteps also provides a Person–Item Map, which puts parameters of test-takers and items on the same logit scale. This procedure enables a more direct and intuitive comparison between person ability and item difficulty, an assessment of the item difficulty hierarchy, identification of redundant items and gaps for more items.

Results and Discussion

Results of Rasch Data Analysis

Table 3.2 shows the person reliability, item reliability, Cronbach's alpha, person ability and item difficulty estimates, number of misfitting items and the eigenvalue

TABLE 3.2 Summary of the results of Rach analyses of the FL aptitude test

Task	Misfitting items	Eigenvalue of the first component	Person ability	Item difficulty	Person reliability/ separation index	Item reliability/ Separation index	Alpha
1NL	2	3.3	0.13	0.62	0.87/2.6	0.84/2.28	0.92
2SC	0	2.7	0.38	0.88	0.82/2.15	0.91/3.19	0.91
3PS	3	2.2	1	1.2	0.68/1.46	0.87/2.63	0.82
4PA	0	1.9	1.64	0.6	0.65/1.37	0.86/2.44	0.85
5WS	2	2	0.8	1.36	0.71/1.58	0.96/4.75	0.86
6LA	2	2.1	0.38	1.11	0.64/1.35	0.95/4.27	0.77

Note: NL = Number Learning, SC = Spelling Clues, PS = Phonetic Script, PA = Paired Associates, WS = Words in Sentences, LA = Language Analysis.

of the first component of Rasch model residuals. Overall, the six subtests showed a good fit to the Rasch model, especially Subtest 2-Spelling Clues and Subtest 4-Paired Associates, as all the items showed good model–data fit. However, for the other subtests, two or three misfitting items were identified.

The eigenvalue of the first component of the Rasch model residuals for the first subtest was 3.3. After removing the two misfitting items, the eigenvalue was still 3.3, which suggests a second dimension underlying the data. By examining the two groups of items that had negative and positive loadings on the first component, it was found that for some items the students not only needed to recall the meanings of the sounds but also to infer the correct places of digits. However, for other items, the students did not need to infer digit places. For example, for the number "306", besides being able to recall the two digits "3" and "6", the test-taker also needed to infer the correct places of the two digits based on the sounds that indicate place values of digits. However, for another number "326", as there are already three nonzero digits, the test-taker did not need to infer the correct places of these digits. Carroll (1965, 1981) hypothesized that the corresponding MLAT-I measures both auditory memory and inductive language learning ability. We hypothesized that those numbers that require inferences on digit valued measured inductive language learning ability in addition to auditory rote memory. The Rasch model provided evidence for multidimensionality of this subtest.

Subtest 3-Phonetic Script had three misfitting items (with infit >2). A closer examination of these three items revealed that there was one recording error for one syllable. In another item, the four sounds required strong ability in differentiating sounds with high similarity. According to Carroll (1965), ability in differentiating sounds is different from phonetic coding ability, which might explain the misfit of this item. The misfit of the third item was due to a print error. After removing the three misfitting items, the other items showed a good fit to the model.

In Subtest 5-Words in Sentences, two items showed misfit. By examining the item characteristic curve of one misfitting item, we found that a small number of test-takers with ability estimates much lower than the item difficulty estimates answered this item correctly. A closer look at this item revealed that one option provided clues to the correct answer. Analysis of another item showed that the item had two correct answers. After removing the two misfitting items, the remaining items showed a good fit to the model.

The two misfitting items for Subtest 6-Language Analysis happened to be the two most difficult items. An analysis of the two items revealed that they provided clues to the correct answer, resulting in unexpected correct answers from low-ability students.

In terms of unidimensionality, the eigenvalue of the first component was less than 3 for all subtests except Subtest 1-Number Learning. This finding suggests that Subtests 2–6 measured one dimension. In terms of difficulty, the most difficult subtests were Subtest 1-Number Learning (with average person ability estimate at 0.13), Subtest 2-Spelling Clues and Subtest 6-Language Analysis (both with average person ability estimate at 0.38). Subtest-1 Number Learning measured students' auditory memory ability. This subtest also measured students' acuity in response to sounds. For students who are used to memorizing FL words visually, this subtest was a challenge. While administering the test to the college students, the researchers observed that one student did not write even one word. In an informal interview, this student explained that he was used to memorizing words visually and found it very hard to memorize words by simply listening to their sounds. This finding also shows that though Number Learning and Paired Associates were both designed to measure memory ability, they might reflect different preferences among learners in memorizing language materials. Grigorenko et al. (2000) also designed two ways (orally and visually) of presenting language materials to test-takers to reflect differences in modes of processing FL materials. Subtest 2-Spelling Clues and Subtest 6-Language Analysis showed a good match with the ability of the test-takers, and their abilities were also more varied. Though the students' estimated ability in Subtest 5-Words in Sentences was also varied, this subtest was easier for them. The easiest subtest was Paired Associates. The estimated person ability was 1.64, and 16 students obtained full scores. This might also be the reason for the low reliability of this subtest. From the feedback of test-takers on this subtest, we learned that the practice part of the subtest made the test much easier than other subtests.

In terms of reliability, Cronbach's alpha for the subtests ranged from 0.77 to 0.92, suggesting satisfactory internal reliability. Item reliability for the subtests ranged from 0.84 to 0.96, while person reliability ranged from 0.64 to 0.87. Subtest 4-Language Analysis had the lowest person reliability, which might be due to the small number of items in this subtest. However, overall, person reliability and item reliability of the test were satisfactory.

The Item–Person Map showed the match between person ability and item difficulty and the hierarchy of item difficulty (see Appendix). There was a good match between person ability and item difficulty for Subtests 1, 2 and 6. The easiest subtest was Part 4-Paired Associates. About half of the test-takers had ability estimates higher than the difficulty of the most difficult items, which also made it hard to reliably measure these students' ability. From the first figure in the Appendix, we could also see that the difficulty range for Subtest 1-Number Learning was quite narrow. Students with either high or low ability cannot be reliably measured by this subtest, which might be caused by the limited number of digits used to measure students' memory ability. More difficult and easier items could be designed to increase the difficulty range of this subtest.

Correlations Among FL Aptitude Subtests

Table 3.3 shows the correlations among students' FL aptitude subtest scores. Except for Subtest 2-Spelling Clues, all subtests showed weak to moderate correlations. The result also lends support to Carroll's (1965) theory, which claims that these aptitude components are correlated with, yet independent of, each other. However, Subtest 2-Spelling Clues had the lowest correlation with the total aptitude score (0.539) and had weak significant correlations with Subtest 1-Number Learning and Subtest 4-Paired Associates, but had a nonsignificant correlation with Subtest 3-Phonetic Script. The result suggests that Subtest 2-Spelling Clues may only weakly measure Chinese language vocabulary and phonetic coding ability. The correlation of Subtest 2 with the two subtests (Number Learning and Paired Associates) measuring memory ability might be attributed to its task characteristics. In Subtest 2, to be able to retrieve the correct set phrase, students needed to keep the sounds of those alternative characters in memory temporarily, which is similar to the tasks in Number Learning and Paired Associates.

Furthermore, though Subtest 1-Number Learning and Subtest 4-Paired Associates measured rote memory ability, the former had the highest correlation with Subtest 3-Phonetic Script, which measured phonetic coding ability, and also had

TABLE 3.3 Correlation matrix among the six FL aptitude subtests

Task	2 SC	3 PS	4 PA	5 WS	6 LA	Total
1 NL	.234**	.510**	.415**	.408**	.308**	.754**
2 SC		.146	.262**	.097	.130	.539**
3 PS			.311**	.376**	.346**	.655**
4 PA				.289**	.309**	.657**
5 WS					.450**	.619**
6 LA						.653**

Note: **, *p* < 0.01 (two-tailed); NL = Number Learning, SC = Spelling Clues, PS = Phonetic Script, PA = Paired Associates, WS = Words in Sentences, LA = Language Analysis.

moderate correlations with Subtest 5-Words in Sentences and Subtest 6-Language Analysis. The result suggests that Subtest 1-Number Learning measured more than rote learning ability. It might also tap inductive language learning ability.

Subtest 5-Words in Sentences and Subtest 6-Language Analysis had a moderate correlation at 0.45, which supports Skehan's (1998) hypothesis of the close association between the two components. Both subtests might have measured general verbal intelligence. However, further studies are needed to examine the relationship between general intelligence, grammatical sensitivity and inductive language learning ability.

Correlations Between FL Aptitude and English Language Achievement

Table 3.4 shows the descriptive statistics of the midterm English examination scores and FL aptitude scores for both the 10th- and 12th-grade high school students. The mean FL aptitude score of the 12th-grade students was higher than that of the 10th-grade students. As mentioned earlier, the 12th-grade students were from an elite high school in Beijing and had passed strict exams before entering the high school. Their academic ability and general intelligence might be higher on average than that of the 10th-grade students, who were from the nonelite school. The 12th graders' better performance on the FL aptitude test could also be partly ascribed to the age factor. The MLAT manual (2002) shows that students' FL aptitude increases with age and stabilizes after 18 years of age. In terms of English achievement scores, we also found that there was more variability among the 10th-grade students than the 12th-grade students in their aptitude scores.

TABLE 3.4 Descriptive statistics of FL aptitude scores and English achievement scores of the high school students

Task	10th Grade				12th Grade			
	Min	Max	Mean	SD	Min	Max	Mean	SD
1 NL	−4.72	2.16	−.80	1.37	−1.23	4.59	2.25	1.73
2 SC	−4.64	1.14	−.75	1.51	−3.29	4.38	1.27	2.28
3 PS	−1.30	4.08	.78	1.38	−.39	4.08	2.09	1.33
4 PA	−.75	3.29	1.08	1.13	−.18	4.52	2.59	1.49
5 WS	−2.18	1.94	−.16	.99	−1.10	4.03	1.74	1.26
6 LA	−4.48	2.64	−.97	1.83	−2.00	2.64	1.06	1.52
Aptitude	−1.31	.89	−.14	.55	.38	3.84	1.83	.87
English	78.00	140.00	115.20	14.52	100.00	141.00	121.41	10.22

Note: **, p < 0.01 (two-tailed); NL = Number Learning, SC = Spelling Clues, PS = Phonetic Script, PA = Paired Associates, WS = Words in Sentences, LA = Language Analysis.

TABLE 3.5 Correlations between FL aptitude and English achievement of the high school students

English Achievement	NL	SC	PS	PA	WS	LA	Aptitude
10th Grade	.399★	.000	.374★	.572★★	−.021	.186	.612★★
12th Grade	.034	−.070	.170	.004	.336	.024	.114

Note: ★, $p < 0.05$, ★★, $p < 0.01$ (two-tailed); NL = Number Learning, SC = Spelling Clues, PS = Phonetic Script, PA = Paired Associates, WS = Words in Sentences, LA = Language Analysis; the number of students in 10th grade and 12th grade were 32 and 29, respectively.

Table 3.5 shows the correlations between the two groups of students' aptitude scores and English achievement scores.

As shown in Table 3.5, there was a strong correlation between 10th-grade students' total aptitude score and their midterm English examination score (coefficient of 0.612). Among the aptitude subtests Subtest 1-Number Learning, Subtest 3-Phonetic Script and Subtest 4-Paired Associates had the strongest correlation with their English achievement scores (coefficients of 0.3999, 0.374 and 0.572, respectively). These findings provide evidence for the external validity of the aptitude test and suggest that aptitude is an important individual variable in FL learning (Skehan, 1998; Stansfield & Winke, 2008). In addition, Skehan (1998) hypothesized that memory ability and phonetic coding ability are particularly important at the beginning stage of FL learning. We speculate that the 10th-grade students' English proficiency was at the low to intermediate level, which might be the reason why memory ability and phonetic coding ability correlated more strongly with their English achievement.

However, the aptitude scores of the 12th-grade students were not related to their English achievement scores. This finding may be due to the fact that all the students scored high on the aptitude test and there was little variability in their English exam scores. Another reason might be that when students reach 12th grade, other individual factors like motivation might begin to play a more important role in their language learning. For example, Sick (2007) studied a group of Japanese high school students for three years and found that though both aptitude and motivation were important predictors of FL learning, the influence of motivation was stronger than that of aptitude from 11th grade on. Students with low aptitude began to spend more time on FL learning, which also made the gap in English proficiency between them and those with stronger FL aptitude smaller. Subtest 6-Language Analysis was not correlated with students' English achievement for either group. This finding might be due to the smaller number of items. After removing two misfitting items, only seven items remained, which were too few to reliably measure students' ability. Furthermore, this subtest was found to be too easy for the 12th-grade students (two-thirds of the student obtained full scores). Low variability in their aptitude scores also contributed to the nonsignificant correlation between FL aptitude scores and their English achievement. Subtest 2-Spelling Clues exhibited little correlation with their English achievement. In view of this result, we speculate that the ability measured by this subtest may not be able to predict students' FL learning.

Conclusion

This study developed an FL aptitude test for Chinese learners of FLs. The result of the preliminary validation study showed that most of the items demonstrated good fit to the Rasch model and most subtests showed unidimensionality, high reliability, and internal consistency. There was a good match between overall test difficulty and students' ability. However, the Rasch model also helped to identify some misfitting items and items that might be redundant and/or should be added. The significant intercorrelations among the aptitude subtests and their correlation with one group of students' English achievement also provided evidence for the structural and external validity of the test. It was also found that Subtest 4-Paired Associates was too easy for the students and Subtest 2-Spelling Clues may have failed to measure any of the aptitude components. Future studies could remove Subtest 2-Spelling Clues and increase the difficulty of Subtest-4 Paired Associates (e.g., by removing the practice part). Though the aptitude test needs to be revised and more validity studies need to be conducted, this study provided evidence for the validity of using Carroll's (1981) theory in developing an FL aptitude test in a language markedly different from English. Admittedly, differences between language systems might be one of the causes for the difficulty of validly measuring some aptitude components (e.g., phonetic coding ability), yet this can also be an interesting topic for further exploration in this area.

This study has several limitations. First, we did not examine the validity and reliability of the school English achievement tests of the high school students. This limitation may directly affect the correlations obtained between FL aptitude and FL achievement. Second, we did not measure the English achievement of the college students in our study. Third, though FL is considered relatively stable (Carroll, 1981), as the students in our study had studied English for years, it is possible that their aptitude might have undergone some changes as their FL learning experience grew, which would make it difficult to interpret the correlation between aptitude and achievement as evidence of the validity of the test result.

In view of the limitations, it is suggested that future studies use standardized tests to measure students' language achievement. Additionally, unless there is firm and unanimous evidence showing that FL aptitude is stable and impervious to language learning, it would be best to investigate the predictive validity of new aptitude tests by administering them to individuals who have never studied any FLs but are going to studying a new FL and then compare their performance in the aptitude test and their FL achievement after some period of study.

References

Alagumalai, S., & Curtis, D. (2005). Classical test theory. In S. Alagumalai, D. Curtis & N. Hungi (Eds.), *Applied Rasch measurement: A book of exemplars* (pp. 1–14). Dordrecht, The Netherlands: Springer.

Bond, T. G., & Fox, C. M. (2015). *Applying the Rasch model: Fundamental measurement in the human sciences* (3rd ed.). Mahwah, NJ: Lawrence Erlbaum Associates, Inc.

Carroll, J. B. (1965). The prediction of success in intensive Foreign language training. In R. Glaser (Ed.), *Training, research, and education* (pp. 87–136). New York, NY: Wiley.

Carroll, J. B. (1981). Twenty-five years of research on Foreign language aptitude. In K. C. Diller (Ed.), *Individual differences and universals in language learning aptitude* (pp. 83–118). Rowley, MA: Newbury House.

Carroll, J. B., & Sapon, S. (2002). *Modern language aptitude test manual.* North Bethesta, MD: Second Language Testing Inc.

Dai, Y. (2006). The effects of language aptitude on second language acquisition. *Foreign Language Teaching and Research*, *38*(6), 451–459.

Dai, Y., & Cai, J. (2008). Research on language aptitude in SLA: History, state of the art, reflection and prospect. *Journal of Foreign Languages*, *31*(5), *80–90*.

DeKeyser, R. M. (2000). The robustness of critical period effects in second language acquisition. *Studies in Second Language Acquisition*, *22*(4), 499–533.

Doughty, C. J., Campbell, S. G., Mislevy, M. A., Bunting, M. F., Bowles, A. R., & Koeth, J. T. (2010). Predicting near-native ability: The factor structure and reliability of Hi-LAB. In M. Prior, Y. Watanabe, & S. Lee (Eds.), *Second language research forum 2008 proceedings* (pp. 10–31). Somerville, MA: Cascadilla Press.

Ellis, N. C., & Beaton, A. (1993). Psycholinguistic determinants of foreign language vocabulary learning. *Language Learning*, *43*(4), 559–617.

Fan, L., & Du, G. (2001). Language aptitude and its impact on language learning. *Shandong Foreign Language Journal*, *22*(2), 65–68.

Gajar, A. H. (1987). Foreign language learning disabilities: The identification of predictive and diagnostic variables. *Journal of Learning Disabilities*, *20*(6), 327–330.

Grigorenko, E. L., Sternberg, R. J., & Ehrman, M. E. (2000). A theory-based approach to the measurement of Foreign language learning ability: The CANAL-F theory and test. *The Modern Language Journal*, *84*(3), 390–405.

Harley, B., & Hart, D. (1997). Language aptitude and second language proficiency in classroom learners of different starting ages. *Studies in Second Language Acquisition*, *19*(3), 379–400.

Horwitz, E. K. (1987). Linguistic and communicative competence: Reassessing Foreign language aptitude. In B. Van Patten, T. R. Dvorak, & J. F. Lee (Eds.), *Foreign language learning: A research perspective* (pp. 146–157). Cambridge, MA: Newbury House.

Li, L. (2015). Can PLAB be used to measure Chinese students' Foreign language aptitude? A Rasch-based study. *Foreign Language Testing and Teaching*, (2), 11–20.

Li, S. (2015). The associations between language aptitude and second language grammar acquisition: A meta-analytic review of five decades of research. *Applied Linguistics*, *36*, 385–408.

Linacre, J. M. (2002). What do infit and outfit mean-square and standardized mean? *Rasch Measurement Transactions*, *16*(2), 878.

Linacre, J. M. (2012a). *Winsteps (Version 3.74.0).* Beaverton, OR: Winstep.com.

Linacre, J. M. (2012b). *Winsteps Rasch measurement computer program User's Guide.* Beaverton, OR: Winsteps.com.

Linck, J. A., Hughes, M. M., Campbell, S. G., Smith, B. K., Bunting, M. F., & Doughty, C. J. (2013). Hi-LAB: A new measure of aptitude for high-level language proficiency. *Language Learning, 63*(3), 530–566.

Liu, J., & Jiang, N. (2006). A report on English language aptitude test among Chinese learners. *Foreign Languages in China, 3*(4), 63–68.

Liu, T., Liu, L., & Deng, J. (2005). A correlational study on the test index of grammatical sensitivity in language aptitude. *Journal of Southwest University for Nationalities, 26*(10), 292–295.

Ma, Z., & Wang, T. (2011). The effects of language aptitude and working memory on L2 reading comprehension. *Shandong Foreign Language Journal, 32*(3), 41–47.

Parry, T. S., & Child, J. R. (1990). Preliminary investigation of relationship between VORD, MLAT and language proficiency. In T. Parry, & C. W. Stansfield (Eds.), *Language aptitude reconsidered* (pp. 30–66). Englewood Cliffs, NJ: Prentice-Hall.

Petersen, C. R., & Al-Haik, A. R. (1976). The development of the Defense Language Aptitude Battery (DLAB). *Educational and Psychological Measurement, 36*(2), 369–380.

Pienemann, M. (1998). *Language processing and second language development: Processability Theory* (Vol. 15). Amsterdam, The Netherlands: John Benjamins Publishing Company.

Pienemann, M. (2005). *Cross-linguistic aspects of processability theory* (Vol. 30). Amsterdam, The Netherlands: John Benjamins Publishing Company.

Pimsleur, P. (1966). *Pimsleur language aptitude battery*. New York, NY: Harcourt Brace Jovanovich.

Ranta, L. (2002). The role of learners' language analytic ability in the communicative classroom. In P. Robinson (Ed.), *Individual differences and instructed language learning* (pp. 159–180). Amsterdam, The Netherlands: John Benjamins Publishing Company.

Rasch, G. (1960). *Probabilistic models for some intelligence and achievement tests*. Copenhagen: Danish Institute for Educational Research.

Robinson, P. (2005). Aptitude and second language acquisition. *Annual Review of Applied Linguistics, 25*(1), 46–73.

Robinson, P. (2007). Aptitudes, abilities, contexts, and practice. In R. DeKeyser (Ed.), *Practice in a second language: Perspectives from applied linguistics and cognitive psychology* (pp. 256–286). Cambridge: Cambridge University Press.

Sawyer, M., & Ranta, L. (2001). Aptitude, individual differences, and instructional design. In P. Robinson (Ed.), *Cognition and second language instruction* (pp. 319–353). Cambridge: Cambridge University Press.

Sick, J. (2007). *The learner's contribution: Individual differences in language learning in a Japanese high school* (Unpublished doctoral dissertation). Temple University, Philadelphia.

Skehan, P. (1998). *A cognitive approach to language learning*. Oxford: Oxford University Press.

Skehan, P. (2002). Theorising and updating aptitude. In P. Robinson (Ed.), *Individual differences and instructed language learning* (pp. 69–94). New York, NY: Lawrence Erlbaum Associates, Inc.

Sparks, R., & Ganschow, L. (2001). Aptitude for learning a Foreign language. *Annual Review of Applied Linguistics, 21*, 90–111.

Stansfield, C. W., & Reed, D. J. (in press). Looking back on 60 years of the MLAT. In Z. Wen, P. Skehan, A. Biedroń, S. Li, & R. L. Sparks (Eds.), *Rethinking language aptitude: Contemporary insights and emerging trends*. London: Routledge.

Stansfield, C. W., & Winke, P. (2008). Testing aptitude for second language learning. In E. Shohamy (Ed.), *Language testing: Encyclopedia of language and education Vol. 7* (pp. 81–94). Boston, MA: Kluwer Academic Publishers.

Wen, Z. (2005). Foreign language aptitude revisited. *Modern Foreign Language*, (4), 57–66.

Wen, Z. (2012). Foreign language aptitude. *English Language Teaching Journal*, *66*(2), 233–235.

Wesche, M. (1981). Language aptitude measures in streaming, matching students with methods, and diagnosis of learning problems. In K. C. Diller (Ed.), *Individual differences and universals in language learning aptitude* (pp. 119–154). Rowley, MA: Newbury House.

Wu, Y., Liu, R., & Jeffrey, P. (1993). Learner factors and language learning achievement: A survey. *Foreign Language Teaching and Research*, *25*(1), 36–46.

Xia, H. (2011). A language aptitude test for native Chinese: Development and validation. *Shandong Foreign Language Journal*, *32*(5), 52–55.

Appendix: Map of the Six FL Aptitude Subtests

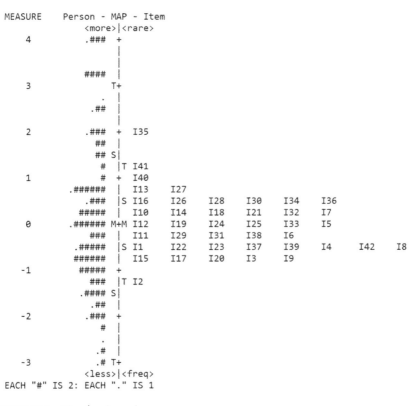

```
MEASURE    Person - MAP - Item
              <more>|<rare>
   4        .###   +
                   |
                   |
                   |
            ####   |
   3             T+
             .     |
            .##    |
                   |
   2        .###   +  I35
            ##     |
            ## S|
             #  |T I41
   1         #  +  I40
          .######  |   I13   I27
            .###  |S I16   I26    I28    I30    I34    I36
           #####  |   I10   I14    I18    I21    I32    I7
   0      .###### M+M I12   I19    I24    I25    I33    I5
            ###   |   I11   I29    I31    I38    I6
          .#####  |S I1    I22    I23    I37    I39    I4    I42    I8
          ######  |   I15   I17    I20    I3     I9
  -1      #####   +
            ###   |T I2
          .#### S|
            .##   |
  -2        .###  +
             #    |
             .    |
            .#    |
  -3        .#   T+
              <less>|<freq>
  EACH "#" IS 2: EACH "." IS 1
```

FIGURE 3.1   Number Learning

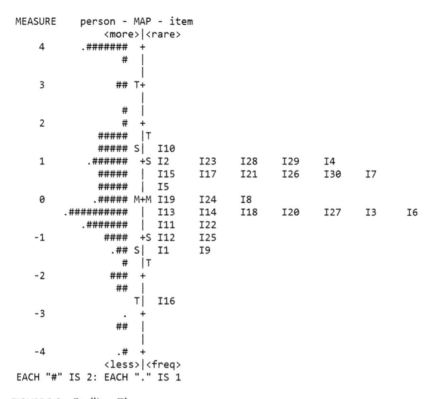

FIGURE 3.2 Spelling Clues

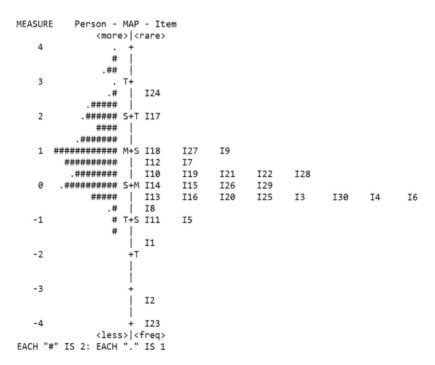

FIGURE 3.3 Phonetic Script

```
MEASURE    Person - MAP - Item
              <more>|<rare>
    4     .######### +
                     |
                   T |
                     |
          .######### |
    3             .  +
                     |
             .####   |
                   S |
                .    |
    2           .### +
                .### |
                 .   |
              .##### |
              .#### M|T
    1          ###### +   I11     I5
          .########## |   I13     I21
              .####   |S  I20
                  .#  |   I14     I15     I16
                 .### S|   I1     I10     I2
    0          #####  +M  I17
                  .#  |   I18     I22     I23     I24     I7
                  .#  |   I6      I9
                   #  |S  I19     I4
                  .#  |   I8
   -1           .  T +
                     |T  I12     I3
                     |
                     |
                     |
   -2                +
              <less>|<freq>
    EACH "#" IS 2: EACH "." IS 1
```

FIGURE 3.4   Paired Associates

```
MEASURE      Person - MAP - Item
                <more>|<rare>
   4            .  +
                   |
                #  |  I26
   3          .## T+
                .  |T I25
            .##### |
   2          ### S+  I30
            ##### |  I7
      ############ |S I17    I31
   1    .######### +  I24    I8
      ########## M|  I12    I18    I23
         .###### |  I27
   0     .####### +M I1     I19    I20
         ##### S|  I11    I14    I22    I28    I9
           .### |  I13    I15    I16    I3
  -1        ### +  I29
            .# T|S I21    I6
            .# |  I10    I4     I5
  -2            +
                |
                |T
  -3            +
                |  I2
                |
  -4            +
             <less>|<freq>
   EACH "#" IS 2: EACH "." IS 1
```

FIGURE 3.5 Words in Sentences

```
MEASURE     Person - MAP - Item
               <more>|<rare>
    4          .####  +
                      |
                      |
    3          .###  T+
                      |
               ###   |T
    2                 +
           ######## S|   I12
                  ## |    I13      I14      I15
    1          ######  +S
        .############  |    I8
               #### M|    I10
    0      .########  +M  I11      I5
           ########  |    I1       I6       I9
                      |    I3       I7
   -1      .#######  S+S
               ####  |
                   . |    I2
   -2      .####   +
                   T|T  I4
                      |
   -3          ##   +
                      |
                      |
   -4             .  +
               <less>|<freq>
   EACH "#" IS 2: EACH "." IS 1
```

FIGURE 3.6   Language Analysis

4

LANGUAGE APTITUDE IMPLICATES LANGUAGE AND COGNITIVE SKILLS[1]

Peter Skehan

The Place of Language Abilities in Foreign Language Aptitude

It may seem a little odd that the theme of this first section is the question as to whether language abilities themselves have any special role in the study of foreign language aptitude. It may seem obvious that this is so. Yet in recent years proposals have been made regarding aptitude which de-emphasise the nature of specifically language skills and instead propose general psychological mechanisms and processes as fundamental. This presents something of a contrast with previous work on foreign language aptitude (Skehan, 1989), on the research which had previously been conducted (Carroll, 1965), and the aptitude batteries and tests which had been constructed (Carroll & Sapon, 1959). For that reason, there is some relevance in re-examining whether language abilities are distinct, and this needs to be integral to aptitude constructs and aptitude tests.

A first point to consider is whether there is a critical period for language learning. If there is no such thing and what have been termed unified approaches are central (Macwhinney, 2005), then the need to posit a special status for language reduces considerably. In contrast, a critical period approach would suggest that early in life predispositions for implicit language learning exist and that after some cut-off point, either suddenly or gradually, the involvement of such specific talents diminishes and general learning mechanisms and processes underlie learning in the domain of language (DeKeyser, 2000). Interestingly, both of these positions (a unified approach and a critical period approach) can be argued to mean that language, in the second language, post-critical period case, is not special, and general learning (and therefore aptitudes based on general learning principles) are what we need to focus on. In this section I want to argue that, despite these possibilities, language is special, even while assuming the existence of a critical period and that a concern to embed language tasks and material within foreign language aptitude tests is indispensable.

We can recast this discussion, first of all, in terms of the status of Universal Grammar (UG), an inbuilt propensity to learn language (Meisel, 2011) which constrains the form of emerging grammatical structures and which enables the first language acquirer to go beyond the input that is received. If one accepts that first language acquisition is influenced importantly (though not totally) by such constraints, then one can, theoretically, try to characterise post-critical period language learning as (a) based on continued full access to this universal grammar, or (b) based on partial access to this grammar (with different proposals as to what 'partial' means) but supplemented by other structures and processes, or (c) based on other structures and processes altogether, with no access to UG still available (Meisel, 2011).

I am going to proceed assuming that (b) is the option that is most suitable for any discussion of foreign language aptitude, and I am broadly going to follow the proposals made in Meisel (2011). Meisel proposes three general influences on second language acquisition. These are:

- The residue of a universal grammar. He assumes partial access, with 'partial' determined by areas not affected in L1 acquisition. The assumption is that parameters which have been set in the L1 case cannot be reset but that aspects of UG not triggered in the L1 can still operate.
- A Language Acquisition Device (LAD). Meisel argues that not all of language acquisition is UG determined and that we have to look more widely for language-relevant predispositions. These include:
  - domain-specific discovery principles, perhaps including a capacity to identify language-as-pattern, and possibly the capacity to deal with language development through implicit learning
  - processing mechanisms, such as the capacity to deal with movement
  - a sound processing capacity
- A language making capacity (LMC). This is concerned with domain-general cognitive operations, including:

  - general implicit or procedural learning
  - working memory
  - general pattern making

The argument, then, is that language continues to be special in a number of ways but that it also implicates a hybrid system in which domain-general and domain-specific capacities co-exist. An important implication of this view is that foreign language aptitude as a construct needs to reflect this diversity and that it needs to contain components which try to probe individual differences in the language acquisition device, certainly, but also the language making capacity that Meisel discusses. We might assume (correctly or incorrectly) that there are not going to be wide differences in any residue of universal grammar (although there might be interesting L1–L2 contrasts, depending on the particular L1–L2 combinations). But it does seem reasonable to expect individual differences in the other areas of the language acquisition device and the language-making capacity. These analyses can also be represented visually, as in Figure 4.1. This figure brings out the movement from a core which is the UG leftover, through the LAD to the domain-general processes and structures of a language-making capacity (LMC).

A contrasting (complementary, rather than conflicting) perspective to this same point, that language, at least partly, continues to be special, derives from the work of J. B. Carroll (1965). Obviously, his work on foreign language aptitude is seminal (and will be discussed later), but he viewed this aptitude research as part of a much wider enterprise—'The study of human cognitive abilities'. Indeed this phrase gave the title of his major publication (Carroll, 1993) which was a massive investigation of a very large number of datasets, using multivariate statistical techniques, with the aim of uncovering the general structure of cognitive abilities. He proposed a three-level structure. At the top is essentially his version of general intelligence, a wide-ranging, general intellectual competence. The intermediate layer is then composed of general abilities (still) but with moderate degrees of specialisation (fluid intelligence, crystallised intelligence, learning and memorial processes, speed, and so on), which Carroll (1993, p. 634) also organises in terms of process, content, and response. Then the lowest level is concerned with abilities which are fairly specific in nature. This includes language, reasoning, auditory factors, and many more specific abilities. Some of these are not particularly relevant to language, but others, such as those just mentioned, clearly are.

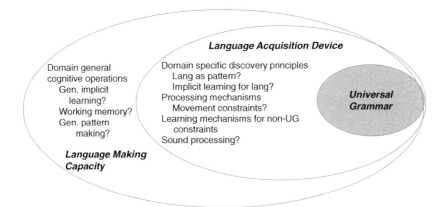

FIGURE 4.1 Underlying linguistic and cognitive abilities

From Skehan's chapter for Wen, Skehan, Sparks, Li, & Biedroń (2019)

Two points are important here. First, methodologically, Carroll used factor analysis (not the more currently fashionable meta-analysis), and his purpose was to explore which cognitive abilities go together and which are more distinct. His analyses revealed how there were clusters of talents. In other words, some individuals seemed to be particularly good within particular domains and not so good in others. He was demonstrating, in other words, that there is not one across-the-board ability, but rather that there are strengths and weaknesses. Second, there are ways that this analysis can be related to Meisel's distinction between a language acquisition device (with domain-specific discovery principles, processing mechanisms, and sound processing) and a language-making capacity (involving general implicit or procedural learning, working memory, and perhaps general pattern making). The language acquisition device and the language-making capacity relate to different specific abilities in the general structure of abilities that Carroll proposed. This also hints at the possibility that different patterns of cognitive ability could be associated with preferences for different styles of learning, as learners play to their strengths (and avoid weaknesses).

All of this seems to me a laborious statement of the obvious, that foreign language aptitude research has, at the very least, to consider the possibility that language itself is part of what determines such an aptitude. Consequently, one might question why there has been so much detail in this section. But relatively recent aptitude research has frequently taken a domain-general viewpoint (cf. much of the HiLAB (Linck et al., 2013), or approaches to language aptitude as co-existing memory systems (declarative and procedural: Morgan-Short & Buffington, this volume), or even research into working memory as aptitude (Wen & Skehan, 2011). So my purpose has been to articulate the alternative viewpoint— that domain-specific language structure and processes still have to be entertained as *possible* components of foreign language aptitude or, more strongly, as *essential* components of such an aptitude. To put this another way, it seems to me that it cannot be assumed that domain-general structures and processes are all there is in a post-critical period context—there is generally value in including domain-specific aptitudes in any research.

Foreign Language Aptitude Research and Acquisitional Processes

Traditional foreign language aptitude research (typical, until, say, 1990) used what I would term a 'macro' approach: an aptitude battery was administered just before a course of instruction (preferably to large numbers of people), the instructional period took place, and then achievement was measured. The aptitude tests were then related to the end-of-course achievement, relationships were revealed, and an account was provided of what aptitudinal factors there are and how these relate to prediction of achievement. What actually happened during the instruction, although not ignored, did not come into focus and typically was not investigated in any detail. This approach underlay Carroll's research (1965), for example. In practice, it produced the Modern Language Aptitude Test (Carroll & Sapon, 1959). More theoretically, it generated Carroll's four-factor theory of foreign language aptitude: phonemic coding ability, grammatical sensitivity, inductive language learning, and associative memory (Skehan, 1989). This work is covered in detail in Stansfield (this volume), which brings out how the four factors emerged from the extensive research programme that Carroll conducted (Carroll, 1965).

In recent years, a contrasting approach has emerged, one that I would term 'micro'. Typically, the research design will be experimental or quasi-experimental, and aptitude measures will be embedded within a focused investigation of instructional comparisons or intervention processes. For example, there may be comparisons between explicit and implicit approaches to instruction, or there may be research into the effects of different feedback types. In these cases, the role of aptitude is to enable new questions to be asked. An example could be the conditions when aptitude is most important, comparing, for example, the different instructional types (explicit-implicit) or different feedback moves. It may also be that different aspects of aptitude are hypothesised to be more or less important for particular circumstances, such as formal and informal learning. Slightly surprisingly, even though the research design is innovative, the actual aptitude measures that are generally used are conservative—either long-established measures, such as the MLAT (Carroll & Sapon, 1959), or newer measures based on the MLAT, such as Llama (Meara, 2005). In addition, working memory is often built in to the research designs which are used.

Micro research has become increasingly commonplace since the first initiatives of this sort, arguably Robinson (1995) and De Graaf (1997). Indeed, now aptitude measures are often 'plugged in' to second language acquisition research designs on something of a routine basis (which is, of course, highly desirable). The research has been illuminating, and I will return to it later. For now, the purpose in mentioning this considerable change in emphasis in aptitude research is to contextualise a viewpoint I have tried to develop: the linkage between acquisitional processes and the fine-grain of aptitude research and aptitude tests.

Figure 4.2 gives an idea of how acquisitional processes can be outlined and then related to aptitude. Two important points are relevant here. First, the acquisitional processes form a sequence, from the beginning of acquisition to fluent and effortless use. But it is important to say that this applies to *any* particular element or sub-system of an L2. In practice, as the many structures and sub-systems of an L2 are being learned, some sub-systems will be well advanced along this sequence, while others will be at earlier points. Second, the point of taking such a micro approach to acquisitional processes is to clarify how aptitudinal sub-tests might be relevant. If, for a particular process within the sequence, there are individual differences, then there is the prospect of an aptitude sub-test being relevant. The fine-grained nature of the sequence then becomes a useful means of exploring existing aptitude sub-tests to see where they might be located and which acquisitional

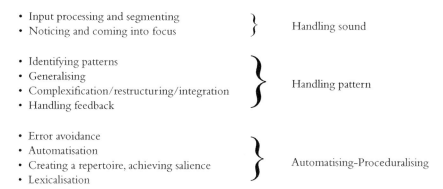

- Input processing and segmenting
- Noticing and coming into focus } Handling sound

- Identifying patterns
- Generalising
- Complexification/restructuring/integration
- Handling feedback } Handling pattern

- Error avoidance
- Automatisation
- Creating a repertoire, achieving salience
- Lexicalisation } Automatising-Proceduralising

FIGURE 4.2   Acquisitional processes and macro-categories

processes they would be most relevant for. It also provides a general framework to locate processes for which there are no or only a small number of foreign language aptitude sub-tests (Skehan, 2016). The sequence of processes, organised in terms of three general, or macro, acquisitional stages, is shown in Figure 4.2.

The three macro-categories are handling sound, handling pattern, and automatising-proceduralising. It is striking that a major linkage is apparent already between Carroll's four-factor view of aptitude and the first two of the macro-categories. Handling sound maps on to phonemic coding ability, and handling pattern to grammatical sensitivity and inductive language learning. Automatising-proceduralising, perhaps, links with associative memory (although this mapping is less successful). Carroll (1965) was concerned with the ability to absorb vocabulary under fairly explicit conditions, and indeed vocabulary development is an important, but often forgotten, component of language learning success. Automatising-proceduralising, in contrast, is more concerned with gaining control over the product of the earlier stages (handling sound, handling pattern). This was not particularly addressed in Carroll's aptitude theorising (although it is quite clearly there in his account of general cognitive abilities (Carroll, 1993)).

The range of micro studies which have been published over the last twenty years have linked features of interaction and feedback to aptitude test scores. These have shown consistent relationships between aptitude and the details of second language acquisition. I reviewed this work in Skehan (2016), so I will not go into detail at this point. The aim in the present discussion is to discuss these macro-categories a little further, but perhaps most important of all, to consider the domain-general vs. domain-specific issue as it applies to these different processes.

Handling Sound

A good starting point for handling sound is Carroll's characterisation of phonemic coding ability: the capacity to analyse sound so that it can be retained. In other words, handling sound is not primarily the capacity to make sound discriminations, but rather an ability to impose some structure on unfamiliar sound *so that it can be retained.* Implicit in this is (a) the claim that sound, and in particular, unfamiliar sound, is a significant challenge and (b) that imposing structure on this sound connects with memorability. Immediately this suggests that we are dealing with something that is domain specific, since the sounds we are dealing with are sounds in language and presumably distinctions made in language. Perhaps it is relevant that infants seem equipped to make all the sound distinctions in language (Eimas, Miller, & Jusczyk, 1987). Developing the sound system of the L1 is a process of *unlearning* the distinctions that do not apply.

It is interesting to consider whether there is a connection between the capacity to handle sound and working memory. Most analyses of working memory suggest it has a componential structure, comprising a central executive, which handles processing, and associated buffer systems (phonological, visuo-spatial, episodic), which enable temporary storage. Measurement alternatives then connect with a processing-storage contrast. A storage-emphasising method of measurement which is relevant to oral language is to use non-word repetition, which is meant to reflect the operation of the phonological buffer in Baddeley's (2007, 2015) model. Processing-oriented approaches emphasise the functioning of the central executive and how working memory reflects operations within consciousness while processing takes place (Cowan, 2013). Measurements which emphasise processing typically require retention while some processing activity is carried out, as with the range of span tests which are available (Conway et al., 2005). The two perspectives are not independent: the more efficient the processing, the more capacity is available for the retention of material.

These alternatives raise questions regarding the relationship between phonemic coding ability and working memory and about any special status for language material. A test of phonemic coding ability will use unfamiliar material as the basis for short-term learning. A phonological memory test will likely use non-words which need to be retained (although there is no emphasis on cumulative learning). The reason non-words are used to measure working memory in this way is to avoid the potential for greater long-term memory involvement if actual words (with associations) had been used. But one could have a test format which brings together these approaches: the use of unfamiliar phonological material (cf. phonemic coding ability), on the one hand, and a focus on working memory, on the other. To exemplify this, Chan, Skehan, and Gong (2011) outline a non-word repetition test (hence measuring phonological memory) but where the non-wordness of the items is determined by the L2 (in these cases, the phonological structure of Cantonese and Mandarin). Such a test builds in the need to process unfamiliar sounds, as phonemic coding ability requires, but it does so within a fairly conventional working memory format.

The more focussed point of this discussion is to build upon the insight that unfamiliar sound is important and then to make a link between phonemic coding ability and phonological memory. But the wider point is to argue that relevant aspects of language need to be primary in any attempt to deal with the processing of sound as a component of foreign language aptitude. There needs to be a way of enabling the participant to bring to bear the capacity to process unfamiliar sound, on the one hand, and memory, on the other. I would argue more generally that working memory tests which emphasise computation and processing lack construct validity where language aptitude is concerned, unless they have clear language components. As we have seen, in the case of first language acquisition, where sound is concerned, what happens is that young children are capable of handling all the distinctions of whatever language they are acquiring, but then they lose some of this ability. It may be that there is variation in how complete this loss is and that phonemic coding ability, or language-sensitive measures of working memory, is able to pick up on the differential fading of this unlearning process.

In the past (Skehan, 1989), I proposed that phonemic coding ability is likely to be of greatest importance at early stages of second language acquisition. Being able to analyse unfamiliar sound is at a premium, both to be able to parse incoming language more effectively and to be able to retain phonological representations that are unfamiliar. Beginners, especially when faced with more realistic language processing conditions, are operating at the limit of their abilities, and so any 'edge' as far as the processing of sound is concerned is vital. This analysis fits in with the first two stages in the sequence shown in Figure 4.2 (input processing and segmenting; noticing and coming into focus) This claim, in itself, still seems straightforward, but the other side of the claim is that as proficiency grows, the abilities to process incoming sound more effectively and then to impose structure on it so that it can be retained would fade somewhat in importance and other features of aptitude would become more important. It is interesting therefore that evidence has emerged more recently which suggests that phonemic coding ability retains its importance beyond beginner levels. Yilmaz and Koylu (2016), for example, report evidence linking phonemic coding ability to the effectiveness of feedback. In an ideal world, when feedback is provided, (a) the input that is provided has to be parsed and analysed, (b) the feedback has to be recognised as feedback, (c) a linkage has to be made between the auditory material that is being held in the phonological buffer and the relevant aspects of long-term memory, and (d), potentially, long-term memory itself has to be changed. Fast, effective, and even automatic processing at the first of these stages provides more attention for the important remaining three stages. So sound-linked operations have to take place and a focus on form brought to bear when all of this might seem irrelevant to ongoing communication. It appears that phonemic coding ability is still relevant when the second language speaker has to try to identify and benefit from feedback, and so this takes us well beyond the beginner level—it is likely to have importance as long as the emerging interlanguage system is flexible.

Another recent study also broadens the contribution that phonemic coding ability might make. Saito (2017) reports that a test of sound–symbol association ability correlates with performance on an oral production task. The strongest correlations are with pronunciation features (production of segmentals, word stress, intonation), but there are also significant correlations with morphological accuracy and (subordination) complexity. Here phonemic coding ability seems relevant to production, as though a capacity to handle L2 sound benefits, perhaps in the assembly buffer (Levelt, 1989), as upcoming speech is being prepared. Perhaps better L2 phonological representations linked to phonemic coding ability reduce attentional demands during speech production.

[handwritten margin note: greater automatisation]

Taken together, these two studies suggest that a greater ability to handle unfamiliar sound continues to have importance beyond the beginner level. It would be nice to think that there is a threshold for the sound system of the L2, after which it no longer poses problems. These recent studies suggest that it is not so easy to reach any such threshold. It also takes us back to the relationship between phonemic coding ability and phonological short-term memory. The non-beginner studies reviewed in Skehan (2015) which showed a relationship between working memory and gain scores after feedback used tests of phonological memory or had a listening span emphasis. It again seems to be the case that the capacity to process sound is important for reception and production at beyond the beginner level and that we are dealing with sound linked to language.

Handling Pattern

The same issue is fundamental here: to consider to what extent the sub-processes involved in handling pattern (identifying pattern, generalising, complexification–restructuring–integrating, handling feedback) need to implicate specifically language material. In Meisel's (2011) terms, this is the distinction between a language acquisition device and a language-making capacity. We have seen that there has been significant growth in the number of micro studies in recent years which have investigated linkages between aptitudinal components and focussed language instruction or feedback. Two articles in 2015 reviewed this literature and built in a comparison between explicit and implicit approaches. Li (2015) conducted a meta-analysis of a range of extant studies which met designated research design criteria. He reported that there is a significant relationship between aptitudinal measures (including working memory) and benefits from instruction and also from feedback. The effect sizes were medium size rather than huge. In addition, they were larger for explicit instructional conditions and explicit feedback than for implicit conditions and feedback. Skehan (2015) conducted a narrative review of the very same studies. He reported that, regarding instruction, aptitude predictors seem to have a greater impact when the focal point for instruction was redundant or lacking in salience. With feedback, redundancy and salience were also important, as was complexity of the L1–L2 relationship. The broad relationships obviously reflected the effect sizes reported in Li (2015), but it was also the case that there could be fairly strong relationships in certain studies even for the implicit instruction or feedback. In other words, within the overall effect sizes, there was quite a lot of variation which is fundamentally yet to be accounted for (and therefore most interesting of all).

The set of studies reviewed in Li (2015) and Skehan (2015) come from a special issue of *Applied Linguistics* juxtaposing meta-analyses and narrative inquiry in several areas, and they provide fascinating insights. Yet it also has to be said that they are limited, since each meta-analysis or narrative inquiry is necessarily based on the research studies in the database identified (and it should be noted that it is the criteria from the meta-analyses which guide the selection of studies). The central problem is that there is no overall guiding research design for the studies (hardly surprising, since they were separate studies), so one has to take what is there, and this inevitably will have shortcomings. There is a lack of systematicity, therefore, in things like the aptitude measures that were used, the L1–L2 combinations, and the age of the participants. There is a degree of systematicity in some other variables, such as the proficiency level, the focal point of instruction or feedback, and the length of the treatment, but in these cases, somewhat perversely, the systematicity is itself a problem. The proficiency level is either beginner or intermediate (and not even high intermediate), but never advanced. The focal point is generally varied, but there is a tendency to avoid more difficult syntax or morphology (though that is not true all the time, and some studies attempt a simple–complex contrast, at least with the studies in instruction, though less so with feedback). But finally there is a clear and strong generalisation regarding length of study—they are all brief, with the longest being fifteen hours, but with most studies under three hours. (This contrasts somewhat with macro aptitude studies, alluded to earlier, where time periods were considerably greater.)

The database, therefore, is not large enough to sustain powerful generalisations even though this has been a fertile area for recent research. It is to be hoped that this vitality continues and that as more studies accumulate, the foundations for claims which are made can become more robust. But we have what we have, and it is possible that some insights can already be gleaned. The first is that although the safest present conclusion is that aptitude is more predictive with explicit conditions (instruction or feedback), this does not mean that aptitude is irrelevant for implicit conditions. Several studies with implicit conditions report strong or moderate to strong (my assessments with the 2015 article correlations). The interest may be to try to uncover if there are additional variables at play which can help to account for the implicit studies with moderate to strong relationships, on the one hand, and studies which show no relationship, on the other. Interestingly, implicit studies which show stronger relationships often involve the MLAT Words in Sentences or a test of inductive language learning ability (Skehan, 2015), although it has to be said that there are implicit studies with these measures which do not show such a relationship.

A second point that needs to be made concerns the length of the studies. As we have seen, this tends to be short (in keeping with the micro nature of these studies). Earlier a sequence of acquisitional processes was outlined. Of course, this is a general list. Some aspects of language learning hardly need to involve restructuring and complexification, for example. Similarly, different aspects of an L2 will be at different stages of development in terms of the sequence. But the range of studies tends to be of quite short duration, and there is more of an emphasis towards simpler and self-contained aspects of language. In other words, the database we have does not easily enable the sequence of processes to come clearly or systematically under scrutiny. The available studies, in other words, tend to be more appropriate when we consider processes such as identifying patterns or generalising, rather than restructuring or complexification, let alone automatisation or proceduralisation.

But some insights are possible, for all that. One of the most interesting comes from Kempe and Brooks (2016). This study showed that a language analytic test (a conventional component of foreign language aptitude) was most effective in predicting pattern identification (with case marking in Russian), whereas a culture-fair intelligence test was better at predicting generalisation of the pattern to new exemplars. This suggests that making first inroads into a language pattern is a language issue, but that working further with that pattern and developing it draw on more general abilities. The first seems to be part of the LAD in Meisel's proposal, and the second part of his LMC. One wonders if the later processes in the sequence proposed here (restructuring, complexification, integration) might similarly have language-specific and domain-general implications. Restructuring might be a linguistic insight, but would then need to be followed by the development of generality for that restructuring. Integration might involve the (linguistically based) incorporation of one element into a larger system and then the need to generalise what could be incorporated in this way. Obviously, all this speaks to the domain-general vs. domain-specific contrast. It might imply that in second language development, language aptitude specifically is implicated in early work and then other abilities come into play to extend and possibly consolidate.

The other insight from Skehan (2015) concerns the focal language point from the different studies. Two interesting features here were redundancy and salience. Redundancy worked the same way for the instruction studies and the feedback studies: higher-aptitude participants did better when the focal point involved redundancy. If the focal point did not seem vital for communication, it seemed advantageous to be high aptitude. Lower-aptitude participants seemed to miss the point in instruction and did not benefit as much as they might have when provided with feedback. Salience also worked with both groups, but in interestingly different ways. In the instruction studies, greater salience proved an advantage for higher-aptitude learners, whereas in the feedback studies lower salience benefitted more from feedback with the higher-aptitude students. In the case of instruction, it seemed that higher aptitude made learners more sensitive to the input, provided that there were already signals in that input. Greater prominence, plus the ability to do something with that prominence, was an advantage. With feedback, low salience (linked to aptitude) was the issue. One assumes that if there is a need for feedback, this is reflective of a point of interlanguage malleability or current readiness—the feedback has to have something to respond to. In this case, it appears that lower prominence is the heart of the problem and that the feedback is needed because the input itself is not sufficiently attention-engaging. In these circumstances, higher aptitude is also an advantage, to capitalise on the signals that the feedback provides. To look at the reverse, lower-aptitude learners, even when provided with feedback, do not seem to engage with the learning opportunities that are provided. Finally, just to hammer this point to death, salience and redundancy were the focal point features which showed relationships with aptitude. Other features, such as amount of movement, clarity of form–function relationship, and so on, did not show such relationships.

It is interesting that, given the range of focal point features that were considered, the two which stood out as connecting with aptitude are rather surface oriented. Each is concerned with the input itself, either its acoustic qualities or its avoidability. They are not, in themselves, implicated in any particular aspect of the language system, and both essentially concern relatively straightforward input processing. To restate this, aptitude, although concerned with the learning of particular focal structures, or the feedback about other focal structures, seems most involved with a *necessary* condition only—the input has to become available for subsequent and deeper processing. I have to confess to finding this slightly disappointing!

There is, though, one other focal point feature which showed a relationship with aptitude. This concerned the complexity of the L1–L2 relationship. Higher-aptitude learners were at an advantage, but only where feedback was concerned (i.e. not in the instruction set of studies) and only in the implicit condition. This, at least, is not an input-dependent feature, but relates more clearly to aspects of an underlying interlanguage system. For all that, there has to be an input-processing dimension. It appears to be the case here that when feedback was provided for some aspect of language where there was a divergence between the L1 and the L2, that feedback was recognised as feedback and it was acted upon to some degree. A more complex aspect of language, a signal that all is not well, and the capacity, i.e. aptitude, is then called upon to do something about it. Again, aptitude may have a triggering effect, highlighting something and catalysing other developmental processes. But it may have a more direct effect also, as the ability which facilitates the way such developmental processes occur.

The major theme introduced earlier, the contrast between domain generality and domain specificity, is slightly, but not extensively, illuminated by this section. I believe that significant progress will only come when we have a much greater database of relevant studies and probably when we are in a position to design studies which do not simply include aptitudinal measures in an unfocussed way, but when particular aptitude-linked hypotheses can be formulated. For now, we seem to see a slight indication that aptitude links with input processing, and so, linked with the discussion of the Kempe and Brooks' (2016) study, it seems that aptitude is important to provide an initial insight into what needs to be learned or developed. In some ways this is close to Schmidt's (1990) conception of noticing. The key issue then becomes what happens afterwards (Skehan, 2013) and consequently what contribution aptitude then makes. To return to the detail of Meisel's characterisation, the contrast is between domain-specificity discovery procedures and general pattern making. Then the issue concerns whether development of any pattern continues with domain-specific or domain-general processes. The evidence from micro studies seems slightly more consistent with domain-specific discovery procedures but is still unclear about what happens at subsequent stages.

An Interim Summary

The sequence of acquisitional processes outlined earlier fell into the three macro-categories of handling sound, handling pattern, and automatising. We have covered the first two of these general categories and will move on to the third next. So this is a moment to broaden the scope and discuss some wider problems that aptitude has to wrestle with. A fundamental issue, vital as we move on to consider automatisation, concerns the nature of the learning that takes place and contrasts an explicit approach with an implicit perspective. There are four possibilities:

- That initial explicit processes become proceduralised so that error is gradually reduced and fluency increases. Effective communication then proceeds based on this automatised base, and so in fluent performance we are dealing with explicit learning used very quickly. DeKeyser (2007) argues for this position.
- That the initial explicit processes do generate explicit knowledge but that over time this knowledge base becomes implicit, and so later communication is based on this implicit base and is below the level of consciousness. This is generally known as the strong interface position within SLA.
- That while explicit processes may occur, significant development draws on implicit processes directly, and so effective and fluent communication is based on an implicit knowledge system, which has been built without any explicit involvement. In this view the explicit learning has a secondary status. This position is most clearly associated with Paradis (2009).
- That initial explicit processes become automatised, as in the first possibility, but that in parallel and separately, direct implicit development can occur. This differs from the third possibility in that the two learning paths have more equivalent status and are each regarded as viable alternatives for second language development. This position has been advocated by Ullman (2005, 2015).

These alternatives are, of course, well known within general second language acquisition. They are relevant for aptitude because they have contrasting implications for the sorts of abilities that might predict success in foreign language learning. The first position is consistent with aptitude tests which capture effectiveness of initial explicit learning and then speed and completeness of the proceduralisation which follows. In this case aptitude sub-tests need to be sensitive to the capacity to speed up rule access and operation, as well as skill at chunking. The fourth position suggests that two systems will co-exist, but that each, in its own way, is worthwhile. In this case, aptitude tests need to cover both possibilities—explicit (as in the first position) and then separately implicit processes. In the second case of the four noted earlier, the assumption is that explicit becomes implicit. In this case, the task for aptitude tests is to measure what is relevant about the initial processes of explicit learning and then develop measures of how what has been explicit is converted into implicit knowledge. The third position essentially portrays explicit learning as a sideshow, and so aptitude tests would need to focus strongly on the prediction of implicit learning processes and knowledge.

Overlaid on these positions, of course, is the possible special role of language. If language is special (as I would argue), then explicit and implicit processes and knowledge give language some centrality in all these positions. For example, in the explicit-becomes-implicit position (the second one), it would lead to the assumption that handling sound and handling pattern mean handling the sounds of language and the patterns of language, specifically, and that what then becomes implicit knowledge emphasises its linguistic nature and continuity from the earlier stages. Interestingly, if one explores the final position with two co-existing systems, declarative and procedural, it even raises the possibility that one, declarative, might be linguistic, and the other, procedural, might be generally cognitive. Complications such as these then have implications for the focus of aptitude tests.

Proceduralisation

Traditional aptitude test batteries do not have a lot to offer with regard to proceduralisation. (I use the term proceduralisation for shorthand convenience, but I intend it to cover automatisation and implicit learning, unless a particular term is used for specific relevance.) There may be occasional concern for cumulative learning. The tests of phonemic coding ability in the MLAT do this a little (Carroll & Sapon, 1959), as does the inductive language learning in the PLAB (Pimsleur, 1966). Llama also builds this in slightly, in Llama D. Perhaps the clearest example is in CANAL-F (Grigorenko, Sternberg, & Ehrman, 2002) where there is continuity of learning across different sub-tests. But even with these glimpses of more proceduralised learning, there are no focussed measures of the area, and the coverage seems somewhat unsystematic. The emphasis in these batteries tends to be on the processing of sound and of pattern in ways already discussed.

There is some focus on memory more generally in existing batteries. The clearest example here is MLAT V, Paired Associates. This particular sub-test has been widely used in recent research in the sorts of micro studies reviewed in

Skehan (2015), but also in recent work on declarative-procedural influences on language learning, where it has been used as a measure of declarative memory (Faretta-Stutenberg & Morgan-Short, 2017). Proposals such as Ullman (2015) and Paradis (2009) locate vocabulary within declarative memory, and so MLAT V is seen as a predictor of the capacity to learn vocabulary. This is, however, only associative memory, and there would seem scope to broaden the aspects of declarative memory which feature within potential foreign language aptitude tests (Skehan, 1982, 1989).

A more relevant approach is to consider research into automatisation in a second language context. As indicated earlier, DeKeyser (2007) proposes that post-critical period second language learning is driven by explicit processing which, when there is success, is progressively automatised. To that end he has explored (Suzuki, 2017; Suzuki & DeKeyser, 2017) developing measurement options which distinguish between declarative knowledge, which has been automatised, and implicit knowledge. Measurements of the former use different types of time-pressured grammatical judgement tasks, and the latter use variants of real-world comprehension tasks, such as word monitoring and self-paced reading. In these latter, eye tracking can play an important role. This research targets greater understanding of the relationship between explicit, implicit, and automatised processes, but potentially the distinctions recast what is needed in developing measures of aptitudes for automatisation and for the capacity to develop implicit knowledge. These test formats of automatised and implicit knowledge might lend themselves to the development of sub-tests which could function within aptitude batteries.

The insight from these studies is that distinguishing between automatised and implicit knowledge is feasible, important, and relevant for aptitude. They suggest value in a dual approach to developing aptitude tests targeting the capacity for proceduralisation. However, most other developments in aptitude research have focussed more on ways of predicting the capacity to develop implicit knowledge. Granena (2013), for example, proposes that Llama D, sound recognition, measures implicit learning (and contrasts markedly therefore with all other Llama sub-tests (F, E, and B). Within the HiLAB (Linck et al., 2013), a serial reaction time task is used to measure implicit learning, and indeed this is one of the tests which distinguishes between the two target groups in the study, with higher scores for the very talented learner group as opposed to the merely successful group. (The two others which do this are a test of phonological working memory and a test of associative memory.)

The most systematic area for the investigation of proceduralisation relates to Ullman's (2015) dual-system theories. Under this approach, proceduralisation may best be characterised as a shift in reliance from the declarative memory system to the procedural memory system. A series of studies (Morgan-Short, Faretta-Stutenberg, Brill-Schuetz, Carpenter, & Wong, 2014; Morgan-Short, Deng, Brill-Schuetz, Faretta-Stutenberg, & Wong, 2015; Faretta-Stutenberg & Morgan-Short, 2018) have explored the extent to which measures of declarative memory and measures of procedural memory relate to foreign language learning success. Interestingly, these studies often measure declarative memory by using the MLAT V Paired Associates test, often supplemented by the Continuous Visual Memory Task (Morgan-Short et al. (2014). Procedural memory is measured by tests taken from general cognitive psychology, such as the Weather Prediction task or the Towers of London task. In addition, a serial reaction task is frequently used (cf. the HiLAB, which also uses this format). Generalising across these declarative-procedural studies, the tendency is for declarative memory to be more likely to account for variance at earlier stages of learning, in more formal learning contexts, and with more complex rules. Procedural memory scores, in contrast, are better in accounting for later stages of learning, in less formal contexts, and with simpler rules. (Bear in mind that Ullman's (2015) argument is that the two systems can function in parallel and be complementary but also with some degree of competition.)

Morgan-Short et al. (2015) link the two memory systems to different brain structures. Declarative memory is linked to the medial temporal lobe, whereas procedural memory is linked to the frontal lobe as well as the basal ganglia, suggesting clear anatomical differences between the two systems. Another interesting feature of this set of research studies is the suggestion that it is profitable to identify different types of learners—referred to in one study as learners, simplifiers, and non-learners (Ettinger, Bradow, & Wong, 2014). It is also proposed that different types of learners show different sorts of change in brain responses. (There is an interesting, if general, correspondence here with Skehan (1986) who used cluster analysis, based on aptitude profiles, to identify different learner types—analytic vs. memory oriented in this case.) Finally, an intriguing aspect of the declarative-procedural research studies is that they sometimes use a more macro approach to research design—administer aptitude tests, then allow learning time to elapse, and then measure change, with this final measurement based on general tests (Faretta-Stutenberg et al., 2017), rather than the more focussed grammatical points of the micro studies reviewed in Li (2015) and (Skehan, 2015).

The sequence of processes in Figure 4.2 ended with creating a repertoire/achieving salience and finally lexicalisation. These suggest how a second language speaker will be able to make language choices which are similar to those made by native speakers, and even beyond that, that the second language speaker can develop a repertoire of formulaic language which can then ease processing pressures. These last two stages (native speaker choices and formulaic repertoires) are well beyond the scope of this discussion and are mentioned here only for completeness. They can possibly be discussed more in terms of very high-level accomplishment (Hyltenstam, Bartning, & Fant, in press).

The challenge for aptitude tests is clear, if daunting. Most existing aptitude tests emphasise handling sound or handling pattern—the earlier stages. Significant progress has been made in each of these areas, and undoubtedly, more is to come. The major challenge for the future is to develop measurement procedures in the area of automatisation-proceduralisation which have comparable construct and predictive validity. Such research will need to compare language-focussed and general cognition-focussed assessment formats, to explore whether the processes proceduralisation and automatisation are different in each case. Once again, the question of any special status for language arises.

Conclusions

We have now examined the three macro processes: sound processing, pattern making, and automatisation, and within each tried to integrate a range of aptitude research and theorising. Some major issues emerge from this discussion, and this final section will try to address these. In turn, they are the place of language in language aptitude, the way insights into automatisation can be incorporated into aptitude research and theorizing, and a potential to re-invigorate more macro and longitudinal research designs.

The issue of aptitude as language linked or as general cognition has been lurking throughout this chapter. Regarding sound, the issue concerned phonemic coding ability relative to general working memory. The proposal that phonological working memory might be a compromise here would be a way of bringing general cognitive operations and a focus on sound a little more together, particularly if non-words consistent with the L2 were used (Chan et al., 2011). Regarding pattern, earlier macro studies and more recent micro studies both show relationships between aptitude sub-tests emphasising language and success, either over a longer term, with macro studies, or with specific aspects of language, in the micro studies. Old, established aptitude tests have been (surprisingly) successful in these micro studies. It would be interesting to see if newer proposals, e.g. a pattern-oriented aptitude test based on Pienemann's ideas on sequence (Pienemann, 1998), would be even more successful (Chan & Skehan, ms), and perhaps more useful at more advanced levels. An intriguing possibility that emerges from the micro studies (Kempe & Brooks, 2016) is that domain specificity and domain generality may each have a role to play. The suggestion here is that new pattern making may be domain specific, whereas extensions of an original insight might have more domain-general qualities.

The language-is-special perspective also has relevance at the proceduralisation stage. But we saw that a major factor here is how the relationship is theorised between explicit language focus (which is typical of most pattern-oriented aptitude tests) and subsequent proceduralisation. Strong or weak interface positions see continuity here, and so one might look for language-oriented aptitude tests to capture ability to proceduralise. This is less so of the other positions which argue for important roles for implicit learning. The sorts of procedures which are advocated to measure procedural memory (e.g. weather prediction; serial reaction time, eye-movement based tests) do not have an obvious connection with language-as-pattern. It is interesting therefore that Llama D, sound based as it is, is proposed as a measure of implicit learning (Granena, 2013) and this is clearly language oriented. Perhaps there is scope to explore if language-oriented methods of assessing aptitude for proceduralisation can be developed. In such cases, the patterns that would be the focus for direct proceduralisation or direct development of implicit knowledge would be language patterns.

The second concluding point concerns tests of proceduralisation more generally. The results which have emerged in this area in recent years are consistent and powerful. Tests of procedural memory, such as the Weather Prediction task or reaction time tasks (with little explicit concern for language), have shown interesting connections with language learning success, as indicated earlier: greater for later stages of learning, in informal contexts, and with simpler rules. So there are interesting and important results to work with here. But there is the additional potential, through the study of tests of proceduralisation, to make major contributions in developing our understanding of the nature of second language learning more generally. We have seen the different positions that have been advocated (strong interface, parallel systems, and so on). Developing aptitude tests which probe the relevance of the different positions can make contributions to theory which go well beyond simple prediction of language learning success. They can clarify the nature of language learning itself.

But if that is to occur, considerable measurement progress needs to be made. We have seen claims for procedures to measure automatisation (Suzuki, 2017; Suzuki & DeKeyser, 2017). There are also tests which are portrayed as measuring implicit learning ability, such as Llama D (Granena, 2013). We have also seen tests used extensively within a declarative-procedural framework (Morgan-Short & Buffington, this volume). If these tests can produce fine-grained measurements of different aspects of what happens when learners achieve greater speed and control with an L2, then we may be able to use them to explore what is going on at later stages of learning. This, in turn, may clarify the relationship between the sorts of concerns in the handling sound and handling pattern stages for aptitude tests, on the one hand, and the later stages of learning, on the other. In other words, successful aptitude measurement could clarify which of the different models (explicit to implicit; automatisation; declarative-procedural) account for language learning success. Such improved measurement might also clarify how different models apply differently to different learner types. It may even be possible that different models apply, but at different times or different stages, to the very same learner.

A final point I would make in this regard concerning measurement progress is that there is room to develop methods of assessing capacity for automatisation, for proceduralisation, and for the development of implicit knowledge which are more specifically language focussed. We have seen non-language-oriented procedures show interesting relationships in this regard. But language-oriented tests have not been tried, or are yet to be developed. Absence of evidence is not evidence of absence—a relevant adage here. It may be that such tests, if developed, could produce even better results than the more cognitively oriented tasks such as weather prediction.

The third concluding point concerns the research designs which are used in aptitude studies. This takes us back to macro studies. Classic macro studies, such as those conducted by Carroll (1965), typically used large numbers of aptitude tests, and then two things happened. Of course, the aptitude tests were related to language learning success. But in addition, it was typical to examine the inter-relationships of the component tests in the aptitude battery that was used. This achieved three things. It eliminated the failures which did not correlate with success. It identified duplicates amongst the aptitude battery. And third, the use of broadly composed aptitude batteries enables the structure of aptitude itself to be explored. Hence, for example, the development of Carroll's four-factor theory of aptitude. The more micro-oriented studies which have dominated aptitude research in recent years, and which have made huge contributions, may now need to be supplemented by a return to a more macro approach. Obviously, a research design which relates aptitude measures to actual achievement is desirable, but the separate point I want to make here is that the use of a well-composed aptitude battery, drawing on the insights and measurement procedures which have been developed more recently, would be extremely revealing about the structure of aptitude. We now have important new measurement devices of working memory and of automatisation-proceduralisation. It would be very revealing to see how these function together and also relate to the range of older aptitude sub-tests focussed on phonemic coding ability and language-as-pattern. Measurement of (linguistic) declarative memory could also figure here. This might make it possible for a new structure of aptitude to be developed.

As a concluding point I would suggest that if this is done, it might connect with what has been a background issue in aptitude research—that there may be different types of learners. I argued this some time ago with the distinction between analysis-oriented learners and memory-oriented learners (Skehan, 1986). Ettinger et al. (2014) have made comparable points through their depiction of learners, simplifiers, and non-learners, and they have also related learner type to different brain responses. It may be that if we have a better view of the structure of aptitude, this may provide the framework to see more clearly how not all learners are created equal, but have profiles of strengths and weaknesses.

Note

1   The author would like to thank Alan Juffs, Kara Morgan-Short, and Charles Stansfield for comments on an earlier version of this chapter.

References

Baddeley, A. D. (2007). *Working memory, thought and action*. Oxford: Oxford University Press.
Baddeley, A. D. (2015). Working memory in second language learning. In Z. Wen, M. Borges Mota, & A. McNeill (Eds.), *Working memory in second language acquisition and processing*. Clevedon and Avon: Multilingual Matters.

Carroll, J. B. (1965). The prediction of success in intensive Foreign language training. In R. Glaser (Ed.), *Training, research, and education*. New York, NY: Wiley.

Carroll, J. B. (1993). *Human cognitive abilities: A survey of factor-analytic studies*. Cambridge: Cambridge University Press.

Carroll, J. B., & Sapon, S. M. (1959). *Modern languages aptitude test—form a*. New York, NY: The Psychological Corporation.

Chan, E., & Skehan, P. (ms.) *Developing an aptitude test based on Pienemann's Processability Theory*. London: Birkbeck College.

Chan, E., Skehan, P., & Gong, G. (2011). Working memory, phonemic coding ability and Foreign language aptitude: Potential for construction of specific language aptitude tests—the case of Cantonese. *Ilha Do Desterro: A Journal of English language, literatures and cultural studies, 60*, 45–73.

Cowan, N. (2013). Working memory and attention in language use. In J. Guandouzi, F. Loncke, & J. Williams (Eds.), *The handbook of psycholinguistics and cognitive processes*. London: Psychology Press.

Conway, A. R. A., Kane, M. J., Bunting, M. F., Hambrick, D. Z., Wilhem, O., & Engle, R. W. (2005). Working memory span tasks: A methodological review and user's guide. *Psychonomic Bulletin & Review, 12*(5), 769–786.

de Graaff, R. (1997). The eXperanto experiment: Effects of explicit instruction on second language acquisition. *Studies in Second Language Acquisition, 19*(2), 249–276.

DeKeyser, R. (2000). The robustness of critical period effects in second language acquisition. *Studies in Second Language Acquisition, 22*, 499–533.

DeKeyser, R. (2007). Skill acquisition theory. In B. Van Patten & J. Williams (Eds.), *Theories in second language acquisition: An introduction* (pp. 97–112). Mahwah, NJ: Lawrence Erlbaum Associates, Inc.

Eimas, P. D., Miller, J. L., & Jusczyk, P. W. (1987). On infant speech perception and the acquisition of language. In S. Harnad (Ed.), *Categorical perception* (pp. 161–195). New York, NY: Cambridge University Perss.

Ettinger, M., Bradow, A., & Wong, P. (2014). Variability in the learning of complex morphophonology. *Applied Psycholinguistics, 35*(4), 807–831.

Faretta-Stutenberg, M., & Morgan-Short, K. (2018). The interplay of individual differences and context of learning in behavioural and neurocognitive second language development. *Second Language Research, 34*, 67–101.

Granena, G. (2013). Individual differences in sequence learning ability and second language acquisition in early childhood and adulthood. *Language Learning, 63*, 1–39.

Grigorenko, E. L., Sternberg, R. J., & Ehrman, M. (2002). A theory based approach to the measurement of Foreign language learning ability: The Canal-F theory and test. *Modern Language Journal, 84*(3), 390–405.

Hyltenstam, K., Bartning, I., & Fant, L. (in press). *High-level language proficiency in second language and multilingual contexts*. Cambridge: Cambridge University Press.

Kempe, V., & Brooks, P. (2016). Miniature nature language learning in L2 acquisition research. In G. Granena, D. O. Jackson, & Y. Yilmaz (Eds.). *Cognitive individual differences in second language processing and acquisition* (pp. 41–68). Amsterdam, The Netherlands: John Benjamins Publishing Company.

Levelt, W. J. M. (1989). *Speaking: From intention to articulation*. Cambridge: Cambridge University Press.

Li, S. (2015). The associations between language aptitude and second language grammar acquisition: A meta-analytic review of five decades of research. *Applied Linguistics, 36*(3), 385–408.

Linck, J. A., Hughes, M. M., Campbell, S. G., Silbert, N. H., Tare, M., Jackson, S. R., . . . Doughty, C. J. (2013). Hi-LAB: A new measure of aptitude for high-level language proficiency. *Language Learning, 63*(3), 530–566.

MacWhinney, B. (2005). A unified model of language acquisition. In J. F. Kroll & A. M. B. De Groot (Eds.), *Handbook of bilingualism: Psycholinguistic approaches* (pp. 49–67). Oxford: Oxford University Press.

Meara, P. (2005). *LLAMA language aptitude tests: The manual.* Lognostics: University of Swansea. Retrieved from www.lognostics.co.uk/tools/llama

Meisel, J. M. (2011). *First and second language acquisition.* Cambridge: Cambridge University Press.

Morgan-Short, K., & Buffington, J. (this volume). *Declarative and procedural memory in second language aptitude.*

Morgan-Short, K., Deng, Z, Brill-Schuetz, K. A., Faretta-Stutenberg, M. F., & Wong, P. C. M. (2015). A view of the neural representation of second language syntax through artificial language learning under implicit contexts of exposure. *Studies in Second Language Acquisition, 37,* 383–419.

Morgan-Short, K., Faretta-Stutenberg, M., Brill-Schuetz, K. A., Carpenter, H., & Wong, P. C. M. (2014). Declarative and procedural memory as individual differences in second language acquisition. *Bilingualism, Language, and Cognition, 17*(1), 56–72.

Paradis, M. (2009). *Declarative and procedural determinants of second languages.* Amsterdam, The Netherlands: John Benjamins Publishing Company.

Pienemann, M. (1998). *Language processing and second language development: Processability theory.* Amsterdam, The Netherlands: John Benjamins Publishing Company.

Pimsleur, P. (1966). *The pimsleur language aptitude battery.* New York, NY: Harcourt, Brace, Jovanovich.

Robinson, P. (1995). Learning simple and complex rules under implicit, incidental, rule-search, and instructed conditions. *Studies in Second Language Acquisition, 18,* 27–67.

Saito, K. (2017). Effects of sound, vocabulary and grammar learning aptitude on adult second language speech attainment in Foreign language classrooms. *Language Learning, 62*(3), 665–693.

Schmidt, R. (1990). The role of consciousness in second language learning. *Applied Linguistics, 11,* 129–158.

Skehan, P. (1982). *Memory and motivation in language aptitude testing* (Unpublished PhD dissertation), University of London.

Skehan, P. (1986). Cluster analysis and the identification of learner types. In V. Cook (Ed.), *Experimental approaches to second language acquisition.* Oxford: Pergamon.

Skehan, P. (1989). *Individual differences in second language learning.* London: Edward Arnold.

Skehan, P. (2013). Nurturing noticing. In J. M. Bergsleithner, S. N. Frota, & J. Yoshioka (Eds.), *Noticing and second language acquisition: Studies in honor of Richard Schmidt* (pp. 169–180). Honolulu, HI: University of Hawaii Press.

Skehan, P. (2015). Foreign language aptitude and its relationship with grammar: A critical overview. *Applied Linguistics, 36*(3), 367–384.

Skehan, P. (2016). Foreign language aptitude, acquisitional sequences, and psycholinguistic processes. In G. Granena, D. O. Jackson, & Y. Yilmaz (Eds.). *Cognitive individual differences in second language processing and acquisition* (pp. 17–40). Amsterdam, The Netherlands: John Benjamins Publishing Company

Suzuki, Y. (2017). Validity of new measures of implicit knowledge: Distinguishing implicit knowledge from automatized explicit knowledge. *Applied Psycholinguistics, 38,* 1229–1261.

Suzuki, Y., & DeKeyser, R. (2017). The interface of explicit and implicit knowledge in a second language: Insights from individual differences in cognitive abilities. *Language Learning, 67*(4), 747–790.

Ullman, M.T. (2005). A cognitive neuroscience perspective on second language acquisition: The declarative/ procedural model. In C. Sanz (Ed.), *Mind and context in adult second language acquisition: Methods, theory and practice* (pp. 141–178). Washington, DC: Georgetown University Press.

Ullman, M. T. (2015). The declarative/procedural model: A neurobiologically-motivated theory of first and second language. In B. VanPatten & J. Williams (Eds.), *Theories of second language acquisition: An introduction* (pp. 135–158). Mahwah: NJ: Lawrence Erlbaum Associates, Inc.

Wen, Z., & Skehan, P. (2011). A new perspective on Foreign language aptitude: Building and supporting a case for 'working memory as language aptitude'. *Ilha do Desterro: A Journal of English Language, Literatures, and Cultural Studies, 60,* 15–44.

Yilmaz, Y., & Koylu, L. (2016). The interaction between feedback exposure condition and phonetic coding ability. In G. Granena, D. O. Jackson, & Y. Yilmaz (Eds.). *Cognitive individual differences in second language processing and acquisition* (pp. 303–326). Amsterdam, The Netherlands: John Benjamins Publishing Company.

5

SIX DECADES OF LANGUAGE APTITUDE RESEARCH

A Comprehensive and Critical Review

Shaofeng Li

Introduction

In this chapter, I provide an overview of the research on language aptitude that has accumulated over the past six decades. This reflective piece is based primarily on the data and findings of the three meta-analyses or research syntheses I have conducted (Li, 2015, 2016, 2017) of the empirical studies on various aspects of language aptitude. Li (2015) aggregated the results of all the empirical studies on the associations between aptitude and second language grammar learning. Li (2016) investigated what research had demonstrated about the nature of language aptitude in terms of its associations with learning outcomes and with other individual difference variables. The outcome measures of the meta-analysis went beyond grammar learning and included overall proficiency as well as specific aspects of learning, such as the learning of language skills (writing, speaking, listening, and reading) and linguistic knowledge (grammar and vocabulary); the other individual difference variables included motivation, anxiety, and working memory. Li (2017) synthesized the studies on the associations between language aptitude and various aspects of second language interaction, especially the effects of corrective feedback. The research synthesis sought to provide a holistic picture of the substantive domain by integrating meta-analysis and traditional narrative review. These meta-analyses, which are based on the totality of the research, provided precise numeric estimates of the various relationships subjected to empirical investigation; they also showed what factors moderated the investigated relationships. In this chapter, I aim to conduct a comprehensive, critical overview of the research on language aptitude based on the data I have collated for the three meta-analyses. However, the chapter is not simply a summary of the meta-analytic findings; rather, it goes beyond the meta-analyses and discusses various other aspects surrounding the construct of language aptitude, including the theories, research methodology, and pedagogy, in addition to research findings. I will start with a discussion of the theories underlying aptitude research.

Theory

The Carrollian Approach

The Carrollian approach is named after Carroll, who developed the MLAT (the Modern Language Aptitude Test) (Carroll & Sapon, 1959)—the most influential aptitude test that has dominated aptitude research in the past six decades. The theoretical foundation of this approach is behaviorism, which in turn underlies the audiolingual approach to language teaching characterized by mechanical drills, rote learning, and grammar instruction. Although Carroll did not associate his conceptualization of aptitude with behaviorism or the audiolingual approach, the MLAT was developed based on his observations about what was important for learning success in audiolingual classes, and the test was validated with learners in those classes. For example, rote learning is a defining feature of audiolingual instruction, and accordingly a central component of aptitude in Carroll's approach is rote memory, which is measured through the Paired Associates subtest of the MLAT. Under this approach, aptitude is conceived as a predictor of learning rate; that is, other things being equal, learners with higher aptitude learn faster within a given period. The purpose of aptitude testing was initially to identify learners who could master a foreign language within a short period in state-funded language programs. The research that was subsequently conducted, which can be called predictive research, sought primarily to ascertain whether aptitude was correlated with learning success operationalized as course grades or scores on proficiency tests.

The Carrollian approach has the following characteristics. First, aptitude is a determinant of learning success, regardless of context or instruction type. The focus is placed on the outcome, not the process, of learning. Second, aptitude is a unitary construct. Although Carroll conceived aptitude as componential and the MLAT that he developed consists of several subtests, he had discussed aptitude as a holistic concept and discussed the validity of the construct by referring to learners' composite aptitude scores. One implication of the unitary view is that a learner is either a high- or low-aptitude learner; in other words, a scenario in which one is strong in one aptitude component but weak in another does not exist. Third, the aptitude conceptualized by Carroll is a learner trait that is implicated in the initial stages of learning. However, this does not mean aptitude is not important in advanced learning; rather, the kind of aptitude that is sensitive to advanced learning might be different from traditional aptitude or the components measured by existing aptitude tests. Fourth, given that the subtests of the MLAT all require conscious processing of linguistic materials, the underlying abilities seem more relevant to explicit learning than implicit learning. Fifth, all the subtests of the MLAT concern primarily the formal aspects of language and require little form–meaning mapping. Also, they concern learning through discrete item practice, not practice in a meaning context. Sixth, the measured abilities only concern the linguistic aspects of L2 learning, not pragmatic competence, or the ability to use the second language appropriately in different communicative contexts. Seventh, the MLAT is purely comprehension based and only involves understanding linguistic materials; no language production (speaking or writing) is involved.

The Linguistic Coding Difference Hypothesis (LCDH)

The LCDH, which is proposed by Sparks and his colleagues (see Chapter 7), is a variant of the Carrollian approach. A central tenet of the theory is that first and second language learning draw on the same pool of cognitive abilities, and aptitude for second language learning is the remnant of the aptitude for first language learning. The principles of the theory are well represented in the following statement from Ganschow and Sparks (1996, p. 201): "Skills in one's native language in the phonological/orthographic, syntactic, and semantic codes provide the basic foundation for foreign language learning". The theory was first proposed as Linguistic Coding *Deficit* Hypothesis to account for foreign language learning disabilities, but later the term *deficit* was changed to *difference* to reflect the idea that individual differences stand in a continuum. The theory was justified on the following grounds. First, two subtests of the MLAT—Spelling Clues and Grammatical Sensitivity—measure test-takers' knowledge about vocabulary and grammar, respectively, in English, which is the targeted learners' native language. (The MLAT was developed for foreign language learners in the United States.) Second, learners' first language skills were found to be predictive of their foreign language aptitude (Sparks et al., 1998). Third, learners' first language skills were predictive of their foreign language achievements (Sparks, Patton, Ganschow, Humbach, & Javorsky, 2006).

Some further comments are in order. First, what constitutes first language skills needs to be clarified. In Sparks's studies, they were operationalized as IQ, phonemic awareness, achievements in one's first language such as vocabulary and reading comprehension, and so on. However, vocabulary and reading comprehension are achievements, and it is theoretically unreasonable to consider them to be cognitive abilities. Second, the fact that first language skills are correlated with foreign language aptitude does not mean they are identical. It may mean that the shared variance is due to a third, untested variable such as motivation. Therefore, the correlations or predictive relationships the researchers identified between first language skills, foreign language aptitude, and second language achievements need to be clarified. Finally, the LCDH is essentially a variant and extension of the

Carrollian approach in that the primary concern is the correlations between aptitude measures and learning outcomes.

ATI (Aptitude–Treatment–Interaction)

While the Carrollian approach emphasizes the predictive power of aptitude for learning outcomes, the ATI approach attaches importance to the interface between aptitude and learning conditions (Snow, 1991). Snow argues that learners with different aptitude profiles may benefit differently from different types of instruction depending on whether there is a fit between one's aptitude strengths and the processing demands of the learning condition. Low-aptitude learners, for example, may benefit more from materials that are clearly structured, while high-aptitude learners may learn more from instruction that encourages them to extrapolate patterns and rules via their own cognitive resources. However, in Snow's conceptualization, aptitude refers to any individual difference factor that affects the learner's readiness for a learning situation. It not only includes cognitive factors such as intelligence but also affective factors such as anxiety, motivation, and learner beliefs. In second language research, however, aptitude has a narrower scope, and often it is considered to be a cognitive variable.

Although Snow's definition of aptitude is different, the ATI approach she proposed has valuable implications and profound influence on aptitude research in the field of second language acquisition. Robinson (2002a) pioneered the initiative to introduce and extend the ATI approach in second language research. He proposed the so-called Aptitude Complexes hypothesis, which states that different learning conditions draw on different clusters of cognitive abilities. These abilities exist in a hierarchy: first-order abilities, which are measured through aptitude tests, form variables at a higher level, which are called latent variables in educational psychology. For example, learning from recasts, an implicit type of corrective feedback, implicates two abilities: noticing the gap and memory for contingent speech. Noticing the gap comprises two first-order abilities: perceptual speed and pattern recognition. Memory for contingent speech subsumes phonological working memory and speed of phonological working memory.

A related idea of Robinson's approach that has not heeded aptitude researchers' attention is the Fundamental Similarity hypothesis, according to which learning under different conditions draws on the same "general cognitive abilities contributing to focal attention allocation, 'noticing' (Schmidt & Frota, 1986), and rehearsal in memory" (2002a, p. 124). The theory suggests that adults learn a second language in similar ways under different learning conditions—they learn consciously and draw on attention-driven cognitive resources. The differential relationships between aptitude and learning effects are due to the nature of the instruction or treatment. Therefore, this theory suggests that language learning is conscious and accordingly involves abilities related to explicit learning and that the various components of traditional aptitude are important for explicit learning.

The Fundamental Difference Hypothesis (FDH)

The FDH, which is derived from Chomsky's theory about first language acquisition, is proposed by Bley-Vroman (1990), who made the following claim:

> First language development is controlled by an innate language acquisition system which no longer operates in adults. Adult language learning resembles general adult learning. This is the explanation advocated here: the fundamental difference hypothesis.
>
> *(p. 23)*

Thus, according to this theory, children are endowed with a language acquisition device that enables them to acquire a language efficiently, effortlessly, and unconsciously. Via this device, the outcome of first language acquisition is uniform: mastery. The kind of ability possessed by children is domain specific. Adults, however, have lost the domain-specific language learning ability, and they learn a language by drawing on domain-general analytic abilities, which often result in failure and a high degree of individual variation in terms of the outcome of learning. These domain-general analytic abilities are components of language aptitude or traditional aptitude. This theory has spawned a stream of research examining the interface between age and aptitude, represented in two hypotheses: (1) language aptitude (the domain-general abilities) is correlated with adult language learning but not with the learning outcomes of those who start to learn a second language at a young age; (2) adult learners who achieve a high level of attainment in a second language have exceptional aptitude, whereas early starters with high achievements are varied in terms of aptitude. The purpose of this line of research (e.g. Abrahamsson & Hyltenstam, 2008; DeKeyser, 2000) is to examine age effects on second language learning, which are represented in the Critical Period hypothesis, which claims that (1) children and adults learn through different mechanisms and (2) child language acquisition is uniformly successful, whereas adult language learning is subject to high variability.

However, it is important to point out that if we assume that language aptitude— the kind of ability adults draw on to learn a second language—is distinct from abilities for academic learning in general, or intelligence, then it is domain specific. In other words, both children and adults draw on domain-specific cognitive devices, but the two devices are different in nature. For children, the device is language acquisition or universal grammar (UG); it is essential for implicit learning. For adults, it is called language aptitude and is important for explicit learning. However, we cannot assume that UG is the only device for child language acquisition, as children may learn explicitly. Carroll, for example, developed a parallel version of the MLAT, called EMLAT (with E representing "elementary"), to measure children's ability to learn a second language. The subtests of the EMLAT are similar to the MLAT, which has proven sensitive to explicit learning (Li, 2015).

By the same token, adults may learn implicitly and they may differ in their ability to do so (Granena, 2015), hence the term "implicit aptitude" (see Chapter 12).

The Staged Model

The staged model is proposed by Skehan (2002, 2012), who divides L2 development into four macro stages that involve different aptitude components. The macro stages were subdivided into some micro stages, but in order to have a clear understanding of the mapping between L2 stages and aptitude components, we focus on the macro stages here. The first stage is noticing, which refers to the cognitive process of attending to and detecting linguistic forms. Skehan posits the relevance of phonemic coding and working memory to this initial stage of learning. The second stage is patterning, where learners extrapolate rules and patterns based on noticed linguistic forms. This stage requires the application of language analytic ability, which, according to Skehan, is insufficient, because rule learning also involves restructuring existing knowledge, such as by incorporating information contained in corrective feedback. The third stage is controlling, during which learners proceduralize their L2 knowledge; proceduralization, according to information processing theory, refers to the application of rule-based knowledge in actual linguistic behaviors during oral or written performance. Skehan did not elaborate what aptitude components might be relevant for proceduralization, although he mentioned the concept of cumulative learning, which he said seems to be measurable by the York aptitude test and the CANAL-F (Grigorenko, Sternberg, & Ehrman, 2000). The final stage is lexicalizing, which is similar to the concept of automatization in the framework of information processing theory. At this stage, learners build a system that enables them to have speedy access to the linguistic information required in real-life performance. Because of the automatized nature of such a system, it is accessible in similar ways as lexical items or as holistic, unanalyzed chunks. Skehan argued that the memory component of aptitude, especially the ability to retrieve information, is responsible for lexicalization. He further contended that neither rote memory (associative memory) nor working memory is about information retrieval; however, he did not propose an alternative.

As with Robinson, Skehan regards aptitude as a componential rather than a unitary construct (Carroll, 1981), arguing that different aptitude components are drawn upon at different stages. His model is explanatory rather than predictive in that he tries to map aptitude components onto stages of learning defined in L2 theories. However, although the claims are theoretically appealing, it is difficult to empirically verify them because the hypothesized stages cannot be easily operationalized and because the theory did not offer concrete ideas on how to measure the newly proposed aptitude components (e.g. proceduralizing ability) and what they entail. However, the claims are insightful and inspiring. One valuable implication is that different aptitude components might be differentially predictive of the learning outcomes at different proficiency levels, which echoes the idea of the Hi-LAB (Linck et al., 2013), an aptitude battery aiming to measure cognitive abilities essential for advanced L2 proficiency. However, there is a lack of research on the interaction between aptitude and proficiency.

Research

In general, two strands of research can be observed: those examining the relationships between aptitude and learning outcome and those examining the relationships between aptitude and other individual difference variables. The bulk of the research falls into the former category, and based on the research design, the studies in this category can be further divided into predictive research and interactional research (Li, 2015, 2016). The predictive research is rooted in the Carrollian approach and investigates the influence of aptitude on learning rate. Typically in these studies learners are tested in terms of aptitude and L2 proficiency (either general proficiency or specific aspects of proficiency such as grammar, reading, etc.), and analyses of a correlational nature are conducted to identify the links between learners' aptitude scores and learning outcomes. The interactional research adopts an ATI approach, investigating the differential relationships between aptitude and instructional treatments. Typically learners are divided into groups and receive different types of treatments, which are consistently manipulated and operationalized according to certain learning theories (such as implicit vs. explicit; inductive vs. deductive). Learners are given pretests and posttests to assess learning gains resulting from the treatments in addition to taking tests of aptitude. Analyses are conducted separately for different learning conditions to ascertain whether aptitude is associated with learning gains in different ways.

The research examining the relationships between aptitude and other cognitive and affective variables is limited and often integrated into the research on aptitude–learning associations. In many cases, the primary purpose of the study is to examine how aptitude and other variables influence learning, but the correlations between aptitude and those variables are also reported; the data can then be drawn upon to shed light on the construct validity of aptitude. In the following, I start with these studies, then proceed to discuss the findings on aptitude–learning associations, and finally conclude with a discussion of some methodological concerns.

Aptitude and Other Individual Difference Variables

The relationships between aptitude and other individual difference variables in the affective and cognitive domains are revealing about the validity of such a construct. Li's (2016) aggregation of the correlations (based on MLAT scores) reported in the primary research showed that aptitude is distinct from motivation ($r = .16$), negatively correlated with anxiety ($r = -.35$), strongly correlated with intelligence

(r = .64), and weakly correlated with working memory (r = .37, .16 for executive working memory and phonological short-term memory, respectively). We will discuss these results in turn. First, the finding that aptitude is uncorrelated with motivation constitutes counter-evidence for the assumption that high aptitude leads to stronger motivation and suggests that aptitude and motivation make unique contributions to L2 learning. Indeed, the research has shown that among all individual difference variables, aptitude and motivation have been shown to be the two most consistent, powerful predictors of L2 attainment—a point to be revisited.

Second, the negative correlations between anxiety and aptitude are in line with their opposite effects on learning outcomes: while anxiety has been found to have a consistently unfavorable impact, aptitude has proven to be facilitative of learning. The causes for the negative correlations between the two variables are unclear. If we assume that they share the same pool of resources, we can posit a reciprocal relationship between them; that is, high anxiety depletes cognitive resources and low aptitude leads to high anxiety. In a similar vein, we can also argue that anxiety primarily affects online performance under a time constraint, such as in a testing setting; therefore, the negative correlations may result from the possibility that learners with high anxiety did poorly on aptitude tests.

Moving on to the strong correlations between aptitude and intelligence, there seems to be an overlap between language learning abilities and abilities for academic learning in general. Several factor analytic studies (Granena, 2012; Sparks, Patton, Ganschow, & Humbach, 2011, 2011; Wesche, Edwards, & Wells, 1982) also showed that language aptitude and intelligence were not entirely separate. The overlap is likely due to similar subtests included in the test batteries for the two constructs. For example, tests of language aptitude and intelligence both include a subtest of L1 vocabulary and a subtest of memory. Despite the overlap, the correlation, which is around .6, is not strong enough for the two variables to be considered identical. Also, the research has shown that aptitude is more predictive of L2 proficiency than intelligence when the two variables were entered into the same model (Granena, 2012; Sparks, Patton, Ganschow, & Humbach, 2009). However, I would like to conclude this section by expressing a concern over the large overlap between language aptitude and intelligence. The validity of the construct of language aptitude is questionable if it is not separable from abilities for other academic subjects. I therefore make a call for more research in this regard, including initiatives to develop tests that measure abilities that are exclusively important for language learning.

Finally, with respect to the links between aptitude and working memory, the weak correlations suggest that they are separate constructs. The finding is further confirmed by Yalçın, Çeçen, and Erçetin's (2016) study, which showed that working memory as measured by two reading span tests and one operation span test loaded on a factor separate from language aptitude measured through the LLAMA test (Meara, 2005). Similarly, Hummel (2009) showed that working memory, measured through a nonword repetition test, was separate from language aptitude, which was gauged through a French version of the MLAT. The findings challenge the suggestion that working memory be considered an aptitude component in replacement of rote memory. Moreover, theoretically, working memory is a domain-general cognitive device essential for academic learning in general and is therefore supposedly different from the domain-specific language aptitude. This claim has been borne out by the evidence generated by Li's research synthesis (2017) showing that language aptitude is a stronger predictor of language learning than working memory. The conclusion we may reach based on available evidence seems that working memory is implicated in language learning but that it is better not to consider it an aptitude component because its role is not restricted to language learning.

Aptitude and Language Learning

Predictive research. As previously mentioned, in general the studies on how aptitude relates to learning outcomes falls into two categories: predictive and interactional. Predictive research focuses on the associations between aptitude and learning outcomes, whereas interactional research investigates how aptitude mediates the effects of different instructional treatments in different ways. Li (2016) aggregated the findings of all predictive studies and found that aptitude measured through whole test batteries was correlated with general L2 proficiency at around .50, which means approximately 25% of the variance was explained. The correlation is considered a large effect based on Cohen's criteria (1988) and in comparison with the effects of other individual difference variables. For example, Linck et al.'s (2013) meta-analysis showed that the mean correlations between working memory and L2 proficiency were .17 and .27 for phonological short-term memory and executive working memory, respectively. In another meta-analysis, Masgoret and Gardner (2003) reported that the mean correlation between motivation and L2 learning gains was .37. Horwitz (2001) synthesized the research on foreign language anxiety, pointing out that overall anxiety is negatively correlated with L2 proficiency, with the correlation coefficient being approximately .20. These findings constitute evidence for the strong predictive power of language aptitude compared with other variables in the affective and cognitive domains. One caveat relating to the predictive power of aptitude as a global construct for general L2 proficiency is that when aptitude was measured through adapted versions of the MLAT, it was significantly less predictive than the original MLAT. Therefore, although those tests were modelled on the MLAT, they were not validated, and the results based on the tests should be interpreted with caution.

How predictive is overall aptitude for specific aspects of L2 learning? Li (2016) revealed that the average correlations were in the range of .30 and .39 for the learning of L2 skills such as listening, speaking, and reading and the learning of L2 grammar. However, it had a weak correlation with vocabulary learning (.15) and a nonsignificant correlation with L2 writing. But we cannot conclude that traditional aptitude is not important for these two aspects of learning because they were predicted by aptitude components (subtests of aptitude tests). For example, phonetic coding was a significant predictor for vocabulary learning ($r = .38$), and two subtests of the MLAT—Number Learning and Spelling Clues—were significantly predictive of writing ($r = .42$ for both). The results suggest that there is a need for more research on the role of overall aptitude in vocabulary learning and writing and that for the predictive power of aptitude for specific aspects of learning, it is perhaps more meaningful to examine aptitude components rather than overall aptitude.

Concerning the influence of overall aptitude, Li (2015, 2016) reported that it was more strongly correlated with the L2 achievements of high school foreign language learners than those of university learners. Li argued that this may mean that aptitude is more relevant for initial than later stages of learning, confirming Carroll's (1981) speculation that traditional aptitude constitutes initial readiness for language learning that primarily relates to learning from scratch. Note that these findings are based on meta-analysis, where the studies were divided into two groups based on whether the participants were high school or university learners. There has been very limited primary research on the influence of learner proficiency on aptitude–learning associations. Hummel (2009) is probably the only published study that investigated proficiency as an independent variable. Hummel reported that overall aptitude was a significant predictor of general L2 proficiency but that after the learners were divided into high and low proficiency based on their median scores, it was no longer a significant predictor for either proficiency level. Hummel further reported that working memory was predictive of the proficiency scores of low-level learners but not those of high-level learners. Similarly, Serafini and Sanz (2016) found that working memory was predictive of beginning but not intermediate and advanced foreign language learners' grammar knowledge. These findings suggest that language aptitude, together with other cognitive abilities such as working memory, are more, if not only, relevant for initial language learning.

Whereas this discussion focused on the effects of overall aptitude, the following section centers on those of aptitude components: phonetic coding, analytic ability, and rote memory (Li, 2016). In terms of overall proficiency, rote memory was found to be the least predictive among the three aptitude components. In terms of specific aspects of learning, the following patterns were obtained. First, phonetic coding was the strongest predictor for vocabulary learning, suggesting the importance of encoding novel sounds in learning the vocabulary in a second language. Second, language analytic ability was the strongest predictor for grammar learning, which is not surprising given its posited importance in rule learning. Third, rote memory was the least predictive of all aspects of L2 learning, including vocabulary learning, for which memory is often assumed to be critical. The finding that rote memory is a consistently weak predictor for L2 learning is counter-evidence for the assumption that language learning is a matter of rote learning—a main feature of traditional audiolingual instruction.

Finally, one stream of predictive research has investigated the relationship between aptitude and age to test the Fundamental Difference hypothesis (Bley-Vroman, 1990), which seeks explanations for why children are more successful language learners than adults. A core idea of the theory is that children learn a language through domain-specific, unconscious learning mechanisms, whereas adults, who have lost the abilities children possess, have to rely on conscious, analytic abilities, such as those contained in language aptitude. As mentioned earlier in the chapter, the theory makes two predictions: (1) language aptitude is only correlated with adult language learning but not child language learning and (2) adult learners with high L2 achievements have exceptional aptitude. In general, the claims of the theory have been confirmed despite some mixed findings for the first claim. With regard to the first claim, both DeKeyser (2000) and Granena and Long (2013) reported that aptitude was only predictive of adult learners' L2 achievements but not with child language learners'. However, Abrahamsson and Hyltenstam (2008) found that aptitude was predictive of the L2 attainment of both age groups. For the second claim, DeKeyser (2000) and Abrahamsson and Hyltenstam (2008) both reported that adults with exceptional language achievements also had exceptional aptitude.

Interactional Research

There have been three major streams of interactional research investigating the mediating effects of language aptitude on the effectiveness of (1) corrective feedback, (2) implicit and explicit instruction, and (3) deductive and inductive instruction. Corrective feedback refers to responses to errors learners commit in their L2 production (Li, 2014). Corrective feedback can be explicit or implicit depending on whether learners' attention is overtly drawn to the errors they make. For example, the recast, which refers to the reformulation of an erroneous sentence without changing the meaning, is relatively implicit. Meta-linguistic feedback, which entails a comment on the learner's language use, is explicit. Li (2017) meta-analysed all the empirical studies on the role of language aptitude in mediating the effects of corrective feedback and found that aptitude as a global construct (when measured using whole test batteries) showed stronger associations with the effectiveness of explicit feedback than that of implicit feedback ($r = .59$ vs. $r = .32$), and the gap was larger when aptitude was operationalized as language analytic ability ($r = .51$ vs. $r = .09$), which is not surprising given the importance of this aptitude component in learning L2 morphosyntax—the target of the feedback research. In the same research synthesis, Li (2017) also aggregated the results for working memory, which showed overall weaker associations with the effects of corrective feedback. The correlations between executive working memory and explicit and implicit feedback were .34 and .23, respectively; for phonological short-term memory, the correlations were .19 and .23. Referring to the overall small effect for working memory on L2 learning in general based on Linck, Osthus, Koeth, and Bunting's (2014) meta-analysis, Li (2017) concluded that as a domain-general cognitive device, working memory is less important than language aptitude—a domain-specific ability that is exclusively important for language learning.

The greater importance of aptitude for explicit instruction than implicit instruction receives further support from the studies that investigated explicitness/implicitness of instruction as an independent variable. The studies in this category all investigated both explicit and implicit instruction delivered via the computer, and they all showed a stronger effect for aptitude under explicit learning conditions. For example, Carpenter (2008) found a significant correlation between aptitude and the effects of an explicit treatment that asked learners to learn the grammar rules of an artificial language but not the effects of an implicit treatment that only exposed learners to some exemplars of the language without any rule explanation. Robinson (1997, 2002b) reported a stronger effect for aptitude under conditions where learners were asked to process or search for grammar rules than conditions where they memorized linguistic exemplars or engaged in comprehension tasks. One study that is seemingly at odds with the other studies is de Graaff (1997), who found that aptitude was drawn on in both explicit and implicit treatments. However, the implicit treatment, which involved form-focused activities (such as gap filling, target structure comprehension, etc.), may have encouraged learners to engage in conscious processing of the L2.

Three studies (Erlam, 2005; Hwu & Sun, 2012; Hwu, Wei, & Sun, 2014) have investigated the interface between aptitude, on one hand, and deductive and inductive instruction, on the other, and yielded the following findings. The distinction between deduction and induction originated in philosophy, with the former referring to a process that is general to specific and the latter to a process that is specific to general. In second language research, deductive instruction is often operationalized as rule explanation followed by practice activities where the rule is applied; inductive instruction requires the learner to induce the grammar rule from linguistic exemplars. It must be pointed out that both deductive and inductive instruction constitute explicit instruction because they require learners to process linguistic materials. This strand of research yields the following findings. First, aptitude is less likely to be implicated in deductive instruction, which affords external support and which poses less processing or cognitive burden on the learner. Conversely, inductive instruction requires the learner to rely on his or her own cognitive resources, hence a stronger correlation between aptitude and the gains resulting from the instruction (Erlam, 2005). Erlam (2005) further pointed out that input-based instruction, which requires the learner to process linguistic materials, is more likely to draw on aptitude than output-based instruction, where the requirement for production may neutralize the effects of aptitude. Second, high-aptitude learners benefit more from inductive instruction, whereas low-aptitude learners benefit more from deductive instruction (Hwu & Sun, 2012; Hwu et al., 2014). These findings constitute evidence for Snow's (1991) claim that low-aptitude learners benefit more from instruction that is more structured and that provides more assistance to learners.

Methodological Concerns

The large amount of empirical research on aptitude has generated valuable findings enhancing our understanding of L2 acquisition and pedagogy. However, the findings are subject to the methodological heterogeneity observed among the studies in terms of the measurement of the predictor variable (aptitude) and the outcome variable (learning gains) and the implementation of instructional treatments. Li's meta-analyses/research syntheses (2015, 2016, 2017) showed that aptitude had been measured via a variety of measures, including the MLAT (and its adapted versions in other languages), PLAB, LLAMA, VORD, and Language Analysis Test, among others. The extent they measure the same construct remains unknown, and to date no research has been conducted to cross-validate these tests. To exemplify, both Abrahamsson and Hyltenstam (2008) and DeKeyser (2000) examined the relationship between aptitude and age, but in the former study aptitude was measured via the LLAMA test (whole battery), whereas in the latter it was measured through the Words in Sentences subtest of a Hungarian aptitude battery. This disparity is perhaps partly responsible for their different findings: Abrahamsson and Hyltenstam's study showed a significant correlation between aptitude and child language learners' ultimate L2 attainment, whereas DeKeyser's study did not. Similarly, both de Graaff (1997) and Robinson (1997) investigated the relationship between aptitude and the effects of computerized implicit and explicit instruction; however, de Graaff measured aptitude using a hybrid aptitude test consisting of a test asking learners to infer eXperanto (an artificial language) words from context and the Dutch versions of the MLAT 4 and MLAT 5, while Robinson tested learners' aptitude using the original MLAT, which is in English—the learners' L2.

The empirical studies also measured learning outcomes differently. For example, in predictive research, general L2 proficiency has been measured through course grades (Curtin, Avner, & Smith, 1983), TOEFL (Ross, Yoshinaga, & Sasaki, 2002), cloze (Harley & Hart, 1997), etc. In interactional research, treatment effects have been measured through sentence making (Lado, 2008); composite scores of dictation, writing, and error correction (Sheen, 2007); oral picture description (Trofimovich, Ammar, & Gatbonton, 2007); and so on. Also, the outcome measures were not distinguished in terms of whether they measure explicit or implicit knowledge (Ellis, 2005); the former refers to knowledge that is conscious and accessible under controlled tasks (e.g. grammaticality judgment test), and the latter to knowledge that is unconscious and available for use in spontaneous production (e.g. oral production). It is possible that aptitude and aptitude components have differential associations with L2 learning depending on how learning gains are measured.

The instructional treatments in interactional research are equally heterogeneous. For example, both Sheen (2007) and Trofimovich et al. (2007) investigated whether the effects of recasts were related to language analytic ability. However, the nature of recasts is different across the two studies. In Sheen's study, recasts were given in a classroom setting and were provided only when the learners made errors, while in Trofimovich et al.'s study, the instruction was delivered via the computer, recasts (or the correct versions of the expected utterances) were given regardless of whether errors were existent, and for each item, learners were asked to report whether there was a difference between the audio recast and their own utterance. In a similar vein, both Erlam (2005) and Hwu & Sun (2012; Hwu et al., 2014) examined the relationship between aptitude and deductive vs. inductive instruction. However, in Erlam's study the inductive group never received any grammar explanation, but in Hwu et al.'s study the inductive instruction contained meta-linguistic feedback, which is equivalent to grammar explanation.

To conclude this section, I would like to make two calls. One is for unifying the methodology of the research so as to reach firmer conclusions about the examined questions. Researchers are encouraged to consult existing literature thoroughly, be fully aware of the methodology of previous research, and align their methods with similar studies if they claim to examine the same variables as previous studies. The other call is for acknowledging the differences between their and other studies, making the differences transparent, and interpreting the results accordingly. It is misleading for a researcher to make claims about the same variable or research question if the methods are different. Of course, variation is unavoidable, and a certain level of variation increases the external validity of the research, but it must remain within the boundary of the examined construct and be transparent.

Pedagogy

The literature on aptitude contains very little information on how to apply the research findings to classroom teaching, except for some tips on how teachers and program administrators may use learners' aptitude scores (Carroll, Sapon, Reed, & Stansfield, 2010; Skehan, 2012) based on aptitude's predictive and diagnostic functions, which are elaborated in the following. First, aptitude scores can be used to select elite learners for programs that expect or require learners to master a foreign language within a short period. Second, teachers may use learners' aptitude scores to provide counselling informing them of the right way to study based on their aptitude profiles. For example, for learners with high analytic ability but poor memory, perhaps it is advisable to learn a foreign language analytically instead of trying to memorize linguistic materials. Third, aptitude tests can be used to diagnose learning disabilities, and learners who fail to meet a certain threshold may be waived foreign language requirements. Fourth, results of aptitude tests may serve as a basis for placement decisions; that is, students in different classes or streams should have comparable aptitude scores to ensure they progress at similar rates and to ensure the objectiveness of teaching or program evaluation (that is, the superior performance of one group is not because of their high aptitude, and vice versa).

A more promising application of aptitude findings is to match learners' aptitude profiles with the appropriate instruction type. Matching can happen on a macro level and a micro level. Macro matching means dividing learners into groups based on their aptitude profiles and provide them with the type of instruction that matches the whole group's aptitude strengths in a consistent manner over a long period (e.g. throughout the program of study), as reported in Wesche's (1981) study. However, although Wesche stated that the matched groups showed superior performance than the unmatched groups, the implementation of the investigated instruction types was not strictly monitored, and overall the study was not rigorously conducted. To date, except for Wesche's study, there has been no other empirical research on the feasibility and effects of long-term or macro aptitude–instruction matching.

Micro matching refers to the use of different instructional techniques in a class with mixed aptitude profiles. For example, given the finding that high-aptitude learners benefit more from inductive instruction and low-aptitude learners more from deductive instruction, the teacher may assign different tasks to different learners when they work in groups. For low-aptitude learners, for instance, they may receive a priori explanation in a handout. Similarly, for learners with strong memory or analytic ability, they may receive tasks that fit their aptitude strengths. However, similar to macro matching, to date there has been no research on the practicality and effectiveness of matching instruction with aptitude profiles in a class with mixed aptitude profiles. The research in this regard is therefore badly needed.

It must be pointed out that the idea of matching is based on the existence of aptitude–instruction interaction, that is, the comparative effectiveness of instruction types depends on learners' aptitude profiles. If there is no interaction—that is, for example, Type A instruction is always more effective than Type B instruction regardless of learners' aptitude—then the former instruction type should be opted for.

Another way to cater to learners' individual differences is to adopt an eclectic approach, using a variety of approaches and techniques. For example, if deductive instruction benefits low-aptitude learners and inductive instruction favors high-aptitude learners, it might be ideal to mix deductive and inductive instruction in order not to disadvantage high- or low-aptitude learners. Similarly, if high-aptitude learners benefit more from explicit corrective feedback than from implicit corrective feedback and the reverse is true for low-aptitude learners, then teachers should provide a variety of feedback instead of a single genus (Li, 2018; Lyster &

Ranta, 2013). However, an eclectic approach does not mean teachers can be blind to research findings. Teachers would need to be aware of the distinction between the different instruction types/devices and know how to implement them, as well as the fact that aptitude interacts with the instruction types/devices.

Still another way to cater to learners' aptitude differences is to use the type of instruction whose effects are not related to aptitude but which is equally, if not more, effective as other instruction types. For example, Li, Ellis, and Zhu (under review) showed that language analytic ability was drawn upon in the absence of pretask or posttask grammar instruction and that it had no correlation with the effects of instruction when learners received grammar instruction either before or after performing communicative tasks. Moreover, those who received form-focused instruction learned more than those who did not (Li, Ellis, & Zhu, 2016a, 2016b). Therefore, it would seem that a certain dose of grammar instruction is advisable, given that it cancels the effects of aptitude without sacrificing learning gains.

Conclusion

The chapter started with a discussion of the current theories on language aptitude, including the Carrollian approach, the Linguistic Coding Difference Hypothesis, the ATI approach, the Fundamental Difference hypothesis, and the staged model. Then it provided an overview of the findings on language aptitude based on three meta-analyses (Li, 2015, 2016, 2017). Aptitude has been found to be distinct from other individual difference variables, which, together with the fact that it is also more predictive of learning outcomes than other variables, suggests that it is a domain-specific language learning device. The predictive research shows that overall aptitude is a strong predictor of learning success, but it seems less predictive of L2 writing and vocabulary learning. Among the three components of aptitude, rote memory is the least predictive of learning outcomes; language analytic ability is more predictive of grammar learning than other components of aptitude; and phonetic coding is a stronger predictor of vocabulary learning. Moreover, aptitude seems more predictive of learning at initial stages than higher stages of learning, and it is more predictive of adult language learning than child language learning. The interactional research demonstrates that aptitude is more correlated with the effects of explicit instructional treatments than implicit treatments and that it has stronger associations with deductive instruction than inductive instruction. The section on research findings ended with a discussion of the methodological limitations of the primary research. The following section focused on how the research findings can be applied to classroom teaching. Several strategies were proposed, including matching instruction with aptitude profile, adopting an eclectic approach, and utilizing techniques and instruction types that are insensitive to aptitude. However, these suggestions are tentative, and more research is warranted on how to integrate research findings into pedagogical practice.

References

Abrahamsson, N., & Hyltenstam, K. (2008). The robustness of aptitude effects in near-native second language acquisition. *Studies in Second Language Acquisition, 30*(4), 481–509.

Bley-Vroman, R. (1990). The logical problem of Foreign language learning. *Linguistic Analysis, 20,* 3–49.

Carpenter, H. S. (2008). *A behavioural and electrophysiological investigation of different aptitudes for L2 grammar in learners equated for proficiency level* (Ph.D. dissertation). Washington, DC: Georgetown University.

Carroll, J. (1981). Twenty-five years of research on Foreign language aptitude. In K. Diller (Ed.), *Individual differences and universals in language learning aptitude* (pp. 83–118). Rowley, MA: Newbury House.

Carroll, J., & Sapon, S. (1959). *Modern language aptitude test.* New York, NY: The Psychological Corporation/Harcourt Brace Jovanovich.

Carroll, J., Sapon, S., Reed, D. J., & Stansfield, C. W. (2010). *Manual for the MLAT.* Bethesda, MD: Second Language Testing, Inc.

Cohen, J. (1988). *Statistical power analysis for the behavioral sciences,* 2nd ed. Hillsdale, NJ: Lawrence Erlbaum Associates.

Curtin, C., Avner, A., & Smith, L. A. (1983). The pimsleur battery as a predictor of student performance. *The Modern Language Journal, 67*(1), 33–40.

De Graaff, R. (1997). The eXperanto experiment: Effects of explicit instruction on second language acquisition. *Studies in Second Language Acquisition, 19,* 249–276.

DeKeyser, R. M. (2000). The robustness of critical period effects in second language acquisition. *Studies in Second Language Acquisition, 22*(4), 499–533.

Ellis, R. (2005). Measuring implicit and explicit knowledge of a second language: A psychometric study. *Studies in Second Language Acquisition, 27,* 141–172.

Erlam, R. (2005). Language aptitude and its relationship to instructional effectiveness in second language acquisition. *Language Teaching Research, 9*(2), 147–171.

Ganschow, L., & Sparks, R. L. (1996). Anxiety about Foreign language learning among high school women. *Modern Language Journal, 80*(2), 199–212.

Granena, G. (2012). *Age differences and cognitive aptitudes for implicit and explicit learning in ultimate second language attainment* (Ph.D. dissertation), The University of Maryland, College Park, MD.

Granena, G. (2015). Cognitive aptitudes for implicit and explicit learning and information-processing styles: An individual differences study. *Applied Psycholinguistics, 37,* 577–600.

Granena, G., & Long, M. H. (2013). Age of onset, length of residence, language aptitude, and ultimate L2 attainment in three linguistic domains. *Second Language Research, 29*(3), 311–343.

Grigorenko, E., Sternberg, R., & Ehrman, M. (2000). A theory-based approach to the measurement of Foreign language learning ability: The Canal-F theory and test. *The Modern Language Journal, 84,* 390–405.

Harley, B., & Hart, D. (1997). Language aptitude and second language proficiency in classroom learners of different starting ages. *Studies in Second Language Acquisition, 19*(3), 379–400.

Horwitz, E. K. (2001). Language anxiety and achievement. *Annual Review of Applied Linguistics, 21,* 112–126.

Hummel, K. (2009). Aptitude, phonological memory, and second language proficiency in nonnovice adult learners. *Applied Psycholinguistics, 30,* 225–249.

Hwu, F., & Sun, S. (2012). The aptitude-treatment interaction effects on the learning of grammar rules. *System, 40,* 505–521.

Hwu, F., Wei, P., & Sun, S. (2014). Aptitude-treatment interaction effects on explicit rule learning: A latent growth curve analysis. *Language Teaching Research, 18,* 294–319.

Lado, B. (2008). *The role of bilingualism, type of feedback, and cognitive capacity in the acquisition of non-primary languages: A computer-based study* (Ph.D. dissertation), Georgetown University, Washington, DC.

Li, S. (2014). Recasts, working memory, and the choice of target structure. In Z. Han (Ed.), *Second language acquisition of Chinese: A series of empirical studies* (pp. 103–125). Buffalo: Multilingual Matters.

Li, S. (2015). The associations between language aptitude and second language grammar acquisition: A meta-analytic review of five decades of research. *Applied Linguistics, 36,* 385–408.

Li, S. (2016). The construct validity of language aptitude. *Studies in Second Language Acquisition, 38,* 801–842.

Li, S. (2017). The effects of cognitive aptitudes on the process and product of L2 interaction: A synthetic review. In L. Gurzynski-Weiss (Ed.), *Expanding individual difference research in the interaction approach: Investigating learners, instructors, and other interlocutors* (pp. 41–70). Amsterdam: John Benjamins Publishing Company.

Li, S. (2018). Corrective feedback in L2 speech production. In J. Liontas (Ed.), *The TESOL encyclopaedia of English language teaching* (pp. 1–9). Hoboken, NJ: Blackwell Publishing.

Li, S., Ellis, R., & Zhu, Y. (under review). The associations between cognitive ability and L2 development under five different instructional conditions.

Li, S., Ellis, R., & Zhu, Y. (2016a). The effects of the timing of corrective feedback on the acquisition of a new linguistic structure. *Modern Language Journal, 100,* 276–295.

Li, S., Ellis, R., & Zhu, Y. (2016b). Task-based versus task-supported language instruction: An experimental study. *Annual Review of Applied Linguistics, 36,* 205–229.

Linck, J., Linck, J. A., Hughes, M. M., Campbell, S. G., Silbert, N. H., Tare, M., . . . Doughty, C. J. (2013). Hi-LAB: A new measure of aptitude for high-level language proficiency. *Language Learning, 63*(3), 530–566.

Linck, J., Osthus, P., Koeth, J., & Bunting, M. (2014). Working memory and second language comprehension and production: A meta-analysis. *Psychonomic Bulletin & Review, 21*(4), 861–883.

Lyster, R., & Ranta, L. (2013). Counterpoint piece: The case for variety in corrective feedback research. *Studies in Second Language Acquisition, 35,* 167–184.

Masgoret, A., & Gardner, R. (2003). Attitudes, motivation, and second language learning: A meta-analysis of studies conducted by Gardner and associates. *Language Learning, 53,* 123–163.

Meara, P. (2005). *LLAMA language aptitude tests.* Swansea: Lognostics.

Robinson, P. (1997). Individual differences and the fundamental similarity of implicit and explicit adult second language learning. *Language Learning, 47,* 45–99.

Robinson, P. (2002a). Learning conditions, aptitude complexes, and SLA. In P. Robinson (Ed.), *Individual differences and instructed language learning* (pp. 113–133). Amsterdam and Philadelphia: John Benjamins Publishing Company.

Robinson, P. (2002b). Effects of individual differences in intelligence, aptitude and working memory on adult incidental SLA. In P. Robinson (Ed.), *Individual differences and instructed language learning* (pp. 212–266). Amsterdam and Philadelphia: John Benjamins Publishing Company.

Ross, S.,Yoshinaga, N., & Sasaki, M. (2002). Aptitude-exposure interaction effects on Wh-movement violation detection by pre-and-post-critical period Japanese bilinguals. In P. Robinson (Ed.), *Individual differences and instructed language learning* (pp. 267–299). Amsterdam, The Netherlands: John Benjamins Publishing Company.

Schmidt, R., & Frota, S. (1986). Developing basic conversational ability in a second langauge: A case study of an adult learner of Portuguese. In R. Day (Ed.), *Taking to learning: Conversation in second langauge learning* (pp. 237–322). Rowley, MA: Newbury House.

Serafini, E., & Sanz, C. (2016). Evidence for the decreasing impact of cognitive ability on second language development as proficiency increases. *Studies in Second Language Acquisition, 38,* 607–646.

Sheen,Y. (2007). The effects of corrective feedback, language aptitude, and learner attitudes on the acquisition of English articles. In A. Mackey (Ed.), *Conversational interaction in second language acquisition* (pp. 301–322). Oxford: Oxford University Press.

Skehan, P. (2002). Theorizing and updating aptitude. In P. Robinson (Ed.), *Individual differences and instructed language learning* (pp. 69–94). Amsterdam, The Netherlands: John Benjamins Publishing Company.

Skehan, P. (2012). Language aptitude. In S. Gass & A. Mackey (Eds.), *Handbook of second language acquisition* (pp. 381–395). New York, NY: Routledge.

Snow, R. E. (1991). Aptitude-treatment interaction as a framework for research on individual differences in psychotherapy. *Journal of Consulting and Clinical Psychology, 59,* 205–216.

Sparks, R. L., Artzer, M., Ganschow, L., Siebenhar, D., Plageman, M., & Patton, J. (1998). Differences in native-language skills, Foreign-language aptitude, and Foreign-language grades among high-, average-, and low-proficiency Foreign-language learners: Two studies. *Language Testing, 15*(2), 181–216.

Sparks, R. L., Patton, J., Ganschow, L., & Humbach, N. (2009). Long-term relationships among early first language skills, second language aptitude, second language affect, and later second language proficiency. *Applied Psycholinguistics, 30*(4), 725–755.

Sparks, R. L., Patton, J., Ganschow, L., & Humbach, N. (2011). Subcomponents of second-language aptitude and second-language proficiency. *Modern Language Journal, 95*(2), 253–273.

Sparks, R. L., Patton, J., Ganschow, L., Humbach, N., & Javorsky, J. (2006). Native language predictors of Foreign language proficiency and Foreign language aptitude. *Annals of Dyslexia, 56*(1), 129–160.

Trofimovich, P., Ammar, A., & Gatbonton, E. (2007). How effective are recasts? The role of attention, memory, and analytical ability. In A. Mackey (Ed.), *Conversational interaction in second language acquisition.* Oxford: Oxford University Press.

Wesche, M. (1981). Language aptitude measures in streaming, matching students with methods, and diagnosis of learning problems. In K. Diller (Ed.), *Individual differences and universals in language learning aptitude* (pp. 119–175). Rowley, MA: Newbury House Publishers.

Wesche, M., Edwards, H., & Wells, W. (1982). Foreign language aptitude and intelligence. *Applied Psycholinguistics, 3*(2), 127–140.

Yalçın, Ş., Çeçen, S., & Erçetin, G. (2016). The relationship between aptitude and working memory: An instructed SLA context. *Language Awareness, 25,* 144–158.

PART II

Emerging Insights on Age and Ultimate Attainment

6

DIFFICULTY AND EASE IN LEARNING FOREIGN LANGUAGES AT THE PRIMARY SCHOOL LEVEL

General Learning Ability, Language Aptitude, or Working Memory?

Amelia Lambelet and Raphael Berthele

Introduction

The effectiveness of foreign language teaching at school is a topic of societal interest in many regions. In Switzerland, a country with four national languages and where language rights are granted territorially to each language communities, this question is of particular concern. Many school hours are devoted to the learning of at least two foreign languages starting at the primary school level (one national language and English), often with rather disappointing results in terms of proficiency attained at the end of compulsory education. Students are expected to achieve level A1.2 ("breakthrough") of the Common European Framework of Reference (CEFR) at the end of primary school (i.e. grade 6) and CEFR level A2.2 ("waystage") at the end of compulsory education (grade 9). Those two levels are rather basic and allow only very simple communication: At level A2, students are expected to

> understand sentences and frequently used expressions related to areas of most immediate relevance (e.g. very basic personal and family information, shopping, local geography, employment) [. . .] communicate in simple and routine tasks requiring a simple and direct exchange of information on familiar and routine matters [. . .] describe in simple terms aspects of [their] background, immediate environment and matters in areas of immediate need.
>
> *(Persons, 2001, p. 2)*

In a recent study aiming to evaluate the levels of French and English proficiency attained at the end of grades 6 and 8 in German-speaking children, Peyer,

Andexlinger, Kofler, and Lenz (2016) found that at both times of data collection and particularly in the national language (French), the proficiency levels defined as learning objectives were far from being achieved. At the end of grade 6, around half of the children had not yet attained the learning objective for French written comprehension and production, and two-thirds of them had not attained the learning objective for oral comprehension and production. At the end of grade 8, one-quarter of the children had still not attained the learning objective for grade 6 in oral and written comprehension, and one-third of them had not attained the learning objective for grade 6 in oral and written production.

This type of result is worrying in a country that ideologically constructs proficiency in the other national language(s) as part of its cohesion and shared identity and puts increased emphasis on foreign language learning at school. Therefore, linguistic educational policies are debated politically and publicly on a regular basis. In particular, three aspects of the linguistic educational policies are often discussed: the order of foreign languages introduced in the curriculum (i.e. should a national language be taught first, or should it be English?), the age at which foreign language teaching should begin (i.e. should both languages be taught at the primary school level, or can/should the teaching of one or both languages be pushed to the secondary school level?), and cognitive overload (i.e. is the teaching of two languages at school too cognitively demanding for some students?).

This last question is the topic of this chapter and the center point of the Language Aptitude at the Primary School Level (LAPS) project, in which we aim to develop a battery of aptitude tests adequate for predicting foreign language learning achievement in primary school. In the following, we intend to give a theoretical overview of the factors predicting success in foreign language learning and present and discuss the results of a study investigating foreign language aptitude in German-speaking children learning French as a foreign language in primary school (grade 4 and grade 5).

Foreign Language Aptitude Research

Research on foreign language learning aptitude dates at least back to the 1920s when colleges and universities in the United States developed an interest in individual differences among foreign language students due to high failure rates and the need to optimize the return on investment by selecting the "apt" students for foreign language instruction (Spolsky, 1995). Later, in the 1950s, government initiatives were aimed at developing tests that improve selection procedures for expensive programs in foreign language learning. In this context, John B. Carroll and his colleague Stanley M. Sapon worked on the abilities needed to learn foreign languages in short and intensive foreign language training courses for military purposes. Their works resulted in the definition of foreign language aptitude as consisting of four dimensions: *phonetic coding ability* (the ability to discriminate and identify new language sounds), *grammatical sensitivity* (the awareness of the grammatical function of the different elements constituting a sentence), *inductive ability* (the ability to identify grammatical/meaning patterns in unknown language samples), and *rote memory* (the ability to learn a large number of items in a short time). These dimensions resulted from factorial analyses of the participants' responses to a series of tests predicting achievement in the target-language courses.

Based on their results, Carroll and Sapon designed a series of tests aimed at measuring language aptitude, the Modern Language Aptitude Test (MLAT). After Carroll and Sapon's MLAT, other test batteries were developed and tested following the same data-driven principles (mostly based on factor analysis, for instance, Pimsleur's (1966) PLAB, Doughty et al.'s (2010) Hi-LAB, etc.). Since then, MLAT and MLAT-based test batteries have proved their predictive power on a variety of students' L1 and target languages in studies aiming to investigate interindividual differences in foreign language learning in a (high) school context (among others, Cochran, McCallum, & Bell, 2010; Doughty et al., 2010; Erlam, 2005; Hummel, 2009; Kiss & Nikolov, 2005; Linck et al., 2013; Muñoz, 2014; Safar & Kormos, 2008). Foreign language aptitude at the primary school level has nevertheless rarely been studied. It is also worth mentioning that in a recent meta-analysis of 33 studies investigating the link between aptitude (as measured by MLAT or "quasi-MLAT" aptitude tests) and the acquisition of L2 grammar, Li (2015) found an overall moderate effect of aptitude and higher predictive effect of the language analytic abilities than of phonetic coding abilities and rote memory. This result suggests that other dimensions of aptitude not covered in conventional test batteries might play an important role in L2 learning achievement.

Moving Beyond Traditional Conceptualization of Foreign Language Learning Aptitude

The four componential dimensions of aptitude as defined by Carroll have been discussed both theoretically and empirically. Skehan (1998, 2002), for instance, proposed a model of aptitude in three dimensions: auditory processing, language analysis, and memory, instead of Carroll's initial four dimensions and, more importantly, associated these dimensions with processing stages in SLA. Other authors, basing their research on theory, proposed aptitude measures completely different from Carroll's initial dimensions. In this respect, Grigorenko, Sternberg, and Ehrman (2000) argued for one central ability required for foreign language learning based on Sternberg's (1999, 2002) model of intelligence: the ability to cope with novelty and ambiguity in linguistic materials, and developed a test of foreign language aptitude (CANAL-FT) aiming to assess this particular ability.

More generally, two important discussions have emerged in the field of foreign language learning abilities in the last decades. The first one concerns the role of working memory in foreign language learning, while the second one concerns the role of affective factors (motivation, but also foreign language anxiety).

Working Memory

One of the more widespread critiques of Carroll and Sapon's MLAT consists of its measure of (rote) memory, considered by Carroll as the "ability to store information passively" (Erlam, 2005, p. 149). This conceptualization of memory as static and passive has been challenged with the advancement in cognitive sciences, and in particular, since Baddeley and Hitch's (1974) research and their definition of working memory as consisting of several components and slave systems, which not only store information but also process it in real time and serve as a gateway to long-term memory. Several recent studies added measures of working memory to well-established aptitude measures and found working memory to "exercise consistent and distinctive influences on various aspects of L2 acquisition and processing" (Wen, Biedroń, & Skehan, 2017, p. 19). Nevertheless, following several authors, the importance of working memory still deserves more empirical testing (for instance Li, 2015; Safar & Kormos, 2008; Singleton, 2014; Wen et al., 2017; Wen & Skehan, 2011).

Affective Factors

Following several scholars, affective factors can also be conceived as a subcomponent of aptitude (see for instance Sparks, Humbach, Patton, & Ganschow, 2011), but these two dimensions have rarely been investigated in close relation one to another. The results of the few studies investigating foreign language aptitude in relation to affective factors showed that adding affective factors to aptitude test batteries results in explaining more variance in foreign language learning success than models with aptitude alone, even though aptitude still remains the more important predictor (Bialystok & Fröhlich, 1978; Kiss & Nikolov, 2005; Sparks, Patton, Ganschow, & Humbach, 2009).

The influence of affective factors on foreign language achievement has furthermore been researched independently in a wide range of studies. In particular, motivation has been widely investigated in the last decade, and its theoretical underpinning has been substantially developed, moving from Gardner's (1985) Integrative Motive Theory, which states that L2 learning is dependent on the learner's desire to integrate a valued speech community, to theories such as the L2 Motivational Self System, which sees L2 learning as the result of the learner's projection of themselves (ideal self), their extrinsic motivation, and their L2 learning experience (Dörnyei, 2009). But, as is the case for research on foreign language aptitude, research on affective factors has principally investigated populations of high school students. As noted by Boo, Dörnyei, and Ryan (2015) in their literature review of motivational studies, only 5.6% of the research projects taken into account focus on primary school–level students. In Switzerland, one study investigated the role of motivation in foreign language learning at the primary school level with a longitudinal design. In this study, the development of

German-speaking primary school students' motivational and attitudinal disposi-tions with respect to English and French was investigated. Three factors were found to influence primary school children's language learning motivation and language attitudes: self-concept, beliefs about language learning, and anxiety (Heinzmann, 2013).

Other affective, or personality, dimensions have appeared sporadically in the literature to explain difficulties in L2 attainment. Among them, *locus of control*, a psychological trait that refers to an individual's perception of their own respon-sibility of an outcome: individuals with an *internal* locus of control tend to think that they are personally responsible for what happens to them, whereas individuals with an *external* locus of control think that their achievement/failures are deter-mined by factors external to them. In relation to foreign language learning, it can be hypothesized that students with an internal locus of control will attain a higher level of proficiency, as they will tend to take responsibility in their learning and therefore study more thoroughly (Biedroń, 2010; Chang & Ho, 2009; Peek, 2016; Sparks & Ganschow, 1993).

Foreign Language Aptitude and General Learning Abilities

From a larger perspective, an important question on foreign language aptitude we would like to address consists of its link to general learning/cognitive abili-ties (among which working memory is one, as well as other cognitive skills and dimensions of intelligence). Besides foreign language aptitude, we believe that other factors may have an impact on foreign language learning in school. Those factors, which are part of general intelligence and more generally cognitive abili-ties, have an impact on success in school-related learning, and their link with foreign language aptitude has been discussed since the first works of Carroll and colleagues (see for instance Carroll, 1964). Among these cognitive factors, *field (in-)dependence* seems to have an impact. Research on field (in-)dependence has been conducted in psychology since Witkin's pioneering works in the 1940s. It is a cognitive trait describing the way an individual treats (new) information from the environment, with field-dependent individuals perceiving the organization of the field as a whole, while field-independent individuals are "able to perceive items as discrete from the organized field of which they are a part" (Witkin, 1967, p. 236). Field-dependent individuals are also more sensitive to social cues and interested in others than field-independent individuals. A link between field-independent personalities' analytical way of apprehending their environment and success in foreign language learning has been investigated in several studies (Bialystok & Fröhlich, 1978; Chapelle & Roberts, 1986; Farsi, Bagheri, Sharif, & Nematollahi, 2014; Johnson, Prior, & Artuso, 2000; Stansfield & Hansen, 1983; see also Gardner, Tremblay, & Masgoret, 1997; Skehan, 1991, for discussion), but it has also been postulated that field-dependent individuals' social skills favor their foreign language learning (see Gardner et al., 1997, p. 346)

In conclusion, research on aptitude has evolved in the last decades to take into account cognitive abilities and particularly working memory. Affective factors, on the other hand, are believed to influence language learning, but they have rarely been investigated in research on aptitude. Yet, as Singleton (2014) recalls, Stansfield already mentioned possible links between aptitude in the narrow sense and other factors affecting language learning in 1998:

> the aptitude tests currently in use . . . do not take into account new insights . . . on the human learning process in general and on the language learning process in particular. Nor do they take into account . . . the relation of attitudes, motivation, personality, and other emotional characteristics and predispositions to second language learning.
>
> *(Stansfield, 1998, pp. 3–4; cited in Singleton, 2014)*

These factors potentially affecting foreign language learning are investigated in the LAPS project from the Institute of Multilingualism (University of Fribourg/ University of Teaching Education, Fribourg, Switzerland) from which the data discussed in this chapter come from.

The LAPS Study

In the LAPS study, we investigate the effect of three dimensions of factors on foreign language learning in a school context: language learning abilities, general learning abilities, and affective factors. Among language learning abilities, we investigate three principal dimensions.

The first one, *inductive ability*, is the capacity of an individual to identify grammatical or meaning patterns in unknown language samples and to deduce rules allowing for the generalization of these patterns. It is one of the dimensions covered by the MLAT and PLAB tests but that doesn't appear in the MLAT-Elementary (designed for grades 3 to 6). For the study, we therefore adapted form 4 of the PLAB for the age and language of our participants. In this task, the test-takers are confronted with strings of words in an artificial language[1] and have to inductively understand the artificial language's rules to be able to "translate" new sentences into the artificial language (see "Test Battery" later).

Grammatical sensitivity is another important dimension of aptitude. It is the capacity of an individual to identify grammatical structures and their grammatical functions and therefore to learn grammatical rules and apply them to understand/ produce sentences in a foreign language. To test this ability, we translated and adapted Part 2 of MLAT-E, a test in which the participants have to understand the function of keywords in sentences (ibid.).

Finally, *phonemic discrimination* is the ability to perceive sounds from a new language and store them in memory. In our project, we assess phonemic discrimination in relation to *phonological working memory* with LLAMA-E, a task in which test-takers learn the spelling of phonemes in an unknown language (ibid.).

Besides those language learning abilities, we investigate the impact of general learning abilities on foreign language learning with a test of fluid intelligence consisting of arithmetic sequences the test-takers must complete, complemented by the Group Embedded Figure Test (GEFT) to assess field (in-)dependence. As working memory seems to play an important role in (foreign/second) language learning, we have decided to test two dimensions of it via the Forward Digit Span and the Corsi Blocks. Both of these tasks require participants to remember strings of items (numbers in the Forward Digit Span; lighted squares in the Corsi Blocks). And finally, we have included a test of creative thinking to the test battery to account for task-based approaches to foreign language learning in the Swiss curricula. This teaching method asks students to solve communicative tasks by using known elements of the language and applying them to new contexts, an exercise that requires the ability to generate ideas, as well as imagination, originality, risk-taking, flexibility, and the ability to create new classifications of knowledge (Sternberg, 1985), all of which are cognitive processes underpinning creative thinking (see Finke, Ward, & Smith, 1992; Sternberg, 1985, 2002).

To investigate the affective factors, a participant questionnaire combining items measuring (extrinsic and intrinsic) motivation, self-concept, dedication, anxiety, and (parental and teacher) encouragement with a standardized measure of locus of control has been developed. The parents of the participants furthermore completed a questionnaire on their children's language environment and the socioeconomic (SES) status of the family.

The LAPS project contains two main studies. The first one, the object of this chapter, is cross-sectional: we investigate the influence of aptitude (in a wide sense) on German-speaking primary school students' achievement in French taught in school as a foreign language. The second one, beginning in fall 2017, is longitudinal and investigates the predicting power of the same test battery on learning of English as a foreign language in German-speaking students between grade 4 and grade 6.

The Present Study

Aims and Research Question

In this chapter, we will present the results of LAPS Study 1. Our main goal is to answer the following two research questions:

1.) *What is the internal dimensionality of the aptitude-related tests administered in Study 1? How many factors can we identify, and which dimension of cognitive ability do they represent?*
2.) *To what extent do these abilities covary with the German-speaking primary school students' proficiency in French (measured by C-tests)?*

The test battery (described in detail in Table 6.1) allows us furthermore to disentangle foreign language learning potential or difficulty from general learning abilities and difficulties, thanks to the combination of traditional aptitude dimensions and tests of general learning abilities. It also allows us to discuss the role of affective factors in foreign language learning in a school context.

Method

The data collection took place in April 2017 in 10 school classes of the German-speaking part of the canton of Fribourg (Switzerland). Tests were administered by two to three fieldworkers depending on the size of the class. In each class, four lessons were dedicated to the study (2×2 lessons). The test sequence was organized to allow for alternation between more and less cognitively demanding tasks. All instructions were recorded and played via speakers to have a maximal control over the elicitation situation, e.g. neutralize the impact of potential differences among communicative styles of different fieldworkers giving instructions.

Participants

Participants were 174 children living in the German-speaking part of Switzerland attending grade 4 ($n = 57$) or grade 5 ($n = 117$). One hundred and thirty of the participants grew up in a German-only-speaking family, 14 in families where another language is the family language, and 29 were from mixed (German and other languages) families. The languages other than (Swiss) German spoken by the children at home are rather diverse, and there is no dominant group of a particular heritage language in our sample.

Test Battery

The test battery was composed of eight tests measuring language linked abilities and general learning abilities. Participants also completed a questionnaire aiming to assess the affective factors having an impact on language learning (motivation, anxiety, self-concept, dedication, parental and teacher encouragement, the locus of control), as well as an evaluation of their level of proficiency in the school language and a target-language proficiency test. The test battery is described in Table 6.1.

Results

First, a factor analysis was carried out to investigate the internal dimensionality of the tests administered (Research Question 1). Using the factors that emerge from this analysis, a regression model was fitted to the data to test the association between these cognitive abilities and the achievement scores in French as a foreign language (Research Question 2).

Descriptives and Reliability

Most of the scores obtained with the test battery were transformed into scores between 0 and 1, except for the memory span tests that produce values on a theoretically open scale (see Table 6.2; reliability measures are given where they are applicable).

TABLE 6.1 Description of the LAPS test battery

Dimensions	Subdimensions	Tests	Time (incl. instructions)	Description of the task
Initial aptitude dimensions	Inductive ability	"Language detective" (based on PLAB, Form 4, adapted for age and artificial language)	15'	Participants are presented with words and small sentences in an artificial language, as well as their translation in the school language. Participants' task is to infer regularities and translate sentences following the same pattern from the school language to the artificial language.
	Grammatical sensitivity	"Matching words" (based on MLAT-E, Part 2)	26'	Participants are presented with two sentences. In the first one, one word is highlighted. Participants' task is to find in the second sentence the word with the same function as the highlighted word in the first sentence.
	Phonemic discrimination and phonemic working memory	LLAMA-E	Ind.	Participants have two minutes to learn how sounds are "spelled" in an artificial language (training phase).

(*Continued*)

TABLE 6.1 (Continued)

Dimensions	Subdimensions	Tests	Time (incl. instructions)	Description of the task
				Participants' task is then to listen to bisyllabic words in the artificial language and choose their correct spelling between two solutions.
General learning abilities	Visuospatial working memory	Corsi Block task	Ind.	Participants are asked to remember the order of an increasing number of squares lit up out of a matrix of squares.
	Verbal working memory	Forward Digit Span	Ind.	Participants are asked to reproduce series of numbers of increasing length. Stimuli are presented both visually and auditorily.
	Creative thinking	TCT-DP	14'	The task consists of six pictural fragments on the basis of which the test-takers are asked to complete a drawing.
	Field (in-)dependence	Group Embedded Figures Test (GEFT)	20'	Participants have to find simple geometrical figures embedded in more complex figures under time pressure.

Factor	Construct	Instrument	Time	Description
	General intelligence	CFT 20-R Number sequences	15'	Participants are asked to calculate basic arithmetic operations (number sequences).
Affective factors	Locus of control	Translation of the N-S Personality scale (based on Nowicki-Strickland, 1973)	Ind.	Participants are asked to agree or disagree (yes/no) to 20 statements.
	Motivation, anxiety, self-concept, dedication, parental and teacher encouragement	Questionnaire	Ind.	Participants respond on 4-point Likert scales to statements assessing the motivational, dedicational, self-concept, and external encouragement dimensions.
Sociobiographical factors	Language environment, migration status, and SES	Parental questionnaire: SES		
Linguistic proficiency	School language = German	ELFE	20'	
	Target language = French	C-tests	20'	

TABLE 6.2 Descriptives of the tasks administered in the LAPS test battery

Subdimension	Test	# of subscores/items	Interpretation of scores[2]	Mean (sd)	Reliability std.alpha (if applicable)
Inductive ability	Language detective	15 items	high = high aptitude	0.43 (0.21)	0.72–0.76
Grammatical sensitivity	Matching words	30 items	high = high aptitude	0.63 (0.18)	0.82–0.84
Phonemic discr. and phonemic WM	LLAMA–E	NA	high = high aptitude	0.39 (0.28)	NA
Visuospatial WM	Corsi Block Task (# of correct responses)	NA	high = high capacity	6.621 (2.35)	NA
Verbal WM	Forward Digit Span (# of correct responses)	NA	high = high capacity	5.11 (2.07)	NA
Creative thinking	TCT	14 criteria	high = high creativity	0.29 (0.12)	NA
Field (in-)dependence	GEFT	9 items	high = high field independence	0.30 (0.23)	NA
General intelligence	CFT 20—Number sequences	NA	high = high fluid intelligence	0.56 (0.24)	NA
Locus of control	N-S Personality scale	22 items	high = external locus	0.41 (0.15)	0.52–0.60
Self-concept L2 (French)	Questionnaire	3 items	high = highly motivated	0.64 (0.19)	NA
Self-concept L1/school language (German)	Questionnaire	4 items	high = highly motivated	0.81 (0.15)	NA
Anxiety	Questionnaire	5 items	high = high FL anxiety	0.57 (0.17)	
Intrinsic motivation	Questionnaire	4 items	high = highly motivated	0.59 (0.18)	
Extrinsic motivation	Questionnaire	7 items	high = highly motivated	0.62 (0.14)	NA
Extrinsic motivation (lingua franca)	Questionnaire	3 items	high = highly motivated	0.69 (0.19)	NA
Parental encouragement	Questionnaire	5 items	high = highly motivated	0.76 (0.15)	NA

Teacher encouragement	Questionnaire	5 items	high = highly motivated	0.76 (0.15)	NA
Dedication	Questionnaire	4 items	high = highly dedicated	0.78 (0.15)	NA
Linguistic proficiency school language (German)	ELFE	3 subscores	high = high achievement in reading German	0.56 (0.13)	0.71–0.88
Linguistic proficiency target language (French)	C–Tests 4th	4 × 20 gaps	high = high achievement in French	0.35 (0.24)	0.91–0.92
Linguistic proficiency target language (French)	C–Tests 5th	4 × 20 gaps	high = high achievement in French	0.42 (0.21)	0.90–0.93

Factor Analysis

All variables described earlier, except for the C-Tests in French, were fed into a factor analysis using the factanal function in R (R Core Team, 2017). The correlations between variables range from -0.53 to 0.57 (Table 6.3). The requirements of Bartlett's test (Chisq = 643, $p < 0.001$) and the Kaiser-Meyer-Olkin factor adequacy tests (overall MSA = 0.69 and MSA for each item between 0.56 and 0.85) are met (cf. Field, Miles, & Field, 2012).

A factor analysis producing five factors was first carried out. As Raîche, Walls, Magis, Riopel, and Blais (2013) argue, several different strategies are used to determine the number of components that should be retained in a factor analysis. We applied the four strategies generally used (eigenvalues: six factors, parallel analysis: four factors, optimal coordinates: four factors and acceleration factor: two factors) using the nFactors library (Raiche, 2010) and chose the mode, i.e. four factors. The factor loadings of this four-factor solution are given in Table 6.4.

The Chi-square test of the four-factor solution yields a p-value of 0.12, which means that we cannot reject the hypothesis of the perfect fit.

As Table 6.5 shows, the variance explained by the four factors is relatively modest. This means that the abilities measured by the test battery used in the LAPS project cannot easily be mapped onto a small number of components but represent rather different abilities that are often only weakly related among each other.

A closer look at the loadings in Table 6.4 allows us to tentatively label underlying abilities that correspond to the four components. The first factor is characterized by relatively high loadings of all language aptitude tests (Matching words, Language detective, LLAMA-E), but also of memory-related tasks (Corsi and Digit Span) as well as intelligence (Number sequences) and field independence (GEFT). This first factor thus is associated with general cognitive-linguistic abilities. The second factor is determined by high loadings of mostly extrinsic motivational measures (extrinsic motivation for learning French, lingua-franca use of French, teachers and parents' role as motivators, as well as dedication to learning French). The third factor is related to the self-concept of being a good learner of French, intrinsic motivation to learn French, and foreign language anxiety. This factor thus represents the pupils' construal of their French-learning selves and the pleasure they have in learning French. The last factor is related, again, to foreign language learning anxiety and to an external locus of control. Thus, we can summarize the four factors as follows:

- Factor 1—"Cognition": Modern language learning aptitude, intelligence, and memory
- Factor 2—"Extrinsic motivation": Motivation, mostly extrinsic
- Factor 3—"Self-concept, fun, anxiety": Self-concept, intrinsic motivation, and foreign language learning anxiety
- Factor 4—"External locus of control": Foreign language learning anxiety and external locus of control

TABLE 6.3 Correlation coefficients for all variables in the test battery

	2	3	4	5	6	7	8	9	10	11	12	13	14	15	16	17	18	19
1 Linguistic proficiency school language	0,21	0,00	0,19	0,11	0,13	0,20	0,02	0,04	0,20	-0,12	-0,10	0,10	0,09	-0,01	0,09	0,11	0,15	0,20
2 Grammatical sensitivity		0,35	0,38	0,24	0,32	0,31	0,13	0,11	0,19	-0,18	-0,26	-0,13	0,00	0,03	0,04	0,02	0,38	0,25
3 Inductive ability			0,28	0,19	0,19	0,27	0,16	0,20	0,01	-0,11	-0,08	-0,11	-0,01	0,09	-0,06	-0,03	0,32	0,14
4 Phonemic discr. and phonemic WM				0,21	0,32	0,25	0,10	0,05	0,18	0,00	-0,13	-0,02	0,06	-0,02	0,11	0,01	0,17	0,07
5 Visuospatial WM					0,33	0,34	-0,03	0,00	0,07	-0,11	-0,13	-0,11	-0,01	-0,17	-0,10	-0,16	0,25	0,05
6 Verbal WM						0,33	-0,04	-0,04	0,14	-0,05	-0,19	-0,05	-0,08	-0,03	0,05	-0,08	0,28	0,05
7 General intelligence							0,47	-0,01	0,13	-0,20	-0,29	-0,03	-0,04	-0,12	-0,12	-0,08	0,42	0,07
8 Intrinsic motivation								0,57	0,15	-0,46	-0,23	0,28	0,38	0,10	0,29	0,39	-0,06	0,05
9 Self-concept L2 (French)									0,06	-0,53	-0,11	-0,01	0,20	0,13	0,18	0,18	0,00	0,12
10 Self-concept L1/school language										-0,19	-0,15	-0,05	0,03	-0,11	0,21	0,10	0,02	-0,08
11 Anxiety											-0,19	0,46	0,01	0,20	0,01	-0,15	-0,14	-0,13
12 Locus of control												0,28	0,12	0,28	-0,01	-0,12	-0,15	-0,14
13 Extrinsic motivation													0,12	-0,09	-0,01	-0,04	-0,11	-0,01
14 Extrinsic motivation (lingua franca)														0,41	0,36	0,18	0,35	-0,01
15 Parental encouragement															0,30	0,32	0,44	0,08
16 Teacher encouragement																0,39	0,38	0,12
17 Dedication																	0,52	-0,06
18 Field (in-)dependence																		0,28
19 Creative thinking																		1,00

TABLE 6.4 Loadings of the four-factor solution. Boldface indicates the factor on which the test had the highest absolute loading.

Variable	Factor1	Factor2	Factor3	Factor4
Grammatical sensitivity	**0.614**	0.018	0.11	0.139
General intelligence	**0.587**	−0.119	−0.158	0.34
Verbal WM	**0.564**	−0.033	−0.129	0.146
Field (in-)dependence	**0.532**	−0.147	−0.023	0.14
Phonemic discr. and phonemic WM	**0.521**	0.113	0.023	0.003
Inductive ability	**0.505**	−0.025	0.241	−0.073
Visuospatial WM	**0.436**	−0.162	−0.022	0.102
Creative thinking	**0.239**	−0.002	0.136	0.056
Linguistic proficiency school language	**0.236**	0.113	−0.027	0.215
Dedication	−0.12	**0.689**	0.112	0.336
Extrinsic motivation (lingua franca)	0.004	**0.604**	0.138	0.061
Teacher encouragement	−0.025	**0.601**	0.082	0.107
Extrinsic motivation	−0.052	**0.595**	−0.082	−0.118
Parental encouragement	−0.01	**0.552**	0.046	−0.126
Self-concept L2 (French)	0.045	0.131	**0.828**	0.061
Intrinsic motivation	0.037	0.394	**0.6**	0.245
Self-concept L1/school language	0.149	0.08	0.028	**0.258**
Anxiety	−0.021	0.239	−0.62	**−0.744**
Locus of control	−0.223	0.005	−0.123	**−0.503**

TABLE 6.5 Variance explained by the four factors

Variance explained	Factor 1	Factor 2	Factor 3	Factor 4
Proportion	0.118	0.115	0.086	0.070
Cumulative	0.118	0.233	0.319	0.389

Some tasks are not associated strongly with any of the four factors, most notably so the creativity test (TCT). Also, linguistic proficiency in school language (measured as reading skills with the ELFE test) is only weakly associated with the first and the fourth factors. This is surprising since from the point of view of a holistic conception of the linguistic repertoire (Cook, 1992), we would have expected foreign language abilities to be more strongly predicted by first[3] language abilities.

Regression Analysis

In the next step, we used the four components identified in the factor analysis in a regression model. The goal of this analysis is to estimate the degree of association of these four components with the pupils' achievement in learning French as a foreign language. As argued in an earlier section, most studies on foreign language learning aptitude focus on older learners. A question relevant from the point of view of curriculum planning in primary and lower secondary schools is to what extent individual differences that can or cannot be changed by pedagogical measures are related to success or failure in learning a foreign language. Whereas e.g., working memory or intelligence are probably less affected by pedagogical impact, motivational components—most notably extrinsic motivation—are dependent on the interaction of the pupil with her or his social and institutional environment (teachers, parents, language ecology, etc.). It seems thus important to understand the relative association of the components described in an earlier section with achievement in foreign language learning.

The dependent variable in this regression model is the mean score of the four C-tests (see Table 6.1 for details). These four tests were not the same for the fourth and the fifth graders since they had to be adapted in terms of difficulty to the difference in exposure time of the two grade levels. Therefore, two separate regression models need to be fitted for the two groups of pupils.

We fitted the linear mixed models using the lmer function of the lme4 package (Bates, Mächler, Bolker, & Walker, 2014). As predictors, we used the regression scores produced by the factanal function (see the "Factor Analysis" section). Random intercepts[4] by the teacher were modeled to account for the clustered nature of the sample.

As Table 6.6 and Figure 6.1 show, factors 1 (cognition) and 3 (self-concept and fun) are positively associated with the scores in the C-tests. No significant effects are found for the two remaining factors that involve the degree of extrinsic motivation, the locus of control, and foreign language learning anxiety. Figure 6.1 only shows the effects of the subsample of the fifth graders (the larger group with seven school classes of children), but the model for the fourth graders is very similar (see Table 6.7).

TABLE 6.6 Fixed effects of the four factors on the French C-test score

	4th grade			*5th grade*		
Fixed effects	Estimate	±SE	P	Estimate	±SE	p
Intercept	0.44	0.033	<0.001	0.04	0.029	<0.001
Cognition	0.14	0.036	<0.001	0.10	0.019	<0.001
Extrinsic.motivation	−0.03	0.032	=0.308	0.00	0.018	=0.824
Selfconcept.fun. anxiety	0.13	0.033	<0.001	0.08	0.019	<0.001
External.locus	0.01	0.031	=0.754	0.00	0.019	=0.832

TABLE 6.7 Random effect adjustments by the teacher

Random effects	4th grade	5th grade
	modeled standard deviation	
Random intercept by the teacher	0.000[5]	0.003

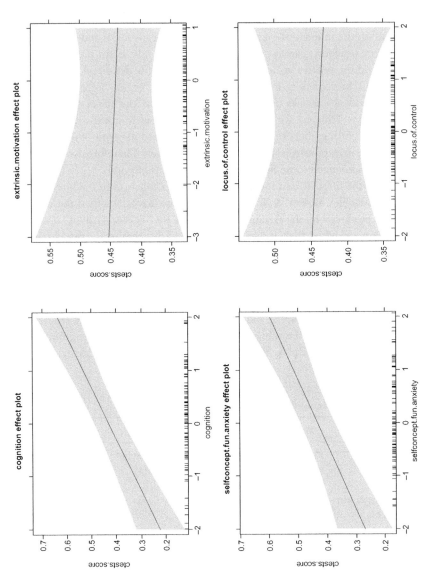

FIGURE 6.1 Effects of the regression with the fifth graders

The two regression models thus yield the same overall picture: scores pertaining to factors 1 and 3 are positively associated with the French proficiency measure, whereas factors 2 and 4 are not.

Summing Up the Statistical Findings

The factor analysis carried out in the earlier section yields four factors that can be distinguished in the correlation matrix of the variables analyzed in the LAPS project. This solution suggests that, as the literature on motivation advocates, different types of motivation can be distinguished roughly along the lines of intrinsic enjoyment of learning vs. extrinsic motivation to learn the foreign language. Also, general cognitive abilities and specific linguistic abilities as measured by the language aptitude tests load on the same factor, which suggests that second/foreign language learning is not independent of general cognitive abilities, including working memory capacities.

The regression models that analyze the larger group of the fifth graders and the smaller group of the fourth graders separately yield very similar results, which suggests that they stand for robust linear associations: cognition and language learning ability, as well as intrinsic enjoyment, self-concept, and foreign language learning anxiety predict the achievement scores, whereas the two other factors related to extrinsic motivation and locus of control are not significantly associated with the French scores.

Discussion and Outlook

The results presented in this chapter raise two main discussion points. The first one concerns the dimensionality encountered in our data and, in particular, the fact that foreign language aptitude measures and general learning ability measures don't appear to load on different factors. This suggests that the language ability is not fundamentally different from other cognitive dimensions, as pupils scoring high on the conventional aptitude dimensions also score high on measures of crystallized intelligence, working memory, and GEFT (i.e. tend to be field independent). This result reminds us of the early studies on foreign language learning aptitude that showed strong correlations between the ability to learn foreign languages and intelligence (see Spolsky, 1995). Our results do not seem to corroborate the view that language learning ability is domain specific, as was claimed later by Carroll[6] (see for instance Skehan, 1998, p. 186–196 for a discussion). The domain-specific view of language aptitude has since then been widely shared in the field. However, it should be noted that intelligence, as aptitude, covers several dimensions and that studies have shown that some components of intelligence are related to particular components of aptitude (see for instance Granena, 2013; Wesche et al., 1982, also Carroll (1990, p. 20) for a discussion of the link between grammatical sensitivity and intelligence). Thus, it is also possible that as one of the reviewers of this chapter pointed out, other aptitude test components or whole tests administered would have yielded other correlational patterns. This may well be the case, and future research on early foreign language learning aptitude will hopefully provide more evidence on the relationship of these constructs.

The other discussion point concerns the results of the regression analysis and in particular the null effect for extrinsic motivation (factor 2) and locus of control (factor 4) on French proficiency. Foreign language learning anxiety loads on both factors 3 and 4, and its negative association with the French scores is already taken into account by the effect of factor 3 in the regression model. Locus of control therefore does not seem to explain any additional variance in the outcome variable. Whereas locus of control is considered a psychological trait and cannot easily be affected by changes in the pedagogical measures taken, the items contained in factor 2 are the variables more susceptible to be influenced by the (pedagogical) environment. Their lack of effect on French attainment is therefore intriguing in an applied perspective. It would mean that success in foreign language learning is dependent on cognitive abilities (specific for language and general) and intrinsic motivation to learn the language, but not on teachers' and parents' encouragement or attitudes towards the language and classroom interactive settings. Among these variables related to the pedagogical setting, only foreign language anxiety, which arguably also depends on the way the foreign language is taught, seems to be associated with the French scores. This does not mean that pedagogy has no effect on foreign language learning, but the finding nevertheless raises doubts on a too-optimistic view of the role of extrinsic and therefore environmentally shapeable motivation on language learning in class, at least at the early stages of language development.

This study has taken place in a particular context marked by high expectations on the social effect of teaching two foreign languages at the primary school level. As discussed in the introduction, even if the goals set in terms of proficiency level to be attained are not ambitious, many pupils are unable to achieve them. Understanding why some pupils attain better levels than others is therefore important. The LAPS study is furthermore one of the few studies investigating aptitude at the primary school level and does it with a comprehensive test battery tapping into a wide range of cognitive abilities. The next phase of the project will replicate the results presented here with a larger sample and a longitudinal design. Our goal will be to predict success and difficulties in learning English as a foreign language in Swiss-German–speaking fourth and fifth graders (at the beginning of the study) with a very similar test battery.

Acknowledgments

We gratefully acknowledge the help and contribution to this chapter from our colleagues involved in the LAPS project: Isabelle Udry and Jan Vanhove from the

University of Fribourg, as well as Carina Steiner and Hansjakob Schneider from the University of Teaching Education, Zurich.

We also would like to thank the students who helped for the data collections: Thomas Aeppli, Kinga Dobrowolska, Laura Hodel, Patricia Isler, Alexandra Jaszkowski, Bente Lowin Kropf, Pauline Robert-Charrue, Fabio Soares, and Carina Steiner.

Notes

1 The artificial language was created in a postgraduate seminar by Jan Vanhove and his students (University of Fribourg).
2 The scores, except for the open-ended memory tests (Visuospatial and Verbal WM), can be read as percentages of correctly resolved items or as strength of motivation in the case of the questionnaire items.
3 German is the first language of most of the pupils if the Swiss-German variety most of them grow up with is not counted as a separate language.
4 The comparison of a model with all random slopes and random intercepts (21 Df, random effects: +(1+ cognition+extrinsic.motivation+selfconcept.and.fun+anxiety. and.external.locus | Teacher)) to the simpler model with random intercepts only (7 Df, random effects: +(1 | Teacher)) yields clearly better fit measures for the simpler model (AIC, BIC, Chisq n.s.).
5 Since there are only 3 classes/teachers of 4th graders, the random intercepts by the teacher cannot be estimated. A regular linear model could be fitted (which would yield the same results).
6 "[F]acility in learning to speak and understand a foreign language is a fairly specialized talent (or group of talents) relatively independent of those traits normally included under 'intelligence'" (Carroll 1962, p. 89 quoted by Wesche, Edwards, & Wells, 1982, p. 131).

References

Baddeley, A. D., & Hitch, G. (1974). Working memory. In G. H. Bower (Éd.), *Psychology of learning and motivation* (Vol. 8). Cambridge, MA: Academic Press.

Bates, D., Mächler, M., Bolker, B., & Walker, S. (2014). Fitting linear mixed-effects models using lme4. *arXiv preprint arXiv:1406.5823.*

Bialystok, E., & Fröhlich, M. (1978). Variables of classroom achievement in second language learning. *The Modern Language Journal, 62*(7), 327–336.

Biedroń, A. (2010). Awareness, responsibility and control as prerequisites of autonomy in second language acquisition. *Beyond Philology, 7*, 305–325.

Boo, Z., Dörnyei, Z., & Ryan, S. (2015). L2 motivation research 2005–2014: Understanding a publication surge and a changing landscape. *System, 55*, 145–157.

Carroll, J. B. (1962). The prediction of success in intensive Foreign language training. In R. Glaser (Ed.), *Training research and education.* Pittsburgh, PA: University of Pittsburgh Press.

Carroll, J. B. (1964). The prediction of success in intensive Foreign language training. In R. Glaser (Ed.), *Training, research, and education* (pp. 87–136). New York, NY: Wiley.

Carroll, J. B. (1990). Cognitive abilities in Foreign language aptitude: Then and now. *Language Aptitude Reconsidered*, 11–29.

Chang, M. M., & Ho, C. M. (2009). Effects of locus of control and learner-control on web-based language learning. *Computer Assisted Language Learning, 22*(3), 189–206. https://doi.org/10.1080/09588220902920094

Chapelle, C., & Roberts, C. (1986). Ambiguity tolerance and field independence as predictors of proficiency in English as a second language. *Language learning, 36*(1), 27–45.

Cochran, J. L., McCallum, R. S., & Bell, S. M. (2010). Three A's: How do attributions, attitudes, and aptitude contribute to Foreign language learning? *Foreign Language Annals, 43*(4), 566–582.

Cook, V. J. (1992). Evidence for multicompetence. *Language Learning, 42*(4), 557–591.

Dörnyei, Z. (2009). The L2 motivational self system. *Motivation, Language Identity and the L2 Self, 36*(3), 9–11.

Doughty, C. J., Campbell, S. G., Mislevy, M. A., Bunting, M. F., Bowles, A. R., & Koeth, J. T. (2010). Predicting near-native ability: The factor structure and reliability of Hi-LAB. In M. T. Prior, et al. (Eds.), *Selected proceedings of the 2008 second language research forum* (pp. 10–31). Somerville, MA: Cascadilla Proceedings Project.

Erlam, R. (2005). Language aptitude and its relationship to instructional effectiveness in second language acquisition. *Language Teaching Research, 9*(2), 147–171.

Farsi, M., Bagheri, M. S., Sharif, M., & Nematollahi, F. (2014). Relationship between field dependence/independence and language proficiency of female EFL students. *International Journal of Language Learning and Applied Linguistics World, 6*(3), 208–220.

Field, A., Miles, J., & Field, Z. (2012). *Discovering statistics using R.* London: Sage Publications.

Finke, R. A., Ward, T. B., & Smith, S. M. (1992). *Creative cognition: Theory, research, and applications.* Cambridge, MA: MIT Press.

Gardner, R. C. (1985). *Social psychology and second language learning: The role of attitudes and motivation.* London: Arnold.

Gardner, R. C., Tremblay, P. F., & Masgoret, A. (1997). Towards a full model of second language learning: An empirical investigation. *The Modern Language Journal, 81*(3), 344–362.

Granena, G. (2013). Cognitive aptitudes for second language learning and the LLAMA Language Aptitude Test. *Sensitive Periods, Language Aptitude, and Ultimate L2 Attainment, 35*, 105.

Grigorenko, E. L., Sternberg, R. J., & Ehrman, M. E. (2000). A theory-based approach to the measurement of Foreign language learning ability: The Canal-F theory and test. *The Modern Language Journal, 84*(3), 390–405. https://doi.org/10.1111/0026-7902.00076

Heinzmann, S. (2013). *Young language learners' motivation and attitudes: Longitudinal, comparative and explanatory perspectives.* London: Bloomsbury Publishing.

Hummel, K. M. (2009). Aptitude, phonological memory, and second language proficiency in nonnovice adult learners. *Applied Psycholinguistics, 30*(2), 225–249.

Johnson, J., Prior, S., & Artuso, M. (2000). Field dependence as a factor in second language communicative production. *Language Learning, 50*(3), 529–567.

Kiss, C., & Nikolov, M. (2005). Developing, piloting, and validating an instrument to measure young learners' aptitude. *Language Learning, 55*(1), 99–150.

Li, S. (2015). The associations between language aptitude and second language grammar acquisition: A meta-analytic review of five decades of research. *Applied Linguistics, 36*(3), 385–408.

Linck, J. A., Hughes, M. M., Campbell, S. G., Silbert, N. H., Tare, M., Jackson, S. R., Doughty, C. J. (2013). Hi-LAB: A new measure of aptitude for high-level language proficiency. *Language Learning, 63*(3), 530–566.

Muñoz, C. (2014). The association between aptitude components and language skills in young learners. In *Essential topics in applied linguistics and multilingualism* (pp. 51–68). New York, NY: Springer.

Peek, R. (2016). Exploring learner autonomy: Language learning locus of control in multilinguals. *International Journal of Multilingualism, 13*(2), 230–248.

Persons, D. L. I. (2001). *Common European framework of reference for languages: Learning, teaching, assessment.* Retrieved from www.memorbalia.it/poseidonpercorso3/Documenti/contestid'uso.pdf

Peyer, E., Andexlinger, M., Kofler, K., & Lenz, P. (2016). *Projekt Fremdsprachenevaluation BKZ: Schlussbericht zu den Sprachkompetenztests.* Fribourg: Institut de plurilinguisme.

Pimsleur, P. (1966). *Pimsleur language aptitude battery (form S).* San Diego: Harcourt, Brace and world, Incorporated.

R Core Team. (2017). *R: A language and environment for statistical computing.* Vienna, Austria: R Foundation for Statistical Computing.

Raiche, G. (2010). nFactors: An R package for parallel analysis and non graphical solutions to the Cattell scree test. *R Package Version, 2*(3).

Raîche, G., Walls, T. A., Magis, D., Riopel, M., & Blais, J. G. (2013). Non-graphical solutions for Cattell's screen test. *Methodology: European Journal of Research Methods for the Behavioral and Social Sciences, 9*(1), 23.

Safar, A., & Kormos, J. (2008). Revisiting problems with Foreign language aptitude. *IRAL-International Review of Applied Linguistics in Language Teaching, 46*(2), 113–136.

Singleton, D. (2014). Apt to change: The problematic of language awareness and language aptitude in age-related research. *Studies in Second Language Learning and Teaching, IV*(3), 557–571.

Skehan, P. (1991). Individual differences in second language learning. *Studies in Second Language Acquisition, 13*(2), 275–298.

Skehan, P. (1998). *A cognitive approach to language learning.* Oxford: Oxford University Press.

Skehan, P. (2002). Theorising and updating aptitude. *Individual differences and instructed Language Learning, 2*, 69–94.

Sparks, R., & Ganschow, L. (1993). Searching for the cognitive locus of Foreign language learning difficulties: Linking first and second language learning. *The Modern Language Journal, 77*(3), 289–302.

Sparks, R. L., Humbach, N., Patton, J. O. N., & Ganschow, L. (2011). Subcomponents of second-language aptitude and second-language proficiency. *The Modern Language Journal, 95*(2), 253–273.

Sparks, R. L., Patton, J. O. N., Ganschow, L., & Humbach, N. (2009). Long-term relationships among early first language skills, second language aptitude, second language affect, and later second language proficiency. *Applied Psycholinguistics, 30*(4), 725–755.

Spolsky, B. (1995). Prognostication and language aptitude testing, 1925–62. *Language Testing, 12*(3), 321–340.

Stansfield, C., & Hansen, J. (1983). Field dependence-independence as a variable in second language cloze test performance. *Tesol Quarterly, 17*(1), 29–38.

Sternberg, R. J. (1985). *Beyond IQ: A triarchic theory of human intelligence.* Cambridge: Cambridge University Press Archive.

Sternberg, R. J. (1999). The theory of successful intelligence. *Review of General Psychology, 3*(4), 292.

Sternberg, R. J. (2002). The theory of successful intelligence and its implications for language-aptitude testing. In P. Robinson (Ed.), *Individual differences and instructed language learning.* Amsterdam, The Netherlands: John Benjamins Publishing Company.

Wen, Z., Biedroń, A., & Skehan, P. (2017). Foreign language aptitude theory: Yesterday, today and tomorrow. *Language Teaching, 50*(1), 1–31.

Wen, Z., & Skehan, P. (2011). A new perspective on Foreign language aptitude research: Building and supporting a case for" working memory as language aptitude". *Ilha do*

Desterro a Journal of English Language, Literatures in English and Cultural Studies, (60), 15–44. doi:10.5007/2175-8026.2011 n60p015

Wesche, M., Edwards, H., & Wells, W. (1982). Foreign language aptitude and intelligence. *Applied Psycholinguistics, 3*(2), 127–140.

Witkin, H. A. (1967). A cognitive-style approach to cross-cultural research. *International Journal of Psychology, 2*(4), 233–250. https://doi.org/10.1080/00207596708247220

7

LANGUAGE APTITUDE

Insights From US High School Students

Richard L. Sparks, Jon Patton, and Julie Luebbers

In a recent review, Dixon et al. (2012) synthesized relevant research about second language (L2) learning in the United States from four different areas—foreign language education, child language research, sociocultural studies, and psycholinguistics.[1] One of those areas, psycholinguistics, examines the mental processes used for L2 acquisition, component skills used to build L2 competency, and cognitive skills that aid transfer from L1 to L2. Their review of investigations from psycholinguistic research indicated that L2 learners with strong L2 aptitude, motivation, and L1 skills are more successful language learners.

The Linguistic Coding Differences Hypothesis (LCDH) (Sparks, Ganschow, & Pohlman, 1989, 1993) fits squarely within the framework of psycholinguistic research. The major premise underlying the LCDH is that the primary causal factors in more and less successful L2 learning are linguistic. Specifically, Sparks and Ganschow proposed that a) L1 skills serve as the foundation for L2 learning; b) both L1 and L2 learning depend on basic language learning mechanisms; c) problems with one component of language have a negative effect on both L1 and L2 learning; and d) individuals with lower levels of L1 skills exhibit lower L2 aptitude and proficiency. Conceptually, the LCDH is similar to Cummins's Linguistic Interdependence Hypothesis, which proposes that L1 and L2 are interdependent and have a common underlying proficiency, and Threshold Hypothesis, which proposes that L2 proficiency is moderated by the level of attainment in L1 (Cummins, 1979).

Since 1991, empirical studies conducted with US secondary students in L2 courses have provided strong support for LCDH and Cummins's hypotheses (see reviews by Sparks, 2012, 2013). These studies have found individual differences in L1 skills among high-, average-, and low-achieving L2 learners and strong relationships among L1 skills, L2 aptitude, and L2 proficiency. The studies have not yet investigated the roles of working memory (WM), phonological short-term memory (PSTM), and metacognitive knowledge (MK) with US L2 learners. WM, the capacity to simultaneously store and process information (Wen, Mota, & McNeill, 2015), and PSTM, the phonological loop responsible for coding information in temporary storage (Hummel, 2009), have been found to be important for L2 learning (Wen & Skehan, 2011). MK, awareness of one's cognitive processes, is a good predictor of L2 reading comprehension (van Gelderen, Schoonen, Stoel, Glopper, & Hulstijn, 2007). In addition, no studies have investigated how well US high school students achieve in a L2 when their performance is compared to native speakers of the target language.

In the present study, US students completing high school Spanish courses were administered a large battery of L1 tests, an L2 aptitude test, standardized measures of WM and PSTM, and an MK measure. At the end of each year, their L2 skills were assessed using a standardized measure of Spanish achievement normed on native Spanish speakers. The aims of the study were to examine a) the latent structure underlying the test battery; b) the factors that best predicted Spanish achievement; and c) differences in L1 skills, WM, PSTM, MK, and L2 achievement when students were grouped by L2 aptitude level (MLAT).

In the literature review, the authors describe the US context for L2 learning and summarize evidence supporting L1–L2 relationships. Then they use evidence from L1 and L2 reading to examine the notion that learning language is qualitatively different from other cognitive skills. Comprehensive reviews for the studies reviewed are cited in Sparks (2012, 2013), Sparks and Patton (2013), and Sparks, Patton, Ganschow, and Humbach (2009, 2011).

Review of the Literature

Social Context for L2 Learning in the United States

Although there are a small number of dual immersion language programs in US elementary schools, the social context for L2 learning is unlike other countries in several ways: a) most students begin L2 study until high school; b) the L2 is studied in largely monolingual academic and social environments; c) most students live in a home where the target language is not spoken; d) students are taught academic subjects in English, not the L2; e) the L2 is studied to meet a requirement, not to become fluent or literate; f) the large majority of students finish only two years of L2 courses; g) L2 study is not mandatory; and h) the United States has no national policy for L2 learning or teaching. On one hand, the US social context is problematic because students have little opportunity to establish L2 proficiency. On the other hand, the context provides a unique opportunity to investigate long-term relationships between L1 skills learned many years earlier and L2 learning beginning many years later.

Evidence Supporting L1–L2 Relationships

Starting in the early 1990s, Sparks and Ganschow conducted *comparison* studies demonstrating that high-achieving L2 students displayed significantly stronger L1 skills than average- and low-achieving L2 learners. High-achieving learners exhibited above-average L1 reading, spelling, writing, and vocabulary skills. Although there were significant L1 differences among the groups, the results showed that low-achieving learners did not exhibit deficits in their L1 skills, but their L1 skills were in the low-average range. In all studies, high-achieving L2 learners with stronger L1 skills exhibited significantly stronger L2 aptitude on the MLAT than average- and low-achieving learners.

Retrospective studies in which high school L2 learners' scores on testing measures in 4th and 6th grades were collected from school records showed that high- and low-achieving learners exhibited significant differences on L1 literacy and language measures as early as 4th grade, on the MLAT in 9th grade, and in L2 achievement in 10th grade. In another study using cluster analysis, three distinct learner profiles emerged in which students in the high-achieving cluster scored in the above-average range, the average-achieving cluster scored in the average range, and the low-achieving cluster scored in the low-average range on all L1 skill, MLAT, and L2 proficiency measures.

In the early 1990s, Sparks and Ganschow began a longitudinal *prospective* study that followed students over 10 years from 1st grade through two years of L2 courses in 10th grade. The students were administered L1 measures in 1st to -5th grades and 10th grade, the MLAT and L2 anxiety and L2 motivation measures in 9th grade, and L2 proficiency measures after second-year L2 courses in 10th grade. Comparison studies with high-, average-, and low-proficiency L2 groups revealed significant group differences in all L1 skills as early as 2nd grade, in 10th-grade L1 reading, and on the MLAT. *Prediction* studies showed that L1 literacy and L1 vocabulary skills in elementary school explained 73% of the variance in L2 aptitude, and early L1 reading skills alone explained 40% of the variance in oral and written L2 proficiency. In other prediction studies, early L1 word decoding and L1 spelling skills explained over half the variance in L2 word decoding and L2 spelling in 10th grade, and the MLAT alone predicted 56% of the variance in L2 proficiency. Like Skehan (1998), Sparks et al. proposed that the MLAT "cuts out" variance in L2 proficiency explained by L1 variables because it taps into students' ability to learn from decontextualized material and serves as a proxy for their language analytic ability and metalinguistic skills. Another study using hierarchical regressions found that L1 print exposure explained significant unique variance in L2 proficiency. Prediction results suggested the possibility of long-term, cross-linguistic transfer of early L1 skills to later L2 aptitude and proficiency.

Sparks and Ganschow proposed that *affective* variables, i.e., motivation, anxiety, are unlikely to play a causal role in L2 proficiency and instead are related to learners' L1 skill and L2 aptitude levels, e.g., students with high L2 anxiety and low L2 motivation will have lower L1 skills and L2 aptitude. In several studies, their findings have shown that low-anxiety (or high-motivation) groups exhibit significantly stronger L1 skills as early as 2nd grade and stronger L2 aptitude on the MLAT than high-anxiety (low-motivation) learners. In another study using path analysis and hierarchical regressions, results showed that an L2 anxiety survey (FLCAS; Horwitz, Horwitz, & Cope, 1986) administered in high school explained significant unique variance in L1 skills administered in elementary school (1st to 5th grades). These findings suggest that affective surveys are likely measuring individual differences in students' language skills rather than motivation or anxiety.

Sparks and Ganschow's *factor analytic* studies have found that L2 aptitude is componential. These analyses have yielded separate language-based factors related to *phonological/orthographic* (sound–symbol) skills, including L1 skill measures and MLAT subtests (Phonetic Coding, Spelling Clues), and *language analysis*, including measures of L1 vocabulary and language comprehension and MLAT subtests (MLAT Words in Sentences, Number Learning). In a recent longitudinal study, measures of L1 skills in elementary school were loaded on these factors with MLAT subtests administered in 9th grade, suggesting long-term relationships between early L1 skills and later L2 aptitude.

Language Is Special for L2 Skills: Evidence From L1 and L2 Reading

Language aptitude tests assume that language is special – that is, learning a language requires talent for language, an assumption shared by the LCDH. Both Skehan (1998) and Sparks et al. (2011) have supported the view that language is qualitatively different from other cognitive skills and cited evidence which shows that learners routinely exhibit different profiles in a) cognitive skills, e.g., poor readers can have good math skills; b) the same cognitive skill, e.g., readers can exhibit strong word decoding but poor reading comprehension; and c) cognitive processing skills, e.g., poor language learners can have strong visual-spatial ability. Evidence from exceptional learners shows unique separation between language skills and other cognitive abilities, e.g., brain-damaged individuals with extraordinary L2 talent, individuals with very low cognitive ability who demonstrate impressive skills in one or more language components (see Sparks & Artzer, 2000).

Like L2 aptitude, research has found that reading is a language-based skill; that is, language is special for the development of reading skill (see Perfetti & Harris, 2013). However, reading also depends on the writing system that encodes the language. Learning to read is both *explicit*, i.e., requires overt instruction, and *implicit*, i.e., requires that individuals notice the regularities of language for e.g., phonology, morphology, words, and word and letter sequences. Seidenberg (2017) explains that learning to read is "the process of acquiring the several types of statistical knowledge [of language] that support rapid and efficient comprehension, starting with phonological structure, orthographic structure, the mappings between orthography and phonology, vocabulary, and grammar" (p. 88) and that deficits in language skills impede reading progress. Voluminous evidence has shown that a problem with one component of language (phonological processing) will have a negative effect on the development of skills that rely on this component (word decoding) but, over time, will affect other language skills necessary for skilled reading (vocabulary knowledge, language comprehension) (Stanovich, 2000).

The Simple View of Reading (SVR) model (Gough & Tunmer, 1986; Hoover & Gough, 1990) provides an empirically based account of the language skills necessary for learning to read. The SVR posits that reading is the product of word decoding and language (listening) comprehension and that these two components make separate, independent contributions to reading skill. Evidence has supported the model for L1 reading skill in many languages with varying orthographic depths, including English (Catts, Adolf, & Weismer, 2006), French (Megherbi, Seigneuric, & Ehrlich, 2006), Greek (Kendou, Papadopoulos, & Kotzapoulou, 2013); Hebrew (Joshi, Ji, Breznitz, Amiel, & Yulia, 2015), Norwegian (Hóien-Tengesdal, & Hóein-Tengesdal, 2012), and Dutch (Verhoeven & van Leeuwe, 2012). Research has also found that word decoding explains more variance in the early stages of learning to read but the contribution of language comprehension increases in later grades (Droop & Verhoeven, 2003; García & Cain, 2014). L2 reading researchers have found that the SVR model is relevant for explaining L2 reading in other alphabetic languages (see Koda, 2008; Verhoeven & van Leeuwe, 2012) and for reading acquisition in bilingual language-minority children learning a transparent second language (Bonifacci & Tobia, 2017).

The idea that L2 reading is componential and that these components make separate, independent contributions to reading skill was demonstrated with US high school students in two recent studies. Sparks (2015) found that US high school students exhibited large differences of 3 to 4 *SD*s between their Spanish word decoding and Spanish reading comprehension even after two years of L2 study, i.e., word decoding skills were over 3 *SD*s higher than reading comprehension. Sparks and Patton (2016) found that Spanish word decoding and Spanish reading comprehension made separate, independent contributions to Spanish reading skill and explained over 70% of the variance in Spanish reading.

In sum, studies with US high school L2 learners have found a) individual differences in L1 skills and L2 aptitude among high- and low-achieving L2 learners; b) students with stronger L1 skills exhibit stronger L2 aptitude; c) students with stronger L1 skills and higher L2 aptitude exhibit stronger L2 proficiency; d) L1 skills and L2 aptitude explain significant variance in L2 proficiency; e) affective variables are linked to one's level of L1 skills and L2 aptitude; f) long-term, cross-linguistic transfer between L1 and L2 skills; and g) L2 aptitude and reading are componential and dependent on language skill.

Purpose of Study

The studies reviewed have yielded consistent results with different populations of L2 learners but have not compared US students' L2 proficiency to native speakers of the target language or examined US students' L1 WM, PSTM, and MK. In this study, monolingual US high school students studying Spanish were administered standardized measures of L1 skills, L2 aptitude (MLAT), WM, PSTM, and an MK survey and followed over three years of Spanish courses. At the end of each year, they were administered a standardized measure of Spanish achievement normed with native Spanish-speaking students. The purposes of the study were to a) analyze the latent structure underlying the test battery; b) conduct regression analyses to determine the factors that best predicted Spanish achievement; and c) determine whether there would be differences in L1 skills, L2 achievement, WM, PSTM, and MK when students were grouped by their level of L2 aptitude on the MLAT.

Method

Participants

The study began with 307 participants chosen randomly enrolled in first-year Spanish courses at one of four high schools in a large suburban school district near a metropolitan US city. There were 154 males and 153 females whose mean age was 15 years, 7 months (ages ranged from 13 years, 7 months to 17 years, 6 months) enrolled in 9th, 10th, and 11th grades at the beginning of the study. Participants included 299 Caucasian, five African American, and three East Asian students. Two hundred and ninety-three of the 307 students completed first-year Spanish, 268 students (of the 293) completed second-year Spanish, and 51 students (of the 268) completed third-year Spanish (22 males and 29 females). All participants were monolingual English speakers who had no prior experience with Spanish, were not routinely exposed to Spanish outside school, and spoke no language other than English. Parental permission was obtained for each participant.

Instruments for Factor Analysis: Predictor Variables

L1 Skills

L1 Word Decoding The measure of L1 word decoding was the Woodcock Reading Mastery Test-Revised Basic Skills Cluster (Woodcock, 1998). The Basic Skills Cluster is composed of two subtests, Word Identification, on which a student reads aloud a list of increasingly difficult words, and Word Attack, on which a student reads a list of increasingly difficult pseudowords. For a response to be correct, the student had to produce a natural reading (pronunciation) of the word or pseudowords.

L1 Word Decoding Fluency   The measure of L1 word decoding fluency was the Test of Word Reading Efficiency (Torgesen, Wagner, & Rashotte, 1999). The test is composed of two subtests, Sight Word Efficiency, on which a student reads aloud from a list of real printed words with a 45-second time limit, and Phonemic Decoding Efficiency, on which a student reads aloud from a list of printed pseudowords with a 45-second time limit. For a response to be correct, the student had to produce a natural reading (pronunciation) of the word or pseudoword.

L1 Reading Comprehension   The measure of L1 reading comprehension was the Stanford Achievement Test 10 (Pearson, 2007). The test is a timed, group-administered, standardized measure of reading comprehension. The student reads passages silently and answers multiple-choice questions after reading a passage.

L1 Vocabulary   The measure of L1 vocabulary was the Woodcock-Johnson-III/ NU Picture Vocabulary subtest (Woodcock, Shrank, McGrew, & Mather, 2001), on which a student was shown a series of pictures and asked to identify aloud the name of the picture. The student is not penalized for mispronunciations resulting from articulation errors, dialect variations, or regional speech patterns. The words increase in difficulty as the test progresses.

L1 Language Analysis   The measure of language analysis was the Test of Language Competence-Expanded Edition Figurative Language subtest (Wiig & Secord, 1989). This subtest is designed to measure the ability to interpret figurative expressions (idioms and metaphors), e.g., *It's all behind us now.* The examiner reads the expression aloud, and the student interprets the meaning of the expression. Then the examiner reads aloud four metaphoric expressions (printed on the page) to the student, who chooses the expression closest in meaning to the previous metaphoric expression.

L1 Phonological Memory   The measure of PSTM was the Comprehensive Test of Phonological Processing (CTOPP) (Wagner, Torgesen, & Rashotte, 1999). The Phonological Memory (PM) Composite measures the ability to code information phonologically for temporary storage in working or short-term memory. The Nonword Repetition subtest measures the ability to listen to recorded pseudowords of three to fifteen sounds and repeat the words exactly as heard. The Memory for Digits subtest assesses an individual's ability to repeat a series of two to eight digits in order when presented at the rate of two digits per second.

L1 Working Memory   The measure of WM, the Woodcock-Johnson-III/ NU Working Memory Cluster (Woodcock, Shrank, McGrew, & Mather, 2005), assesses the ability to hold information in immediate awareness while performing a mental operation on the information. On the Auditory WM subtest, the student listens to a series of numbers and words and then reorders the information into two discrete categories in a particular order, i.e., says the words first, then says the numbers in the same order presented, e.g., *3-word-8-table* becomes *word-table-3-8*. On the Numbers Reversed subtest, the student is asked to hold a series of digits in memory and then repeat the digits backwards. The items become increasingly difficult on both subtests.

L1 Writing   The measure of L1 writing was the On-Demand Writing assessment, a state-required outcomes assessment that is a timed, group-administered, standardized measure of writing. A student responds in writing to two types of prompt stimuli: a short prompt outlining a situation and an extended prompt that includes a reading passage. The score is determined by performance in three domains of writing: content, structure, and writing conventions.

Metacognitive Knowledge   Participants' MK was measured using a questionnaire consisting of statements that were either correct or incorrect. The questionnaire was designed by van Gelderen et al. (2007). The questionnaire included 64 items assessing knowledge about texts, reading, and writing. Since the original questionnaire was about Dutch texts, the wording of some items was changed to reflect English conventions. The student was asked to read each item and decide whether she or he agreed or disagreed (*yes* or *no*). Examples of correct and incorrect statements are *To be able to understand a text properly, you sometimes need to know things that are not said in the text* (yes); *If you read a text to find a specific piece of information quickly (e.g., a date), it is sensible to read the text thoroughly* (no).

L2 Skills

L2 (Spanish) Phoneme Awareness   The Spanish phoneme awareness measure was an author-designed phoneme deletion test with 20 items composed of one-syllable Spanish pseudowords. The items were recorded and presented to participants, who listened with headphones on a computer. The items were designed so that initial (say *plas* with the /p/), final (say *duat* without the /t/), and medial (say *plan* without the /l/) phonemes were deleted.

L2 Aptitude   The measure of L2 aptitude was the Modern Language Aptitude Test (MLAT) (Carroll & Sapon, 1959). This standardized test measures L2 aptitude with a simulated format to provide an indication of the probable degree of success in learning an L2. The Long Form consists of five subtests: Number Learning, Phonetic Script, Spelling Clues, Words in Sentences, and Paired Associates.

Outcome Variables: Measures of L2 Achievement

A standardized measure of Spanish achievement, the *Batería III Woodcock-Muñoz Pruebas de aprovechamiento* (Woodcock, Muñoz-Sandoval, McGrew, & Mather, 2004) designed for students whose native language is Spanish, was used for measuring the participants' oral and written Spanish skills. Six subtests from this test were used to measure Spanish achievement.

Spanish Word Decoding The measure of Spanish word decoding was the Identificación de letras y palabras subtest on which the student reads aloud a list of increasingly difficult words. For a response to be considered correct, the student had to decode and pronounce the word correctly. The difficulty level of the words ranged from one-syllable (*vez, pan*) to two- and three-syllable (*joven, ciuidado*), and multisyllabic (*desalmado, municipalidad*) words. Testing continued until a student read six consecutive words incorrectly.

Spanish Reading Comprehension The measure of Spanish reading comprehension was the Comprensión de textos subtest. On the first four items, the student reads a phrase (e.g., *casa grande*) and points to one (of four) pictures representing the meaning of the phrase. On the remaining items, the student reads a short passage and identifies a key missing word which makes sense in the context of the passage, e.g., *Luis y Rosa _____ amigos.* The items become increasingly difficult by removing picture stimuli and increasing passage length, level of vocabulary, and complexity of syntactic and semantic cues. Most items consist of one to two sentences. Testing continued until a student answered six consecutive items incorrectly.

Spanish Vocabulary The measure of Spanish vocabulary was the Vocabulario sobre dibujos subtest, which measures an individual's speaking vocabulary in Spanish. On two items, the student points to one (of four) pictures after the examiner says a vocabulary word, e.g., *la estufa.* On the remaining items, the student identifies by name the objects shown in the picture. The items begin with pictures of objects commonly found, e.g., *hand, eye, spoon*, to objects that appear less frequently in the environment, e.g., *sun, pig, hammer, palm tree.* Testing continued until a student was unable to identify six consecutive items.

Spanish Spelling The measure of Spanish spelling was the Ortografía subtest. This subtest measures an individual's ability to correctly spell (in writing) words presented orally. The items increased in difficulty as the test progressed, e.g., *tres,* *por, abuelo, lección, gimnasio.* The test items were recorded and presented to the participants on a computer. Participants listened with headphones and could request items be repeated. Testing continued until a student misspelled six consecutive words.

Spanish (Listening) Comprehension   The measure of oral (listening) comprehension was the Comprensíon Oral subtest. This subtest measures the ability to comprehend a short, audio-recorded passage and supply a missing word using syntactic and semantic cues. The missing word is located at the end of each item. This oral cloze procedure requires use of listening comprehension, verbal reasoning, and vocabulary skills. The test begins with simple sentences, e.g., *Los niños estudian en la* _____, and progresses gradually to more complex passages, e.g., *Los vientos traen aire, los ríos traen* _____. Each item could be repeated twice. Testing continued until a student responded incorrectly to six consecutive items.

Spanish Writing   The measure of writing was the Muestras de redaccíon subtest. For each item, a participant is given a verbal direction in English. In some cases, the item is accompanied by a picture. The individual writes sentences in Spanish evaluated with respect to their quality. The difficulty of the items increases by increasing length, level of vocabulary, grammatical complexities, and level of concept abstraction. For example, a student is shown a picture of a *cat* and writes the correct word in a blank, i.e., *Éste es un* _____. On a difficult item, the student is asked to write a sentence that describes three things she or he would like to do on vacation. The student is not penalized for errors in spelling or punctuation.

Procedure

The predictor variables were administered to participants at different times over the course of the study. Figure 7.1 presents the timeline for administration of all measures. All measures were administered and scored by the first and third authors and graduate students trained by them. Participants' scores on the L1 reading comprehension and L1 writing measures were obtained from school records.

The outcome measures of Spanish achievement were administered at the end of first-, second-, and third-year Spanish courses by the first and third authors and graduate students. Participants' raw scores for the six measures were transformed to standard scores ($M = 100$, $SD = 15$) using the *Woodcock-Johnson-III* Normative Update Compuscore and Profiles Program Version 3.1 (Schrank & Woodcock, 2008). Because the *Woodcock-Munoz* is a standardized, norm-referenced test calibrated to measure the skills of native Spanish-speaking test-takers, norms were available for a range of grade levels (Schrank, McGrew, Ruef, Alvarado, Muñoz-Sandoval, & Woodcock, 2005). Participants' scores on the six

Measure	8th grade	Beginning of Spanish I (9th grade)	End of Spanish I (9th grade)	End of Spanish II (10th grade)	End of Spanish III (11th grade)
L1 Reading Comprehension	X				
L1 Writing	X				
MLAT		X			
L1 Word Decoding		X			
L1 Word Decoding Fluency		X			
L1 Vocabulary		X			
L1 Language Analysis		X			
L1 Phonological Memory		X			
L1 Working Memory		X			
L1 Metacognitive Knowledge		X (texts)	X (writing)	X (reading)	
L2 Phoneme Awareness			X		
Woodcock-Muñoz Subtests			X	X	X

FIGURE 7. 1   Timeline for administration of predictor and outcome measures

subtests could be compared to a range of native Spanish-speaking students from 1st to 11th grades. For this study, participants were compared to 9th-grade native Spanish speakers.

Results

Table 7.1 reports mean scores of the participants on the predictor variables. Appendices A, B, and C present correlations among the predictor and outcome variables for students completing first-, second-, and third-year Spanish courses. Because of space constraints, correlations are presented when participants' scores on the predictor variables were correlated with their 9th-grade *Woodcock-Muñoz* scores. Correlations among the predictor and outcome variables when participants' *Woodcock-Muñoz* scores were compared to 1st- to 8th-grade and 10th- to 11th-grade native Spanish speakers revealed little difference in the strength of the correlations.

TABLE 7.1 Means and standard deviations on the predictor variable measures for participants who completed first-year Spanish ($n = 293$)

Measure	M	SD	Minimum	Maximum
L1 Word Decoding [a]	104.0	11.1	72	139
L1 Word Decoding Fluency [a]	96.9	11.9	63	128
L1 Vocabulary [a]	93.2	10.5	60	129
L1 Working Memory [a]	98.6	11.9	64	141
L1 Phonological Memory [b]	95.8	12.7	63	127
L1 Language Analysis [b]	9.3	1.7	1	12
L1 Reading Comprehension [a]	108.2	12.4	63	135
L1 Writing [c]	10.9	2.0	5	16
L1 Metacognitive Knowledge [d]	51.1	5.0	30	62
Spanish Phoneme Awareness [d]	16.9	2.8	4	20
MLAT Number Learning [d]	26.4	10.0	3	45
MLAT Phonetic Script [d]	22.3	3.4	12	30
MLAT Spelling Clues [d]	11.8	5.6	1	37
MLAT Words in Sentences [d]	11.7	3.7	3	23
MLAT Paired Associates [d]	11.5	5.2	0	24

[a] Standard Scores, $M = 100$, $SD = 15$
[b] Standard Scores, $M = 10$, $SD = 3$
[c] Standard Scores, $M = 10.1$, $SD = 2.9$ (range 0–16)
[d] Raw Scores

To determine the latent structure underlying the test battery predicting L2 proficiency, a factor analysis with promax rotation was selected (Brown, 2009). The purpose of promax rotation is to simplify factors by maximizing the variance of the loading within each factor across variables. The spread in loadings is maximized so loadings that are high after extraction become higher after rotation and loadings that are low become lower. To select the number of factors to analyze, a minimum eigenvalue of 1.0 was used (Tabachnick & Fiddell, 1996). The analysis examined the relationship among and between observed variables and their relationship to a set of unobserved components or theoretical constructs. This relationship appears as a factor loading with a range of 0 to 1.0. The higher the loading of the observed variable, the more important the variable is to the factor.

Initially, an exploratory factor analysis was conducted by randomly dividing the dataset of students completing first-year Spanish ($n = 268$) into two parts. The results of the exploratory factor analysis were then subjected to a confirmatory factor analysis with remaining participants. This procedure was used to determine whether the confirmatory factor analysis would validate the results of the exploratory factor structure. Analyses were conducted using SAS version 9.4 (SAS Institute, Cary, NC).

To examine the predictive relationship between the factors and dependent (outcome) variables, a standard multiple regression analysis was performed using the factor scores derived from the factor analysis as independent variables and the L2 achievement measures as the dependent variables.

Factor Analysis

Three factors based on the 15 testing measures emerged from the exploratory factor analysis and explained 50.3% of the variance in the model. The confirmatory factor analysis validated the three factors, $x^2 = 132.45$ ($df = 87$, $p < .01$, *Bentler Comparative Fit Index* = .912, *RMSEA* = .062. The chi-square statistic was significant due to the large sample size. Table 7.2 shows the three factors, the testing measures, their factor leadings, and the commonality estimates for each of the testing measures. Factor 1 (26% of the variance) was defined as a *Phonological/ Orthographic/Working Memory* dimension. Factor 2 (21.5% of the variance) was defined as a *Language Analysis* dimension. Factor 3 (19.3% of the variance) was defined as an *L2 Aptitude* dimension. Table 7.2 presents the results of the factor analysis.

Regression Analyses

Results of the regression analyses for the six *Woodcock-Muñoz* testing measures are reported under separate headings in Tables 7.3 to 7.8. Each table presents results for first-, second-, and third-year Spanish participants, including the R^2, significant factors in the model, semipartial R^2, and p-values. As described earlier,

TABLE 7.2 Principal components solution with promax rotation and communality estimates for test battery

Variable	Factor 1	Factor 2	Factor 3	Communality Estimates
L1 Word Decoding	**.78**	.18	−.04	.717
L1 Word Decoding Fluency	**.74**	−.03	.06	.571
L2 Phoneme Awareness	**.70**	−.03	.17	.586
L1 Working Memory	**.62**	.11	.12	.527
L1 Phonological Memory	**.59**	.27	−.27	.466
L1 Metacognitive Knowledge	−.02	**.70**	.06	.502
L1 Writing	.21	**.65**	.06	.536
L1 Reading Comprehension	.06	**.63**	.05	.453
L1 Language Analysis	−.02	**.43**	.35	.374
L1 Vocabulary	.24	**.36**	.15	.337
MLAT Words in Sentences	−.27	.28	**.70**	.570
MLAT Spelling Clues	.11	−.08	**.66**	.467
MLAT Number Learning	.08	.29	**.56**	.550
MLAT Paired Associates	.41	−.37	**.49**	.461
MLAT Phonetic Script	.24	.24	**.39**	.425

the first-, second-, and third-year participants were compared to native Spanish speakers at several grade levels, i.e., 1st to 11th. Because of space constraints, only the regression analyses for the 1st- and 9th-grade levels are reported in the tables and the text. However, the results (R^2, *semipartial* R^2, F, p value) for first-, second-, and third-year students at other grade levels are similar to those reported for the 9th-grade level.

L2 Word Decoding   The regression analysis for first-year participants yielded a solution that resulted in an R^2 of .29, F (2, 261) = 53.78, $p <$ .0001. The regression analysis for second-year participants yielded a solution that resulted in an R^2 of .37, F (3, 261) = 50.17, $p <$ .0001. The regression analysis for third-year participants yielded a solution that resulted in an R^2 of .32, F (2, 49) = 9.20, $p <$ .0004.

L2 Reading Comprehension   The regression analysis for first-year participants yielded a solution that resulted in an R^2 of .10, F (2, 262) = 11.38, $p <$ .0001. The regression analysis for second-year participants yielded a solution that resulted in an R^2 of .22, F (2, 262) = 35.57, $p <$ .0001. The regression analysis for third-year participants yielded a solution that resulted in an R^2 of .30, F (2, 49) = 9.75, $p <$ .0003.

L2 Vocabulary   The results for the first-year participants yielded a solution that resulted in an R^2 of .14, F (2, 262) = 20.30, $p <$ .0001. The regression analysis for second-year participants yielded a solution that resulted in an R^2 of .25, F (2, 262) = 42.75, $p <$ .0001. The regression analysis for third-year participants yielded a solution that resulted in an R^2 of .37, F (3, 48) = 8.76, $p <$ .0001.

L2 Listening Comprehension   The regression analysis for first-year participants yielded a solution that resulted in an R^2 of .22, F (2, 261) = 37.49, $p <$ .0001. The regression analysis for second-year participants yielded a solution that resulted in an R^2 of .30, F (3, 261) = 39.13, $p <$ .0001. The regression analysis for third-year participants yielded a solution that resulted in an R^2 of .36, F (2, 49) = 12.85, $p <$ .0001.

L2 Spelling   The regression analysis for first-year participants yielded a solution that resulted in an R^2 of .32, F (3, 261) = 40.00, $p <$ .0001. The regression analysis for second-year participants yielded a solution that resulted in an R^2 of .40,

F (3, 261) = 57.24, $p <$ .0001. The regression analysis for third-year participants yielded a solution that resulted in an R^2 of .28, F (2, 49) = 9.16, $p <$ .0004.

L2 Writing   The regression analysis for first-year participants yielded a solution that resulted in an R^2 of .14, F (2, 262) = 21.30, $p <$ .0001. The regression analysis for second-year participants yielded a solution that resulted in an R^2 of .23, F (2, 262) = 37.98, $p <$ .0001. The regression analysis for third-year participants yielded a solution that resulted in an R^2 of .17, F (1, 50) = 9.86, $p <$ .003.

MLAT Group Comparisons

To determine group differences on L1 skill and L2 achievement measures, participants were classified into three groups—High, Average, and Low Aptitude—based on their MLAT Long Form scores (M = 100, SD = 15), which were transformed into z scores. Students scoring more than 1.0 standard deviation (SD) above the sample mean were identified as High; +.99 and -.99 SDs were identified as

TABLE 7.3 Results of regression analyses for *Woodcock-Muñoz* L2 word decoding measure

Year	Grade	R^2	Factors	Semipartial R^2	p-value
1	9	.30	Phono/Ortho/WM	.272	<.0001
			L2 Aptitude	.020	.007
			Language Analysis	.006	.14
2	9	.37	Phono/Ortho/WM	.324	<.0001
			L2 Aptitude	.029	.001
			Language Analysis	.013	.06
3	9	.32	Language Analysis	.205	.03
			L2 Aptitude	.081	.07
			Phono/Ortho/WM	.030	.16

TABLE 7.4 Results of regression analyses for *Woodcock-Muñoz* L2 reading comprehension measure

Year	Grade	R^2	Factors	Semipartial R^2	p-value
1	9	.08	Phono/Ortho/WM	.067	.001
			Language Analysis	.013	.053
2	9	.22	L2Aptitude	.159	<.0001
			Language Analysis	.055	<.0001
3	9	.30	L2 Aptitude	.191	.009
			Language Analysis	.107	.01

TABLE 7.5 Results of regression analyses for *Woodcock-Muñoz* L2 vocabulary measure

Year	Grade	R^2	Factors	Semipartial R^2	p-value
1	9	.14	L2 Aptitude	.102	.0001
			Language Analysis	.033	.002
2	9	.25	L2 Aptitude	.171	<.0001
			Language Analysis	.075	<.0001
3	9	.37	L2 Aptitude	.226	.001
			Language Analysis	.103	.004
			Phono/Ortho/WM	.037	.11

TABLE 7.6 Results of regression analyses for *Woodcock-Muñoz* L2 listening comprehension measure

Year	Grade	R^2	Factors	Semipartial R^2	p-value
1	9	.22	L2 Aptitude	.172	<.0001
			Language Analysis	.051	<.0001
2	9	.31	Language Analysis	.246	<.0001
			L2 Aptitude	.056	.0003
			Phono/Ortho/WM	.008	.07
3	9	.36	Language Analysis	.231	.003
			L2 Aptitude	.128	.004

TABLE 7.7 Results of regression analyses for *Woodcock-Muñoz* L2 spelling measure

Year	Grade	R^2	Factors	Semipartial R^2	p-value
1	9	.32	Phono/Ortho/WM	.283	<.0001
			Language Analysis	.024	.009
			L2 Aptitude	.010	.054
2	9	.40	Phono/Ortho/WM	.347	<.0001
			Language Analysis	.041	.0002
			L2 Aptitude	.009	.049
3	9	.30	Phono/Ortho/WM	.191	.02
			L2 Aptitude	.110	.02

TABLE 7.8 Results of regression analyses for *Woodcock-Muñoz* L2 writing measure

Year	Grade	R^2	Factors	Semipartial R^2	p-value
1	9	.14	L2 Aptitude	.114	<.0001
			Language Analysis	.026	.005
2	9	.23	L2 Aptitude	.185	<.0001
			Language Analysis	.040	.0004
3	9	.17	Language Analysis	.173	.003

Average; more than 1.0 *SD* below the sample mean were identified as Low. For each of the four group comparisons conducted, i.e., L1 Skills, L2 Achievement-Year 1, L2 Achievement-Year 2, L2 Achievement-Year 3, a separate multiple analysis of variance procedure (MANOVA) determined overall differences among the groups. All four MANOVAs revealed significant overall differences among the High, Average, and Low Aptitude groups on the L1 skills and L2 achievement measures. Since the MANOVAs were significant, one-way analyses of variance (ANOVAs) were used to compare the three aptitude groups on the L1 skills and L2 achievement measures. The criterion for significance for all analyses was $p \leq .05$. To reduce the possibility of Type I error, a Scheffe procedure was used in comparing between-group differences on each measure.

There were significant differences between the High and Low Aptitude groups on all L1 skills ($d = 0.73$–1.69) and L2 achievement ($d = 0.91$–2.18) measures at the end of first-, second-, and third-year Spanish. There were significant differences between the High and Average Aptitude groups on all L1 measures except reading comprehension ($d = .51$–$.92$), all L2 achievement tests at the end of first- and second-year Spanish ($d = .50$–1.04), and most L2 achievement measures at the end of third-year Spanish ($d = .99$–1.37). There were significant differences between the Average and Low Aptitude groups on all L1 measures except PSTM and writing ($d = .44$–$.81$), all L2 achievement tests in first-year Spanish except vocabulary ($d = .37$–$.52$), and all L2 achievement tests in second-year Spanish ($d = .56$–$.80$). There were no significant differences between the Average and Low Aptitude groups on all L2 achievement tests at the end of third-year Spanish.[2]

Discussion

Studies with US high school L2 learners have consistently found individual differences in language learning skills (Sparks, 2012, 2013). In this study when participants were grouped by L2 aptitude, there were significant group differences in *all* L1 skills, WM, PSTM, MK, and L2 phoneme awareness. L1 differences between the high and low L2 aptitude groups ranged from .65 *SD* to 1.33 *SD* with effect sizes ranging from $d = .73$ to 1.69. (In previous studies, differences were found even after controlling for IQ.) Even so, the low L2 aptitude group's L1 skills were still in the low-average range. Previous studies with US students have found language differences among L2 learners whether they were grouped by L1 skills, L2 anxiety or L2 motivation levels, L2 teachers' perceptions of students' L2 achievement, or parents' perceptions of their student's L1 skills. Moreover, individual differences between high- and low-achieving L2 learners are apparent by 2nd grade, and L1 skills in primary school were predictive of L2 aptitude in 9th grade.

There were also significant differences in L2 achievement among the three L2 aptitude groups. Students with stronger L2 aptitude attained significantly higher levels of achievement at the end of first-, second-, and third-year Spanish. L2 achievement differences among low and high L2 aptitude groups ranged from .53

SD to 1.60 *SD* at the end of first-year Spanish (*d* =.91–1.65) and from .80 *SD* to 2.0 *SD* at the end of second-year Spanish (*d* = 1.21–1.62). Even among third-year Spanish learners, there were significant differences among the three aptitude groups on most L2 achievement measures. The finding that L2 aptitude differences are strongly related to both L1 skill and L2 achievement differences lends support to the notion of long-term, cross-linguistic relationships among early L1 skills, later L2 aptitude, and subsequent L2 achievement.

Even though there were group differences in WM and PSTM among the high-, average-, and low-aptitude groups, these variables did not load as a separate factor. Instead, WM and PSTM loaded on the factor with L1 word decoding and L2 phoneme awareness. This finding is consistent with L1 reading research, which has found that PSTM, or the phonological loop, is important for learning to read words (e.g., see Boada & Pennington, 2006) and learning new written and spoken vocabulary (Baddeley, Gathercole, & Papagno, 1998) but is more relevant for novice L2 learners (French & O'Brien, 2008). The finding is consistent with L2 research, which has shown that WM is more important at advanced stages of L2 acquisition because its function is to activate information stored in long-term memory (Cowan, 1999; Wen & Skehan, 2011). All participants in this study were beginning L2 learners who had little knowledge of Spanish stored in long-term memory for activation.

Two additional factors, *Language Analysis* and *L2 Aptitude*, emerged from the analysis. In previous studies, a language analysis factor composed of L1 vocabulary, L2 reading and listening comprehension, and L1 grammar has consistently emerged as a separate factor. L1 writing and MK also loaded on the *Language Analysis* factor. These findings were expected because language analysis skills are more relevant for the initial stages of L2 learning (Li, 2015). A new finding is that *L2 Aptitude*, composed of the five MLAT subtests, emerged as a separate factor. In previous studies, the MLAT subtests loaded with the *Phonological/Orthographic* factor (Phonetic Script, Spelling Clues), the *Language Analysis* factor (Words in Sentences, Number Learning), or on a separate factor paired with IQ (Paired Associates). The finding of a separate aptitude factor suggests that L2 aptitude as conceptualized in the MLAT may also be more important for the initial stages of L2 acquisition (see Wen, Biedroń, & Skehan, 2017).

Regression analyses showed that the *Phonological/Orthographic/Working Memory* factor predicted the largest amount of variance for L2 word decoding and L2 spelling, a finding replicating L1 (Stanovich, 2000; Snowling & Hulme, 2008) and L2 (Sparks, Patton, Ganschow, Humbach, & Javorsky, 2008) research, which found that letter–sound knowledge and PSTM predict L1 word decoding and spelling. By third-year Spanish, the *Language Analysis* and *L2 Aptitude* factors predicted L2 word decoding skill, a result consistent with L1 reading research, which has shown that language comprehension explains the largest amount of variance in reading once word decoding is established (Garcia & Cain, 2014; Verhoeven & van Leeuwe, 2012). In contrast, the *Language Analysis* and *L2 Aptitude* factors predicted the variance in

L2 reading comprehension, vocabulary, listening comprehension, and writing. These findings suggest that L2 learning may be componential; that is, different L2 skills rely on different components of language (Sparks, 2012, 2013; Sparks et al., 2011).

The results of this study also support the idea that language is special for L2 learning, particularly for L2 reading. Evidence from L1 reading researchers has shown that reading is a language-based skill that relies on word decoding and language comprehension and that both components make separate, independent contributions to reading skill, i.e., the Simple View of Reading model (SVR). Decoding relies on phonological and orthographic processing skills, and language comprehension relies on language analysis skills, e.g., vocabulary, grammatical knowledge, background knowledge. The SVR model also claims there are four types of readers: *Good* (good word decoding, good language comprehension), *Dyslexic* (poor word decoding, good language comprehension), *Hyperlexia* (good word decoding, poor language comprehension), and *Garden Variety* (poor word decoding, poor comprehension) (see Figure 7.2). Studies over several years in L1 have validated the types of reader profiles proposed by the SVR model (e.g., see Catts et al., 2006; Catts, Hogan, & Fey, 2003). In a recent study with US high school L2 learners, Sparks and Luebbers (in press) tested the SVR model and found that the large majority (96%) of students completing one, two, and three years of Spanish fit the *hyperlexic* profile, but there were *no* good or dyslexic readers. Most students learned to decode Spanish words relatively well but demonstrated very poor comprehension when listening and reading. The finding that students' Spanish reading comprehension is so poor was directly related to their very poor acquisition of Spanish vocabulary. These findings suggest that L2 reading may also be componential.

Moreover, in the present study, there were strong correlations between participants' L1 word decoding skills and L2 decoding skills that increased from first- (.41) to second- (.52) to third-year (.58) courses and between their L2 word decoding skills and L2 spelling skills (.63, .50, .60), both of which rely on

Decoding

		Poor	Good
Language Comprehension	Good	Dyslexia Specific decoding deficit	No deficits
	Poor	Garden Variety Decoding and comprehension deficits	Hyperlexia Specific language comprehension deficit

FIGURE 7.2 Types of readers proposed by the SVR model

phonological processing and orthographic knowledge (see Sparks et al., 2008). Likewise, there were strong correlations between Spanish reading comprehension and Spanish vocabulary that increased from first- (.31) to second- (.47) to third-year (.66) courses; between Spanish vocabulary and Spanish listening comprehension that increased each year (.43 to .56 to .68); and between Spanish reading comprehension and Spanish listening comprehension that increased each year (.38 to .56 to .75). In a recent meta-analysis, Jeon and Yamashita (2014) found that both L2 vocabulary knowledge and L2 listening comprehension were strong predictors of L2 reading comprehension. Vocabulary has been found to be a critical determinant of reading and listening comprehension (Lervåg & Aukrust, 2010). These findings support research which has found that L2 listening comprehension and L2 vocabulary are strong predictors of L2 reading comprehension (Jeon & Yamashita, 2014). These results provide additional evidence that L2 reading may be componential, i.e., separable and independent word decoding and language comprehension skills supported by different cognitive processes.

In sum, the cumulative evidence from studies with US L2 learners suggests that the question raised by Alderson (1984), *Is L2 reading skill a reading problem or a language problem?* should be revised to ask the following question: *Is L2 reading a word decoding problem, a language comprehension problem, both a decoding and language comprehension problem, or neither a decoding or language comprehension problem?*

L2 Aptitude: Insights From L1 and L2 Reading Research With US Students

Studies with US high school L2 learners and from L1/L2 reading research have the potential to provide a framework for L2 aptitude testing. For several years, L2 aptitude has been hypothesized to include domain-specific and general cognitive processes. L2 aptitude researchers can acknowledge that language is "special" for L2 learning but also that general cognitive processing skills are needed for L2 learning. In their early work, Sparks and Ganschow (1993, 1995) used the concept of the Assumption of Specificity (AOS) to explain this point. In the L1 reading literature, the AOS states that the poor reader has a cognitive deficit that is specific to reading, a language-based task (see Stanovich, 1988). The deficit does not extend into other domains of cognitive functioning because it would depress intelligence as well as other skills, e.g., math, nonverbal ability, that are unrelated to the reading task. The AOS applied to L2 aptitude suggests that the reasons for different levels of proficiency in L2 learning (or failure to advance to higher levels of L2 learning) are specific to the L2 task, that is, they are language related. In our view, this is the primary reason that the MLAT has been found to predict the largest amount of variance in L2 learning, that is, the MLAT measures language specific skills.

However, general cognitive processing skills are not specific to language. Skills such as working memory, attentional control, processing speed, and motivation have been found to be important for L2 learning. But these skills are needed for proficiency in other domains, e.g., math, nonverbal ability. Although language skills have been found to explain larger amounts of variance for L2 learning than general cognitive processing skills, general cognitive processing skills are also necessary for more skilled (advanced) L2 learning. For example, an individual may score at the 95th percentile on the MLAT. But the same individual may score at the 45th percentile on measures of working memory. Although she or he may do well in L2 learning, his or her average working memory skills may hinder more advanced L2 achievement. Likewise, another individual may score at the 45th percentile on the MLAT and at the 95th percentile on working memory measures. In this case, she or he may have less ability to achieve at more advanced levels of L2 learning because of average L2 aptitude.

Like L1 and L2 reading, L2 learning is a language-based skill, that is, language is *necessary* for L2 learning. However, research shows that language skills alone are not *sufficient* for L2 learning; that is, general cognitive processes are also necessary for skilled L2 learning. In a recent study investigating the SVR model, Kim (2017) shows that word decoding and listening comprehension are "upper-level" skills built upon multiple language *and* cognitive component skills that are necessary for assessment and instruction. Likewise, we suggest that domain-specific and general cognitive processes are "upper-level" skills built upon multiple language (domain specific) and general cognitive processes (domain general), both of which are necessary for skilled L2 learning. Thus, we propose a "simple view" of L2 aptitude in which researchers work to develop L2 aptitude tests that measure the multiple language (domain-specific) and general cognitive processing (domain-general) skills necessary for L2 learning. Then, longitudinal studies should be conducted to determine the domain-specific and domain-general profiles that are most predictive of skilled L2 learning.

Notes

1 This chapter is dedicated to the memory of Leonore Ganschow, who was the first author's mentor, colleague, and friend.
2 Due to space constraints, the tables reporting means, *SD*s, *df*, *F*, and Cohen's *d* are not included in this chapter. Readers interested in these results can write to the first author and request the tables (email to Richard.sparks@msj.edu).

References

Alderson, J. (1984). Reading in a Foreign language: A reading problem or a language problem? In J. Alderson & A. Urquhart (Eds.), *Reading in a Foreign language* (pp. 1–24). London: Longman, Brown, and Co.

Baddeley, A., Gathercole, S., & Papagno, C. (1998). The phonological loop as a language learning device. *Psychological Review, 105*, 158–173.

Boada, R., & Pennington, B. (2006). Deficient implicit phonological representations in children with dyslexia. *Journal of Experimental Child Psychology, 95*, 153–193.

Bonifacci, P., & Tobia, V. (2017). The simple view of reading in bilingual language-minority children acquiring a highly transparent second language. *Scientific Studies of Reading, 21*, 109–119.

Brown, J. (2009). Choosing the right type of rotation in PCA and EFA. *Shiken: JALT Testing and Evaluation SIG Newsletter, 13*, 20–25.

Carroll, J., & Sapon, S. (1959, 2000). *Modern language aptitude test (MLAT): Manual*. San Antonio, TX: Psychological Corp. Republished by Second Language Testing, Inc., www.2LTI.com.

Catts, H., Adolf, S., & Weismer, S. (2006). Language deficits in poor comprehenders: A case for the simple view of reading. *Journal of Speech, Language, and Hearing Research, 49*, 278–293.

Catts, H., Hogan, T., & Fey, M. (2003). Subgrouping poor readers on the basis of reading-related abilities. *Journal of Learning Disabilities, 36*, 151–164.

Cowan, N. (1999). An embedded-processes model of working memory. In A. Miyake & P. Shah (Eds.), *Models of working memory: Mechanisms of active maintenance and executive control* (pp. 62–101). Cambridge: Cambridge University Press.

Cummins, J. (1979). Linguistic interdependence and the educational development of bilingual children. *Review of Educational Research, 49*(2), 222–251.

Dixon, L., Zhao, J., Shin, J., Shuang, W., Su, J., Burgess-Brigham, R., . . . Snow, C. (2012). What we know about second language acquisition: A synthesis from four perspectives. *Review of Educational Research, 82*, 1–50.

Droop, M., & Verhoeven, L. (2003). Language proficiency and reading ability in first- and second-language learners. *Reading Research Quarterly, 38*, 78–103.

French, L. M., & O'Brien, I. (2008). Phonological memory and children's second language grammar learning. *Applied Psycholinguistics, 29*, 463–487.

García, R., & Cain, K. (2014). Decoding and reading comprehension: A meta-analysis to identify which reader assessment characteristics influence the strength of the relationship in English. *Review of Educational Research, 84*, 74–111.

Gough, P., & Tunmer, W. (1986). Decoding, reading, and reading disability. *Remedial and Special Education, 7*, 6–10.

Høein-Tengesdal, I., & Høein-Tengesdal, T. (2012). The reading efficiency model: An extension of the componential model of reading. *Journal of Learning Disabilities, 45*, 467–479.

Hoover, W., & Gough, P. (1990). The simple view of reading. *Reading and Writing: An Interdisciplinary Journal, 2*, 127–160.

Horwitz, E., Horwitz, M., & Cope, J. (1986). Foreign language classroom anxiety. *Modern Language Journal, 70*, 125–132.

Hummel, K. (2009). Aptitude, phonological memory, and second language proficiency in nonnovice adult learners. *Applied Psycholinguistics, 30*, 225–249.

Jeon, E., & Yamashita, J. (2014). L2 reading comprehension and its correlates: A meta-analysis. *Language Learning, 64*, 160–212.

Joshi, R., Ji, X. R., Breznitz, Z., Amiel, M., & Yulia, A. (2015). Validation of the simple view of reading in Hebrew. *Scientific Studies of Reading, 19*, 243–252.

Kenedou, P., Papadopoulos, T., & Kotzapoulou, M. (2013). Evidence for the early emergence of the simple view of reading in a transparent orthography. *Reading and Writing, 26*, 189–204.

Kim, Y. (2017). Why the simple view of reading is not simplistic: Unpacking component skills of reading using a direct and indirect model of reading (DIER). *Scientific Studies of Reading, 21*, 310–333.

Koda, K. (2008). Impacts of prior literacy experience on second-language learning to read. In K. Koda & A. Zehler (Eds.), *Learning to read across languages* (pp. 68–96). New York, NY: Routledge. http://dx.doi.org/10.1080/10888438.2017.1291643

Lervåg, A., & Aukrust, V. (2010). Vocabulary knowledge is a critical determinant of the difference in reading comprehension between first and second language learners. *Journal of Child Psychology and Psychiatry*, *51*, 612–620.

Li, S. (2015). Working memory, language analytical ability, and L2 recasts. In Z. Wen, M. Mota, & A. McNeill (Eds.), *Working memory in second language acquisition and processing* (pp. 139–159). Bristol, UK: Multilingual Matters.

Megherbi, H., Seigneuric, A., & Ehrlich, M. (2006). Reading comprehension in French in 1st and 2nd grade children: Contribution of decoding and language comprehension. *European Journal of Psychology of Education*, *21*, 135–147.

Pearson Education. (2007). *Stanford Achievement Test 10*. New York, NY: Author.

Perfetti, C., & Harris, L. (2013). Universal reading processes are modulated by language and writing system. *Language Learning and Development*, *9*, 296–316.

Schrank, F., McGrew, K., Ruef, M., Alvarado, C., Muñoz-Sandoval, A., & Woodcock, R. (2005). Overview and technical supplement. *Batería III Woodcock-Munoz Assessment Service Bulletin*, (1).

Schrank, F., & Woodcock, R. (2008). Woodcock interpretation and instructional interventions program (WIIIP, Version 1.0) [Computer software]. Rolling Meadows, IL: Riverside.

Seidenberg, M. (2017). *Language at the speed of sight: How we read, why so many cannot, and what can be done about it*. New York, NY: Basic Books.

Skehan, P. (1998). *A cognitive approach to language learning*. Oxford: Oxford University Press.

Snowling, M., & Hulme, C. (Eds.). (2008). *The science of reading: A handbook* (Vol. 9). Malden, MA: Blackwell.

Sparks, R. (2012). Individual differences in L2 learning and long-term L1—L2 relationships. *Language Learning*, *62*(Suppl. 2), 5–27.

Sparks, R. (2013). Individual differences in learning a Foreign (second) language: A cognitive approach. In D. Martin (Ed.), *Researching dyslexia in multilingual settings: Diverse perspectives* (pp. 36–54). Bristol, UK: Multilingual Matters.

Sparks, R. (2015). Language deficits in poor L2 comprehenders: The Simple View. *Foreign Language Annals*, *48*, 635–658.

Sparks, R., & Artzer, M. (2000). Foreign language learning, hyperlexia, and early word recognition. *Annals of Dyslexia*, *50*, 189–211.

Sparks, R., & Ganschow, L. (1993). Searching for the cognitive locus of Foreign language learning difficulties: Linking first and second language learning. *The Modern Language Journal*, *77*, 289–302.

Sparks, R., & Ganschow, L. (1995). A strong inference approach to causal factors in foreign language learning: A response to MacIntyre. *Modern Language Journal*, *79*, 235–244.

Sparks, R., Ganschow, L., & Pohlman, J. (1989). Linguistic coding deficits in Foreign language learners. *Annals of Dyslexia*, *39*, 177–195.

Sparks, R., & Luebbers, J. (in press). How many U.S. high school students have a Foreign language reading "disability"? Reading without meaning and the Simple View. *Journal of Learning Disabilities*. doi:10.1177/0022219417704168

Sparks, R., & Patton, J. (2013). Relationship of L1 skills and L2 aptitude to L2 anxiety on the Foreign language classroom anxiety scale. *Language Learning*, *63*, 870–895.

Sparks, R., & Patton, J. (2016). Examining the Simple View of Reading (SVR) model for U.S. high school Spanish students. *Hispania*, *99*, 17–33.

Sparks, R., Patton, J., Ganschow, L., & Humbach, N. (2009). Long-term cross linguistic transfer of skills from L1 to L2. *Language Learning*, *59*, 203–243.

Sparks, R., Patton, J., Ganschow, L., & Humbach, N. (2011). Subcomponents of second-language aptitude and second-language proficiency. *The Modern Language Journal, 95*, 253–273.

Sparks, R., Patton, J., Ganschow, L., Humbach, N., & Javorsky, J. (2008). Early first-language reading and spelling skills predict later second-language reading and spelling skills. *Journal of Educational Psychology, 100*, 162.

Stanovich, K. (1988). The right and wrong places to look for the cognitive locus of reading disability. *Annals of Dyslexia, 38*(1), 154–177.

Stanovich, K. (2000). *Progress in understanding reading: Scientific foundations and new frontiers.* New York, NY: The Guilford Press.

Tabachnick, B., & Fiddell, L. (1996). *Using multivariate statistics.* New York, NY: Harper Collins.

Torgesen, J., Wagner, R., & Rashotte, C. (1999). *TOWRE: Test of word reading efficiency.* Austin, TX: PRO-ED.

van Gelderen, A., Schoonen, R., Stoel, R., Glopper, K., & Hulstijn, J. (2007). Development of adolescent reading comprehension in language 1 and language 2: A longitudinal analysis of constituent components. *Journal of Educational Psychology, 99*, 477–491.

Verhoeven, L., & van Leeuwe, J. (2012). The simple view of second language reading throughout the primary grades. *Reading and Writing: An Interdisciplinary Journal, 25*, 1805–1818.

Wagner, R., Torgesen, J., & Rashotte, C. (1999). *CTOPP: Comprehensive test of phonological processing.* Austin, TX: PRO-ED.

Wen, Z., Biedroń, A., & Skehan, P. (2017). Foreign language aptitude theory: Yesterday, today and tomorrow. *Language Teaching, 50*, 1–31.

Wen, Z., Mota, M., & McNeill, A. (2015). *Working memory in second language acquisition and processing.* Bristol, UK: Multilingual Matters.

Wen, Z., & Skehan, P. (2011). A new perspective on foreign language aptitude research: Building and supporting a case for "working memory as language aptitude." *Ilha do Desterro: a Journal of English Language, Literatures in English and Cultural Studies, 60*, 15–44.

Wiig, E., & Secord, W. (1989). *Test of language competence-expanded edition.* New York, NY: Psychological Corporation.

Woodcock, R. (1998). *Woodcock reading mastery tests—revised/normative update.* Circle Pines, MN: American Guidance Service.

Woodcock, R., McGrew, K., & Mather, N. (2001). *Woodcock-Johnson-III tests of achievement, tests of cognitive abilities.* Itasca, IL: Riverside.

Woodcock, R., Muñoz-Sandoval, A., McGrew, K., & Mather, M. (2004, 2007). *Batería-III Woodcock-Muñoz.* Rolling Meadows, IL: Riverside.

Appendix A: Intercorrelations Among Predictor Variables and Outcome Variables for Students Completing First-Year Spanish

Measure	1	2	3	4	5	6	7	8	9	10	11	12	13	14	15	16	17	18	19	20	21
1. L1 Word Decoding	--	.57	.38	.44	.37	.	.32	.33	.27	.43	.27	.40	.35	.25	.16	.52	.20	.19	.33	.56	.23
2. L1 Decode Fluency	--	--	.23	.42	.27	.22	.32	.27	.18	.32	.20	.28	.33	.25	.20	.45	.21	.18	.27	.40	.21
3. L1 Vocabulary	--	--	--	.22	.22	.35	.22	.15	.23	.22	.20	.29	.24	.20	.13	.25	.23	.31	.32	.31	.26
4. L1 Working Memory	--	--	--	--	.49	.23	.21	.23	.36	.34	.36	.32	.23	.20	.12	.36	.10	.12	.26	.39	.17
5. L1 Phono Memory	--	--	--	--	--	.26	.15	.18	.24	.23	.23	.18	.14	.16	.03	.18	.02	.03	.14	.26	.09
6. L1 Lang Analysis	--	--	--	--	--	--	.33	.25	.26	.19	.24	.23	.20	.29	.17	.23	.07	.12	.20	.27	.13
7. L1 Reading Comp	--	--	--	--	--	--	--	.33	.22	.12	.24	.16	.15	.25	.05	.24	.11	.11	.21	.24	.13
8. L1 Writing	--	--	--	--	--	--	--	--	.34	.21	.18	.26	.18	.26	.15	.20	.10	.15	.23	.32	.17
9. Meta Knowledge	--	--	--	--	--	--	--	--	--	.15	.26	.29	.15	.29	.20	.19	.03	.22	.21	.22	.21
10. L2 Phon Awareness	--	--	--	--	--	--	--	--	--	--	.35	.38	.16	.14	.18	.42	.18	.23	.26	.44	.21
11. MLAT Numb Learn	--	--	--	--	--	--	--	--	--	--	--	.36	.20	.23	.20	.28	.09	.21	.25	.30	.25

(Continued)

(Continued)

Measure	1	2	3	4	5	6	7	8	9	10	11	12	13	14	15	16	17	18	19	20	21
12. MLAT Phon Script	--	--	--	--	--	--	--	--	--	--	--	--	.25	.28	.36	.36	.23	.29	.31	.40	.30
13. MLAT Spell Clues	--	--	--	--	--	--	--	--	--	--	--	--	--	.33	.10	.22	.04	.15	.26	.26	.16
14. MLAT Words Sent	--	--	--	--	--	--	--	--	--	--	--	--	--	--	.15	.16	.12	.17	.26	.12	.16
15. MLAT Pair Assoc	--	--	--	--	--	--	--	--	--	--	--	--	--	--	--	.21	.13	.26	.25	.16	.29
16. L2 Word Decoding	--	--	--	--	--	--	--	--	--	--	--	--	--	--	--	--	.28	.29	.41	.50	.31
17. L2 Read Comp	--	--	--	--	--	--	--	--	--	--	--	--	--	--	--	--	--	.31	.38	.31	.42
18. L2 Vocabulary	--	--	--	--	--	--	--	--	--	--	--	--	--	--	--	--	--	--	.43	.28	.56
19. L2 Listen Comp	--	--	--	--	--	--	--	--	--	--	--	--	--	--	--	--	--	--	--	.43	.37
20. L2 Spelling	--	--	--	--	--	--	--	--	--	--	--	--	--	--	--	--	--	--	--	--	.31
21. L2 Writing	--	--	--	--	--	--	--	--	--	--	--	--	--	--	--	--	--	--	--	--	--

Note: L1 = English/native language; L2 = Spanish/foreign language; MLAT = Modern Language Aptitude Test.

Note: All correlations ≥ .16 are significant at $p < .01$; all correlations from ≥ .11 to .15 are significant at $p < .05$ level; all correlations below .11 are $p > .05$.

Appendix B: Intercorrelations Among Predictor Variables and Outcome Variables for Students Completing Second-Year Spanish

Measure	1	2	3	4	5	6	7	8	9	10	11	12	13	14	15	16	17	18	19	20	21
1. L1 Word Decoding	--	--	--	--	--	--	--	--	--	--	--	--	--	--	--	.58	.36	.31	.42	.61	.33
2. L1 Decode Fluency	--	--	--	--	--	--	--	--	--	--	--	--	--	--	--	.54	.31	.27	.39	.48	.27
3. L1 Vocabulary	--	--	--	--	--	--	--	--	--	--	--	--	--	--	--	.26	.25	.37	.33	.33	.32
4. L1 Work Memory	--	--	--	--	--	--	--	--	--	--	--	--	--	--	--	.37	.26	.24	.30	.41	.24
5. L1 Phono Memory	--	--	--	--	--	--	--	--	--	--	--	--	--	--	--	.22	.10	.11	.10	.27	.14
6. L1 Lang Analysis	--	--	--	--	--	--	--	--	--	--	--	--	--	--	--	.23	.16	.21	.26	.31	.17
7. L1 Reading Comp	--	--	--	--	--	--	--	--	--	--	--	--	--	--	--	.30	.27	.24	.37	.36	.18
8. L1 Writing	--	--	--	--	--	--	--	--	--	--	--	--	--	--	--	.32	.32	.24	.37	.34	.20
9. Meta Knowledge	--	--	--	--	--	--	--	--	--	--	--	--	--	--	--	.23	.25	.29	.31	.25	.27
10. L2 Phon Awareness	--	--	--	--	--	--	--	--	--	--	--	--	--	--	--	.42	.20	.36	.34	.46	.30
11. MLAT Numb Learn	--	--	--	--	--	--	--	--	--	--	--	--	--	--	--	.25	.21	.31	.25	.31	.29
12. MLAT Phon Script	--	--	--	--	--	--	--	--	--	--	--	--	--	--	--	.43	.34	.39	.34	.33	.34
13. MLAT Spell Clues	--	--	--	--	--	--	--	--	--	--	--	--	--	--	--	.30	.18	.16	.21	.27	.22

(Continued)

(Continued)

Measure	1	2	3	4	5	6	7	8	9	10	11	12	13	14	15	16	17	18	19	20	21
14. MLAT Words Sent	--	--	--	--	--	--	--	--	--	--	--	--	--	--	--	.22	.25	.23	.29	.21	.24
15. MLAT Pair Assoc	--	--	--	--	--	--	--	--	--	--	--	--	--	--	--	.20	.29	.33	.26	.20	.33
16. L2 Word Decoding	--	--	--	--	--	--	--	--	--	--	--	--	--	--	--	--	.41	.33	.48	.60	.35
17. L2 Read Comp	--	--	--	--	--	--	--	--	--	--	--	--	--	--	--	--	--	.47	.56	.50	.51
18. L2 Vocabulary	--	--	--	--	--	--	--	--	--	--	--	--	--	--	--	--	--	--	.53	.38	.62
19. L2 Listen Comp	--	--	--	--	--	--	--	--	--	--	--	--	--	--	--	--	--	--	--	.49	.56
20. L2 Spelling	--	--	--	--	--	--	--	--	--	--	--	--	--	--	--	--	--	--	--	--	.43
21. L2 Writing	--	--	--	--	--	--	--	--	--	--	--	--	--	--	--	--	--	--	--	--	--

Note: L1 = English/native language; L2 = Spanish/foreign language; MLAT = Modern Language Aptitude Test.

Note: All correlations ≥ .16 are significant at $p < .01$; all correlations from ≥ .11 to .15 are significant at $p < .05$ level; all correlations below .11 are $p > .05$.

Appendix C: Intercorrelations Among Predictor Variables and Outcome Variables for Students Completing Third-Year Spanish

Measure	1	2	3	4	5	6	7	8	9	10	11	12	13	14	15	16	17	18	19	20	21
1. L1 Word Decoding	--	--	--	--	--	--	--	--	--	--	--	--	--	--	--	.41	.37	.19	.43	.46	.30
2. L1 Decode Fluency	--	--	--	--	--	--	--	--	--	--	--	--	--	--	--	.44	.45	.17	.36	.31	.38
3. L1 Vocabulary	--	--	--	--	--	--	--	--	--	--	--	--	--	--	--	.28	.31	.42	.32	.18	.19
4. L1 Work Memory	--	--	--	--	--	--	--	--	--	--	--	--	--	--	--	.21	.14	−.04	.04	.22	−.03
5. L1 Phono Memory	--	--	--	--	--	--	--	--	--	--	--	--	--	--	--	.24	.18	−.06	.07	.41	.28
6. L1 Lang Analysis	--	--	--	--	--	--	--	--	--	--	--	--	--	--	--	.30	.36	.25	.44	.22	.35
7. L1 Reading Comp	--	--	--	--	--	--	--	--	--	--	--	--	--	--	--	.35	.26	.24	.36	23	.40
8. L1 Writing	--	--	--	--	--	--	--	--	--	--	--	--	--	--	--	.37	.31	.19	.31	.21	.22
9. Meta Knowledge	--	--	--	--	--	--	--	--	--	--	--	--	--	--	--	.19	.25	.28	.18	.27	.18
10. L2 Phon Awareness	--	--	--	--	--	--	--	--	--	--	--	--	--	--	--	.27	.34	.26	.36	.37	.01
11. MLAT Numb Learn	--	--	--	--	--	--	--	--	--	--	--	--	--	--	--	.46	.46	.49	.37	29	.08
12. MLAT Phon Script	--	--	--	--	--	--	--	--	--	--	--	--	--	--	--	.18	.31	.39	.32	.25	.11
13. MLAT Spell Clues	--	--	--	--	--	--	--	--	--	--	--	--	--	--	--	.28	.25	.13	.27	.34	−.01

(*Continued*)

(Continued)

Measure	1	2	3	4	5	6	7	8	9	10	11	12	13	14	15	16	17	18	19	20	21
14. MLAT Words Sent	--	--	--	--	--	--	--	--	--	--	--	--	--	--	--	.09	.19	.05	.11	.12	.18
15. MLAT Pair Assoc	--	--	--	--	--	--	--	--	--	--	--	--	--	--	--	.32	.30	.46	.38	.28	.24
16. L2 Word Decoding	--	--	--	--	--	--	--	--	--	--	--	--	--	--	--	--	.56	.48	.68	.63	.34
17. L2 Read Comp	--	--	--	--	--	--	--	--	--	--	--	--	--	--	--	--	--	.66	.75	.67	.51
18. L2 Vocabulary	--	--	--	--	--	--	--	--	--	--	--	--	--	--	--	--	--	--	.68	.45	.36
19. L2 Listen Comp	--	--	--	--	--	--	--	--	--	--	--	--	--	--	--	--	--	--	--	.69	.51
20. L2 Spelling	--	--	--	--	--	--	--	--	--	--	--	--	--	--	--	--	--	--	--	--	.55
21. L2 Writing	--	--	--	--	--	--	--	--	--	--	--	--	--	--	--	--	--	--	--	--	--

Note: L1 = English/native language; L2 = Spanish/foreign language; MLAT = Modern Language Aptitude Test; $\star$ $p \leq .05$; $\star\star$ $p \leq .01$.

Note: All correlations $\geq .16$ are significant at $p < .01$; all correlations from $\geq .11$ to .15 are significant at $p < .05$ level; all correlations below .11 are $p > .05$.

8

LANGUAGE APTITUDE

Insights From Hyperpolyglots

Michael Erard

Introduction

Over the centuries, an untold number of high-intensity language learners known as "polyglots" or "hyperpolyglots" have undertaken natural experiments into the limits of second language acquisition and multilingualism by learning and maintaining a high number of languages over their lifetimes. It is sometimes assumed that hyperpolyglots must be talented language learners or possess high levels of aptitude for foreign language learning. Otherwise, how to explain their persistent, apparently successful, accumulation and use of a large linguistic repertoire?

Thus far, the role of language aptitude in hyperpolyglots' learning outcomes has not been clearly defined, mainly because massive multilinguals have not been a population of interest in theoretical or applied linguistics. Any attention came in the form of case studies of exceptional learners who had accumulated large linguistic repertoires (Novoa, Fein, & Obler, 1988; Krashen & Kiss, 1996; Smith & Tsimpli, 1995; Biedroń & Szczepaniak, 2009). Other studies of exceptional learners (e.g., Schneiderman & Desmarais, 1988a; Schneiderman & Desmarais, 1988b; Marinova-Todd, 2003) have mainly looked at how they achieve native-like abilities in a single second language learned after puberty, not multiple subsequent languages learned to varying degrees of proficiency. Thus, hyperpolyglots have not been studied in adequate detail to understand whether or not individual variation in general cognitive or specifically linguistic abilities explains their outcomes and, if so, in what stage of the learning process and developmental course those abilities might be most salient. Moreover, it is not clear that aptitude for learning languages is even necessary for multilingual outcomes. Multilingual populations exist all over the world, and in those real-world contexts aptitude is not required for learning multiple languages. Therefore, it is important to consider other reasons for building and maintaining a large linguistic repertoire. For example, an individual might possess normal language aptitude but have a high tolerance for repetitive learning activities, or they might possess some neurocognitive factor that is neither language specific nor included in existing aptitude constructs. In other words, hyperpolyglots and learners with high language aptitudes may be nonoverlapping populations.

Overall, the population of hyperpolyglots is highly relevant to the field of second language acquisition studies, and particularly to the re-emerging interest in language aptitude from a neuroscience perspective (Reiterer, Pereda, & Bhattacharya, 2009; Reiterer, 2009; Biedroń, 2015; Biedroń & Pawlak, 2016). New research contributions on language aptitude will come not from the development of new constructs but in increased attention to understudied subpopulations of language learners across a range of cognitive, neurological, and behavioral profiles, from the impaired to the gifted. As language researchers seek to explore individual variation using innovations in data mining, brain imaging, and genomics, it is important that they explore the full range of language outcomes, from impairments to exceptional achievements. Speech language pathology, psycholinguistics, and cognitive psychology have developed a rich taxonomy of impairments and are evaluating the effectiveness of interventions. In the same way, the field of second language acquisition should build a taxonomy of extraordinary language learners and exceptional language users, both as phenotypes of their own and as co-occurring with other talents or disorders. In this taxonomy, the hyperpolyglot would be only one type of exceptional learner. Clearly, the hyperpolyglot is exceptional. But what does the hyperpolyglot have to do with aptitude?

This chapter explores their connection to aptitude along three paths. The first is backward looking: I will present how hyperpolyglots of different historical eras understood the origins of their language learning abilities and whether they considered the influence of aptitude or other organic brain-based factors. The second considers results from an online survey conducted in 2009–2010 about contemporary perception about the role of aptitude, motivation, and other factors. The third is future looking: it will briefly discuss opportunities and barriers to the search for a genetic basis of hyperpolyglottism (and, by extension, to language aptitude).

What Is a Hyperpolyglot?

The most salient attribute of the hyperpolyglot appears to be their language repertoire size. Consequently, one question that immediately arises is what repertoire size qualifies an individual as a hyperpolyglot. Another way to phrase the question is to ask, "What distinguishes the hyperpolyglot from the ordinary community multilingual?" In 2004 University College London linguist Richard Hudson proposed that because five languages appeared to be the normative number of languages spoken in multilingual communities, a repertoire of six or more languages represents an exceptional level of human performance (Hudson, personal communication). Therefore, he suggested six languages or more as the quantitative limit for hyperpolyglot status. However, based on an online survey of hyperpolyglots and their repertoires, Erard (2012) suggested that another good candidate limit is 10 or 11 languages. In a sample of 172 respondents reporting 6 or more languages, the number of people reporting repertoires larger than 11 languages dropped significantly (Figure 8.1). Though repertoire sizes drop after 6 languages, language accumulation appears to be considerably rarer after one has learned 10 languages. This is the territory that researchers should explore further.

Apart from repertoire size, the hyperpolyglot demonstrates other cognitive and behavioral traits as well. Some of these traits seem to overlap with elements of well-known aptitude constructs by John Carroll, Peter Robinson (2001, 2005), and Peter Skehan (1998). That is, hyperpolyglots appear to learn grammatical structures and phonological rules quickly because they are good at recognizing and producing patterns, and they retain learned items easily. For example, Skehan (1998) in particular showed how his aptitude construct could account for exceptional learners who possess "an unusual degree of language learning talent that is mediated by particular patterns of neuropsychological development" (Skehan, 1998, p. 215). These are essentially memory-driven learners who are motivated by an "interest in the form of language" (Skehan, 1998, p. 215). Their talent is not specifically on language material but derives from central processing and memory strengths (Skehan, 1998, p. 233). Such exceptional learners "have a high range of lexicalized exemplars, considerable redundancy in their memory systems, and multiple representations of lexical elements" and possess "unusual memories, particularly for the retention of verbal material" (Skehan, 1998, p. 233). He also posited that exceptional learners, according to his model, do not seem

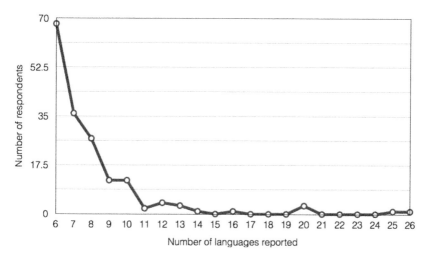

FIGURE 8.1   Language repertoire size from online sample (N=172)

to have "unusual abilities with respect to input or central processing" (Skehan, 1998, p. 233). It is necessary to add that some of the pattern-learning abilities of hyperpolyglots are the effects of metalinguistic knowledge as well as learner self-awareness. Therefore, future aptitude research on hyperpolyglots should separate organic aptitude levels from enhanced learning processes.

Hyperpolyglots also possess other traits that are not necessarily considered in the aptitude literature. For instance, hyperpolyglots report being able to reactivate previously learned lexical items and linguistic structures. As a result, they often possess a dormant language repertoire that is larger than the actively maintained repertoire that is either productive or receptive. Also, many of them are autodidacts, engaged in assembling methods and using materials that suit their personal preferences and self-perceived "cognitive style." Additionally, they can be adept at switching among languages in their active repertoire with facility. They readily learn languages across their lifespans, changing learning methods and adapting desired outcomes as they age. However, not all hyperpolyglots are alike. Some are able to mimic native speaker pronunciations, whereas others are not. Some appear to focus on languages with certain typological features, which raises the additional question of how certain populations of learners may be better suited for certain types of languages (Dediu, 2015). Taken together, these observations suggest that hyperpolyglots' exceptionality is not entirely captured by aptitude constructs as they are currently formulated.

The Case of Historical Polyglots

Attention to hyperpolyglots' stated beliefs about language learning provides an additional piece of the puzzle in determining the role that language aptitude plays in their pursuits. Of course, contemporary scientists should not use statements from historical or contemporary hyperpolyglots as data about their status or abilities. Not surprisingly, historical hyperpolyglots often attributed their abilities according to guiding ideologies of their day. Take the case of the arguably pre-eminent hyperpolyglot of the eighteenth and nineteenth centuries, Cardinal Giuseppe Mezzofanti (1774–1859), a humble son of a local carpenter who lived through the Napoleonic Wars in his native Bologna, then went to the Vatican in Rome. In both Bologna and Rome (Mezzofanti did not travel outside of Italy), historical circumstances, institutional contexts, and his own personal fame provided him with resources for learning to speak multiple languages. His total repertoire was said to number between 61 and 72, and observers agreed that he had "mastered" 30 of these languages (Russell, 1858; Watts, 1859).

In Mezzofanti's era, "mastery" and "fluency" were defined through correctness of forms; grammatical accuracy; and nativelikeness of accent, lexicon, and idiom, usually as judged by native speakers themselves (Watts, 1859). Also, oral performance was prized over interpersonal interaction, and literacy and translation abilities were prized over speaking abilities. Yet Mezzofanti's ability to switch among languages rapidly and without error was widely noted by commentators (Russell, 1858). Mezzofanti's memory was reportedly prodigious, and he could switch among languages rapidly in the same social context, about which numerous anecdotes exist. For instance, in 1820, the Hungarian astronomer Baron Franz Xavier von Zach visited Mezzofanti, who addressed him in Hungarian so excellent, the surprised Baron said he felt "stupefied." Then (as he wrote later), "he afterwards spoke to me in German, at first in good Saxon, and then in the Austrian and Swabian dialects, with a correctness of accent that amazed me to the last degree" (Watts, 1859, p. 243). Mezzofanti went on to speak English in conversation with a visiting Englishman, and Russian and Polish with a visiting Russian prince. He did all of this, wrote Zach, "not stuttering and stammering, but with the same volubility as if he had been speaking his mother tongue" (Watts, 1859, p. 243). In other encounters, his interlocutors often felt as if Mezzofanti had spoken their language the most fluently. And he was reportedly able to learn a new language in a remarkably short time, using neither dictionaries nor grammars. Even without a shared language to help him translate, Mezzofanti asked a speaker to repeat the Lord's Prayer until he grasped the language's sounds and rhythms. Then he would break it into the parts of speech (Russell, 1858, p. 48).

When asked about the source of his abilities, Mezzofanti was willing to credit divine intervention and the presence of an explicable "gift" that he possessed (Russell, 1858, p. 157). He was asked once by a visitor how he could speak 45 languages. "I cannot explain it," he reportedly replied. "Of course God has given me this peculiar power: but if you wish to know how I preserve these languages, I can only say, that, when once I hear the meaning of a word in any language, I never forget it" (Russell, 1858, p. 343). At other times he said that God had given him "a good memory and a quick ear" (Russell, 1858, p. 342).

By contrast, the American polyglot Elihu Burritt (1810–1879) attributed his linguistic repertoire solely to his own hard work. Burritt was an American laborer born and living in New England who taught himself to read 50 languages in a compulsive display of aspiration that lasted about a decade and a half. Starting at the age of 22, he became fascinated by resemblances between Latin, Greek, and French and began studying in earnest. Within a year's time, he had made substantial progress. During the most intense period, he spent four hours a day studying multiple languages simultaneously (as diverse as French, Hebrew, Syriac, Swedish, and Celtic) at the same time he worked as a blacksmith over eight hours a day (Tolis, 1968). "His compulsive and erratic study of languages was not an end in itself," wrote his biographer Peter Tolis, "but a means of social escalation, a kind of intellectual stunt he used to emancipate himself from the blacksmith shop" (Tolis, 1968). Burritt's passion for self-improvement was common in his day. Historian Merle Curti has called it the "cult of self-improvement" (Curti, 1937), and its practitioners were convinced that any mind could be elevated, morally and intellectually, through persistent application. Burritt himself said that "All that I have accomplished, or expect, or hope to accomplish, has been and will be by the plodding, patient, persevering process of accretion which builds the ant-heap—particle by particle, thought by thought, fact by fact" (Burritt, 1839).

Similarly, the Hungarian polyglot and translator Lomb Kato (1909–2003) argued extensively in her memoir, *Polyglot: How I Learn Languages* (2008), against "the idea of an 'innate ability' for language learning" (Lomb, 2008, p. 19). One entire chapter, peppered with personal observations and anecdotes, titled "The Language Gift," argues that talent or aptitude does not exist. She wrote:

> The complaint "I have no talent for languages" usually means that someone can only memorize new words with difficulty, after several tries. The term "good at languages" is given those who imitate the sounds of a foreign language with a parrot-like skill. The language student who solves written exercises without a mistake is proclaimed a "genius" because she can quickly find her bearings in the morphological and syntactic tangles of a language.
>
> *(Lomb, 2008, p. 174)*

In her argument, individual differences are not intrinsic or biological but personal and contextual; different outcomes arise because individuals have different resources, time, and motivation. Her tenth "commandment" for learning languages is also telling in this regard:

> Be firmly convinced that you are a linguistic genius. If the facts demonstrate otherwise, heap blame on the pesky language you aim to master, on the dictionaries, or on this book, not on yourself.
>
> *(Lomb, 2008, p. 161)*

Lomb allows for only two intrinsic factors: the first is the negative emotion of "inhibition," when "the fear of making mistakes prevents you from speaking and also when you are aware that you are transferring the structure of your mother tongue to the new language" (Lomb, 2008, p. 176). The second, interestingly, is gender. She claims that men have more inhibition at speaking than women, who also talk more than men, talk faster than men, and have a "closer relationship to words" (Lomb, 2008, p. 152). Women also have an innate desire to "emphasize femininity" (Lomb, 2008, p. 154) when they speak by shifting all consonants to sibilants and using "heightened emotional emphasis on the syntactic level" (Lomb, 2008, p. 154). Her antipathy toward an aptitude for learning languages may be expected. But explaining her willingness to ascribe different behaviors and outcomes to women would require more information about gender attitudes in post–World War II Soviet bloc nations.

Attitudes of Contemporary Hyperpolyglots

Three thumbnail portraits of hyperpolyglots in three different historical and cultural contexts demonstrate the shared attributes that can help inform research on contemporaneous exceptional language learning. They also suggest a spectrum of attitudes about organic advantages itself. If one were to ask hyperpolyglots if they possess "talents," "gifts," or organic "aptitudes" for learning languages, they will be apt to respond that they do not. However, it also appears that the more languages a person claims to know, the more likely they are to claim "talent" as a factor in their outcomes and to downplay social, environmental, or familial factors.

This was demonstrated in an online survey that ran from January 2009 to January 2010 as part of research for a book on hyperpolyglots (Erard, 2012). The goal of the survey was to provide a holistic picture of the phenomenon with respect to overall repertoire size, demographic measures, cognitive psychological attributes, and linguistic typological attributes. A convenience sample ($N = 390$) of people from around the world responded to the survey. Group 1 ($n = 172$) reported knowing six or more languages, and Group 2 ($n = 289$) people reported that learning languages was easier for them than for others (based on a question that Loraine Obler used in her own research, finding it a reliable informal probe, of the probable existence of language learning aptitude [Obler, personal communication.])

Even among people who say they know many languages, there are two subgroups of high performers. One subgroup (hereafter "Subgroup A") were respondents who said they know six or more languages and who also reported that learning languages was easier for them ($n = 157$). A second subgroup, labeled here "Subgroup B," were 17 respondents who reported knowing 11 or more languages. The reported attitudes of these two subgroups are reported here.

There is information about attitudes related to aptitude because participants who responded "yes" to the question, "Do you learn languages more easily than others?" were asked this follow-up question: "To what do you attribute your relative ease?" and given seven possible reasons to select. Participants could select more than one option. Results for Subgroup A appear in Figure 8.2. Slightly more than 50% of the sample identified "I have an innate talent" as a factor in their outcomes, while nearly 60% identified "I am more motivated" as a factor, and nearly 90% identified "I like languages" as a factor. In general, the traits within an individual's locus of control were reported more frequently than those outside an individual's locus of control, with one exception: half of the sample was willing to claim an innate talent for languages.

Interestingly, these attitudes toward talent, work, motivation, and the admittedly poorly defined "liking languages" differed among individuals with larger language repertoires. Figure 8.3 compares the responses from Subgroup A and Subgroup B to the question, "To what do you attribute your relative ease?" Those

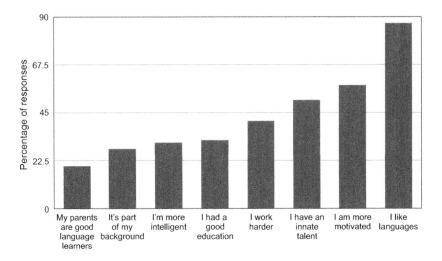

FIGURE 8.2   To what do you attribute your ease of learning? (n=157)

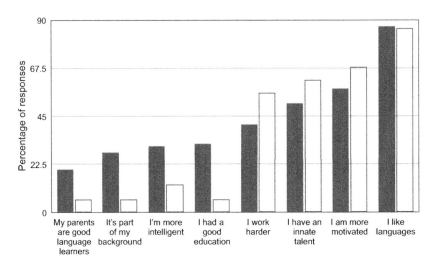

FIGURE 8.3   To what do you attribute your relative ease (of learning)? Subgroup A
(n=157) vs. Subgroup B (n=17)

with more than 10 languages in their repertoire more readily claimed working
harder, having innate talent, and motivation. Also notable were the less frequent
choices of "my parents are good language learners," "it's part of my background,"
"I'm more intelligent," and "I had a good education." The claiming of internal
locus of control factors was much greater for Subgroup B, whose language repertoires ranged from 10 to 26, than for Subgroup A.

Information about hyperpolyglots' attitudes about aptitude comes from another set of survey results. Respondents were asked to rate their agreement with attributes of a good language learner from Joan Rubin's 1975 article, "Lessons that Good Language Learners Can Teach Us," then they were asked in an open text field what else good language learners needed. Respondents from both Subgroup A and Subgroup B supplied 92 comments, which were thematically organized and analyzed. Overall, respondents overwhelmingly listed personal qualities of the individual learner (e.g., "curiosity," "discipline," "openness," "eagerness," "relaxation," "an interest in the culture," "passion," "obsession") before environmental ones. However, among these individual attributes, no cognitive abilities (such as "memory," which is mentioned only nine times in 92 comments), metacognitive strategies, or innate talents (for example, "having an ear," which was mentioned in 3 comments, or "a special personal drive due to his psychological makeup," mentioned only once.

Taken together, these results show that concepts that might map onto the constructs of language learning aptitude are not linked in the minds of contemporary hyperpolyglots to either learning processes or outcomes. Aptitude in the way that applied linguists would discuss it has limited salience to them as they pursue their goals. Though they prefer to explain outcomes in terms of individual characteristics, not environmental factors, the individual characteristics they prefer are more related to culturally salient traits of motivation and hard work, not to cognitive traits. Apart from the fact that it is not possible to accurately measure one's cognitive abilities introspectively, contemporary hyperpolyglots are less likely to consider an innate talent or ability, but instead attribute their differential outcomes to a personal factor. Such impressionistic judgments about mental states and cognitive abilities have been obsolete in psychology for over a century, but they do provide clues about the lived experience of learning many languages that could help with the construction of dimensional aptitude that explains hyperpolyglot outcomes. Descriptions such as these could also help assemble a neurophenotype for the hyperpolyglot more accurately. Most importantly, research on hyperpolyglot phenotypes can be hampered if researchers' recruitment and consent procedures do not take these beliefs into account. These are people who do not suffer a deficit or impairment, so do not need therapeutic intervention as an incentive for involvement.

The Genetics of Hyperpolyglots

As an exceptional learner, the hyperpolyglot is a multidimensional neurophenotype that can contribute to determining the range of phenotypes that underpin the phenomenon of multilingualism in the world. It remains novel to locate the etiology of certain types of language behavior in the genes, not in the social environment, particularly exceptional forms of behavior. This effort is built on studies of the heritability of aptitude in a variety of skills (e.g., Vinkhuyzen et al., 2009;

Pulli et al., 2008) and is aided by recent advances in the neurocognitive basis of language aptitude and exceptional language learning, such as Reiterer (2009), Hu et. al. (2013), and Biedroń and Pawlak (2016). It is also aided by evolving understandings of the genetic basis of language itself (Fisher & Vernes, 2015; Graham & Fisher, 2015).

The next phase of research that will connect hyperpolyglots to language aptitude will consist of accurately defining their neurophenotype, acquiring genetic samples, and exploring the genomes for the presence of genetic variants that are associated with significant statistical power with the phenotype. However, research into developmental language phenotypes is in its infancy (Rice & Tager-Flusberg, 2017; Fisher & Vernes, 2015) and still faces numerous challenges (Mountford & Newbury, 2017). Any excitement about studying the genetic components of hyperpolyglottism and language aptitude must be tempered by the fact that searching across the human genome has not identified robust signals between genetic variants and any language abilities (St Pourcain et al., 2014). Moreover, the genes that influence developmental phenotypes are currently unknown (St Pourcain et al., 2014). Although some progress has been made, it is necessary to understand the challenges faced by genetic explorations that apply to hyperpolyglots and gifted language learners alike.

Numerous reviews on the genetics of language warn of the need for very large samples of participants—in the range of tens of thousands—that are needed to detect gene variants linked to language abilities in genome-wide association studies (GWASs). Because the prevalence of hyperpolyglottism as a form of exceptional language learning appears to be very low, acquiring a large enough sample to achieve the necessary statistical power poses a significant challenge. However, it is necessary to recognize that individuals who possess the phenotype may have lacked exposure to environmental factors that enable high-intensity foreign language learning, e.g., access to pedagogical materials, a social niche conducive to accumulating and using a large linguistic repertoire, and the formation of an identity as an empassioned language learner. As a result, researchers should develop screening tools that do not rely on sizable language repertoires as the central feature of the phenotype.

A more significant challenge is the large number of genes from coding and non-coding regions of the genome that can influence the risk of acquiring disorders (or exceptional abilities). Thus far, 22 genes have been implicated in language disorders in genetic linkage and candidate gene-sequencing studies (Mountford & Newbury, 2017). Only three of the 22 genes (*FOXP1*, *FOXP2*, and *TM4SF20*) lead directly to a language disorder because a mutation leads to absence of a coded protein. Such gene variants were found in single families because the gene mutation and subsequent protein deficiency directly produce a disease state. These were anomalous discoveries, however, and are unlikely to be repeated (Graham & Fisher, 2015). The remaining 19 genes were identified via GWAS surveys of large samples of individuals who are not related to each other but who share the same phenotype (Mountford & Newbury 2017).

Some genetic studies have looked at language abilities more generally, not just language disorders. Harlaar et al. (2014) reported on a GWAS study of the receptive language ability of 12-year-old children that found a possible association with two genes, while St Pourcain et al. (2014) reported that a common variant near *ROBO2* is associated with expressive vocabulary in 15-month-old infants. St Pourcain et al. (2014) also reported a significant genetic association for social communication ability at age 17.

What has emerged from all this work is a rich picture of how gene variants may interact with each other, either conferring, magnifying, or neutralizing susceptibility. Adding to the complexity is the fact that some or all of these variants are triggered or modified by environmental factors. Both language aptitude and language disorders involve "complex inheritance." This means that gene variants, even if they were to be discovered, could explain only a small part of observable individual differences.

Other lessons can be learned from the genetics of language disorders. One challenge has been the lack of standardized diagnostic definitions for disorders and their severity (Mountford & Newbury, 2017), which limits large-scale studies. This terminological disorder affects the study of hyperpolyglottism as well as language aptitude in second language acquisition. Studying genetic associations in language acquisition outcomes is challenging because of rapid changes to the phenotype (St Pourcain et al., 2014). This may also be a challenge in studying hyperpolyglots, whose phenotype can change in terms of both learning and atrophy of proficiency.

Graham and Fisher (2015) described how the co-occurrence of language disorders with developmental disorders suggests a shared genetic influence. This may be a promising route for studying language aptitude, which has been connected to working memory. Thus far, working memory abilities are the most exciting dimension of the hyperpolyglot phenotype to have been examined for heritable links (see Luciano et al., 2001; Friedman et al., 2008; Blokland et al., 2011; Blokland et al., 2017; Wen, 2018). Rice and Tager-Flusberg (2017) mention other language phenotypes: discourse phenotypes (using the Children's Communication Checklist) and brain phenotypes (such as hemispheric asymmetries in morphology or activation levels) (Rice & Tager-Flusberg, 2017, pp. 237–238). However, the latter phenotypes are restricted to specific language impairment (SLI) and autism spectrum disorders (ASD), not to language learning aptitude or other exceptional outcomes.

Another possibility for discovering the heritability of language aptitude given the existing constraints is to look for relevant measures in existing genetic databases. However, very few language measures are included in GWAS databases, and those that are included are not relevant to hyperpolyglottery or even to language aptitude. This stems in part from the clinical nature of these investigations, whose focus on impairment and pathology means that measures are designed to capture details about pathologies that can be used for diagnostic and therapeutic purposes. Similarly, the

painstaking work of mapping pathways for genetic influences on language development has been mainly focused on impairment and pathology. Both issues are on display in the Phenotypes and Exposures project (PhenX), funded by the US National
Institutes of Health, which was developed to help geneticists exploring links to
disease conditions by providing standardized, high-quality measures for 21 medical research domains. One domain was speech and hearing. The language-relevant
measures in the PhenX speech and hearing toolkit were the following:

1. Family history questionnaire
2. Onset and early childhood speech and language (which was monolingual)
3. Grammatical impairments (assessed via three tools: a sentence imitation task,
   the Rice-Wexler test of early grammatical impairment, and the Rice Gram-
   matically Judgment Task-WH Questions)
4. Vocabulary
5. Phonemic inventory
6. Stuttering
7. Reading words and reading comprehension (assessed via two tasks)
8. Stuttering
9. Verbal memory/nonword repetition

Several of these measures are of potential interest to exploring a hyperpolyglot
phenotype (family history questionnaire;,child language onset, phonemic inventory, reading words and reading comprehension, verbal memory/nonword repetition). However, they distinguish impaired and normal performance only and
do not measure the full range of possible variation. Neither are they designed to
measure high levels of behavior or abilities represented by all types of exceptional
language learners, not just hyperpolyglots.

Despite these challenges, geneticists of language continue to pursue gene variants for a variety of important theoretical and applied reasons with wide-ranging
implications. It is important for second language acquisition researchers to know
that this work now takes place in large interdisciplinary and multi-institutional
consortia that enable them to leverage institutional resources and laboratory spe-
cialties. These collaborations have led to rapid uptake of new technologies, the
building of databases, and the linking of genomic information with functional
brain imaging data. This method of working may be unfamiliar to many linguists.
Applied linguists who wish to participate in these consortia should familiarize
themselves with the fundamentals of genetic variation and the role of genes in
language; an excellent textbook is *An Introduction to Genetics for Language Scientists:
Current Concepts, Methods, and Findings* (Dediu, 2015).

Conclusion

We need to understand language learning aptitude not only as the preference of a
brain for a certain part of the learning curve and for certain language structures but

also as a trait that may exist in some populations and not others. However, in order to do this, we need more culturally sensitive and cognitively informed studies of the distribution of proficiency in multiple languages in community settings. These would show us population-level distributions of individual variations in language performance and cognitive traits and help us understand multilingual communities as linguistically and cognitively heterogeneous, not homogeneous. Also, in order to gather adequate data on the phenotypes of exceptional learners in a developmental frame, we need language-related measures that distinguish exceptional performances as well as impairments. Finally, we need better measures for determining the complexity of individual linguistic systems. We also need a way to account for the existence of aptitude that is not realized across populations because of cultural values, access to resources, or environmental factors that affect the development of individuals. Societies should aim to discover aptitude where it exists and develop it, as human cognitive abilities are our most important natural resources.

References

Biedroń, A. (2015). Neurology of foreign language aptitude. *Studies in Second Language Learning and Teaching, 1*(1), 13–40.

Biedroń, A., & Pawlak, M. (2016). New conceptualizations of linguistic giftedness. *Language Teaching, 49*(2), 151–185.

Biedroń, A., & Szczepaniak, A. (2009). The cognitive profile of a talented foreign language learner. A case study. *Psychology of Language and Communication, 13*(1), 53–71.

Blokland, G., McMahon, K. L., Thompson, P. M., Martin, N. G., de Zubicaray, G. I., & Wright, M. J. (2011). Heritability of working memory brain activation. *Journal of Neuroscience, 31*(30), 10882–10890.

Blokland, G., Wallace, A. K., Hansell, N. K., Thompson, P. M., Hickie, I. B., Montgomery, G. W., . . . Wright, M. J. (2017, May). Genome-wide association study of working memory brain activation. *International Journal of Psychophysiology, 115*, 98–111. doi:10.1016/j.ijpsycho.2016.09.010

Burritt, E. (1839). Autobiography of the Author. In *Ten-Minute Talks on All Sorts of Topics.* Boston: Lee and Shepard (Reprinted in 1873).

Curti, M. (Ed.). (1937). *The learned blacksmith: Letters and Journals of Elihu Burritt.* New York, NY: Wilson Erickson.

Dediu, D. (2015). *An introduction to genetics for language scientists: Current concepts, methods, and findings.* Cambridge: Cambridge University Press.

Erard, M. (2012). *Babel no more: The search for the world's most extraordinary language learners.* New York, NY: Free Press.

Fisher, S., & Vernes, S. (2015). Genetics and the language sciences. *Annual Review of Linguistics, 1*, 289–310.

Friedman, N. P., Miyake, A., Young, S. E., DeFries, J. C., Corley, R. P., & Hewitt, J. K. (2008). Individual differences in executive functions are almost entirely genetic in origin. *Journal of Experimental Psychology, 137*(2), 201–225.

Graham, S., & Fisher, S. (2015). Understanding language from a genomic perspective. *Annual Review of Genetics, 49*, 131–160.

Harlaar, N., Meaburn, E. L., Hayiou-Thomas, M. E., Davis, O. S. P., Docherty, S., Hanscombe, . . . Plomin R. (2014). Genome-wide association study of reeptive language ability of 12-year-olds. *Journal of Speech, Language, and Hearing Research, 57*, 96–105.

Hu, X., Ackermann, H., Martin, J., Erb, M., Winkler, S., & Reiterer, S. (2013). Language aptitude for pronunciation in advanced second language (L2) Learners: Behavioural predictors and neural substrates. *Brain & Language, 127*(3), 366–376.

Krashen, S., & Kiss, N. (1996). Notes on a polyglot: Kató Lomb. *System, 24*(2), 207–210.

Lomb, K. (2008). *Polyglot: How I learn languages.* (Trans. Adám Szegi and Kornelia DeKorne, Ed. Scott Alkire). Berkeley, CA: TESL-EJ.

Luciano, M., Wright, M. J., Smith, G. A., Geffen, G. M., Geffen, L. B., & Martin, N. G. (2001). Genetic covariance among measures of information processing speed, working memory, and IQ. *Behavioral Genetics, 31*(6), 581–592.

Marinova-Todd, S. (2003). *Comprehensive analysis of ultimate attainment in adult second language acquisition* (Unpublished PhD dissertation), Harvard University.

Mountford, H., & Newbury, D. (2017). The genomic landscape of language: Insights into evolution. *Journal of Language Evolution*, lzx019. https://doi.org/10.1093/jole/lzx019

Novoa, L., Fein, D., & Obler, L. K. (1988). Talent in Foreign languages: A case study. In: Obler, L. K. & Fein, D. A. (Eds.), *The neuropsychology of talent and special abilities* (pp. 294–302). New York, NY: The Guildford Press.

Pulli, K., Karma, K., Norio, R., Sistonen, P., Göring, H. H. H., & Järvelá, I. (2008). Genome-wide linkage scan for loci of musical aptitude in Finnish families: Evidence for a major locus at 4q22. *Letters to BMJ.* Retrieved August 1, 2017, from http://jmg.bmj.com/content/45/7/451.short

Reiterer, S. M. (2009). Brain and language talent: A synopsis. In G. Dogil & S. Reiterer (Eds.), *Language talent and brain activity. Trends in applied linguistics 1* (pp. 155–191). Berlin: Mouton de Gruyter.

Reiterer, S. M., Pereda, E., & Bhattacharya, J. (2009). Measuring second language proficiency with EEG synchronization: How functional cortical networks and hemispheric involvement differ as a function of proficiency level in second language speakers. *Journal of Second Language Research, 25*(1), 77–106.

Rice, M., & Tager-Flusberg, H. (2017). Language phenotypes. In V. Jagaroo & S. Santangelo (Eds.), *Neurophenotypes: Advancing psychiatry and neuropsychology in the "OMICS" era* (pp. 227–243). New York, NY: Springer.

Robinson, P. (2001). Individual differences, cognitive abilities, aptitude complexes and learning conditions in second language acquisition. *Second Language Learning, 17*(4), 368–392.

Robinson, P. (2005). Aptitude in second language acquisition. *Annual Review of Applied Linguistics, 25*, 46–73.

Rubin, J. (1975). What the "good" language learner can teach us. *Tesol Quarterly, 9*(1), 41–51.

Russell, C. (1858). *The life of cardinal mezzofanti, with an introductory memoir of eminent linguists, ancient and modern.* London: Longman, Brown, and Co.

Schneiderman, E. I., & Desmarais, C. (1988a). The talented language learner: Some preliminary findings. *Second Language Research, 4*(2), 91–109.

Schneiderman, E. I., & Desmarais, C. (1988b). A neuropsychological substrate for talent in second language acquisition. In L. K. Obler & D. A. Fein (Eds.), *The neuropsychology of talent and special abilities* (pp. 103–126). New York, NY: The Guilford Press.

Skehan, P. (1998). *A cognitive approach to language learning.* Oxford, UK: Oxford University Press.

Smith, N., & Tsimpli, I. (1995). *The mind of a savant: Language learning and modularity.* London: Wiley-Blackwell.

Smith, N., Tsimpli, I., Morgan, G., & Woll, B. (2011). *The signs of a savant: Language against the odds*. Cambridge, UK: Cambridge University Press.

St. Pourcain, B., Cents, R., Whitehouse, A., Haworth, C., Davis, O., O'Reilly, P., . . . Smith, G. (2014, September). Common variation near ROBO2 is associated with expressive vocabulary in infancy. *Nature Communications, 16*(5), 4831. doi:10.1038/ncomms5831

Tolis, P. (1968). *Elihu burritt: Crusader for brotherhood*. Hamden, CT: Archon Press.

Vinkhuyzen, A. E., van der Sluis, S., Posthuma, D., & Boomsma, D. I. (2009). The heritability of aptitude and exceptional talent across different domains in adolescents and young adults. *Behavioral Genetics, 39*(4), 380–392.

Watts, T. (1859). On Dr. Russell's Life of Cardinal Mezzofanti. *Transactions of the Philological Society*, 227–256.

Wen, Z. (2019). Working memory as language aptitude: The phonologica/executive model. In Z. Wen, P. Skehan, A. Biedroń, S. Li, & R. Sparks (Eds.), *Language aptitude: Advancing theory, testing, research and practice*. Abingdon: Routledge.

9

LANGUAGE APTITUDE

Insights From L2 Adult Exceptional Learners

Adriana Biedroń

Introduction

There is a reasonable degree of variability in ultimate foreign language attainment. Achieving near-native-like proficiency in a foreign language or a few languages is rare and usually restricted to some linguistic areas. Therefore, an analysis of cases of people attaining very high levels of proficiency in more than one foreign language (for a review see Erard, 2012; Chapter 8 this volume; Hyltenstam, 2016b, 2016c) certainly evokes questions pertaining to their alleged exceptional giftedness. Does their higher-than-average level of foreign language aptitude (FL aptitude) enable them to acquire languages faster, more effortlessly and to high proficiency levels? If so, is there a link between their expertise in language learning and their aptitude level (Biedroń & Birdsong, forthcoming; Granena, Jackson, & Yilmaz, 2016; Singleton, 2017; Thompson, 2013)? What is the importance of other factors, such as personality or learning strategies? And last but not least: Do exceptional learners possess some specific cognitive-affective profiles that differentiate them from less talented individuals (Biedroń, 2012)? These and other questions concerning linguistic giftedness have been gaining popularity in the research and theory of FL aptitude recently (for a detailed review see Biedroń & Pawlak, 2016; Hyltenstam, 2016a). This chapter is an attempt to present both contemporary and historical cases of these outstanding individuals from different perspectives. We will briefly describe cognitive, personality and neurological features that make them exceptional and demonstrate both similarities and differences between them.

Terminology

In second language acquisition (SLA) research, a number of terms are used with reference to high achievement in language learning, namely *ability, aptitude, giftedness* and *talent*. The first two are related in meaning and measured by standardized tests, such as the Modern Language Aptitude Test (MLAT, Carroll & Sapon, 1959/2002), and intelligence and memory scales. Ability is termed as real potential, that is what a person is able to do, provided environmental conditions are optimal, whereas aptitude refers to a cognitive ability that is prognostic of future success in learning. The latter two terms, giftedness and talent, originate in psychology and are more arbitrary. Giftedness is defined as an untrained, exceptional inborn ability, and talent, probably the most difficult to define, refers to an excellent mastery of an innate gift (Gagné, 2011; Renzulli, 1986). According to Gagné, those placed within the top 10% of a population are regarded as gifted or talented. Naturally, there are different criteria for the identification of giftedness for different age groups. As our review focuses on adult gifted learners, the most relevant information is who can be classified as gifted in this age group. Gifted adults are detected based on extraordinary achievements in a field of activity, which is estimated as a sufficient indicator of high abilities (Housand, 2009). This means that the evaluation is based on socially grounded subjective criteria. Two main factors contributing to the development of talent are adequate educational opportunities and high cognitive ability.

Summing up, giftedness and talent are relatively subjective terms, regarded as a continuum and identified based on various qualitative and quantitative criteria, including factors other than cognitive, such as resilience, motivation, perseverance, commitment and creativity and, the most important, high achievements in a given domain (Erard, 2012; Gagné, 2011; Hyltenstam, 2016c; Renzulli, 1986). Evidently, there is a gap between psychological terminology and research on giftedness in SLA. Hyltenstam (2016c), for example, raises a question whether polyglots possess a specific kind of intellectual functioning that differentiates them from individuals gifted in other domains. Due to this terminological ambiguity, researchers in the field of SLA use a variety of terms and perspectives referring to high achievers, such as ultimate attainment[1] (Birdsong, 2004; Bongaerts, 2005; Bylund, Hyltenstam, & Abrahamsson, 2013), native-like pronunciation (Birdsong, 2007), near-native ability (Doughty et al., 2010), extraordinary abilities (Hyltenstam, 2016c), giftedness (Biedroń, 2012; Biedroń & Pawlak, 2016), accomplished multilingualism (Biedroń & Szczepaniak, 2012), high-level language proficiency (Linck et al., 2013a), talent (Hu & Reiterer, 2009; Novoa, Fein, & Obler, 1988; Perani, 2005; Schneiderman & Desmarais, 1988), polyglotism (Hyltenstam, 2016a), hyperpolyglotism (Erard, 2012) and savantism (Smith, Tsimpli, Morgan, & Woll, 2011). These terms imply an exceedingly high level of FL aptitude of the subjects, on the one hand, and the potential for achieving a near-native level of competence in one or more languages, on the other. Unfortunately, this variability of angles is connected with inconsistency in research methodology and terminology and, consequently, terminological ambiguity.

Foreign Language Aptitude

According to Granena et al. (2016), SLA is intensely affected by individual variation, which concerns L2 learning outcomes, learning rate and processing. This variability has been ascribed to a variety of individual differences in cognitive abilities, among which FL aptitude comes to the fore. Recently, this factor has witnessed renewed enthusiasm across various disciplines of educational psychology, SLA and cognitive neuroscience (Wen, Biedroń, Skehan, 2017).

FL aptitude is now defined as an amalgamation of cognitive and perceptual abilities (i.e., aptitudes) (Robinson, 2007; Skehan, 1998; Yilmaz & Granena, 2016), an extremely high level of which indicates linguistic giftedness/talent (Biedroń, 2012; Biedroń & Pawlak, 2016; Hyltenstam, 2016b, 2016c). The concept of FL aptitude traditionally ascribed to its originator, Carroll (1959), has evolved strongly over the past 20 years, progressively becoming a hybrid construct related to a number of cognitive factors creating a composite gauge regarded as the general capacity to master a foreign language (cf. Dörnyei, 2005, p. 33; DeKeyser & Koeth, 2011). Among many theories of FL aptitude, Processing Stage Model by Skehan (1998, 2002, 2016) and Aptitude Complex Model by Robinson (2002) are considered the most influential ones. Both models include a number of different cognitive abilities, such as working memory, and noticing which contribute differently to learning outcomes at different processing stages and in different learning conditions. Recently, the focus of attention in this field has shifted to different types of memory and memory factors regarded as new FL aptitudes (Wen, 2016), which is also reflected in aptitude testing (Hi-Lab; Doughty et al., 2010; Linck et al., 2013a), where working memory is a predictor of high levels of proficiency in foreign language learning.

The Factor of Age in Ultimate Attainment

The discussion of attaining a near-native level in a foreign language is inevitably linked to the constraints imposed by critical periods/sensitive periods (CP/SP) (Long, 1990, 2013). In FL aptitude research, the factor of age is regarded as a crucial developmental aspect determining the ultimate attainment. Since Lenneberg (1967) presented his Critical Period Hypothesis (CPH), which claims that abilities to acquire an L2 after a certain age deteriorate, evidence for this has accumulated, which does not mean that there is no controversy surrounding this theory (Abrahamsson & Hyltenstam, 2008, 2009; Birdsong, 2007; DeKeyser, 2000; Harley & Hart, 1997; Long, 2005, 2013; Moyer, 2014; Muñoz & Singleton, 2011). Basically, the discussion revolves around an apparently uncontroversial claim that the consequence of starting to learn a foreign language after the closure of CP is non-native attainment in a foreign language. Studies on ultimate attainment have provided evidence for a negative correlation between the age of onset of acquisition and ultimate attainment of L2 proficiency (Abrahamsson & Hyltenstam, 2008, 2009; DeKeyser, 2000; Granena & Long, 2013). What is more, recorded native-like proficiency is usually limited to certain phonetic or morphosyntactic aspects of a foreign language (Birdsong, 2007, 2009; Bongaerts, van Summeren, Planken, & Schils, 1997; van Boxtel, Bongaerts, & Coppen, 2003).

Still, the argument whether it is or is not possible to gain a native-like proficiency level is as ardent as always.

CP or SP denotes the phase of heightened sensitivity when one can gain a native-like level of proficiency in a language. After the closure of this period, language learning ability deteriorates. Many researchers agree that this process is not rapid, but rather continuous and refers mainly to grammar and pronunciation, but there is no consensus regarding the beginning of the decline. Most probably there are multiple SPs for different linguistic areas. In Long's (2013) estimation, the shape representing the decline of SPs for learning an L2 resembles a stretched 'Z', where years of peak sensitivity occurring after birth precede a period of gradual decline, the offset, lasting until the end of the SP. After the offset there is a time when the decline is slower and less evident, and attainment depends on other factors, such as length of residence or amount of exposure. Contrary to CPs in animals, human sensitivity for language learning is characterized by residual plasticity after the end of the SP and is influenced by individual differences, such as FL aptitude, intelligence or motivation, as well as external possibilities, for example, exposure and training. That is why, according to Long (2013), it is more reasonable to refer to multiple SPs rather than one CP in an L2 learning.

Long (1990, 2013) represents a strong and stable position on the existence of SPs for language areas. For phonology the likelihood of attaining native-like level occurs at the age of 0 to 6, much earlier than for syntax and lexis, and after the age of 12 this probability equals zero. Phonological abilities are believed to be the most susceptible to the SPs. Even those speakers whose proficiency level is assessed as native-like usually fail to achieve native-like pronunciation, especially non-salient features (cf. Abrahamsson & Hyltenstam, 2009; Long, 1990). For syntax and morphology, the offset is a little more extended and lasts until the age of 15 plus or minus 2. Vocabulary acquisition, in general, is not limited by age effects and depends on other factors, such as literacy. However, idioms and collocations are the most difficult-to-master aspects of a foreign language, with the offset ending at the age of 9 to 10, even earlier than for morphosyntax (Abrahamsson & Hyltenstam, 2009; Long, 2013; Granena & Long, 2013).

Even though there is a cumulative body of evidence in favor of the CP, there are researchers who doubt its existence (Bialystok & Hakuta, 1994; Birdsong, 2004, 2007, 2009; Bongaerts, 2005; Singleton, 2014, 2017; van Boxtel et al., 2003). If there really was a CP for an L2, no second language learners with the age of onset after its closure should demonstrate achievement of native-like levels of ultimate L2 attainment (Bongaerts, 2005, p. 259). The opponents attribute adult learners' success to social, psychological and educational factors or to the effects of bilingualism (Birdsong, 2005). They quote a number of studies presenting evidence for high incidence of native-like attainment beyond the CP in both pronunciation and morphosyntax (Birdsong, 2006, 2007; Bongaerts, Mennen, & van der Silk, 2000; van Boxtel et al., 2003). According to Birdsong (2006), more than 20 studies reported the incidence of native-likeness up to 45% among late L2 learners. This opinion remains in contrast to the views of those researchers who consider exceptional foreign language learners, that is, those attaining native-like levels, evidence in support of the CPH due to the shortage of this phenomenon (Abrahamsson & Hyltenstam, 2008; DeKeyser, 2000; Long, 2013).

The rare incidence of adult native-like or near-native-like attainment in an L2 is in many studies attributed to an exceptional FL aptitude (Abrahamsson & Hyltenstam, 2008, 2009; DeKeyser, 2000; Harley & Hart, 1997; Ioup, Boustagui, El Tigi & Moselle, 1994; Novoa et al., 1988; Sawyer & Ranta, 2001). DeKeyser (2000) claims that adults have no access to implicit learning mechanisms so they have to rely on problem-solving skills, which are characterized by significant individual differences. Therefore, in contrast to children, who, independently of FL aptitude always achieve a native level of competence in an L1, only adults with above-average aptitude have a chance to be on a par with native speakers. This means that only adult learners with high verbal ability are able to bypass the constraints of the CP, whereas aptitude has no significance in ultimate attainment by children.

In contrast to DeKeyser's claim that child acquirers inevitably succeed in L2 learning, irrespective of their aptitude, Abrahamsson and Hyltenstam (2008, 2009) found that aptitude has small but significant effects in child SLA. They observed a significant correlation between L2 grammatical proficiency and FL aptitude among early L2 learners (the age of onset of 1 to 11 years). This tendency was absent among native controls. The researchers conclude that even for child L2 learners an early age of onset is not a guarantee that they will achieve full native-like proficiency. In Granena and Long's (2013) study, the results were less evident, as FL aptitude correlated with the ultimate attainment only if the age of onset was over 16 years, and only in pronunciation and lexis, but not in morphosyntax. These results are difficult to interpret and suggest that many questions related to the SP remain unanswered.

A body of neurological research offers indirect evidence in support of the CPH (Dehaene et al., 1997; Indefrey & Gullberg, 2006; Reiterer et al., 2011a, Reiterer, Pereda, & Bhattacharya, 2011b). Many studies confirmed that there are significant differences between even very proficient L2 speakers and native speakers and that absolutely native-like patterns in L2 learners are rarely found. Moreover, there are different neural correlates for an L1 and L2. Most studies have provided evidence that in contrast to an L1, which always activates the same areas in the left hemisphere, an L2 activates a more extended or bilateral areas of the brain (Dehaene et al., 1997). This observation is usually not ascribed to differences in FL aptitude, but to the age of onset and level of proficiency. In neurological studies (Kim, Relkin, Lee, & Hirsch, 1997; Golestani & Zatorre, 2004; Indefrey & Gullberg, 2006; Reiterer et al., 2011a, 2011b; Sebastián-Gallés et al., 2012; Wong, Perrachione, & Parrish, 2007), late-onset, low-proficiency L2 learners have exhibited greater right hemisphere activation, whereas in early-onset, more proficient learners the areas of L1 and L2 activation overlapped. This is because effort required in

L2 processing increases activation, which suggests that learners might compensate for lower efficiency in an L2 by driving particular brain regions more intensely or activating a bigger number of neurons to perform a task, whereas automatized activities involved in a more proficient language processing demand less effort and, accordingly, less activation. However, counter-evidence to the SP also exists.

In their recent study, Reiterer, Hu, Sumathi, and Singh (2013) challenge the existence of the CP in the field of phonetic aptitude in the case of very gifted learners, who, unlike average ones, seem to experience no interference in phonological learning from the L1 due to their higher neurocognitive flexibility. According to the researchers, these gifted learners seem to have avoided the CP constraints.

The Dynamic Character of FL Aptitude

Traditionally, FL aptitude was considered a stable and, consequently, untrainable inborn capacity (Carroll, 1981), a residue of L1 ability and skills (Skehan, 1986; Sparks, Humbach, Patton, & Ganschow, 2011). Nevertheless, its alleged stability is very poorly researched and has been regularly criticized over the last decade (Rogers et al., 2016; Meara, Barnett-Legh, Curry, & Davie, 2017; Sáfár & Kormos, 2008; Singleton, 2014, 2017). The most significant factor that is potentially capable of changing the magnitude of FL aptitude is the L2 learning experience, which is likely to have a training effect on FL aptitude test scores (Ganschow & Sparks, 1995; Sáfár & Kormos, 2008; Sparks, Ganschow, Artzer, & Patton, 1997). It has been found that learners with previous language learning experience outperformed inexperienced learners (Grigorenko, Sternberg, & Ehrman, 2000; Planchón & Ellis, 2014; Thompson, 2013; cf. Harley & Hart, 1997). Also, instruction significantly increased learners' scores on the MLAT and other FL aptitude tests (Ganschow & Sparks, 1995; Sáfár & Kormos, 2008; Sparks et al., 1997).

Evidence for FL aptitude increase as a result of instruction has accumulated over the last 20 years. A milestone in the discussion on FL aptitude trainability was research by Sparks and Ganschow (Ganschow & Sparks, 1995; Sparks & Ganschow, 1995; Sparks et al., 1997). They observed a long-term increase in not only FL aptitude scores but also L1 skills after L2 instruction. Grigorenko et al. (2000), based on Sternberg's (2002) triarchic theory of human intelligence, correlated a number of languages spoken with aptitude test scores (the CANAL FT). Results revealed that the larger the number of languages spoken, the higher the CANAL FT scores, which confirms the trainability effect of instruction. Sáfár and Kormos (2008) evaluated the effect of intensive L2 English instruction in a bilingual Hungarian high school. Results showed that the bilingual school students' L2 aptitude measures were significantly higher than the monolingual high school students. The authors attributed this result to intensive instructed language learning, which had a strong practice effect on L2 aptitude test scores.

Three studies investigated the link between multilingualism and FL aptitude test scores. Thompson's (2013) study confirmed that L2 learning experience leads to increases in FL aptitude test scores. Having investigated the relationship between multilingualism and FL aptitude, he found that multilinguals achieved significantly higher scores than bilinguals on a FL aptitude test (the CANAL FT, Grigorenko et al., 2000). It is worth emphasizing that multilinguals with even a slight L2 learning experience outperformed L2 learners with no other than English foreign language learning experience. A study conducted by Planchon and Ellis (2014) examined the effects of bilingualism and formal language training on FL aptitude test scores. This study provided evidence that bilinguals and learners with prior formal training performed better on the FL aptitude test (DLAB, Petersen & Al Haik, 1976) than monolinguals. The authors attributed this result to bilinguals' higher metalinguistic awareness as compared to the monolinguals. Finally, Rogers et al. (2017) attempted to investigate whether bilingualism, monolingualism and instructed foreign language learning would affect the LLAMA (Meara, 2005) scores. The results revealed that prior instruction in a foreign language can account for significant amounts of variance in LLAMA_B (6%) and LLAMA_F (2.6%). Evidently, language learning experience, that is, the number of languages learned and the proficiency achieved in each language, is a significant variable in FL aptitude test outcomes.

Singleton (2014, 2017), a persistent opponent of the CPH, is also questioning the concept of FL aptitude as a fixed trait. Especially in view of the possibility that working memory (Baddeley, 2003, 2015), which is believed to be modifiable as a result of experience and instruction (Gathercole & Alloway, 2008), is another kind of language aptitude (Linck, Osthus, Koeth, & Bunting, 2013b; Wen, 2016). Moreover, as Singleton (2017) emphasizes, the instruments to measure FL aptitude and language awareness appear to encapsulate to some extent the same constructs. Consequently, it appears impossible to make a clear boundary between the terms.

It seems that neurological research can confirm the possibility of the dynamic nature of FL aptitude. There are studies which explain variation in FL aptitude as a result of complementary influences of inborn predispositions and experience—dependent brain flexibility (Golestani, Price, & Scott, 2011; Reiterer et al., 2011a, Reiterer et al., 2011b). This means that although cognitive abilities are most probably inborn, expertise in learning languages affects the efficiency of the neural organization, which, in turn, enhances the learning potential.

Exceptionally Talented Learners

Despite an impressive number of studies in the literature describing exceptionally talented foreign language learners able to speak six, ten or over a hundred foreign languages, limited reliable data about this population are available. This is because most of these cases are anecdotal and based on subjective reports presented in popular science literature. In fact, as Biedroń and Pawlak (2016) observe, in the field of SLA, research into gifted and exceptionally talented language learners is scarce, and, as a result, little is known about this very varied population.

The phenomenon of near-native-like accomplishment in a foreign language is quite exceptional, whilst incomplete competence is a norm; therefore. the cases of accomplished multilinguals must evoke a great interest on the one hand and discussion on the other. Most recent records of talented individuals include those by Erard (2012, see also Chapter 8 in this volume) and Hyltenstam (2016b), both of which refer to their cognitive, personality and social characteristics, as well as learning strategies. Individuals presented by Hyltenstam and Erard are termed polyglots and hyperpolyglots and constitute both empirically scrutinized and anecdotal cases. Other scientific studies of high achievers refer to gifted multi-linguals (Biedroń, 2012; Ioup et al., 1994; Novoa et al., 1988; Schneiderman & Desmarais, 1988) and savants (Smith et al., 2011; Treffert, 2009, 2011).

Both scientists and laypeople have always wondered what makes the brains of talented individuals so exceptional. The first case studies (see Biedroń & Pawlak, 2016, for a review) explained exceptional language learning abilities in terms of greater neurocognitive flexibility and more bilateral language processing. There are four such case studies of gifted foreign language learners, namely two subjects examined by Schneiderman and Desmarais (1988), CJ (Novoa et al., 1988) and Julie (Ioup et al., 1994). Along with traditional ability measures, such as Wechsler Intelligence scales, the MLAT and other ability and personality tests, some of the subjects were compared against Geschwind and Galaburda's (1985) cluster. Geschwind and Galaburda proposed that there are clear individual differences in the degree of lateralization and its nature resulting from testosterone affecting the cortex at a particular point during the prenatal phase of development. Con-sequently, a cluster of features may co-occur, including an abnormal talent for languages. The cluster involves twinning, left-handedness, homosexuality, schizo-phrenia and allergies, among others. Some of these features were found in the studied individuals. Moreover, all the individuals capable of attaining a native-like proficiency level revealed superior verbal memory (also observed in other stud-ies of gifted learners and savants), an uneven profile of abilities and a not very impressive level of intelligence. Similar results were obtained in a study conducted by Biedroń (2012) on 44 gifted multilingual foreign language learners. The sub-jects excelled in cognitive ability tests, including FL aptitudes, intelligence and memory. Their general intelligence, as measured by the Wechsler scale, was high, with the score on the verbal scale (130) being higher than those on the nonverbal and memory scales (118 and 128, respectively). Their personality characteristics included open-mindedness, persistence, self-efficacy, creativity and high motiva-tion. Interestingly, all the aforementioned subjects share one more common char-acteristic, namely, passion for learning languages.

Polyglots constitute an especially fascinating population of gifted individuals, usually defined by the number of languages they speak proficiently. According to Hudson (2012), polyglots are people who are highly proficient in at least six languages. In a similar vein, Hyltenstam (2016c) defines them as people who added at least six languages to their repertoire after puberty and attained a high level of proficiency in all of them. An instantaneous reflection is what exactly is meant by 'highly proficient'? Hyltestam (2016a, p. 4) refers to situations where L2 learners achieve a level of ultimate attainment that is equal or close to that of native speakers. The latter is termed *nonperceivable non-nativeness* to describe apparent native-likeness, or a level of proficiency that cannot be distinguished from native in everyday communication and can only be identified through systematic examination (Abrahamsson & Hyltenstam, 2009). Obviously, the level of languages 'known' by polyglots is highly varied with respect to both the level of proficiency and the range of skills they master. Moreover, there are evident discrepancies between 'self-identified native-likness', that is, a self-image of a person who believes she or he can pass for a native speaker; 'perceived native-likeness', that is, how native speakers perceive the degree of native-likeness in a person; and 'scrutinized native-likeness', when the linguistic data are analyzed in detail (Abrahamsson & Hyltenstam, 2009). In the last case, only a few early learners and none of the late learners exhibit full native-likeness in all linguistic aspects. Erard (2012), based on his survey, commenced a term language super-learners, or *hyperpolyglots*, that is, people who can speak or use in reading or writing at least 11 languages, hence upgrading the standard number of 6 suggested by Hudson.

Many famous people can be found on lists of polyglots presented in the literature (see Erard, 2012; Hyltenstam, 2016b, 2016c, for a review), such as popes John Paul II and Benedict XVI and writers James Joyce, J.R.R. Tolkien and Anthony Burgess. There are also professional linguists, such as Rasmus Christian Rask (fluent in 25 and able to read in 35 languages), André Martinet (12 languages) and Kenneth Hale, who studied over 50 indigenous languages of America and Australia, as well as diplomats – for example, one of the most famous polyglots was Emil Krebs. Unfortunately, women are in the minority in this population. The best-known woman polyglot is Kató Lomb (1909–2003), a Hungarian scientist and translator who attempted to learn about 70 languages and was able to interpret in 9 or 10. It is worth emphasizing that researchers report an interesting tendency in subjects attaining near-native levels of proficiency in an L2, namely, they are keen on issues related to language and language learning (Abrahamsson & Hyltenstam, 2008, p. 500). Many of them chose academic careers connected with languages, for example, senior university students, teachers or professors (Bongaerts, 1999), as well as professional translators, interpreters, language teachers, linguists or language students (Abrahamsson & Hyltenstam, 2008; Biedroń, 2012; Hyltenstam, 2016c; van Boxtel et al., 2003).

Polyglots and hyperpolyglots share the same characteristics as other gifted individuals. Among cognitive factors are the following: extraordinary verbal memory, especially for words; high analytic abilities; superior executive functions; and phonological aptitude. The factor of intelligence is poorly studied; however, case studies indicate that their intelligence profiles are uneven, with dominance of verbal intelligence (Biedroń, 2012). As far as learning styles are concerned, polyglots seem to be systemizers (Baron-Cohen, 2002), which means that they tend to organize and systemize the learned material. They like to discover patterns and rules, make predictions and look for exceptions. It would seem they are able to engage in flow (Csikszentmihalyi, 1990) and actively search for this kind of experience. Flow is a state experienced by people utterly absorbed in a task and performing at the peak or beyond their limits, which involves experiencing spontaneous joy. The most promising source of information on polyglotism and linguistic talent is neurology. It transpires that certain inborn anatomical differences, as well as different patterns of activation of the brain, can indicate high levels of FL aptitude (see Biedroń, 2015, for a review).

Does polyglotism enhance linguistic talent? In many countries everybody is bi- or trilingual, for example, Belgium, where also a significant number of people enjoy learning foreign languages as a hobby. Obviously, a claim that they are all exceptionally gifted would be an overstatement. Two thirds of the hyperpolyglots in Erard's study (see Chapter 8) were raised in monolingual families. On the other hand, among 17 people who declared to have known over 11 languages, 11 were bilingual, which may imply that bilingualism can make a contribution to superb language learning abilities. Probably, all the factors — that is, above-average aptitude, bilingualism and expertise in learning languages — accumulate and, if accompanied by passion, can result in polyglotism. Summing up, a polyglot is most likely a highly linguistically talented person.

Savants constitute the most remarkable and extraordinary group of talented language learners. All of them possess highly selective memory, and many of them experience some symptoms of autism spectrum condition (ASC). There are two cases of linguistic savants described in the literature, namely Christopher Taylor (Smith et al., 2011) and Daniel Tammet (Treffert, 2011). Both possess extraordinary linguistic abilities accompanied by a number of physical and mental disorders.

Christopher, aged 55, is a linguistic savant able to communicate, write, read and translate in more than 20 languages. His intelligence level is low to such a degree that he is classified as mentally retarded, which makes him unable to look after himself. Daniel Tammet is a 37-year-old linguistic savant suffering from Asperger syndrome able to communicate in 11 languages. In contrast to Christopher, his intelligence level is normal. Both of them are characterized by ASC, which corresponds with the Extreme Male Brain Theory of Autism (Baron-Cohen, 2002), characterized by high systemizing skills, particular preferences, narrow interests and specific repetitive behaviors. Both savants possesses highly selective superior memory capacity. Daniel is profoundly gifted not only in languages but also in arithmetic computation. Interestingly, his talents appeared after a series of seizures in his early childhood, which places him among acquired savants, that is, people whose special talent appeared as a result of an injury or disease. Daniel is classified as a high-functioning autistic savant, who possesses one more talent, that is, synesthetic ability, as he can see numbers and words as colors. According to

Baron-Cohen et al. (2007) his savantism might be explained by hyperactivity in the left prefrontal cortex, which results from Asperger syndrome and synesthesia.

Conclusions

An exceptionally high level of foreign language aptitude termed linguistic gifted-ness or a talent for learning languages is a fascinating although poorly examined phenomenon in the field of SLA. Contrary to the concept of FL aptitude, linguistic talent is inadequately defined, quite subjective and, consequently, difficult to measure, which means that no clear criteria as to its categorization can be applied. Many terms are used in the literature to refer to individuals who attain very high levels of proficiency in foreign languages, including high achievers, gifted or exceptional foreign language learners, polyglots and hyperpolyglots. A very specific group of high achievers are savants, who are double exceptional, as they have an extreme gift for learning languages and ASC at the same time. Summing up, there is a high degree of variability and inconsistency, both in terminology and in measurement criteria of linguistic giftedness, which excludes any ultimate conclusions. However, some characteristics are consistently detected in all the described cases, namely absolutely exceptional but highly selective memory; talent for mimicking accents; analytical abilities, also reflected in systemizing style of processing information; and 'rage to master', that is, passion for learning languages.

There seem to be two areas of research that would shed some light on the phenomenon of linguistic talent, namely genetics and neurolinguistics. The role of the genetic factor in talent development and the impact of environment and personality as moderating factors are still inadequately examined. A number of questions are yet to be answered, for example: Are there any thresholds in the level of FL aptitude for linguistic talent to develop? Is linguistic talent different from other cognitive abilities? Another issue is neurological determinants of talent, in particular, anatomical differences between the brains of people with different levels of giftedness, both inborn and acquired. The third aspect worth further investigation is savantism, especially acquired savantism. The existence of acquired savants leads to another question: Does this rare and mysterious phenomenon suggest that we all have potential for linguistic genius?

Note

1 In L1 acquisition 'ultimate attainment' refers to adult native-like command of a language. In L2 acquisition the level of ultimate attainment can vary from near native-like to any lower level on the continuum (Hyltenstam, 2016a, p. 4).

References

Abrahamsson, N., & Hyltenstam, K. (2008). The robustness of aptitude effects in near-native second language acquisition. *Studies in Second Language Acquisition, 30*(1), 481–509. doi:10.1017/S027226310808073X

Abrahamsson, N., & Hyltenstam, K. (2009). Age of onset and native-likeness in a second language: Listener perception versus linguistic scrutiny. *Language Learning*, *59*(2), 249–306. Age of onset and native-likeness in a second language: Listener perception versus linguistic scrutiny. doi:10.1111/j.1467-9922.2009.00507

Baddeley, A. D. (2003). Working memory and language: An overview. *Journal of Communication Disorders*, *36*, 189–208. doi:10.1016/S0021-9924(03)00019-4

Baddeley, A. D. (2015). Working memory in second language learning. In Z. Wen, M. B. Mota, & A. McNeill (Eds.), *Working memory in second language acquisition and processing* (pp. 17–28). Bristol: Multilingual Matters.

Baron-Cohen, S. (2002). The extreme male brain theory of autism. *Trends in Cognitive Sciences*, *6*(6), 248–254. doi:10.1016/S1364-6613(02)01904-6

Baron-Cohen, S., Bor, D., Billington, J., Asher, J., Wheelwright, S., & Ashwin, C. (2007). Savant memory in a man with colour form–number synaesthesia and Asperger syndrome. *Journal of Consciousness Studies*, *14*, 237–251. doi:10.1.1.461.4133

Bialystok, E., & Hakuta, K. (1994). *Psychology of second-language acquisition*. New York, NY: Basic Books.

Biedroń, A. (2012). *Cognitive-affective profile of gifted adult Foreign language learners*. Słupsk: Wydawnictwo Akademii Pomorskiej w Słupsku.

Biedroń, A. (2015). Neurology of Foreign language aptitude. *Studies in Second Language Learning and Teaching SSLLT*, *5*(1), 13–40. doi:10.14746/ssllt.2014.5.1.2

Biedroń, A., & Birdsong, D. (forthcoming). Highly proficient and gifted bilinguals. In A. De Houwer & L. Ortega (Eds.), *The Cambridge handbook of bilingualism*. Cambridge, UK: Cambridge University Press.

Biedroń, A., & Pawlak, M. (2016). New conceptualizations of linguistic giftedness. *Language Teaching*, *49*(2), 151–185. doi:10.1017/S0261444815000439

Biedroń, A., & Szczepaniak, A. (2012). Working-memory and short-term memory abilities in accomplished multilinguals. *Modern Language Journal*, *96*, 290–306. doi:10.1111/j.1540-4781.2012.01332.x

Birdsong, D. (2004). Second language acquisition and ultimate attainment. In A. Davies & C. Elder (Eds.), *Handbook of applied linguistics* (pp. 82–105). London: Blackwell Publishing.

Birdsong, D. (2005). Native-likeness and non-native-likeness in L2A research. *International Review of Applied Linguistics in Language Teaching*, *43*, 319–328. doi:10.1515/iral.2005.43.4.319

Birdsong, D. (2006). Age and second language acquisition and processing: A selective overview. *Language Learning*, *56*, 9–49. doi:10.1111/j.1467-9922.2006.00353.x

Birdsong, D. (2007). Native-like pronunciation among late learners of French as a second language. In O. S. Bohn & M. J. Munro (Eds.), *Language experience in second language speech learning* (pp. 99–116). Amsterdam, The Netherlands: John Benjamins Publishing Company.

Birdsong, D. (2009). Age and the end state of second language acquisition. In W. Ritchie & T. Bhatia (Eds.), *The new handbook of second language acquisition* (pp. 401–424). Amsterdam, The Netherlands: Elsevier.

Bongaerts, T. (1999). Ultimate attainment in L2 pronunciation: The case of very advanced late L2 learners. In D. Birdsong (Ed.), *Second language acquisition and the critical period hypothesis* (pp. 133–159). Mahwah, NJ: Lawrence Erlbaum Associates, Inc.

Bongaerts, T. (2005). Introduction: Ultimate attainment and the critical period hypothesis for second language acquisition. *International Review of Applied Linguistics in Language Teaching*, *43*, 259–267. doi:10.1515/iral.2005.43.4.259

Bongaerts, T., Mennen, S., & van der Silk, F. (2000). Authenticity of pronunciation in naturalistic second language acquisition. The case of very advanced late learners of Dutch as a second language. *Studia Linguistica*, *54*, 298–308. doi:10.1111/1467-9582.00069

Bongaerts, T., van Summeren, C., Planken, B., & Schils, E. (1997). Age and ultimate attainment in the pronunciation of a Foreign language. *Studies in Second Language Acquisition, 19*, 447–465. doi:10.1017%2FS0272263197004026

Bylund, E., Hyltenstam, K., & Abrahamsson, N. (2013). Age of acquisition effects or effects of bilingualism in second language ultimate attainment? In G. Granena & M. H. Long (Eds.), *Sensitive periods, language aptitude, and ultimate L2 attainment* (pp. 69–101). Amsterdam, The Netherlands: John Benjamins Publishing Company.

Carroll, J. B. (1959). Use of the modern language aptitude test in secondary schools. *Yearbook of the National Council on Measurements Used in Education, 16*, 155–159.

Carroll, J. B. (1981). Twenty five years of research on Foreign language aptitude. In K. C. Diller (Ed.), *Individual differences and universals in language learning aptitude* (pp. 83–118). Rowley, MA: Newbury House.

Carroll, J. B., & Sapon, S. M. (1959, 2002). *Modern language aptitude test*. San Antonio, TX: The Psychological Corporation.

Csikszentmihalyi, M. (1990). *Flow: The psychology of optimal experience*. New York, NY: Harper Perennial.

Dehaene, S., Dupoux, E., Mehler, J., Cohen, L., Paulesu, E., Perani, D., . . . Le Bihan, D. (1997). Anatomical variability in the cortical representation of first and second language. *NeuroReport, 8*, 3809–3815.

DeKeyser, R. M. (2000). The robustness of critical period effects in second language acquisition. *Studies in Second Language Acquisition, 22*, 499–533. doi:10.1177/0956797611435921

DeKeyser, R. M., & Koeth, J. (2011). Cognitive aptitudes for second language learning. In E. Hinkel (Ed.), *Handbook of research in second language teaching and learning* (pp. 395–407). New York, NY: Routledge.

Dörnyei, Z. (2005). *The psychology of the language learner: Individual differences in second language acquisition*. Mahwah, NJ: Lawrence Erlbaum Associates, Inc.

Doughty, C. J., Campbell, S. G., Mislevy, M. A., Bunting, M. F., Bowles, A. R., & Koeth, J. T. (2010). Predicting near-native ability: The factor structure and reliability of Hi-LAB. In M. T. Prior, Y. Watanabe, & S. K. Lee (Eds.), *Selected proceedings of the 2008 second language research forum* (pp. 10–31). Somerville, MA: Cascadilla Proceedings Project. Retrieved from www.lingref.com, document #2382

Erard, M. (2012). *Babel no more: In search for the world's most extraordinary language learners*. New York, NY: Free Press.

Gagné, F. (2011). Understanding giftedness as the foundation for talents. In T. L. Cross & J. Riedl-Cross (Eds.), *Handbook for school counselors serving students with gifts and talents* (pp. 3–19). Waco, TX: Prufrock Press.

Ganschow, L., & Sparks, R. (1995). Effects of direct instruction in Spanish phonology on the native language skills and Foreign language aptitude of at risk Foreign language learners. *Journal of Learning Disabilities, 28*(2), 107–120. doi:10.1177/002221949502800205

Gathercole, S. E., & Alloway, T. P. (2008). Working memory and classroom learning. In K. Thurman & K. Fiorello (Eds.), *Cognitive development in K-3 classroom learning: Research applications* (pp. 15–38). Mahwah, NJ: Lawrence Erlbaum Associates, Inc.

Geschwind, N., & Galaburda, A. M. (1985). Cerebral lateralization. Biological mechanisms, associations, and pathology: I, II, III. A hypothesis and a program for research. *Archive of Neurology, 42*(5), 428–459, 521–552, 634–654.

Golestani, N., Price, C. J., & Scott, S. K. (2011). Born with an ear for dialects? Structural plasticity in the expert phonetician brain. *Journal of Neuroscience, 31*(11), 4213–4220. doi:10.1523/JNEUROSCI.3891-10.2011

Golestani, N., & Zatorre, R. J. (2004). Learning new sounds of speech: Relocation of neural substrates. *Neuroimage, 21*, 494–506. doi:10.1016/j.neuroimage.2003.09.071

Granena, G., & Long, M. H. (2013). Age of onset, length of residence, language aptitude, and ultimate attainment in three linguistic domains. *Second Language Research, 29*(1), 311–343. doi:10.1177/0267658312461497

Granena, G, Jackson, D. O., & Yilmaz, Y. (2016). Cognitive individual differences in second language processing and acquisition. In G. Granena, D. O. Jackson, & Y. Yilmaz (Eds.), *Cognitive individual differences in second language learning and processing* (pp. 1–14). Amsterdam, The Netherlands: John Benjamins Publishing Company.

Grigorenko, E. L., Sternberg, R. J., & Ehrman, M. E. (2000). A theory based approach to the measurement of Foreign language learning ability: The Canal F theory and test. *Modern Language Journal, 84*(3), 390–405.

Harley, B., & Hart, D. (1997). Language aptitude and second language proficiency in classroom learners of different starting ages. *Studies in Second Language Acquisition, 19*(3), 379–400.

Housand, A. M. (2009). Adult, gifted. In B. Kerr (Ed.), *Encyclopedia of giftedness, creativity and talent* (pp. 28–31). Thousand Oaks, CA: Sage Publications.

Hu, X., & Reiterer, S. (2009). Personality and pronunciation talent in second language acquisition. In G. Dogil & S. Reiterer (Eds.), *Language talent and brain activity: Trends in applied linguistics 1* (pp. 97–130). Berlin and New York, NY: Mouton de Gruyter.

Hudson, R. (2012). How many languages can a person learn? In E. M. Rickerson & B. Hilton (Eds.), *The five-minute linguist: Bite-sized essays on language and languages* (2nd ed., pp. 102–105). Sheffield: Equinox.

Hyltenstam, K. (2016a). Introduction: Perspectives on advanced second language proficiency. In K. Hyltenstam (Ed.), *Advanced proficiency and exceptional ability in second language* (pp. 1–13). Boston and Berlin: Mouton de Gruyter.

Hyltenstam, K. (2016b). The exceptional ability of polyglots to achieve high-level proficiency in numerous languages. In K. Hyltenstam (Ed.), *Advanced proficiency and exceptional ability in second language* (pp. 241–272). Boston and Berlin: Mouton de Gruyter.

Hyltenstam, K. (2016c). The polyglot—an initial characterization on the basis of multiple anecdotal accounts. In K. Hyltenstam (Ed.), *Advanced proficiency and exceptional ability in second language* (pp. 215–240). Boston and Berlin: Mouton de Gruyter.

Indefrey, P., & Gullberg, M. (2006). Introduction. In M. Gullberg & P. Indefrey (Eds.), *The cognitive neuroscience of second language acquisition* (pp. 1–8). Oxford: Blackwell Publishing.

Ioup, G., Boustagui, E., El Tigi, M., & Moselle, M. (1994). Re-examining the CPH. A case study of successful adult SLA in a naturalistic environment. *Studies in Second Language Acquisition, 16*, 73–98. doi:10.1017/S0272263100012596

Kim, K. H., Relkin, N. R., Lee, K. M., & Hirsch, J. (1997). Distinct cortical areas associated with native and second languages. *Nature, 388*(6638), 171–174. doi:10.1038/40623

Lenneberg, E. H. (1967). *Biological foundations of language.* New York, NY: Wiley.

Linck, J. A., Hughes, M. M., Campbell, S. G., Silbert, N. H., Tare, M., Jackson, S. R., & Doughty, C. J. (2013a). Hi-LAB: A new measure of aptitude for high-level language proficiency. *Language Learning, 63*, 530–566. doi:10.1111/lang.12011

Linck, J. A., Osthus, P. Koeth, J. T., & Bunting, M. F. (2013b). Working memory and second language comprehension and production: A meta-analysis. *Psychonomic Bulletin & Review, 21*(4), 861–883. doi:10.3758/s13423-013-0565-2

Long, M. H. (1990). Maturational constraints on language development. *Studies in Second Language Acquisition, 12*, 251–286. doi:10.1017/S0272263100009165

Long, M. H. (2005). Problems with supposed counter-evidence to the critical period hypothesis. *International Review of Applied Linguistics in Language Teaching, 43*, 287–317.

Long, M. H. (2013). Maturational constraints on child and adult SLA. In G. Granena & M. H. Long (Eds.), *Sensitive periods, language aptitude, and ultimate L2 attainment* (pp. 3–41). Amsterdam, The Netherlands: John Benjamins Publishing Company.

Meara, P. (2005). *LLAMA language aptitude tests: The manual*. Swansea: Lognostics.

Moyer, A. (2014). What's age got to do with it? Accounting for individual factors in second language accent. *Studies in Second Language Learning and Teaching. Special Issue: Age and More, 4*(3), 443–464. doi:10.14746/ssllt.2014.4.3.4

Muñoz, C., & Singleton, D. (2011). A critical review of age-related research on L2 ultimate attainment. *Language Teaching, 44*(1), 1–35. doi:10.1017/S0261444810000327

Novoa, L., Fein, D., & Obler, L. K. (1988). Talent in Foreign languages: A case study. In L. K. Obler & D. Fein (Eds.), *The exceptional brain: Neuropsychology of talent and special abilities* (pp. 294–302). New York, NY: The Guilford Press.

Perani, D. (2005). The neural basis of language talent in bilinguals. *Trends in Cognitive Sciences, 9*, 211–213. doi:10.1016/j.tics.2005.03.001

Petersen, C. R., & Al Haik, A. R. (1976). The Development of the Defense Language Aptitude Battery (DLAB). *Educational and Psychological Measurement, 36*(2), 369–380.

Planchon, A., & Ellis, E. (2014). A diplomatic advantage? The effects of bilingualism and formal language training on language aptitude amongst Australian diplomatic officers. *Language Awareness, 23*(3), 203–219.

Reiterer, S. M., Hu, X., Erb, M., Rota, G., Nardo, D., Grodd, W., . . . Ackerman, A. (2011a). Individual differences in audio-vocal speech imitation aptitude in late bilinguals: Functional neuro-imaging and brain morphology. *Frontiers in Psychology, 2*(271), 1–12. doi:10.3389/fpsyg.2011.00271

Reiterer, S. M, Hu, X., Sumathi, T. A., & Singh, N. C. (2013). Are you a good mimic? Neuro-acoustic signatures for speech imitation ability. *Frontiers in Psychology (Cognitive Science), 4*(782), 1–13. doi:10.3389/fpsyg.2013.00782

Reiterer, S. M., Pereda, E., & Bhattacharya, J. (2011b). On a possible relationship between linguistic expertise and EEG gamma band phase synchrony. *Frontiers in Psychology, 2*(334), 1–11. doi:10.3389/fpsyg.2011.00334

Renzulli, J. (1986). The three-ring conception of giftedness: A developmental model for creative productivity. In R. J. Sternberg & J. E. Davidson (Eds.), *Conceptions of giftedness* (pp. 53–93). Cambridge: Cambridge University Press.

Robinson, P. (2002). Learning conditions, aptitude complexes and SLA: A framework for research and pedagogy. In P. Robinson (Ed.), *Individual differences and instructed language learning* (pp. 113–133). Philadelphia, PA: John Benjamins Publishing Company.

Robinson, P. (2007). Aptitudes, abilities, contexts, and practice. In R. M. DeKeyser (Ed.), *Practice in second language* (pp. 256–286). Cambridge: Cambridge University Press.

Rogers, V. E., Meara, P., Aspinall, R., Fallon, L., Goss, T., Keey, E., & Thomas, R. (2016). Testing aptitude. *EUROSLA Yearbook, 16*(1), 179–210. doi:10.1075/eurosla.16.07rog

Rogers, V., Meara, P., Barnett-Legh, T., Curry, C., & Davie, E. (2017). Examining the LLAMA aptitude tests. *Journal of the European Second Language Association, 1*(1), 49–60. doi:10.22599/jesla.24

Sáfár, A., & Kormos, J. (2008). Revisiting problems with Foreign language aptitude. *International Review of Applied Linguistics in Language Teaching, 46*(2), 113–136. doi:10.1515/IRAL.2008.005

Sawyer, M., & Ranta, L. (2001). Aptitude, individual differences, and instructional design. In P. Robinson (Ed.), *Cognition and second language instruction* (pp. 319–354). Cambridge: Cambridge University Press.

Schneiderman, E. I., & Desmarais, C. (1988). A neuropsychological substrate for talent in second-language acquisition. In L. K. Obler & D. Fein (Eds.), *The exceptional brain: Neuropsychology of talent and special abilities* (pp. 103–126). New York, NY and London: The Guilford Press.

Sebastián-Gallés, N., Soriano-Mas, C., Baus, C., Díaz, B., Ressel, V., Pallier, C., . . . Pujol, J. (2012). Neuroanatomical markers of individual differences in native and non-native vowel perception. *Journal of Neurolinguistics, 25,* 150–162. doi:10.1016/j.jneuroling.2011.11.001

Singleton, D. (2014). Apt to change: The problematic of language awareness and language aptitude in age-related research. *Studies in Second Language Learning and Teaching, 4,* 557–571. doi:10.14746/ssllt.2014.4.3.9

Singleton, D. (2017). Language aptitude: Desirable trait or acquirable attribute? *Studies in Second Language Learning and Teaching, 7*(1), 89–103. doi:10.14746/ssllt.2017.7.1.5

Skehan, P. (1986). Where does language aptitude come from? In P. Meara (Ed.), *Spoken Language* (pp. 95–113). London: Centre for Information and Language Teaching: British Association of Applied Linguistics.

Skehan, P. (1998). *A cognitive approach to language learning.* Oxford: Oxford University Press.

Skehan, P. (2002). Theorizing and updating aptitude. In P. Robinson (Ed.), *Individual differences and instructed language learning* (pp. 69–95). Philadelphia, PA: John Benjamins Publishing Company.

Skehan, P. (2016). Foreign language aptitude. In G. Granena, D. O. Jackson, & Y. Yilmaz (Eds.), *Cognitive individual differences in L2 processing and acquisition* (pp. 381–395). Amsterdam, The Netherlands: John Benjamins Publishing Company.

Smith, N., Tsimpli, I., Morgan, G., & Woll, B. (2011). *The signs of a savant: Language against the odds.* Cambridge: Cambridge University Press.

Sparks, R., & Ganschow, L. (1993). The effects of multisensory structured language instruction on native language and Foreign language aptitude skills of at risk high school Foreign language learners: A replication and follow up study. *Annals of Dyslexia, 43,* 194–216. doi:10.1007/BF02928182

Sparks, R., & Ganschow, L. (1995). Parent perceptions in the screening of performance in Foreign language courses. *Foreign Language Annals, 28*(3), 371–391. doi:10.1111/j.1944-9720.1995.tb00806.x

Sparks, R. L., Ganschow, L., Artzer, M., & Patton, J. (1997). Foreign language proficiency of at risk and not at risk learners over 2 years of Foreign language instruction: A follow up study. *Journal of Learning Disabilities, 30*(1), 92–98. doi:10.1177/002221949703000108

Sparks, R. L., Humbach, N., Patton, J., & Ganschow, L. (2011). Subcomponents of second language aptitude and second language proficiency. *The Modern Language Journal, 95*(2), 253–273. doi:10.1111/j.1540-4781.2011.01176.x

Sternberg, R. J. (2002). The theory of successful intelligence and its implications for language aptitude testing. In P. Robinson (Ed.), *Individual differences and instructed language learning* (pp. 13–44). Amsterdam: Oxford University Press.

Thompson, A. S. (2013). The interface of language aptitude and multilingualism: Reconsidering the bilingual/multilingual dichotomy. *Modern Language Journal, 97,* 685–701. doi:10.1111/j.1540-4781.2013.12034.x

Treffert, D. A. (2009). The savant syndrome: An extraordinary condition. A synopsis: Past, present, future. *Philosophical Transactions of the Royal Society B, 364*(1522), 1351–1357. doi:10.1098%2Frstb.2008.0326

Treffert, D. A. (2011). *Daniel Tammet—Brainman: Numbers are my friends.* Retrieved from www.wisconsinmedicalsociety.org/savant_syndrome/savant_profiles/daniel_tammet

Van Boxtel, S., Bongaerts, T., & Coppen, P. A. (2003). Native-Like attainment in L2 syntax. In S. Foster-Cohen & S. Pekarek-Doehler (Eds.), *Eurosla yearbook 3* (pp. 157–181). University of Canterbury and University of Basel: John Benjamins Publishing Company. doi:10.1075/eurosla.3.10box

Wen, Z. (2016). *Working memory and second language learning: Towards an integrated* approach. Bristol: Multilingual Matters.

Wen, Z., Biedroń, A., & Skehan, P. (2017). Foreign language aptitude theory: Yesterday, today and tomorrow. *Language Teaching, 50*(1), 1–31. doi:10.1017/S0261444816000276

Wong, P. C. M., Perrachione, T. K., & Parrish, T. B. (2007). Neural characteristics of successful and less successful speech and word learning in adults. *Human Brain Mapping, 28*, 995–1006. doi:10.1002/hbm.20330

Yilmaz, Y., & Granena, G. (2016). The role of cognitive aptitudes for explicit language learning in the relative effects of explicit and implicit feedback. *Bilingualism: Language and Cognition, 19*(1), 147–161. doi:10.1017/S136672891400090X

PART III

Redefining Cognitive Constructs and Models

10

WORKING MEMORY AS LANGUAGE APTITUDE

The Phonological/Executive Model

Zhisheng (Edward) Wen

Introduction

In the post–Modern Language Aptitude Test (MLAT; Carroll & Sapon, 1959/2002) era, recurring calls to incorporate the cognitive construct of working memory (WM) as a central component of language aptitude have garnered the most prominence and become most widely accepted (e.g., McLaughlin, 1995; Miyake & Friedman, 1998; Sawyer & Ranta, 2001; Robinson, 2001, 2005; Wen & Skehan, 2011; Skehan, 1998, 2012; Kormos, 2013; Wen, 2012a, 2016; Wen, Biedroń, & Skehan, 2017). Since its inception in the mid-1990s, the proposal of 'WM as language aptitude' has now undergone some over 20 years in the making, and it has come of age to re-examine its rationale and underlying theoretical assumptions, its major arguments, and the supporting empirical evidence, as well as sorting out some remaining issues and looming caveats. These related issues constitute the major themes of this current chapter.

Towards this goal, in the following sections, I will first draw on interdisciplinary insights from cognitive science and language science to describe the WM system, including its nature, structure, and functions, in tandem with implications for general language acquisition and processing. This portrayal of the multiple-faceted WM construct as a language acquisition device (LAD) paves the ground for an integrated framework of WM-second language acquisition (SLA) in the second section. Drawing on previous research in cognitive psychology and SLA, I further examine two key WM components, i.e., phonological WM (PWM) and executive WM (EWM), as two key constructs of language aptitude in light of their distinctive contributions to the SLA process and products. These theoretical alignments of the two key WM components and associative functions with specific SLA domains and skills culminate in the overarching theoretical account, namely, the phonological/executive (P/E) model (Wen, 2012b, 2014, 2015, 2016).

The proposed P/E model consists of two key constructs of language aptitude that give rise to two major hypotheses regarding the distinctive effects of PWM and EWM on specific SLA domains and skills. Specifically, it is postulated that PWM is best conceived as a language learning device that underlies the acquisitional and long-term developmental aspects of L2 knowledge of phonemes, lexis, formulas, and morphosyntactic constructions, while EWM is best conceived as a language processing device that regulates and coordinates attentional resources implicated in L2 comprehension and production activities. Towards the end of the chapter, I recapitulate the perceivable advantages of the proposal of WM as language aptitude couched within the P/E model and further pinpoint some remaining issues and looming caveats. It is believed that through the phonological/executive WM perspective of language aptitude, we can further advance theory construction and methodological innovation in future aptitude research.

WM as a Language Acquisition Device?

The term WM first appeared in Miller, Galanter, and Pribram (1960) and generally refers to the ability to simultaneously store and process a small amount of relevant information in our immediate consciousness in order to complete a cognitive task (Baddeley, 1986; Cowan, 2005). Since the seminal model proposed by the British cognitive psychologists Baddeley and Hitch (1974), research interest into WM has grown exponentially. This is particularly so since the turn of the new century (as shown in Figure 10.1), rendering WM research a central topic in all subdisciplines of cognitive sciences (Miller, 2003) ranging from psychology, linguistics, neuroscience, and computer modeling to anthropology, philosophy, and beyond (Conway, Jarrold, Kane, Miyake, & Towse, 2007; Carruthers, 2013, 2015).

Research endeavors from multiple WM theoretical camps are continuously published, subsequently giving rise to a vibrant propagation of WM models and perspectives (Miyake & Shah, 1999; Andrade, 2001; Baddeley, 2012; Cowan, 2017). Notwithstanding, a review of the history of the evolution of the WM

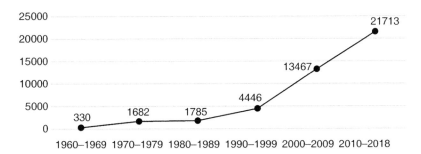

FIGURE 10.1 The number of publications from 1960 to 2018 with "working memory" entered as the search term in the PubMed database (March 2018)

concept and of the staggering number of accumulative literature has also revealed both consensus and controversies over its (a) nature, (b) structure and functions, and (c) inextricable relationship with long-term memory (Baddeley, 2012; Cowan, 2008, 2014, 2016; Jonides et al., 2008; Yuan, Steedle, Shavelson, Alonzo, & Oppezzo, 2006).

Despite controversies and debates, if we put aside the differences in research scope and emphasis, there is scope for compromise within these multiple perspectives with a view to arriving at some unifying characterizations of the WM construct that can be operationalized more readily in practically applied areas of human cognition such as language learning and processing (Wen, 2016; cf. Dehn, 2008; Fenesi, Sana, Kim, & Shore, 2015). More importantly, each of these unifying characterizations of WM can be reconceptualized as relevant for sustaining language acquisition, processing, and development, thus contributing to a comprehensive account of the WM-language association to be portrayed next.

How Do WM Limits Shape Human Language?

In terms of consensus and controversies over the nature of WM, most theoretical models agree that WM has a limited capacity (Conway et al., 2007). Indeed, given its permeating effects on so many essential aspects of human cognition, WM limitations have increasingly become a signature feature of the construct (Klingberg, 2008; Carruthers, 2013, 2015; Gruszka & Necka, 2017). More specifically, the limited capacity of WM manifests itself ostensibly in terms of (a) the restricted amount of information that can be held consciously in our head during task execution (i.e., the 'chunk capacity limit' as conceived by Cowan, 2008); and (b) the short duration of accessibility to this temporarily held information before it disappears completely from our immediate consciousness (i.e., the 'memory decay' conceived by Cowan, 2008).

However, controversies still linger over both properties of this characterization of WM. On the one hand, regarding the exact amount of information that can be held in focal attention, at least two well-known hypotheses regarding its quantification have been proposed, one being Miller's (1956) famous magical number "7 plus or minus 2" and the other being Cowan's (2001) smaller "4 plus or minus 1" (cf. though see Gobet & Clarkson's, 2004, for a magical number 2). On the other hand, WM theorists also disagree on the exact sources of the transient or fleeting nature of information temporarily stored in WM for processing, lasting for around 5 to 12 seconds (Waugh & Norman, 1965; cf. the 'Now or Never' bottleneck effect proposed by Christiansen & Chater, 2016), with some cognitive psychologists attributing this to "memory decay" (Cowan, 2008; Barrouillet & Camos, 2012, 2015; Camos & Barrouillet, 2018), whereas others opt for the "interference" view (Oberauer & Lewandowsky, 2013, 2014).

That said, when the extremes of these arguments are put aside, we can take a compromised stance to accommodate the disparate perspectives (Miyake & Shah,

1999). For example, based on the two views regarding the limited WM capacity, it is fair to say that most WM theorists would agree to accept that the capacity of WM can be set at between four chunks of unrelated items (Cowan's view) and seven units of information (Miller's view), thus arriving at a consensus, albeit compromised quantification of between four and seven. More relevantly for language, this limitation of WM is best conceived as a *universal constraint* on essential aspects of language acquisition and processing (in real time), exerting its pervasive effects on the emergence of such domains as phonology, vocabulary, idioms, or phrase, as well as morphosyntax (i.e., grammar) and even semantics (Jackendoff, 2007, 2011; O'Grady, 2012, 2017).

As a case in point, O'Grady (2017), in his recent commentary on the target article published by Pierce, Genesee, Delcenserie, and Morgan (2017 in *Applied Psycholinguistics*), has cited examples from English, Russian, and Korean to argue that WM limitations not only constrain phonology in language (as already discussed in extensive detail by Pierce et al., 2017) but also constrain the *character* and *acquisition* of many grammatical phenomena, such as the typology of word order and the interpretation of pronouns during language processing. In light of this universal feature of WM, O'Grady (2012) postulates that the limited WM capacity should be the *primary* factor in language design and acquisition, as opposed to being relegated as the *peripheral* ('third') factor by Chomsky (2005) that comes only after the first factor of universal grammar (UG) and the second factor of language experience (also, see Ellis, 2008).

Indeed, accumulating evidence from multiple perspectives seems to converge on the instrumental role of WM limitations in the emergence of variegated language structures and on the way they constrain or shape how human languages are acquired, comprehended, and produced. Some compelling evidence has emerged from recent studies in language typology and big-data corpus studies. For example, Lu (2011) has endorsed Miller's magical number 7 to postulate that any sequence of human speech at any given moment should comprise no more than seven linguistic chunks. For example, the sentence "John carefully read a dictionary in the library for hours yesterday", which is composed of the head noun "John" followed by six phrases (not exceeding seven!). To put it in another way, when the language processing activities go beyond our WM limitation (i.e., contain more than seven linguistic units), it will be extremely difficult, if not impossible, to process such material within our normal capacity. As such, the WM system (in this case, EWM) renders itself as a language processing or parsing device and should be the point of departure for any linguistic structure analysis (Lu, 2011).

In a similar vein, Jackendoff in his 'Parallel Architecture' (2007, 2011) has further proposed that linguistic WM should consist of three subdivisions, or 'departments', corresponding to the processing and construction of three grammatical structures (instead of just only focusing on the 'phonological loop' in Baddeley's classic model): (a) a phonological WM component for constructing and processing phonological structures, (b) a syntactic WM component for processing syntactic structures, and (c) a semantic WM component for processing semantic structures. Interpreted in this way, WM functions as the sort of 'workbench' or *'blackboard'* (Jackendoff, 2011, p. 13) where these grammatical structures are constructed and integrated online in a parallel manner. Unfortunately, WM seems to be held only as a fixed trait construct in this parallel architecture of language processing, and no clues are given as how to operationalize it in the framework.

In recent years, the situation has improved with the advent of big data. The fields of language sciences and cognitive sciences have witnessed large-scale cross-linguistic corpus studies investigating the grammar dependency and local-ity phenomena across a large number of language databases (Gibson, 1998, 2000; also see Futrell, 2017; Liu, 2008; Liu, Xu, & Liang, 2017 for more recent updates). Most of these studies have taken the fundamental assumption and the starting point of the universal constraint of WM capacity limitation (Ferrer-i-Cancho, 2017; Nicenboim, Vasishth, Gattei, Sigman, & Kliegl, 2015). For exam-ple, Liu (2008) measured the average minimum dependency distance (MDD) in 20 languages and found that all fell under the WM capacity of 4 (with Chinese having the greatest MDD of 3.662). In a more recent study, Futrell, Mahowald, and Gibson (2015) included 37 languages and found a similar pattern. Taken together, these large-scale studies shed compelling new light on the general principles of economy (i.e., 'the law of least efforts'; Zipf, 1949) and of com-pression or minimization (towards the tendency of MDD) in general language behavior (Roelcke, 2002), which are presumably all constrained by the lim-ited capacity of WM (Liu et al., 2017; Ferrer-i-Cancho, 2017; Chekaf, Gauvrit, Guida, & Mathy, 2018).

On the reverse side to the constrained WM limits, the two manifestations of the limited WM capacity naturally give rise to two related mechanisms that can be deemed as adaptive and responsive strategies to overcoming the constrain-ing effects of WM limitation through the evolution of language. One of these mechanisms, the *articulatory rehearsal* mechanism or, more recently, the procedure of 'repetition' or 'iteration' (Larsen-Freeman, 2012; cf. Majerus, 2013) is often associated with the phonological component of WM (in Baddeley's view), as it allows information to be maintained much longer before fading away. The other compensatory mechanism offsetting WM limits is the *chunking* process, which is claimed to underpin and facilitate the consolidation process of information in (phonological) WM to form larger units or chunks (Ellis, 1996, 1997, 2012, 2017; Chekaf et al., 2018). Chunking perceived in this way serves as an effective means to expand the limited capacity or span of WM, such as in the most famous case of expert chess playing (Gobet & Simon, 1998; Huang & Awh, 2018; Thalmann, Souza, & Oberauer, 2019).

Following these lines of development, I shall argue in later sections that these two mechanisms are part-and-parcel processes associated with phonological WM (PWM), which in turn carries significant implications for the acquisition and long-term development of key domains of language acquisition and processing such as vocabulary, formulaic sequences, and grammatical constructions in both native and second languages.

How Do WM Components and Functions Contribute to Language Learning?

The second important feature of WM that is simultaneously consensual and controversial concerns its overall design of structure or contents. To begin, Baddeley's structural view of WM (1986; Baddeley & Hitch, 1974) has been the standard model and the benchmark that has dominated most applications of the WM concept in both theoretical and practical aspects of human cognition (D'Esposito & Postle, 2015). In this classical and fractionated model (Baddeley, 1996, 2000), WM is conceived as consisting of four components. There are three storage components, or buffers, that serve to process modality-specific materials, namely, the sound-based phonological loop, the visual-spatial sketchpad, and the integrative episodic buffer. These storage buffers are in turn coordinated by a fourth supervisory component, the central executive whose main job is to regulate and coordinate attention among these storage buffers. Among these components, converging research in cognitive psychology and language sciences (psycholinguistics) has pointed to the essential roles played by the phonological loop and the central executive as being most directly linked to various language learning and processing activities in such areas as acquisition and development of vocabulary, reading comprehension, and production (Baddeley, 2003, 2015, 2017; Gathercole, 2007; Gathercole & Baddeley, 1993). As I shall argue in later sections, these two key WM components also constitute the key constructs of language aptitude to be proposed in this chapter.

In contrast to Baddeley's structural view, however, there is also the functional view of WM that is advocated by most North American–based cognitive psychologists. Two representative models that are often cited in the language science field include Cowan's embedded-processes model (1999, 2005) and the executive control model (e.g., Engle & Kane, 2004). These latter views of WM as attention or executive control are increasingly gaining prominence within cognitive science and seem to be particularly compatible with research findings in cognitive neuroscience (Conway, Moore, & Kane, 2009; Jonides et al., 2008). Accompanying these new trends in WM research is also a paradigm shift in research focus and methodology in language research, for example, from focusing on the phonological loop by the British researchers to focusing more on the central executive functions by North American WM researchers.

Despite such disagreements, these two views, that of WM-as-multiple-components and of WM-as-multiple-functions, can be considered as reflecting differences in research emphasis and scope. One can regard them as complementary rather than contradictory views on the same construct of WM. It can be further argued that an integration of both the structural and functional views that aligns

WM components and functions within a *hierarchical* order may prove to be both feasible and worthwhile to reach a more consensus view of WM that can be applied more readily in practical areas (e.g., Fenesi et al., 2015). In line with this integrative perspective on conceptualizing WM, first, its multiple components include the modality-specific short-term (ST) storage buffers/components plus the domain-general supervisory system (aka, the central executive in Baddeley's conception), while multiple WM mechanisms or functions associated with each WM component can serve as important guidelines for implementing more sensitive WM assessment procedures to measure more finer-grained WM functions (Indrarathne & Kormos, 2018). Such a *hierarchical* view of integrating WM components and functions lays the theoretical foundation for the conceptual framework for understanding and measuring the WM construct in the language sciences in general and in SLA in particular.

How Do WM and LTM Interact to Subserve Language?

Finally, the third characterization of the WM construct that is both consensual and controversial concerns the relationship between WM and the related component of long-term memory (LTM). Though Baddeley (1986, 2012, 2015) tends to distinguish between the two, many of his US counterparts (e.g., Cowan, 1999, 2008; Engle & Kane, 2004) consider WM embedded in LTM, sometimes as the *activated* or *focus-of-attention* portion of LTM (Ruchkin, Grafman, Cameron, & Berndt, 2003). Despite these different stances, it is fair to postulate LTM as playing an integral role in WM and that WM and LTM interact to subserve human cognition as a whole.

Except for a small part of WM that can be considered a special portion of activated LTM and thus embedded therein (Cowan, 1999; cf. LT-WM; Ericcson & Kintsch, 1995; Caplan & Waters, 2013), WM itself as a memory subsystem should still distinguish itself from the permanent LTM system (Norris, 2017; though see Jones & Macken, 2015, 2018 for a different view on the somewhat blurry WM–LTM distinction). LTM is purported to consist of a knowledge-based or fact-based declarative component and a process- or skill-based procedural component (i.e., the 'Declarative/Procedural' model conceived by Ullman, 2001, 2016). As such, future research may need to further explore how WM and LTM interact to subserve SLA. From this perspective, the declarative and procedural WM model as proposed by Oberauer (2009, 2010) may be a way forward.

For the time being, an apt analogy for understanding the WM–LTM relationship is to postulate WM as a gateway to LTM, though how information travels between them (e.g., bidirectionally) remains to be investigated. That said, it is argued here that the WM system is best conceived as possessing first-order short-term storage components and second-order domain-general executive functions, while LTM is best conceived as a permanent storage or a warehouse that virtually holds everything that we know (e.g., including L1 competence and L2 knowledge). More relevant for language acquisition and processing, both WM and LTM may make distinctive contributions in that WM relates more to real-time or online processing aspects of language, while LTM is mainly responsible for storage or representational aspects in the long term. As we shall argue in the next section, such a distinction of the separate roles between WM and LTM carries significant implications for distinguishing the WM effects on the three dimensions of L2 acquisition, processing, and developmental domains, *as opposed to* LTM that is the permanent store or warehouse of L2 knowledge repertoire or L2 proficiency.

Summing Up the WM–Language Association

In summary, the WM construct is now reconceptualized, consistent with existing perspectives and models, and thus can be understood as a *primary* memory subsystem (along with its *secondary* subsystem of LTM) that is composed of multiple components (Baddeley's structural view) and multiple executive functions (Cowan's functional view). The first of these signals a more top-down approach, and the second implicates a more fine-grained bottom-up approach. Overall, it is argued that such a *hierarchical* view of the WM construct (as consisting of multiple components and then associative functions) should have important implications for both theory construction (in terms of integrating with such practical fields as language) and research methodology (in terms of assessment procedures) when it is being conceptualized and implemented in such applied research fields as language research in general (this section) and in SLA research in particular, a theme that will figure more prominently in the next section.

WM and SLA: An Integrated Framework

Building on the discussion of the WM–language association from the previous section, we now turn to extend our integrative perspective to explain the relationship between WM and SLA. To begin with the definition of the two key constructs in the 'WM–SLA nexus' (Wen, 2012b, 2016), the WM system is conceptualized as a multifaceted construct consisting of multiple *components* (which are modality based, following Baddeley's view), with each component encompassing multiple associative mechanisms and executive *functions* (though nonexecutive processes and functions are sometimes possible as well, following the North American tradition; see Dehn, 2008; Cogan et al., 2017). In other words, the current framework adopts a *multifaceted* and hierarchical view of WM as consisting of multiple components and functions (Wen, 2015, 2016; cf. Oberauer, Su¨ß, Schulze, Wilhelm, & Wittmann, 2000; Oberauer , Su¨ß, Wilhelm, & Wittmann, 2003).

Building on these insights, an integrative framework for conceptualizing and measuring WM in SLA research can be constructed (see Figure 10.2 adapted from Wen, 2016). Such an architecture is inspired by Baddeley's recent perspective on the

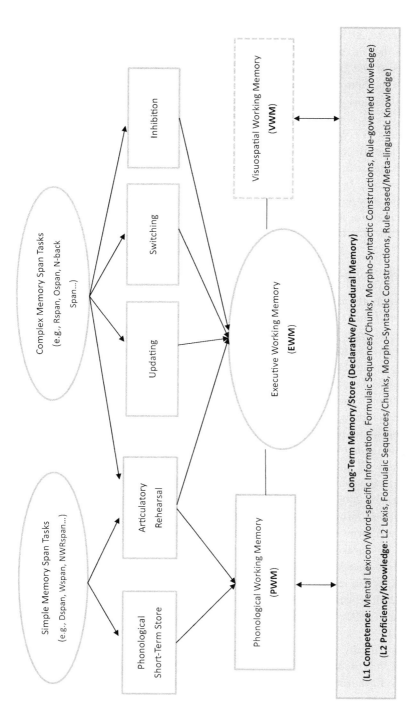

FIGURE 10.2 An integrated framework for WM and SLA (based on Wen, 2016)

WM–LTM distinction as manifested in the blueprint of 'LTM<-->WM<-->Action' (Baddeley, 2015). As demonstrated in the figure, the architecture consists of five levels that aim to integrate LTM (Level I) and Level II (pinning down WM components) and Level III (specifying WM functions with SLA domains and skills). From the bottom level to the top, these comprise Level I, which refers to long-term memory (LTM) that holds L2 proficiency, including an activated portion of LT-WM (the intersecting portion between WM and LTM); Level II, which includes key WM components (PWM, VWM, and EWM) that are fractionated from the overall WM construct; and Level III that encompasses the putative mechanisms/functions associated with each WM component (PWM and EWM in this case). Level IV includes the specification of WM span tasks for measuring the two key putative WM components (PWM and EWM), and Level V indicates SLA domains and skills in real-world practice. Each of these levels and their features are discussed in the following sections.

Level I: Long-Term Memory and L2 Proficiency

At the bottom level lies LTM, and this serves as a permanent storehouse for various forms of long-term knowledge of the two languages (L1 and L2) in the bilingual brain of an (imagined) L2 learner. Supposedly, LTM includes *inter alia*, the bilingual speaker's native language (aka, L1 competence), which subsumes, for example, the mental lexicon and grammatical competence that include phonological knowledge (the sound system), lexical knowledge (individual words or phrases), morphology (knowledge of word formation), semantics (concepts or meanings of words and sentences), and syntax (sentence structures), as well as discourse and pragmatic knowledge (text composition), etc.

Alongside this L1 competence, LTM in the bilingual brain also subserves the learners' L2 knowledge and/or L2 proficiency, though how L1 and L2 coexist in the bilingual brain is still a debatable issue (Li, Farkas, & MacWhinney, 2004; Abutalebi, 2008; Green & Abutalebi, 2013; Abutalebi & Green, 2016; Hamrick, Lum, & Ullman, 2018). In slight contrast to the more implicit L1 mental lexicon and grammatical competence (largely automatic in terms of access or retrieval), bilingual speakers' L2 knowledge or proficiency tends to be more restricted (in terms of knowledge of mental lexicon and mental grammar) and more controlled or explicit in nature, that is, usually constrained by more effortful access or slower retrieval, depending on the developmental stages of L2 proficiency (e.g., see Harrington, 1992; McLaughlin, 1995; Miyake & Friedman, 1998; Wen & Skehan, 2011).

Specifically, organization of the repertoire of L2 knowledge or L2 proficiency in LTM is postulated to encompass various levels of L2 representational domains (lexis, formulas, morphosyntax, Ellis, 1996, 2012; Martin & Ellis, 2012) and L2 processing or use domains (listening, speaking, reading, writing, and translation/interpreting; Wen, 2016; cf. VanPatten, 2013). For example, acquisitional and developmental SLA domains can include, *inter alia*, L2 phonemes (speech sounds and pronunciation), L2 lexis (words or vocabulary items), L2 formulaic sequences (fixed phrases or open-slot expressions), L2 morphosyntactic constructions (morphological and syntactic structures), L2 semantics (meaning mappings of word forms and sentences), L2 grammatical and metalinguistic knowledge (e.g., explicit rules of grammar in L2), and L2 pragmatic knowledge (e.g., Bardovi-Harlig, 2013).

Of most relevance and importance, LTM—as conceptualized in the integrated framework—also contains the activated items of bilingual speakers' L1 and L2 knowledge in WM (the overlapping blurry part of WM and LTM), which can be labeled LT-WM, as opposed to the short-term WM components in the next level (Caplan & Waters, 2013). This idea draws heavily on the LT-WM perspective advocated and pursued by Ericsson and Kintsch (1995) and on the recent reincarnation of the concept in language processing research by Caplan and Waters (2013). Then, in terms of its overall organization, LTM (including LT-WM) in the integrative framework embraces and incorporates the declarative and procedural components in light of the D/P model (Ullman, 2001, 2005, 2016; also Morgan-Short, this volume; cf. Coolidge & Wynn, 2009, 2013). Despite the controversies about the exact nature and structure of the bilingual mind/brain (e.g., Abutelabi, 2008; Abutalebi, Cappa, & Perani, 2001), increasing evidence from multiple disciplines and sources (e.g., behavioral, neurological, genetic, and developmental) is consistent with this declarative/procedural distinction of LTM knowledge in the bilingual brain (cf. Green & Abutalebi, 2013; Paradis, 2009; Hamrick et al., 2018).

More specifically, for example, as conceived in the D/P model of Ullman (2001, 2005, 2016), the declarative memory system mainly subserves idiosyncratic knowledge of the mental lexicon, which includes lexical items and word-specific information such as simple words, irregulars, and complements. In contrast, the procedural memory system is postulated to underlie the rule-governed linguistic knowledge that corresponds more to the grammatical elements, which probably include the rule-governed hierarchical and sequential composition of complex forms. That said, it remains to be seen whether bilingual learners' L1 and L2 knowledge systems reside in the same area of the brain (Li et al., 2004; Abutalebi, 2008; Altarriba & Isurin, 2013; Hamrick et al., 2018).

Level II: WM Components

The mid-level of the integrated architecture consists of the multiple WM components and associated functions that can be fractionated from the general WM system as conceived in Baddeley's (1986, 2003, 2012) multicomponent model and demarcated executive functions based on WM control models (Cowan, 1999, 2005; Engle & Kane, 2004). Following Baddeley's insights (2003, 2015), WM components should include the phonological short-term memory (PWM), the visuospatial sketchpad (VWM), and the episodic buffer (EB), as well as the executive aspects of WM (EWM) that regulate attention among the other buffers.

Although an activated portion of LTM (the overlapping part of WM and LTM) can be deemed a 'special' part of WM (aka, LT-WM; Caplan & Waters, 2013), it is not considered the same as other regular ST-WM components discussed here.

As for other ST-WM components, such as VWM, EB, etc., due to the lack of research and understanding of their roles in current SLA, they are temporarily excluded from the current integrative framework. Even so, the exclusion of VWM, EB, and LT-WM does not indicate their complete absence in SLA. Rather, it is mainly because their respective roles in SLA have not yet been thoroughly studied (as opposed to the two well-established WM components, PWM and EWM; Baddeley, 2003, 2015; Wen, 2015, 2016) that they are excluded. That said, future research in WM and SLA should indeed be directed towards elucidating these relationships. Rudner and Rönnberg (2008), for example, have attempted to explore the links between EB and language processing, so future research can further explore whether such a relationship exists between EB and SLA as well. In a similar vein, although the role of visual WM has received much attention in neuroscientific research with language (which is beyond the scope and focus of the current chapter), relatively few studies have examined its specific role in SLA (cf. Baddeley, 2015). At a purely speculative level, Baddeley (2015, p. 25) hypothesizes its possible role in the acquisition of novel scripts such as those used in Arabic, Hebrew, or Chinese. Similarly, Juffs and Harrington (2011, p. 160), also mention that future WM–SLA research can indeed focus on 'replicable measures of WM in new areas in writing in non-alphabetic scripts', such as Chinese. In light of these insights, more empirical research needs to be conducted so that these underexplored WM components can be incorporated into the current portrayal of the WM–SLA nexus (Wen, 2016).

Based on well-established research syntheses and meta-analyses (Juffs & Harrington, 2011; Linck, Osthus, Koeth, & Bunting, 2014), only two key ST-WM components, namely PWM and EWM, will be highlighted in the integrated framework of WM and SLA, constituting the key constructs of language aptitude. More specifically, as revealed in the meta-analysis of 79 empirical studies (Linck, Osthus, et al., 2014), both WM components were found to be associated with L2 proficiency and learning outcomes (r = .25), though a relatively higher correlation for EWM (r = .27) was found compared to PWM (r = .17), indicating a stronger relationship between the former. As we shall argue, there may be many factors accounting for the overall weak correlation between WM and SLA, and one possible reason can be related to the inconsistency and insensitivity of WM measures adopted in these empirical studies (Wen & Li, 2019; Wen & Juffs, forthcoming).

Level III: WM Mechanisms and Functions

This mid-level of the integrated framework also depicts the multiple mechanisms and executive functions that are associated with the two key WM components discussed earlier (i.e., PWM and EWM). The putative mechanisms associated with PWM (equivalent to Baddeley's phonological loop) encompass a *phonological short-term store* (or phonological memory as it is sometimes called) and *the articulatory rehearsal mechanism* (Baddeley, 1986, 1996, 2012, 2015; Baddeley & Hitch, in press). Indeed, accumulating research pioneered by British WM researchers (Baddeley, Gathercole, etc.) has demonstrated that PWM (usually measured via a simple memory span task such as the nonword repetition span task (Gathercole, Willis, Baddeley, & Emslie, 1994; Gathercole, 2006) is a 'language learning device' in learning novel phonological forms (Baddeley, Gathercole, & Papagno, 1998) and that it plays an instrumental role in various domains and learning activities in native language acquisition and development (Gathercole & Baddeley, 1993; Baddeley et al., 1998), as well as in SLA (Ellis, 1996, 2012; Juffs & Harrington, 2011; Sagarra, 2013; Williams, 2012).

Currently, most SLA researchers have conceptualized PWM as a broad WM component (rather than focusing on the two individual submechanisms) to investigate its effects on L2 learning, especially its role in L2 vocabulary and L2 grammar learning (Wen & Li, 2018). One obvious exception is Ellis and Sinclair (1996), who demonstrated that the articulatory rehearsal mechanism of PWM plays an important role in acquiring vocabulary and syntax. Overall, research from a broad range of disciplines (e.g., psychology, linguistics, education, neuroscience) has confirmed that individual differences (IDs) in PWM are closely linked to variations in language learning outcomes, such as lexis (e.g., Service, 1992; Cheung, 1996), collocations or formulaic chunks (e.g., Foster, Bolibaugh, & Kotula, 2014; Skrzypek, 2009), and grammatical development (French & O'Brien, 2008; O'Brien et al., 2006, 2007), among diverse groups of both typical and nontypical developmental learners (Pierce et al., 2017). Future research can further demarcate the two associative mechanisms of PWM and elucidate their respective roles in SLA domains.

Then, EWM (usually measured via the complex version of memory span tasks such as the reading span task by Daneman & Carpenter, 1980, the operation span task of Turner & Engle, 1989, and their variants) is purported to regulate attention monitoring or control processes, which subsumes such executive functions as information *updating, switching,* and *inhibition* (Miyake & Friedman, 2012; also see Indrarathne & Kormos, 2017). Similar to the situation with PWM, most previous SLA research has merely focused on conceptualizing EWM as a broad WM component (especially among North American WM researchers) to tap its overall effects on SLA, especially, in the L2 subskills learning of listening, speaking, reading, writing, and translation/interpreting, thus rendering it a 'language processing device' or 'language parser' (Wen et al., 2013, 2015; Wen, 2015, 2016; cf. Lu, 2011).

Finally, it is noteworthy that among current empirical studies of WM-SLA (Linck, Osthus, et al., 2014; Wen et al., 2013, 2015; Wen, 2016), very few studies have investigated the individual effects of each of these fine-grained EWM functions (updating, switching, and inhibition) on SLA separately. The few exceptions include studies conducted by Gass and Lee (2011) and Gass, Behney, & Uzum (2013), which found a positive role of inhibitory control in L2 interactions and L2 proficiency in tandem with PWM (cf. Linck & Weiss, 2015). Most recently, Indrarathne and Kormos (2017) corroborated that these combined EWM functions (indexed as a composite EWM score based on separate measures) play a larger role in the acquisition of productive knowledge in explicit learning conditions than implicit conditions. The authors indicate that future research could aim to further examine how these three operations of EWM functions are interrelated and interact with PWM.

Level IV: WM Measures and Procedures

Having identified the two key WM components (Level II) and their associated mechanisms and functions (Level III), the next level of the integrative framework considers corresponding WM measures that can be implemented in nuanced SLA research in the real world. In terms of measuring WM, Dehn (2008, p. 58) has commented, "Until research and measurement tools allow us to further delineate WM processes, it might be safest to define WM as what simple and complex WM span tasks measure". Following Dehn's (2008) suggestion, it is stipulated by the integrative framework that we should adopt separate memory span tasks for assessing PWM and EWM, respectively. Specifically, the 'simple memory span' tasks (e.g., the digit span task and the nonword repetition span task) are postulated to measure PWM, whereas versions of the 'complex memory span' tasks (e.g., the reading span task and its variants, the operation span task, the running memory span task and the N-back span task, etc.) should be adopted to assess EWM.

The rationale for advocating separate measures for assessing the PWM and EWM components builds on discussions of WM–language association in the previous sections (also Conway et al., 2005; Linck, Osthus, et al., 2014). For example, research conducted by British/European WM researchers has demonstrated that the nonword repetition span task approximates the putative mechanisms associated with PWM in the L1 (Gathercole, 2006) and in the L2 (see Ellis, 1996, 2012). On the other hand, numerous studies by the North American WM researchers have demonstrated the close relationships between complex memory span tasks and the attention-regulating or executive areas of WM in language learning (e.g., Daneman & Carpenter, 1980; Turner & Engle, 1989). Conway et al. (2005) conducted reviews of major WM measures and provided general guidelines for administering WM assessment procedures in cognitive psychology, while Juffs (2006), Linck, Osthus, et al.(2014), and Leeser & Sunderman (2016) offered additional insights on implementing WM measures in SLA research (also see Wen, 2016; Wen & Juffs, in preparation).

Another implication from Dehn's comments is that, though currently the simple and complex versions of WM measures are specified by the integrative framework, additional research would be needed to further delineate distinct

WM processes or functions associated with the two components of PWM and EWM. This suggestion is compatible with the recent trend of the increasingly dominant *functional* view of WM (as distinguished from the classical multicomponent view). In particular, more research is necessary to implement WM measures in SLA before the two fields can be integrated more successfully (Wen, 2012b, 2016). For instance, most extant WM measures adopted in current SLA studies are borrowed from the cognitive psychology field, though they have been mainly designed and constructed with monolinguals instead of bilinguals in mind (both the simple version of nonword repetition and complex version of reading span task, etc.). It may sound reasonable to measure WM in the native language, but whether these WM measures are equally applicable for L2 research is an empirical question that needs to be subjected to further scrutiny. Some previous studies have found positive correlations between L1 and L2 WM spans, whereas others have not. Such inconclusive results of the associations between L1- and L2-based WM await further clarification and empirical investigation. Above all, it becomes imperative to tease apart the different hierarchical factors (e.g., information type, encoding modality, and encoding language; Cai & Dong, 2012) influencing the outcomes of WM measures to be implemented in SLA (Wen & Juffs, in preparation).

Level V: SLA Domains and Skills in Action

Besides the appropriate choices of WM measures, the WM–SLA framework is also intended to shed light on 'real-world practice', thus providing insights on how SLA domains and skills are executed in fine-grained research. Presumably, key SLA domains and skills can be categorized to include (a) mental representational domains, which are related to the L2 knowledge or proficiency stored in LTM and likely encompass phonology, lexis, formulas, and morphosyntactic constructions, semantics, and pragmatics, plus L2 metalinguistic knowledge (as opposed to automatic or implicit grammatical knowledge among monolinguals' metalinguistic competence), etc.; and (b) online processing or real-time use aspects of this repertoire of L2 knowledge as manifested in L2 subskills, which likely subsume comprehension processes implicated in listening and reading, as well as production processes implicated in speaking and writing (in this sense, interpreting and translation can be considered a special case of comprehension plus production; Wen, 2016; also see Dong & Wang, 2013).

Within the integrative framework of WM and SLA, it is argued in the following sections that the phonological/executive WM perspective provides insights on three key aspects of the SLA process and learning outcomes: (a) the acquisition(al)/learning aspect, (b) the processing/performance/use aspect, and (c) the long-term developmental aspect (Wen, 2016; cf. VanPatten, 2013). As such, the next section outlines how these two WM components constitute essential constructs of language aptitude and the theoretical and methodological implications therein.

Phonological and Executive WM as Language Aptitude: A Reappraisal

As already discussed in the previous section, the PWM component, conceived as a key construct of language aptitude, can be further demarcated into a phonological short-term store and the articulatory rehearsal mechanism. In addition, PWM has been claimed to play an instrumental role in *acquiring* novel phonological forms and that its two associative mechanisms facilitate the *chunking* process of linguistic sequences of different levels ranging from phonemes, words, and phrases to morphosyntactic constructions. Thus, it is hypothesized by the P/E model that PWM mainly underlies the *acquisitional* and *developmental* aspects of SLA domains such as vocabulary, phrases or formulaic sequences, and morphosyntactic constructions or grammatical structures (Wen, 2016).

Indeed, accumulating evidence from diverse disciplines of cognitive psychology, developmental psycholinguistics, and neurophysiology has pointed to the instrumental role of PWM not just in native language acquisition and development (Cogan et al., 2016; Pierce et al., 2017) but also in L2 acquisition and development of *lexis*, *formula*, and *constructions* among both young and adult L2 learners (Foster et al., 2014; Ellis, 1996, 2012; Wen, 2015, 2016), with its effects particularly evident in early stages of L2 learning, such as among those *ab initio*, beginning- and intermediate-level L2 learners (Serafini & Sanz, 2016; Li, 2017). Thus, a positive association can now be firmly established between PWM and these specific SLA representational domains (especially vocabulary, formulas, and grammar) in both naturalistic settings and laboratory studies, especially among child L2 learners (e.g., Cheung, 1996; Service, 1992; French & O'Brien, 2008). Taken together, these empirical studies lend support to the proposal of our major argument that PWM be considered a *language acquisition device* (Wen, 2016; cf. Baddeley et al., 1998).

Unlike the PWM, which handles *modality-specific* (i.e., sound-based) materials, the executive component of WM (EWM; equivalent to the central executive as originally conceived in the M-model by Baddeley) is purported to subsume such fine-grained executive functions as (information) *updating, task switching,* and *inhibitory control* (Miyake & Friedman, 2012). These *domain-general* functions of EWM are likely to affect attention allocation and supervising or monitoring aspects during language processing activities, especially during some real-time or online performance dimensions (Skehan, 2015) and selective (especially cognitively demanding) offline processes. As such, it is hypothesized in the P/E model that EWM is likely to be essential for subserving some *cognitively demanding aspects* of SLA processing activities and subskill learning during sentence processing and discourse comprehension, production, and interactions. In this sense, EWM is best conceived as a *language processing device*, or simply, a *language processor* within the proposal of WM as language aptitude (Wen, 2016; cf. Lu, 2011, 2012).

Theoretical and Methodological Implications

When compared with previous theories and models of L2 aptitude (e.g., Carroll's four-factor view, 1981, 1990, 1993; Grigorenko et al.'s CANAL-F model, 2000; Sparks's LCDH hypothesis, 1995; Robinson's aptitude complexes view, 2005, 2013; Skehan's macro-SLA aptitude view, 2012, 2016, this volume; the Hi-LAB model by Doughty, 2014 and Linck, Hughes, et al., 2014), the proposal of PWM and EWM as language aptitude has achieved some degree of breakthrough in that it not only allows researchers to *predict* fairly accurately the SLA products or outcomes (Li, 2017 & this volume; Wen et al., 2017; Wen & Li, 2019) but also provides a comprehensive and thorough explanation of its wide-ranging effects on L2 acquisition, processing, and development. In other words, the *explanatory* utility of WM as a component of L2 aptitude in SLA has been greatly enhanced (Wen, 2016; Wen et al., 2017).

As has been mentioned elsewhere (Wen, 2016; Wen et al., 2017), this innovative approach to 'explaining' the process of SLA (Snow, 1992) rather than just 'predicting' the *speed or rate* of L2 learning outcomes (Carroll, 1962, 1981, 1990) could represent a fundamental shift in research focus and a significant theoretical advance in contemporary language aptitude research (Wen et al., 2017). As such, the construct validity and ecological validity of the concept of language aptitude could be enhanced (Li, 2015, 2016), thus rendering WM a *central* topic in individual differences research (Williams, 2015) and in current SLA (R. Ellis, 2004 & Foreword to this volume). For this reason, it may be argued that the proposal of the P/E model of WM as language aptitude constitutes what Richard Snow (1992) has called 'an aptitude theory for tomorrow' (Wen, 2016; Wen et al., 2017). Following Snow's framework, future research should further investigate the pedagogical and clinical implications of WM as language aptitude.

Caveats and Future Directions

As argued earlier, the demarcation of PWM and EWM as two distinctive constructs of language aptitude also raises concerns regarding questionable procedures in measuring WM in SLA (Wen, 2016; Wen & Juffs, in preparation.). For example, some previous studies have opted to obtain a standardized 'composite Z-score of WM' by combining and averaging simple memory span tasks (such as the non-word repetition span task indexing PWM) and complex memory span tasks (such as the operation span task tapping EWM). As explicated in the P/E model, PWM and EWM make distinctive contributions to SLA, so such a practice may run the risk of confounding the differential effects of the two separate WM components. In this case, it may not be advisable to measure WM by combining PWM and EWM span tasks to arrive at a composite WM score in future WM–SLA studies.

On a more speculative level, though, considering the central features of SLA, which implies that a bilingual learner will have two languages at his or her own disposal as opposed to first language acquisition when the speaker is a monolingual, the practice of obtaining a composite score may still be worth exploring provided that it is not combining PWM and EWM (e.g., Wen, 2016). Instead, such a composite score can be obtained from two WM span tasks that are implemented in participants' L1 and L2. That is to say, a composite score that takes into account the bilingual speakers' L1 and L2 WM, i.e., their 'bilingual WM score', then, may tap into the same component or the same function associated with a particular component. In essence, these concerns touch on two core issues: (a) whether WM should be considered a domain-specific or a domain-general construct and what the implications of this are for assessment procedures; and (b) whether a bilingual WM score thus obtained also implicates the effects of LTM or L2 proficiency (cf. Service, Simola, Metsnheimo, & Maury, 2002). For the first issue, it is clear that the P/E perspective accommodates both positions by postulating PWM as domain specific (modality based) and EWM as domain general. For the second issue, the P/E perspective assumes LTM or L2 proficiency will play an integral role in WM performance. That said, future research still needs to solve thorny issues such as how various internal or external factors (information type, encoding modality, encoding language, bilingualism or L2 proficiency, etc.) may affect WM scores in SLA research (e.g., Cai & Dong, 2012).

More importantly, as postulated by the integrative framework, the P/E perspective on language aptitude also suggests that it is not enough to focus just on testing the two WM components (i.e., PWM and EWM) as in most current WM–SLA empirical studies (Linck, Osthus, et al., 2014; Li, this volume; Wen & Li, 2018). Instead, future research should also be directed towards designing more sensitive assessment procedures that will tap into finer-grained WM mechanisms and functions (as shown in Table 10.1). For example, Indrarathne and Kormos (2018) have demonstrated how a number of well-established WM assessment procedures

TABLE 10.1 Measuring WM in SLA: From components to functions

WM Components	Measures of WM Components	WM Mechanisms and Functions	Measures of WM Mechanisms or Functions
PWM	Simple (storage-only) memory span tasks (e.g., digit span, nonword repetition span, etc.)	Phonological short-term store	Serial recall task (e.g., digit span, letter span, nonword span, etc.)
		Articulatory rehearsal mechanism	Articulatory suppression
EWM	Complex (storage plus processing) memory span tasks (e.g., reading span, operation span, etc.)	WM updating	Running memory span/keep track task
		Task switching	Task-switching numbers/the plus-minus task
		Inhibitory control	Antisaccade/Stroop

in cognitive psychology can be implemented to measure putative EWM functions. Overall, positive results have been found regarding their effects on specific L2 learning conditions such as explicit and implicit learning of novel grammar structures. That is, failure to record positive effects of the two WM components should not be taken as conclusive evidence for the null effects of WM, in that the lack of evidence may be due to methodological pitfalls (cf. Calvo, Ibáñez, & García, 2016). Future WM–SLA research needs to further refine WM measures to be implemented in SLA.

Another caveat concerning current WM–SLA research practice was postulated by Juffs (2017) in his recent commentary responding to the target article by Pierce et al. (2017) featuring the relationship between PWM and early language input and development among both typical and nontypical developmental learners. As Juffs argues, the evidence presented by Pierce et al. (2017) suggests that PWM may be an epiphenomenon (i.e., a by-product) arising out of individual differences (IDs) in the robustness and richness of phonological representations in language development, thus rendering the concept of PWM redundant. Juffs also offered suggestions as to how researchers might test this proposal experimentally or in a corpus of child language to dissociate the relationship between phonology and PWM (cf. Service, 1992). Obviously, more empirical studies need to examine the extent to which this claim can be substantiated.

Finally, there is much room for research regarding the reverse relationship between WM and aspects of SLA or bilingualism. For example, instead of looking only at the potential effects or contributions of WM on SLA, future studies can also work out the potential effects of bilingualism on WM (e.g., Calvo et al., 2016). In another line of development, within task-based language teaching (TBLT), though the positive effects of WM have been confirmed (Wen, 2016), how task characteristics and conditions can be designed to overcome the WM limitations in mediating task performance merits further investigation (Ellis, 2019; Skehan, 2015).

Conclusion

To conclude, this chapter has argued that the key tenet and perceivable advantage of proposing "WM as language aptitude" lie in its postulation that the cognitive construct of WM consists of multiple components that can be further demarcated into more finer-grained mechanisms and functions that contribute distinctively to the process of SLA and learning outcomes. More specifically, the two key WM components, PWM and EWM, together with their associative mechanisms and functions, constitute two key constructs of language aptitude that are playing important roles in specific SLA domains and skills. The P/E WM perspective on language aptitude offers a comprehensive account for *predicting* and *explaining* the process and product of L2 acquisition, processing, and development (Wen & Li, 2018; Wen et al., 2017). Furthermore, it was postulated in the P/E model that, given their distinctive contributions to SLA, PWM and EWM should be separately measured in fine-grained WM–SLA studies by implementing separate WM assessment procedures for each. In particular, simple memory span tasks should be adopted to measure PWM, while complex memory span tasks should be used to measure EWM. In addition, it was suggested that future research should develop more sensitive WM measures that tap into finer-grained WM mechanisms and functions. Overall, it was argued that PWM is best conceived as a 'language learning device' and EWM as a 'language processing device' and that both WM components constitute essential constructs within language aptitude. Using the P/E WM perspective, it is hoped that future language aptitude research can be based on a stronger platform for advancing theory, assessment, research, and practice.

References

Abutalebi, J. (2008). Neural aspects of second language representation and language control. *Acta Psychologica, 128*(3), 466–478.

Abutalebi, J., Cappa, S. F., & Perani, D. (2001). The bilingual brain as revealed by functional neuroimaging. *Bilingualism: Language and Cognition, 4*, 179–190.

Abutalebi, J., & Green, D. W. (2016). Neuroimaging of language control in bilinguals: Neural adaptation and reserve. *Bilingualism: Language and Cognition, 19*, 689–698.

Altarriba, J., & Isurin, L. (2013). *Memory, language, and bilingualism: Theoretical and applied approaches.* Cambridge: Cambridge University Press.

Andrade, J. (2001). *Working memory in perspective.* Hove, England: Taylor & Francis.

Atkins, P. W. B., & Baddeley, A. D. (1998). Working memory and distributed vocabulary learning. *Applied Psycholinguistics, 19*, 537–552.

Baddeley, A. D. (1986). *Working memory.* Oxford: Oxford University Press.

Baddeley, A. D. (1996). The fractionation of working memory. *Proceedings of the National Academy of Sciences, USA, 93*, 13468–13472. doi:10.1073/pnas.93.24.13468

Baddeley, A. D. (2000). The episodic buffer: A new component of working memory? *Trends in Cognitive Sciences, 4*, 417–423.

Baddeley, A. D. (2003). Working memory and language: An overview. *Journal of Communication Disorders, 36*(3), 189–208.

Baddeley, A. D. (2012). Working memory: Theories, models and controversies. *Annual Review of Psychology, 63*, 1–30.

Baddeley, A. D. (2015). Working memory in second language learning. In Z. Wen, M. Mota, & A. McNeill (Eds.), *Working memory in second language acquisition and processing* (pp. 17–28). Bristol: Multilingual Matters.

Baddeley A. D. (2017). Modularity, working memory and language acquisition. *Second Language Research, 33*(3), 299–311.

Baddeley, A. D., Gathercole, S. E., & Papagno, C. (1998). The phonological loop as a language learning device. *Psychological Review, 105*, 158–173.

Baddeley, A. D., & Hitch, G. (1974). Working memory. In G. A. Bower (Ed.), *The psychology of learning and motivation* (Vol. 8). New York, NY: Academic Press.

Baddeley, A. D., & Hitch, G. J. (in press). The phonological loop as a buffer store: An update. *Cortex.* doi:10.1016/j.cortex.2018.05.015

Bardovi-Harlig, K. (2013). Developing L2 pragmatics. *Language Learning, 63*, 68–86.

Barrouillet, P., & Camos, V. (2012). As time goes by: Temporal constraints in working memory. *Current Directions in Psychological Science, 21*(6), 413–419.

Barrouillet, P., & Camos, V. (2015). *Working memory: Loss and reconstruction.* Hove: Psychology Press.

Cai, R., & Dong, Y. (2012). Effects of information type, encoding modality, and encoding language on working memory span: Evidence for the hierarchical view (In Chinese). *Foreign Language Teaching and Research, 44*(3), 376–388.

Calvo, N., Ibáñez, A., & García, A. M. (2016). The impact of bilingualism on working memory: A null effect on the whole may not be so on the parts. *Frontiers in Psychology, 7,* 265. doi:10.3389/fpsyg.2016.00265

Camos, V., & Barrouillet, P. (2018). *Working memory in development.* London: Routledge.

Caplan, D., & Waters, G. S. (2013). Memory mechanisms supporting syntactic comprehension. *Psychological Bulletin & Review, 20*(2), 243–268.

Carroll, J. B. (1962). The prediction of success in intensive Foreign language training. In R. Glaser (Ed.), *Training research and education.* Pittsburgh, PA: University of Pittsburgh Press.

Carroll, J. B. (1981). Twenty-five years of research on Foreign language aptitude. In K. C. Diller (Ed.), *Individual differences and universals in language learning aptitude.* Rowley, MA: Newbury House.

Carroll, J. B. (1990). Cognitive abilities in Foreign language aptitude: Then and now. In T. Parry & C. W. Stansfield (Eds.), *Language aptitude reconsidered* (pp. 11–29). Englewood Cliffs, NJ: Prentice-Hall.

Carroll, J. B. (1993). *Human cognitive abilities: A survey of factor-analytic studies.* Cambridge: Cambridge University Press.

Carroll, J. B., & S. Sapon (1959, 2002). *Modern Language Aptitude Test (MLAT).* New York, NY: The Psychological Corporation. (Reprinted in 2002 by Second Language Testing Inc).

Carruthers, P. (2013). The evolution of working memory. *Proceedings of National Academy of Sciences, 110* (Suppl 2), 10371–10378.

Carruthers, P. (2015). *The centered mind: What the science of working memory shows us about the nature of human thought.* Cambridge: Cambridge University Press.

Chekaf, M., Gauvrit, N., Guida, A., & Mathy, F. (2018). Compression in working memory and its relationship with fluid intelligence. *Cognitive Science, 42,* 904–922.

Cheung, H. (1996). Nonword span as a unique predictor of second-language vocabulary learning. *Developmental Psychology, 32*(5), 867–873.

Chomsky, N. (2005). Three factors in language design. *Linguistic Inquiry, 36*(1), 1–22.

Christiansen, M. H., & Chater, N. (2016). *Creating language: Integrating evolution, acquisition, and processing.* Cambridge, MA: MIT Press.

Cogan, G. B., Iyer, A., Melloni, L., Thesen, T., Friedman, D., Doyle, W., Devinsky O, Pesaran, B. (2017). Manipulating stored phonological input during verbal working memory. *Nature Neuroscience, 20*(2), 279–286. doi:10.1038/nn.4459

Conway, A. R. A., Jarrold, C., Kane, M. J., Miyake, A., & Towse, J. N. (Eds.). (2007). *Variation in working memory.* New York, NY: Oxford University Press.

Coolidge, F. L., & Wynn, T. (2009). *The rise of Homo sapiens: The evolution of modern thinking.* Oxford: Oxford University Press.

Coolidge, F. L., & Wynn, T. (2013). The evolution of working memory. In T. P. Alloway & R. G. Alloway, (eds.), *Working memory: The connected intelligence* (pp. 37–60). New York: Taylor & Francis Group.

Conway, A. R. A., Moore, A. B., & Kane, M. J. (2009). Recent trends in the cognitive neuroscience of working memory. *Cortex, 45*(2), 262–268.

Conway, A., Kane, M., Bunting, M., Hambrick, D., Wilhelm, O., & Engel, R. (2005). Working memory span tasks: A methodological review and user's guide. *Psychonomic Bulletin & Review, 12,* 769–786.

Cowan, N. (1999). An embedded-processes model of working memory. In A. Miyake & P. Shah (Eds.), *Models of working memory: Mechanisms of active maintenance and executive control* (pp. 62–101). Cambridge, UK: Cambridge University Press.

Cowan, N. (2001). The magical number 4 in short-term memory: A reconsideration of mental storage capacity. *Behaviour and Brain Sciences, 24,* 87–185.

Cowan, N. (2005). *Working memory capacity.* New York, NY and Hove: Psychology Press.

Cowan, N. (2008). What are the differences between long-term, short-term, and working memory? *Progress in Brain Research, 169,* 323–338.

Cowan, N. (2014). Working memory underpins cognitive development, learning, and education. *Educational Psychology Review, 26,* 197–223.

Cowan, N. (2017). The many faces of working memory and short-term storage. *Psychonomic Bulletin & Review, 24,* 1158–1170. doi:10.3758/s13423-016-1191-6

Daneman, M., & Carpenter, P. A. (1980). Individual differences in working memory and reading. *Journal of Verbal Learning and Verbal Behaviour, 19,* 450–466.

Dehn, M. J. (2008). *Working memory and academic learning: Assessment and intervention.* Hoboken, NJ: John Wiley & Sons, Inc.

D'Esposito, M., & Postle, B. R. (2015). The cognitive neuroscience of working memory. *Annual Review of Psychology, 66,* 115–142.

Dong, Y., & Wang, B. (2013). General versus interpretation-specific language comprehension and production: A two-stage account of the interpreting process (in Chinese). *Chinese Translators Journal* (1), 19–24.

Doughty, C. (2014). Assessing aptitude. In A. Kunnan (Ed.), *The companion to language assessment* (pp. 25–46). Oxford, UK: Wiley-Blackwell.

Ellis, N. C. (1996). Sequencing in SLA: Phonological memory, chunking and points of order. *Studies in Second Language Acquisition, 18,* 91–126.

Ellis, N. C. (1997). The epigenesis of language: Acquisition as a sequence learning problem. In A. Ryan & A. Wray (Eds.), *Evolving models of language: British studies in applied linguistics* (pp. 41–57). Clevedon: Multilingual Matters.

Ellis, N. C. (2008). Phraseology: The periphery and the heart of language. Preface to F. Meunier & S. Granger (Eds.), *Phraseology in language learning and teaching* (pp. 1–13). Amsterdam, The Netherlands: John Benjamins Publishing Company.

Ellis, N. C. (2012). Formulaic language and second language acquisition: Zipf and the phrasal Teddy Bear. *Annual Review of Applied Linguistics, 32,* 17–44.

Ellis, N. C. (2017). Chunking. In M. Hundt, S. Mollin, & S. Pfenninger (Eds.), *The changing english language: Psycholinguistic perspectives* (pp. 113–147). Cambridge: Cambridge University Press.

Ellis, N. C., & Sinclair, S. G. (1996). Working memory in the acquisition of vocabulary and syntax: Putting language in good order. *The Quarterly Journal of Experimental Psychology, 49A*(1), 234–250.

Ellis, R. (2004). Individual differences in second language learning. In A. Davies & C. Elder (Eds.), *The handbook of applied linguistics* (pp. 525–551). Oxford: Blackwell Publishing.

Ellis, R. (2019). Task preparedness. In Wen, Z. & Ahmadian, M. (eds.). *Researching L2 task performance and pedagogy in honour of Peter Skehan.* Amsterdam: John Benjamins.

Engle, R., & Kane, M. (2004). Executive attention, working memory capacity, and a two-factor theory of cognitive control. In B. Ross (Ed.), *The psychology of learning and motivation* (Vol. 44, pp. 145–199). New York, NY: Elsevier.

Ericsson, K. A., & Kintsch, W. (1995). Long-term working memory. *Psychological Review, 102*, 211–245.

Fenesi, B., Sana, F., Kim, J. A., & Shore, D. (2015). Reconceptualizing working memory in educational research. *Educational Psychology Review, 27*(2), 333–351.

Ferrer-i-Cancho, R. (2017). A commentary on "The now-or-never bottleneck: A fundamental constraint on language", by Christiansen and Chater (2016). *Glottometrics, 38*, 116–120.

Foster, P., Bolibaugh, C., & Kotula, A. (2014). Knowledge of nativelike selections in an L2: The influence of exposure, memory, age of onset and motivation in Foreign language and immersion settings. *Studies in Second Language Acquisition, 36*(1), 101–132.

French, L. M., & O'Brien, I. (2008). Phonological memory and children's second language grammar learning. *Applied Psycholinguistics, 29*, 463–487.

Futrell, R. (2017). *Memory and locality in natural language* (Ph.D. thesis), Massachusetts Institute of Technology, Cambridge, MA.

Futrell, R., Mahowald, K., & Gibson, E. (2015). Large-scale evidence of dependency length minimization in 37 languages. *Proceedings of the National Academy of Sciences, 112*(33), 10336–10341.

Gass, S., Behney, J., & Uzum, B. (2013). Inhibitory control, working memory, and L2 interaction gains. In K. Drozdział-Szelest & M. Pawlak (Eds.), *Psycholinguistic and sociolinguistic perspectives on second language learning and teaching* (pp. 91–114). Berlin: Springer Verlag.

Gass, S., & Lee, J. (2011). Working memory capacity, inhibitory control, and proficiency in a second language. In M. Schmid & W. Lowie (Eds.), *From structure to chaos: Twenty years of modeling bilingualism: In honor of Kees de Bot* (pp. 59–84). Amsterdam, The Netherlands: John Benjamins Publishing Company.

Gathercole, S. E. (2006). Nonword repetition and word learning: The nature of the relationship. *Applied Psycholinguistics, 27*(4), 513–543. doi:10.1017.S0142716406060383

Gathercole, S. E. (2007). Working memory and language. In G. Gaskell (Ed.), *Oxford handbook of psycholinguistics* (pp. 757–770). Oxford: Oxford University Press.

Gathercole, S., & Baddeley, A. (1993). *Working memory and language*. Hove, UK: Lawrence Erlbaum Associates.

Gathercole, S. E., Willis, C. S., Baddeley, A., & Emslie, H. (1994). The children's test of nonword repetition: A test of phonological working memory. *Memory, 2*(2), 103–127.

Gibson, E. (1998). Linguistic complexity: Locality of syntactic dependencies. *Cognition, 68*, 1–76.

Gibson, E. (2000). The dependency locality theory: A distance-based theory of linguistic complexity. In Y. Miyashita, A. Marantz, & W. O'Neil (Eds.), *Image, language, brain* (pp. 95–126). Cambridge, MA: MIT Press.

Gobet, F., & Clarkson, G. (2004). Chunks in expert memory: Evidence for the magical number four ... or is it two? *Memory, 12*, 732–747. http://dx.doi.org/10.1080/09658210344000530

Gobet, F., & Simon, H. A. (1998). Expert chess memory: Revisiting the chunking hypothesis. *Memory, 6*, 225–255.

Green, D. W., & Abutalebi, J. (2013). Language control in bilinguals: The adaptive control hypothesis. *Journal of Cognitive Psychology, 25*, 515–530.

Grigorenko, E. L., Sternberg, R. J., & Ehrman, M. (2000). A theory-based approach to the measurement of Foreign language aptitude: The CANAL-F theory and test. *Modern Language Journal, 84*, 390–405.

Gruszka, A., & Necka, E. (2017). Limitations of working memory capacity: The cognitive and social consequences. *European Management Journal, 35*(6), 776–784.

Hamrick, P., Lum, J. A. G., & Ullman, M. (2018). Child first language and adult second language are both tied to general-purpose learning systems. *Proceedings of the National Academy of Sciences (PNAS), 115*(7), 1487–1492. doi:10.1073/pnas.1713975115

Harrington, M. (1992). Working memory capacity as a constraint on L2 development. In R. J. Harris (Ed.), *Cognitive processing in bilinguals* (pp. 123–135). Amsterdam, The Netherlands: North Holland.

Huang, L., & Awh, E. (2018). Chunking in working memory via content-free labels. *Scientific Reports, 8*, 23. doi:10.1038/s41598-017-18157-5

Indrarathne, B., & Kormos, J. (2017). Attentional processing of input in explicit and implicit conditions: An eye-tracking study. *Studies in Second Language Acquisition, 39*, 401–430.

Indrarathne, B., & Kormos, J. (2018). The role of working memory in processing L2 input: Insights from eye-tracking. *Bilingualism: Language and Cognition, 21*, 355–374.

Jackendoff, R. (2007). A Parallel Architecture perspective on language processing. *Brain Research, 1146*, 2–22.

Jackendoff, R. (2011). What is the human language faculty? Two views. *Language, 87*, 586–624.

Jones, G., & Macken, B. (2015). Questioning short-term memory and its measurement: Why digit span measures long-term associative learning. *Cognition, 144*, 1–13.

Jones, G., & Macken, B. (2018). Long-term associative learning predicts verbal short-term memory performance. *Memory & Cognition, 46*(2), 216–229. doi:10.3758/s13421-017-0759-3

Jonides, J., Lewis, R. L., Nee, D. E., Lustig, C. A., Berman, M. G., & Moore, K. S. (2008). The mind and brain of short-term memory. *Annual Review of Psychology, 59*, 193–224.

Juffs, A. (2006). Working memory, second language acquisition and low-educated second language and literacy learners. *LOT Occasional Papers: Netherlands Graduate School of Linguistics*, 89–104.

Juffs, A. (2017). The importance of grain size in phonology and the possibility that phonological working memory is epiphenomenal. *Applied Psycholinguistics, 38*(6), 1329–1333.

Juffs, A., & Harrington, M. (2011). Aspects of working memory in L2 learning. *Language Teaching, 44*, 137–166.

Klingberg, T. (2008). *The overflowing brain: Information overload and the limits of working memory*. Oxford: Oxford University Press.

Kormos, J. (2013). New conceptualizations of language aptitude in second language attainment. In G. Granena & M. Long (Eds.), *Sensitive periods, language aptitude, and ultimate L2 attainment* (pp. 131–152). Amsterdam, The Netherlands: John Benjamins Publishing Company.

Larsen-Freeman, D. (2012). On the roles of repetition in language teaching and learning. *Applied Linguistics Review, 3*, 195–210.

Leeser, M., & Sunderman, G. (2016). Methodological issues of working memory tasks for L2 processing research. In *Cognitive individual differences in second language processing and acquisition* (pp. 89–104). Amsterdam, The Netherlands: John Benjamins Publishing Company.

Li, P., Farkas, I., & MacWhinney, B. (2004). Early lexical development in a self-organizing neural networks. *Neural Networks, 17*, 1345–1362.

Li, S. (2015). The associations between language aptitude and second language grammar acquisition: A meta-analytic review of five decades of research. *Applied Linguistics, 36*(3), 385–408.

Li, S. (2016). The construct validity of language aptitude. *Studies in Second Language Acquisition, 38*(4), 801–842. doi:10.1017/S027226311500042X

Li, S. (2017). Cognitive differences and ISLA. In S. Loewen & M. Sato (Eds.), *The Routledge handbook of instructed second language acquisition* (pp. 396–417). New York, NY: Routledge.

Linck, J. A., Hughes, M. M., Campbell, S. G., Silbert, N. H., Tare, M., Jackson, S. R., . . . Doughty, C. J. (2014). Hi-LAB: A new measure of aptitude for high-level language proficiency. *Language Learning, 63*(3), 530–566.

Linck, J. A., Osthus, P., Koeth, J. T., & Bunting, M. F. (2014). Working memory and second language comprehension and production: A meta-analysis. *Psychonomic Bulletin & Review, 21*(4), 861–883. doi:10.3758/s13423-013-0565-2

Linck, J. A., & Weiss, D. J. (2015). Can working memory and inhibitory control predict second language learning in the classroom? *Sage Open Journal*, 1–11. doi:10.1177/2158244015607352

Liu, H. (2008). Dependency distance as a metric of language comprehension difficulty. *Journal of Cognitive Science, 9*(2), 159–191.

Liu, H., Xu, C., & Liang, J. (2017). Dependency distance: A new perspective on syntactic patterns in natural languages. *Physics of Life Reviews, 21*, 171–193.

Lu, B. (2011). *Working memory and word-order universals.* Keynote presentation at the Workshop on Typological Studies of Languages of China, The University of Hong Kong.

Lu, B. (2012). On the starting point of syntactic analysis: Constraints of the short-term memory span on linguistic constructions. *Chinese Language Learning (in Chinese), 2*, 3–13.

Majerus, S. (2013). Language repetition and short-term memory: An integrative framework. *Frontiers in Human Neuroscience, 7*, 357. doi:10.3389/fnhum.2013.00357

Martin, K. I., & Ellis, N. C. (2012). The roles of phonological STM and working memory in L2 grammar and vocabulary learning. *Studies in Second Language Acquisition, 34*(3), 379–413. doi:10.1017/S0272263112000125

McLaughlin, B. (1995). Aptitude from an information processing perspective. *Language Testing, 11*, 364–381.

Miller, G. (1956). The magical number of seven, plus or minus two: Some limits on our capacity for processing information. *Psychological Review, 63*, 81–97.

Miller, G. (2003). The cognitive revolution: A historical perspective. *Trends in Cognitive Science, 7*(3), 141–144.

Miller, G., Galanter, E., & Pribram, K. H. (1960). *Plans and the structure of behavior.* New York, NY: Holt.

Miyake, A., & Friedman, N. P. (1998). Individual differences in second language proficiency: Working memory as language aptitude. In A. F. Healey & L. J. Bourne (Eds.), *Foreign language learning: Psycholinguistic studies on training and retention* (pp. 339–364). Mahwah, NJ: Lawrence Erlbaum Associates, Inc.

Miyake, A., & Friedman, N. P. (2012). The nature and organization of individual differences in executive functions: Four general conclusions. *Current Directions in Psychological Science, 21*(1), 8–14.

Miyake, A., & Shah, P. (1999). *Models of working memory: Mechanisms of active maintenance and executive control.* New York, NY: Cambridge University Press.

Nicenboim, B., Vasishth, S., Gattei, C., Sigman, M., & Kliegl, R. (2015). Working memory differences in long-distance dependency resolution. *Frontiers in Psychology, 6*, 312. doi:10.3389/fpsyg.2015.00312

Norris, D. (2017). Short-term memory and long-term memory are still different. *Psychological Bulletin, 143*(9), 992–1009.

Oberauer, K. (2009). Design for a working memory. In B. H. Ross (Ed.), *Psychology of learning and motivation: Advances in research and theory* (Vol. 51, pp. 45–100). San Diego, CA: Academic Press.

Oberauer, K. (2010). Declarative and procedural working memory: Common principles, common capacity limits? *Psychologica Belgica, 50*(3–4), 277–308.

Oberauer, K., & Lewandowsky, S. (2013). Evidence against decay in verbal working memory. *Journal of Experimental Psychology: General, 142,* 380–411.

Oberauer, K., & Lewandowsky, S. (2014). Further evidence against decay in working memory. *Journal of Memory and Language, 73,* 15–30.

Oberauer, K., Su¨ß, H. M., Schulze, R., Wilhelm, O., & Wittmann, W. W. (2000). Working memory capacity—facets of a cognitive ability construct. *Personality and Individual Differences, 29,* 1017–1045.

Oberauer, K., Su¨ß, H. M., Wilhelm, O., & Wittmann, W. W. (2003). The multiple faces of working memory: Storage, processing, supervision, and coordination. *Intelligence, 31,* 167–193.

O'Brien, I., Segalowitz, N., Collentine, J., & Freed, B. (2006). Phonological memory and lexical, narrative, and grammatical skills in second language oral production by adult learners. *Applied Psycholinguistics, 27,* 377–402.

O'Brien, I., Segalowitz, N., Collentine, J., & Freed, B. (2007). Phonological memory predicts L2 oral fluency gains in adults. *Studies in Second Language Acquisition, 29,* 557–582.

O'Grady, W. (2012). Three factors in the design and acquisition of language. *Wiley Interdisciplinary Reviews: Cognitive Science, 3,* 493–499.

O'Grady, W. (2017). Working memory and language: From phonology to grammar. *Applied Psycholinguistics, 38*(6), 1340–1343.

Paradis, M. (2009). *Declarative and procedural determinants of second languages.* Amsterdam, The Netherlands: John Benjamins Publishing Company.

Pierce, L. J., Genesee, F., Delcenserie, A., & Morgan, G. (2017). Variations in phonological working memory: Linking early language experiences and language learning outcomes. *Applied Psycholinguistics, 38,* 1265–1302.

Robinson P. (2001). Individual differences, cognitive abilities, aptitude complexes, and learning conditions. *Second Language Research, 17,* 268–392.

Robinson, P. (2005). Aptitude and second language acquisition. *Annual Review of Applied Linguistics, 25,* 46–73.

Robinson, P. (2013). Aptitude in second language acquisition. In C. Chapelle (Ed.), *The encyclopedia of applied linguistics* (pp. 129–133). Oxford: Wiley-Blackwell.

Roelcke, T. (2002). *Efficiency of communication. Glottometrics, 4,* 27–38.

Ruchkin, D., Grafman, J., Cameron, K., & Berndt, S. (2003). Working memory retention systems: A state of activated long-term memory. *Behavioral and Brain Sciences, 26,* 709–728.

Rudner, M., & Rönnberg, J. (2008). The role of the episodic buffer in working memory for language processing. *Cognitive Processing, 9*(1), 19–28.

Sagarra, N. (2013). Working memory in second language acquisition. In Carol A. Chapelle (Ed.), *The encyclopedia of applied linguistics* (pp. 6207–6215). Oxford: Wiley-Blackwell.

Sawyer, M., & L. Ranta. (2001). Aptitude, individual differences, and instructional design. In P. Robinson (Ed.), *Cognition and second language instruction* (pp. 319–353). New York, NY: Cambridge University Press.

Serafini, E. J., & Sanz, C. (2016). Evidence for the decreasing impact of cognitive ability on second language development as proficiency increases. *Studies in Second Language Acquisition, 38*(4), 607–646.

Service, E. (1992). Phonology, working memory and Foreign-language learning. *Quarterly Journal of Experimental Psychology, A, 45*(1), 21–50.

Service, E., Simola, M., Metsnheimo, O., & Maury, S. (2002). Bilingual working memory span is affected by language skill. *European Journal of Cognitive Psychology, 14*, 383–408.

Skehan, P. (1998). *A cognitive approach to language learning.* Oxford: Oxford University Press.

Skehan, P. (2012). Language aptitude. In S. Gass & A. Mackey (Eds.), *Routledge handbook of second language acquisition* (pp. 381–395). New York, NY: Routledge.

Skehan, P. (2015). Working memory and second language performance. In Z. Wen, M. Mota, & A. McNeill (Eds.), *Working memory in second language acquisition and processing* (pp. 189–201). Bristol: Multilingual Matters.

Skehan, P. (2016). Foreign language aptitude, acquisitional sequences, and psycholinguistic processes. In G. Granena, D. O. Jackson, & Y. Yilmaz (Eds.), *Cognitive individual differences in L2 processing and acquisition.* Amsterdam, The Netherlands: John Benjamins Publishing Company.

Skrzypek, A. (2009). Phonological short-term memory and L2 collocational development in adult learners. *EUROSLA Yearbook, 9*, 160–184.

Snow, R. E. (1992). Aptitude theory: Yesterday, today, and tomorrow. *Educational Psychologist, 27*, 5–32.

Sparks, R. (1995). Examining the Linguistic Coding Differences Hypothesis to explain individual differences in foreign language learning. *Annals of Dyslexia, 45*, 187–219.

Thalmann, M., Souza, A. S., & Oberauer, K. (2019). How does chunking help working memory? *Journal of Experimental Psychology Learning Memory and Cognition, 45*(1), 37–55.

Turner, M. L., & Engle, R. W. (1989). Is working memory task dependent? *Journal of Memory and Language, 28*, 127–154.

Ullman, M. T. (2001). The neural basis of lexicon and grammar in first and second language: The declarative/procedural model. *Bilingualism: Language and Cognition, 4*(1), 105–122.

Ullman, M. T. (2005). A cognitive neuroscience perspective on second language acquisition: The declarative/procedural model. In C. Sanz (Ed.), *Mind and context in adult second language acquisition: Methods, theory, and practice* (pp. 141–178). Washington, DC: Georgetown University Press.

Ullman, M. T. (2016). The declarative/procedural model: A neurobiological model of language learning, knowledge and use. In G. Hickok & S. A. Small (Eds.), *The neurobiology of language* (pp. 953–968). Amsterdam: Academic Press.

VanPatten, B. (2013). Mental representation and skill in instructed SLA. In J. Schwieter (Ed.), *Innovations in SLA, bilingualism, and cognition: Research and practice* (pp. 3–22). Amsterdam, The Netherlands: John Benjamins Publishing Company.

Waugh, N. C., & Norman, D. A. (1965). Primary memory. *Psychological Review, 72*, 89–104.

Wen, Z. (2012a). Foreign language aptitude. *ELT Journal, 66*(2), 233–235.

Wen, Z. (2012b). Working memory and second language learning. *International Journal of Applied Linguistics, 22*, 1–22. doi:10.1111/j.1473-4192.2011.00290.x

Wen, Z. (2014). Theorizing and measuring working memory in first and second language research. *Language Teaching, 47*(2), 173–190.

Wen, Z. (2015). Working memory in second language acquisition and processing: The phonological/executive model. In Z. Wen, M. B. Mota, & A. McNeill (Eds.), *Working memory in second language acquisition and processing* (pp. 41–62). Bristol: Multilingual Matters.

Wen, Z. (2016). *Working memory and second language learning: Towards an integrated approach.* Bristol: Multilingual Matters.

Wen, Z., & Li, S. (2019). Working memory in L2 learning and processing. In J. W. Schwieter & A. Benati (Eds.), *The Cambridge handbook of language learning* (pp. 365–389). Cambridge: Cambridge University Press.

Wen, Z., & Juffs, A. (forthcoming). Testing working memory in SLA. In P. Winke & T. (Eds.), *The Routledge handbook of second language acquisition and testing*. London: Routledge.

Wen, Z., Biedroń, A., & Skehan P. (2017). Foreign language aptitude theory: Yesterday, today and tomorrow. *Language Teaching, 50*(1), 1–31.

Wen, Z., Mota, M., & McNeill, A. (2013). Working memory and SLA: Towards an integrated theory. *Asian Journal of English Language Teaching, 23*, 1–18.

Wen, Z., Mota, M., & McNeill, M. (2015). *Working memory in second language acquisition and processing*. Bristol, UK: Multilingual Matters.

Wen, Z., & Skehan, P. (2011). A new perspective on Foreign language aptitude: Building and supporting a case for "working memory as language aptitude". *Ilha Do Desterro: A Journal of English Language, Literatures and Cultural Studies, 60*, 15–44. doi:10.5007/2175-8026.2011n60p015

Williams, J. N. (2012). Working memory and SLA. In S. Gass & A. Mackey (Eds.), *Handbook of second language acquisition* (pp. 427–441). Oxford: Routledge, Taylor & Francis.

Williams, J. N. (2015). Working memory in SLA research: Challenges and prospects. In Z. Wen, M. B. Mota, & A. McNeill (Eds.), *Working memory in second language acquisition and processing* (pp. 301–307). Bristol, UK: Multilingual Matters.

Yuan, K., Steedle, J., Shavelson, R., Alonzo, A., & Oppezzo, M. (2006). *Working memory*, fluid intelligence, and science learning. *Educational Research Review, 1*, 83–98.

Zipf, G. K. (1949). *Human behaviour and the principle of least effort*. Cambridge, MA: Addison-Wesley.

11

DECLARATIVE AND PROCEDURAL MEMORY AS INDIVIDUAL DIFFERENCES IN SECOND LANGUAGE APTITUDE

Joshua Buffington and Kara Morgan-Short

Research in second language (L2) aptitude addresses the components that together constitute aptitude, where aptitude is regarded as a latent construct or trait that predicts outcomes in L2 acquisition (Wen, Biedroń, & Skehan, 2017). Recent approaches to L2 aptitude have considered aptitude to be composed of cognitive abilities (Ellis, this volume; Wen et al., 2017), including constructs such as attentional control and working memory (Robinson, 2007; Skehan, 2016; Wen, this volume). Thus, individual differences in these cognitive abilities would assumedly contribute to differing levels of L2 aptitude among individuals. An emerging line of research suggests that long-term memory may also serve as an individual difference factor in L2 learning. More specifically, declarative and procedural memory, both of which are domain-general, cognitive, long-term memory systems, have been posited to play a role in L2 learning (DeKeyser, 2015; Paradis, 2009; Ullman, 2015), and individual difference research largely supports these claims (e.g., Antoniou, Ettlinger, & Wong, 2016; Faretta-Stutenberg & Morgan-Short, 2018; Hamrick, 2015; Morgan-Short, Faretta-Stutenberg, Brill-Schuetz, Carpenter, & Wong, 2014).

The current chapter considers the role of declarative and procedural memory in L2. First, we provide detailed definitions of declarative and procedural memory and knowledge and then review three theoretical perspectives that posit that declarative and procedural memory contribute to L2 acquisition: Ullman (2015), Paradis (2009), and DeKeyser's Skill Acquisition Theory (DeKeyser, 2015). Subsequently, we provide a review of empirical evidence that examines whether declarative and procedural memory can account for individual differences in L2 learning, as would be predicted by the theoretical perspectives. Finally, we provide a discussion of future research directions with regard to the role of declarative and procedural memory in L2 and conclude that these long-term memory constructs should potentially be considered components of L2 aptitude.

Long-Term Memory Systems

Declarative Memory

Declarative memory is a memory system that supports the acquisition of facts and personal experiences (Cabeza & Moscovitch, 2013; Eichenbaum, 2011; Eichenbaum & Cohen, 2001; Henke, 2010; Morgan-Short, 2013a; Squire & Dede, 2015; Squire & Wixted, 2011; Squire & Zola-Morgan, 1991; Ullman, 2004, 2015, 2016). For example, declarative memory may support the learning of facts such as that the Chicago Cubs won the World Series in 2016, as well as the personal episodic experience of watching the championship baseball game. Declarative memory may be further described by a number of (neuro)cognitive characteristics. For one, knowledge in declarative memory may be explicit, in the sense of being accessible to conscious awareness. However, declarative memory also supports the learning of implicit information (Cabeza & Moscovitch, 2013; Henke, 2010; Squire & Dede, 2015; Squire & Zola-Morgan, 1991; Ullman, 2004, 2015, 2016). Second, learning in declarative memory has been shown to be aided by effortful attention (Foerde, Knowlton, & Poldrack, 2006). Third, the development of knowledge in declarative memory can occur rapidly, often after a single trial of learning (Eichenbaum & Cohen, 2001; Squire & Dede, 2015; Squire & Zola-Morgan, 1991; Ullman, 2004, 2015, 2016). Additionally, knowledge in declarative memory may be used flexibly with other knowledge in declarative memory, as well as with knowledge from other memory systems. Thus, application of knowledge in declarative memory is not limited to the original context of learning, e.g., learning that the Cubs won the World Series in 2016 may be used in a discussion of other unusual events that happened in Chicago during that same year (Squire & Dede, 2015; Squire & Zola, 1996; Ullman, 2004, 2016).

Developmentally, learning abilities in declarative memory (a) mature later than procedural memory learning abilities, (b) improve until early adulthood, (c) remain relatively stable during middle adulthood, and then (d) decline in older adulthood (DiGiulio, Seidenberg, Oleary, & Raz, 1994; Lum, Kidd, Davis, & Conti-Ramsden, 2010; Rönnlund, Nyberg, Bäckman, & Nilsson, 2005; Ullman, 2015, 2016). Anatomically, learning in declarative memory is supported by the medial temporal lobe, which includes the hippocampal formation along with the entorhinal, perirhinal, and parahippocampal cortex (Eichenbaum, 2011; Eichenbaum & Cohen, 2001; Squire & Dede, 2015; Squire & Zola-Morgan, 1991; Ullman, 2004, 2015, 2016). Lastly, cognitive tasks that have been used to assess declarative memory and its role in L2 acquisition include the Modern Language Aptitude Test, Part V (Carroll & Sapon, 1959), the Continuous Visual Memory Task (Trahan & Larrabee, 1988), the LLAMA-B (Meara, 2005), and the visual-auditory learning subtest of the Woodcock-Johnson III Tests of Cognitive Ability (Woodcock, Mather, & McGrew, 2001).

Evidence for the existence of declarative memory as a distinct memory system has been found in work with animal models, amnesic patients, and healthy humans. In animal models such as rats, temporary lesions to the hippocampus prevent the learning of place associations in a maze, whereas rats with functioning hippocampi learn these place associations (Packard & McGaugh, 1996). These results provide evidence for a distinct role of declarative memory in learning arbitrary facts, such as the locations of certain places in a maze. Work with amnesic patients has shown that damage to the medial temporal lobe prevents memory of training materials and episodes, but patients acquire skills such as reading mirror-inverted text and classifying probabilistic stimuli at the same rate as healthy controls (Cohen & Squire, 1980; Knowlton, Mangels, & Squire, 1996). Patients with damage to the striatum—a neural structure that supports procedural memory—but intact hippocampi show the opposite pattern of results. That is, these patients show intact recall of training episodes and materials but impaired skill acquisition (Knowlton et al., 1996). These results provide evidence of a role for declarative memory in recalling facts and personal episodes. Furthermore, work with healthy participants has shown that declarative memory can be involved in probabilistic classification, a task often supported by procedural memory, when there is no distracting task to occupy working memory capacity, demonstrating that declarative memory is often supported by effortful encoding and retrieval in working memory but is also a flexible memory system that can support learning on a wide variety of stimuli (Foerde et al., 2006). Overall, behavioral and neuroscientific research suggests that declarative memory is a distinct memory system primarily responsible for the acquisition of facts and personal experiences but also notably distinguished by its flexibility to acquire a wide range of information.

Procedural Memory

Procedural memory is a type of implicit memory system that supports the acquisition of cognitive and motor skills as well as habits (Ashby, Turner, & Horvitz, 2010; Eichenbaum, 2011; Eichenbaum & Cohen, 2001; Henke, 2010; Morgan-Short, 2013b; Squire & Dede, 2015; Tulving, 1985; Ullman, 2004, 2015, 2016). For example, some motor skills supported by procedural memory include learning to shoot a basketball or to drive a car, and some cognitive skills include learning a new math technique or how to solve a Rubik's cube. Procedural memory may be described by a number of (neuro)cognitive characteristics. By 'implicit' it is meant that learning in procedural memory does not involve conscious awareness (Tulving, 1985; Ullman, 2004, 2015, 2016). Relatedly, learning in procedural memory is not supported by attention, and indeed attention may interfere with learning in procedural memory (Foerde et al., 2006). The development of knowledge in procedural memory occurs gradually and improves over multiple learning trials (Ashby et al., 2010; Ullman, 2004, 2015, 2016). Additionally, knowledge in procedural memory is typically encapsulated, meaning that it is unavailable for use by other memory systems and typically inflexible with respect to the contexts in which it can be applied, e.g., learning how to read mirror-inverted text may not transfer well to learning how to produce mirror-inverted text (Squire & Zola, 1996; Ullman, 2004).

Developmentally, learning abilities in procedural memory (a) mature earlier than learning abilities in declarative memory, (b) tend to be stable during childhood and adulthood, and (c) may decline in older populations, although research on age-related declines in procedural memory has produced a mixed pattern of results (DiGiulio et al., 1994; Lum et al., 2010; Nilsson, 2003; Ullman, 2015, 2016). Anatomically, procedural memory is supported by a striatal-thalamic-frontal circuit, in which information is relayed from the cortex to the striatum (part of the basal ganglia), then to the thalamus, then back to frontal cortex (Ashby et al., 2010; Eichenbaum, 2011). This functional circuit may reflect the planning and execution of skills that have been learned in procedural memory (Ashby et al., 2010; Eichenbaum, 2011; Eichenbaum & Cohen, 2001; Ullman, 2004, 2015, 2016). Lastly, cognitive tasks that have been used to assess procedural memory and its role in L2 acquisition include the Serial Reaction Time Task (Lum & Kidd, 2012), Alternating Serial Reaction Task (Howard & Howard, 1997), Weather Prediction Task (Foerde et al., 2006; Knowlton, Squire, & Gluck, 1994), and the Tower of London (Kaller, Unterrainer, & Stahl, 2012; Unterrainer, Rahm, Leonhart, Ruff, & Halsband, 2003).

Evidence for procedural memory has been found in work with animal models, neuropsychology, and cognitive and neuroimaging research with healthy participants. Work with animal models (McDonald & White, 1993; Packard & McGaugh, 1996), patient H. M. (Scoville & Milner, 1957), and other amnesic patients (Cohen & Squire, 1980; Knowlton et al., 1996) is suggestive of a dissociation between memory of cognitive and motor skills such as mirror drawing and memory of facts or episodes (Eichenbaum & Cohen, 2001; Squire & Dede, 2015). From these studies, researchers have concluded that skill knowledge is supported by a different system from that which supports factual or episodic knowledge, with skill knowledge being supported by procedural memory and factual/episodic knowledge by declarative memory. In a neuroimaging study with healthy humans, Foerde et al. (2006) demonstrated that the role of procedural memory in a probabilistic classification task is modulated by the presence of a secondary task. In this study, subjects learned to classify probabilistic stimuli under either single- or dual-task conditions in a functional magnetic resonance imaging (fMRI) scanner. The dual-task condition involved a secondary task that was designed to occupy working memory and thus reduce the amount of attention that participants were able to give to the probabilistic stimuli. If procedural memory does not depend on attention, then it should be more involved in the dual-task condition compared to the single-task condition, which would allow for attentional mechanisms to focus on the probabilistic stimuli. The results of the study showed a double dissociation in brain regions involved for learning in the single- and dual-task conditions. The striatum (a neural structure known to support procedural memory) was associated with learning in the dual-task condition but not the single-task condition, whereas the medial temporal lobe (a structure involved in declarative memory) supported learning in the single- but not the dual-task condition. The study is informative in that it shows functional and anatomical dissociations between declarative and procedural memory and provides further support for the independence of procedural memory and attention. Overall, the behavioral and neuroscientific research literature suggests that procedural memory is a distinct memory system that operates independently of attention and conscious awareness and is primarily responsible for the acquisition of skills and habits.

Theoretical Perspectives on Declarative and Procedural Memory in L2 Acquisition

Given overviews of the declarative and procedural memory systems, we now outline the three theories that have discussed various roles for declarative and procedural memory and knowledge in L2 acquisition. These theories include DeKeyser's Skill Acquisition Theory (DeKeyser, 2015), Paradis's declarative/procedural model (Paradis, 2009), and Ullman's declarative/procedural model (Ullman, 2004, 2015, 2016). Declarative and procedural memory (in DeKeyser, 'knowledge') play crucial roles in all of the theories discussed here, and yet less is known about the role of these long-term memory systems in L2 than is known about other relevant domain-general cognitive components, such as working memory. For each theory, an overview along with its definitions of declarative and procedural memory or knowledge are provided, followed by a more detailed description of the theory and discussion of the specific roles that declarative and procedural memory play.

The first relevant theory, DeKeyser's Skill Acquisition Theory (DeKeyser, 2015), motivates second language learning as an instance of skill acquisition, with similarities between second language learning and other instances of skill acquisition, such as learning to play a sport or to play the piano. DeKeyser's conception of skill acquisition is consistent with that of other prominent theoretical perspectives on skill acquisition, such as the Adaptive Character of Thought model (ACT-R, Anderson, 1996). Whereas DeKeyser (2015) does not speak of the role of declarative or procedural 'memory' systems in skill acquisition, he does discuss declarative and procedural 'knowledge.' Declarative knowledge is similar to declarative memory in the sense that it is characterized as knowledge 'that' and may be acquired quickly and via observation, i.e., without performance. For example, a learner can acquire declarative knowledge about a skill by watching others perform it, receiving verbal instructions, or undergoing some combination of these two processes. Likewise, procedural knowledge is similar to procedural memory in the sense that both involve the performance of complex skills and both tend to be informationally encapsulated. Procedural knowledge allows the learner to 'chunk' steps from declarative knowledge into a single routine. Note, however, that although declarative and procedural 'memory' and declarative and procedural 'knowledge' are similar, according to DeKeyser, 'knowledge' is the result of learning (cf. Anderson, 1996 where knowledge is the result of encoding information from the environment) and thus is not fully synonymous with 'memory' (DeKeyser, personal communication through review of chapter, December 30, 2017). This is in contrast to the perspective of the declarative and procedural memory system view where these memory systems are involved in both the learning and use of knowledge (Ullman, 2016). The tenets of Skill Acquisition Theory claim that skill learning progresses through the following three stages: the declarative stage, defined by the use of declarative knowledge; the procedural stage, defined by the use of procedural knowledge; and the automatic stage, in which the learner obtains automaticity by practicing the skill to reach a high level of competency where the knowledge becomes fine-tuned so that performance is faster, fewer errors are committed, and less attention is required to perform the task (DeKeyser, 2015). Declarative and procedural knowledge, then, are involved in two initial stages of skill acquisition during which knowledge is acquired about the skill and this knowledge is compiled into a routine for performance, respectively.

Importantly, in DeKeyser's model declarative knowledge does not interface with procedural knowledge in the sense that the output of declarative knowledge becomes the input of procedural knowledge, but rather DeKeyser simply claims that declarative knowledge plays a causal role in the development of procedural knowledge (DeKeyser, 2015, p. 103). This is in much the same way that one needs certain documentation, e.g., proof of residency, birth certificate, in order to obtain a state or national ID. However, it would be silly to argue that proof of residency becomes your state identification; it is simply a necessary condition for obtaining the identification. The same relationship obtains between declarative and procedural knowledge. Additionally, in a large number of studies skill acquisition has been shown to follow the power law of learning, a mathematical formalization of how competency increases with practice. DeKeyser emphasizes, however, that this continuous mathematical function is actually represented as a series of the three qualitatively distinct stages described earlier. In sum, then, DeKeyser's model may be understood to view L2 acquisition as an instance of skill acquisition, in which knowledge proceeds from a declarative to a procedural to an automatic stage. The concepts and predictions in the theory are all derived from this fundamental connection between language and skill acquisition.

A second model of L2 acquisition posits that declarative and procedural memory play crucial roles in learning a second language (Paradis, 2009). Paradis's definitions of declarative and procedural memory are largely consistent with how the terms were defined earlier in the 'Declarative Memory' and 'Procedural Memory' sections. However, it is important to note that for Paradis, declarative memory is synonymous with explicit, i.e., conscious, knowledge, and procedural memory is always implicit, i.e., nonconscious, knowledge, although Paradis accepts other forms of nonconscious knowledge. Note that this one-to-one mapping of declarative memory with conscious knowledge is not accepted by all researchers (Henke, 2010; Ullman, 2015). For L1, Paradis claims that all nongrammatical aspects of language, i.e., vocabulary, as well as any grammatical aspects that are under explicit control, should be supported by declarative memory and that all grammatical aspects that are under implicit control, i.e., syntax, morphology, and phonology, should be supported by procedural memory (Paradis, 2009). Paradis further claims that procedural memory should support lexical knowledge, maintaining a crucial distinction between the lexicon and vocabulary (Paradis, 2009, pp. 14–15). The lexicon, on the one hand, refers to the grammatical properties of lexical items, such as their subcategorization frames, e.g., 'take' requires a direct object. Vocabulary, on the other hand, refers to form–meaning pairings, which should be learned not in procedural memory but in declarative memory. For adult-learned second languages, Paradis predicts that most aspects of language, including grammar, lexicon, and vocabulary, will be learned explicitly in declarative memory. In sum, for L1 Paradis predicts that declarative memory involves learning vocabulary and explicit processing of grammar, whereas procedural memory is responsible for the implicit generation of grammatical structures, which includes syntactic, morphological, phonological, and lexical structures. For L2, Paradis predicts that declarative memory will dominate learning of most aspects of the L2. Indeed, Paradis suggests that the use of procedural memory in adult-learned L2 is rare, although it may be able to be utilized if learning occurs under immersion conditions.

As in DeKeyser's Skill Acquisition Theory, in Paradis's model declarative and procedural memory do not directly interface with each other. The relative reliance on procedural and declarative memory by the learner may change over time, but on logical and empirical grounds Paradis (2009) argues against any sort of interface between these two memory systems. In L1 acquisition, Paradis cites similarities in the processing of motor and cognitive skills and the processing of syntax, as well as clinical dissociations in the ability to learn motor and cognitive skills but the inability to learn new words. Accordingly, this suggests a dissociation between syntax and vocabulary, which map onto procedural and declarative memory, respectively. However, declarative and procedural memory do not always support learning different aspects of a language in L2 acquisition, where analogous knowledge could, in theory, be learned in either system. Indeed, fluency in Paradis's model may be attained either through learning explicit knowledge in declarative memory or through acquiring implicit competence in procedural memory, but the way that learning is represented across these two categories is different. Paradis claims that learning in declarative memory involves "speeded-up controlled use" of grammar, whereas learning in procedural memory involves implicit competence through the internalization of grammar (Paradis, 2009, pp. 7–8). He further notes that most L2 learners use declarative memory to acquire explicit knowledge about their L2, but that with practice a few L2 learners may internalize the grammar and process it in procedural memory. The notion of analogous knowledge but distinct representations across the two memory systems extends the mechanisms by which declarative and procedural memory can contribute to learning a second language and is similar to notions discussed in Ullman's declarative/procedural model (Ullman, 2015), which we turn to next.

Ullman's declarative/procedural model (Ullman, 2004, 2015, 2016) claims that the long-term declarative and procedural memory systems have been co-opted for use in language learning. Ullman's definitions of declarative and procedural memory are consistent with those provided in the memory sections earlier. According to Ullman's model, declarative memory is predicted to be responsible for learning arbitrary pieces of information, such as the meanings of content words, their lexical subcategorization specifications, and their phonological forms, in both L1 and L2, as well as storage of irregular and possibly higher-frequency grammatical forms, especially in L2 (Ullman, 2015). Procedural memory is predicted to be responsible for learning rule-governed sequences and probabilistic information in language, such as rules in the mental grammar, especially at later stages of both L1 and L2 acquisition (Ullman, 2016). Additionally, procedural memory may play a role in the acquisition of syntactic categories as well as in acquiring the phonotactics of a language. Due to the developmental trajectory of procedural memory (see earlier), procedural memory is expected to play a stronger role for language learning in childhood compared to adulthood. In both Paradis's and Ullman's model, then, declarative memory contributes to the acquisition of word meanings and phonological forms, whereas procedural memory contributes to the acquisition of grammatical components of a language. However, the two models differ in their predictions for learning lexical subcategorization properties of words; in Paradis (2009) this information is learned in procedural memory, but in Ullman (2015, 2016) knowledge of subcategorization properties is predicted to be learned in declarative memory.

As in Paradis's and DeKeyser's models, Ullman's model posits that declarative and procedural systems do not interface with one another in the sense of sharing information. However, Ullman discusses two hypotheses concerning the relationship between declarative and procedural memory (Ullman, 2015, p. 139). The first is the redundancy hypothesis, which states that the two memory systems often acquire the same or analogous knowledge, and the second is the competition hypothesis, which claims that the two systems interact competitively such that acquiring knowledge in one system may inhibit learning in the other system. While it is clear that the two hypotheses make opposing predictions, it must also be considered that there are additional variables such as age of acquisition and the learning context that can affect whether declarative and/or procedural memory primarily underlies acquisition. For example, research has shown that the degree to which learners rely on declarative and procedural memory to process grammatical forms varies depending on the learning context, with implicit and immersion learners showing stronger evidence of reliance on procedural memory at later stages of acquisition (Brill-Schuetz & Morgan-Short, 2014; Faretta-Stutenberg &

Morgan-Short, 2018). It should also be noted that the co-presence of knowledge across the two memory systems is not always bidirectional. This is because declarative memory is a much more flexible learning system compared to procedural memory, and thus it is often the case that knowledge learned in procedural memory can also be learned in declarative memory, but the reverse is not always true (Ullman, 2015, 2016). Some of the primary concerns in Ullman's model, then, are not simply what kinds of knowledge can be acquired in which system (declarative or procedural memory) but also how analogous knowledge is maintained across systems as well as how ancillary variables affect learning in both systems.

It should be clear from the preceding discussion that DeKeyser's, Paradis's, and Ullman's models of L2 acquisition all predict roles for declarative and procedural memory and knowledge. In DeKeyser's Skill Acquisition Theory (DeKeyser, 2015), declarative knowledge is used at the beginning of learning to learn about aspects of a second language, and procedural knowledge is expected to develop at an intermediate stage of learning in which learners are practicing a second language but have not yet reached the stage where processing is automatic. In Paradis's model (Paradis, 2009), declarative memory is predicted to be responsible for most aspects of L2 acquisition, but in rare cases L2 learners may internalize grammatical and/or lexical aspects of L2 and process them in procedural memory. Ullman's model (Ullman, 2004, 2015, 2016) also predicts different roles for declarative and procedural memory in L2 acquisition and additionally outlines hypotheses for the relationship between declarative and procedural memory, i.e., redundancy and competition hypotheses, and predicts important contributions from variables such as age of acquisition and the context of learning on the reliance of declarative and/or procedural memory in L2 acquisition. Relatedly, DeKeyser's theory and empirical work are also suggestive of interactions between age of acquisition and verbal aptitude (DeKeyser, 2000; DeKeyser, 2012a; DeKeyser, 2012b; DeKeyser, Alfi-Shabtay, & Ravid, 2010), which would presumably be related to declarative memory, as well as interactions between context of learning and the engagement of declarative and procedural knowledge, i.e., in study-abroad versus classroom contexts (DeKeyser, 2007; DeKeyser, 2010). Although there are some important differences among the models, what all of the models have in common is a view of (a) declarative memory as involved in vocabulary and the initial stages of grammar learning and (b) a stronger role for procedural memory for grammar at later stages of L2 acquisition. Next, an overview of empirical evidence for the role of declarative and procedural memory in L2 acquisition is presented with the intention to examine support for the general claims made across the models discussed here.

Evidence for the Role of Declarative and Procedural Memory in L2 Acquisition

From the theories discussed earlier, it is clear that declarative and procedural memory are expected to play a role in L2 acquisition, but what evidence exists to demonstrate that this is indeed the case? This section reviews evidence on the role of declarative and procedural memory in L2 acquisition, focusing first on evidence from laboratory studies with one training condition and then on those with multiple training conditions, and finally, naturalistic learning studies (see Table 11.1 for summary). We include only studies that directly address predictions generated by declarative/procedural theories of L2 acquisition, but we also note that at least two studies have indirectly provided evidence for these theories by using tasks that we associate with procedural memory, although no claims were made about procedural memory in these two studies (Granena, 2013; Linck et al., 2013). Both of these studies demonstrate that tasks that involve sequence learning (which we believe reflects learning in procedural memory) predict language learning abilities.

Laboratory Studies With a Single Learning Condition

In this first subsection, we will consider laboratory studies that have examined L2 acquisition under a single context of learning. Looking at L2 acquisition under implicit training conditions, Morgan-Short et al. (2014) examined the role of individual differences in declarative memory, as measured by the Modern Language Aptitude Test, Part V (MLAT-V) and the Continuous Visual Memory Task, and procedural memory, as measured by the Tower of London and Weather Prediction Tasks. In order to assess L2 learning ability, the authors used an artificial language paradigm, Brocanto2 (Morgan-Short, Finger, Grey, & Ullman, 2012; Morgan-Short, Sanz, Steinhauer, & Ullman, 2010; Morgan-Short, Steinhauer, Sanz, & Ullman, 2012), which they had adapted from Brocanto (Friederici, Steinhauer, & Pfeifer, 2002), in order to measure syntactic development under implicit training conditions. The findings from this study indicated that declarative memory ability predicted L2 syntactic development at early stages of acquisition and that procedural memory ability predicted L2 syntactic development at later stages of acquisition. In a subsequent analysis of neuroimaging (fMRI) data that had been collected along with the Morgan-Short et al. (2014) study, Morgan-Short et al. (2015) examined the neural circuits associated with L2 acquisition under implicit contexts of exposure. Findings provided evidence of a link between learners who were strong in declarative memory and the use of procedural memory neural circuits in L2 processing at early stages of development. At later stages of development, learners who were low in procedural memory showed neural signatures indicative of effortful and attentional processing but not neural signatures that indicate processing in procedural memory. The authors suggest that learners who are strong in declarative memory are able to quickly engage in a procedural stage of L2 syntactic processing, which provides evidence not only for a link between procedural memory and learning syntactic rules but also for perhaps a complementary relationship between declarative and procedural memory, as predicted by DeKeyser (2015) where strength in declarative memory may lead to rapid acquisition of declarative knowledge that then indirectly facilitates proceduralization.

Using a different artificial language paradigm that involved learning morphophonological rules in a passive, exposure-based condition, Ettlinger, Bradlow, and Wong (2014) examined the relationships between declarative memory, as measured by the visual–auditory learning subtest of the Woodcock-Johnson III test, and procedural memory, as measured by the Tower of London, and L2 acquisition. In this study, the simple rule involved straightforward application of a pattern of morphemes, whereas the complex rule involved vowel changes that could be learned via analogy with words presented in a training phase.[1] As such, learning the pattern rule was predicted to be supported by procedural memory due to the reliance on sequence learning, whereas learning the analogistic rule was predicted to be supported by declarative memory due to the need to recall analogous words to correctly apply this rule. The authors measured learning of the morphophonological rules in a forced-choice test and analyzed the relationship between L2 learning and memory separately in three subgroups: (a) 'learners,' i.e., those participants who learned both the pattern and analogistic rules; (b) 'simplifiers,' i.e., those participants who incorrectly applied the pattern rule for analogistic cases; and (c) 'nonlearners,' i.e., those participants who did not show learning of either pattern or analogistic rules. Findings from this study indicated that participants who learned both the pattern and analogistic rules had high declarative and procedural memory, simplifiers had high procedural memory but low declarative memory, and nonlearners had low declarative and procedural memory. These results suggest that declarative memory is associated with learning the analogistic rule, and procedural memory is associated with learning the pattern rule and has a second-order association with the analogistic rule, such that participants with high procedural memory either scored well below chance on the analogistic rule (simplifiers) or above chance (learners).

Whereas Morgan-Short et al. (2014, 2015) and Ettlinger et al. (2014) looked at the role of declarative and procedural memory in implicit but intentional learning conditions, Hamrick (2015) used an incidental learning condition to examine the role of declarative memory, as measured by the LLAMA-B, and procedural memory, as measured by the Serial Reaction Time Tasks, in L2 acquisition. Participants were exposed to new syntactic structures in a semi-artificial language (Hamrick, 2013) and then given a surprise recognition test that assessed their knowledge of the syntactic rules. The recognition test was given immediately after exposure to the language and after a 1- to 3-week period of no exposure. Findings from this study indicated that immediately after exposure to the semi-artificial language, declarative but not procedural memory abilities were correlated with performance on the surprise test, but after a 1- to 3-week period of no exposure, procedural but not declarative memory abilities were correlated with performance on the test.

Overall, these single learning condition laboratory studies (Ettlinger et al., 2014; Hamrick, 2015; Morgan-Short et al., 2014) provide evidence for a role of declarative and procedural memory in learning syntactic and morphophonological rules under implicit and incidental contexts of exposure.

Laboratory Studies With Multiple Learning Conditions

Next, we move into laboratory studies that look at multiple contexts of learning. The first study that we review, Antoniou et al. (2016), extended Ettlinger et al.'s (2014) research with morphophonological L2 learning under a passive, exposure-based condition and examined whether the role of declarative and procedural memory changes in conditions in which feedback during testing and the order of presentation of the pattern and analogistic L2 rules are manipulated. Declarative memory was measured by the visual-auditory learning subtest of the Woodcock-Johnson III test, and procedural memory was measured by the Tower of London, following Ettlinger et al. (2014). Findings from this study replicated those of Ettlinger et al. (2014) in that declarative memory was associated with learning the analogistic rule and that procedural memory was associated with learning the pattern rule in all conditions, except for when the analogistic rule was presented before the pattern rule. For this ordering of the rules, declarative memory was associated with learning the pattern rule, suggesting that the role of declarative and procedural memory may be mediated by the structure of the input itself.

A few studies have extended previous research with implicit, exposure-based, and incidental conditions to examine whether procedural memory makes different contributions in explicit, instructed conditions. First, examining the effects of implicit vs. explicit training conditions, Brill-Schuetz and Morgan-Short (2014) considered the role of procedural memory, as measured by the Alternating Serial Reaction Task and the Weather Prediction Task, in learning syntactic word-order rules of an artificial language. Their results showed that procedural memory ability interacted with training condition such that participants with high procedural memory were more accurate on a grammaticality judgment task than were participants with low procedural memory, but only in the implicit training condition. A second study examined the role of procedural memory in incidental and instructed conditions using a semi-artificial language with simple and complex word-order rules (Tagarelli, Ruiz, Vega, & Rebuschat, 2016). Procedural memory, as measured by the either the Serial Reaction Time Tasks or the Alternating Serial Reaction Task,[2] was found to be negatively associated with L2 acquisition of syntax, particularly for one complex word-order rule in the incidental but not the instructed learning condition. The authors noted that the use of a semi-artificial language and an untimed grammaticality judgment test to assess L2 knowledge may have biased learners in the incidental condition towards explicit processing, and thus less reliance on procedural memory. Overall, both Brill-Schuetz and Morgan-Short (2014) and Tagarelli et al. (2016) found evidence for both facilitative and interfering roles for procedural memory in implicit and incidental conditions, which is largely consistent with the single-context laboratory studies reviewed earlier. However, no role for procedural memory was evidenced in explicit and instructed conditions.

A final laboratory study, Suzuki (2017), specifically examined the role of procedural memory in explicit training conditions that differed by intersession spacing intervals with 3.3-day or 7-day intervals between sessions. Suzuki measured the automatization of L2 morphology of a miniature language with reaction times and a coefficient of variance (CV)[3] and assessed procedural memory with the Tower of London Task. Results indicated that procedural memory was associated with the speedup of L2 processing, as measured by reaction time, but only in the group given short (3.3-day) intervals of learning. Procedural memory, however, was not associated with more stable processing, as measured by the coefficient of variance, and as such was argued to play a role only in earlier stages of automatization. The results of this study suggest that procedural memory may also play a role in explicit and instructed conditions when reaction time is considered, as opposed to accuracy, which was the L2 measure examined in previous studies that included an explicit or instructed condition (Brill-Schuetz & Morgan-Short, 2014; Tagarelli et al., 2016).

Naturalistic Learning Studies With Multiple Learning Conditions

To our knowledge, only one study has examined the role of declarative and procedural memory in a naturalistic learning context. Faretta-Stutenberg and Morgan-Short (2018) examined the role of declarative memory, as measured by the MLAT-V and Continuous Visual Memory Task, and procedural memory, as measured by the Alternating Serial Reaction Task and Weather Prediction Task, in L2 acquisition of Spanish syntax in a longitudinal study of two naturalistic contexts: study-abroad and at-home university-level L2 learners of Spanish. They assessed both behavioral changes (via a grammaticality judgment task) and neurocognitive processing changes (via event-related potentials). Results from this study did not provide evidence of a link between declarative memory and L2 learning in either context despite L2 improvements for learners in both contexts, but declarative memory was positively correlated with baseline L2 performance, suggesting that declarative memory is important at early stages of learning. Procedural memory predicted to changes in both behavioral performance (improved performance) and neurocognitive processing (N400 and P600 effects) in the second language, but this relationship only held in the study-abroad context of learning. The authors posit that this connection between procedural memory and the study-abroad context may be due to the less instructed and more abundant second language input in study-abroad contexts compared to at-home contexts.

Taken together, laboratory and naturalistic, multiple learning condition studies (Antoniou et al., 2016; Brill-Schuetz & Morgan-Short, 2014; Faretta-Stutenberg & Morgan-Short, 2018; Suzuki, 2017; Tagarelli et al., 2016) of L2 acquisition provide additional evidence for a role for declarative and procedural memory in learning syntactic, morphological, and morphophonological grammatical rules. The results from these studies also suggest that the contributions that these memory systems make may differ by context.

Summary of Evidence

Overall, the studies reviewed implicate roles for declarative and procedural memory in L2 acquisition and begin to shed light on what these roles are (see Table 11.1 for summary). Regarding declarative memory, these studies broadly implicate a positive role for declarative memory (a) at earlier stages of L2 learning (Faretta-Stutenberg & Morgan-Short, 2018; Hamrick, 2015; Morgan-Short et al., 2014); (b) in implicit, exposure-based, incidental, and classroom contexts (Antoniou et al., 2016; Faretta-Stutenberg & Morgan-Short, 2017; Hamrick, 2015; Morgan-Short et al., 2014); (c) in learning analogistic rules when L2 input is not ordered (Antoniou et al., 2016; Ettlinger et al., 2014); and (d) in learning pattern rules when preceded in the input by analogistic rules (Antoniou et al., 2016). Regarding procedural memory, these studies suggest that procedural memory is positively associated with L2 learning (a) at later stages of learning (Brill-Schuetz & Morgan-Short, 2014; Faretta-Stutenberg & Morgan-Short, 2018; Hamrick, 2015; Morgan-Short et al., 2014); (b) in implicit, exposure-based, incidental, and immersion contexts but not in classroom contexts or in explicit contexts (Antoniou et al., 2016; Brill-Schuetz & Morgan-Short, 2014; Ettlinger et al., 2014; Faretta-Stutenberg & Morgan-Short, 2018; Hamrick, 2015; Morgan-Short et al., 2014); (c) in explicit contexts for reaction time measures (Suzuki, 2017); and (d) in learning pattern rules (Antoniou et al., 2016; Ettlinger et al., 2014).

It is important to note that not all of the findings related to the role of declarative and procedural memory are positive or consistent. For example, recall that Tagarelli et al. (2016) evidenced a negative relationship between procedural memory and syntactic development in an incidental condition. Also, recent work in our laboratory that aimed to replicate and extend Ettlinger et al. (2014) has found a positive relationship between pattern rules with declarative memory as well as with procedural memory, as measured by the Weather Prediction Task but not as measured by the Tower of London Task (Buffington & Morgan-Short, 2018). Note, however, that this pattern of results differs from those of Ettlinger et al. (2014) and Antoniou et al. (2016) in that they found a positive relationship between analogistic learning and declarative learning and with pattern learning and procedural memory, as measured by the Tower of London Task. These examples demonstrate that much more replication and extension work will need to

TABLE 11.1 Studies examining the relationship between L2 acquisition and declarative and procedural memory

Reference	Context of learning	L2	Declarative memory (DM) and L2	Procedural memory (PM) and L2
Ettlinger et al., 2014	Passive, exposure-based	Artificial language: morphophonology based on Shimakonde	DM associated with learning analogistic grammatical rule	PM linearly associated with learning pattern grammatical rule; second-order association with learning analogistic grammatical rule
Antoniou et al., 2016	Passive, exposure-based with or without feedback and presentation order	Artificial language: morphophonology based on Shimakonde	DM predicted learning of analogistic rule; DM predicted pattern rule learning when analogistic rule presented before pattern rule	PM predicted learning of pattern rule
Buffington & Morgan-Short, 2018	Passive, exposure-based	Artificial language: morphophonology based on Shimakonde	DM correlated with learning of pattern rule	Only one PM task (Weather Prediction Task) correlated with learning of pattern rule
Suzuki, 2017	Explicit	Artificial language: morphology based on Spanish	NA	PM associated with speedup and early automatization in short-interval learning group

(Continued)

TABLE 11.1 (Continued)

Reference	Context of learning	L2	Declarative memory (DM) and L2	Procedural memory (PM) and L2
Morgan-Short et al., 2014	Implicit	Artificial language: Brocanto2	DM predicted L2 ability at early stage of learning	PM predicted L2 ability at later stage of learning
Morgan-Short et al., 2015	Implicit	Artificial language: Brocanto2	DM ability associated with PM neural circuits at early stage	Low PM ability associated with effortful processing at later stage
Brill-Schuetz & Morgan-Short, 2014	Implicit and explicit	Artificial language: Brocanto2	NA	PM associated with L2 ability in implicit condition
Hamrick, 2015	Incidental	Semi-artificial language: English vocabulary and Persian-based syntax	DM correlated with L2 ability at early stage of learning	PM correlated with L2 ability at later stage of learning
Tagarelli et al., 2016	Instructed and incidental	Semi-artificial language: English vocabulary and German syntax	NA	PM negatively associated with L2 acquisition in incidental group
Faretta-Stutenberg & Morgan-Short, 2018	Study-abroad and at-home/classroom	Spanish syntax	DM correlated with L2 ability at baseline testing	PM predicted L2 learning in study-abroad group

be conducted in order to fully understand the roles of declarative and procedural memory in L2 learning. Overall, though, the evidence reviewed earlier largely converges on the general finding that declarative and procedural memory seem to be related to the ability to learn grammatical structures in a second language but that this role is somewhat contingent on the stage of the learning process, the context of learning, the type of grammatical rule, and potentially even the cognitive task used to assess procedural memory.

Conclusions and Future Directions

This chapter has reviewed theories and evidence on the role of declarative and procedural memory as individual differences in predicting outcomes in L2 acquisition. We offered detailed definitions of declarative and procedural memory and described three theories that predict roles for declarative and procedural memory in L2 acquisition (DeKeyser, 2015; Paradis, 2009; Ullman, 2015). These models all share an expectation that declarative memory will support learning of grammatical structures in L2 at early phases of learning, whereas procedural memory will play an increasingly important role for these structures as L2 proficiency develops. Empirical evidence largely provides support for the claims generated by these models. However, we note that the scope of previous research is limited to syntactic, morphological, and morphophonological grammatical structures, and most studies to date have examined learning in a laboratory-based implicit or exposure-based context. As such, future research would benefit from studying a wider range of linguistic structures, e.g., phonological and lexico-semantic structures, and more systematically studying L2 acquisition in explicit instruction contexts, particularly to examine understudied aptitude/treatment interactions such as the role of declarative memory in explicit environments.

In addition to further exploring when these long-term memory systems play a role in L2 learning, e.g., at what stage, under what contexts, and for which linguistic structures, future research should address what we believe to be important, but underexplored, questions generated by the declarative/procedural theory of L2 acquisition. For one, most empirical work to date is largely consistent with all three declarative/procedural models, but the models also make differing predictions, e.g., regarding the role of declarative memory in learning explicit vs. implicit information. Second, Ullman (2015, 2016) notes that declarative and procedural memory can interact cooperatively and competitively with each other. Although Morgan-Short et al. (2015) provides evidence that suggests that learners high in declarative memory quickly switch to procedural memory neural circuits during L2 acquisition, the cooperation and competition hypotheses should continue to be investigated in future research. For one, it is not known when declarative and procedural memory interact cooperatively in L2 acquisition and when they interact competitively, as well as what mechanisms mediate these relationships. Third, it is important to consider the relative contributions of declarative and procedural to memory to L2 acquisition in light of the contributions of other domain-general constructs such as working memory (Wen, this volume), as well as any domain-specific constructs that contribute to L2 acquisition (Sparks, Patton, & Luebbers, this volume; Yue, this volume). Lastly, an important body of work has examined the contributions of implicit learning (e.g., Granena, 2013; Granena & Yilmaz, this volume; Linck et al., 2013) and statistical learning (e.g., Frost, Siegelman, Narkiss, & Afek, 2013) to L2 acquisition. It is not clear to us how these constructs do or do not map onto declarative and/or procedural memory, and we are not aware of any work attempting to relate these constructs to one another (see Granena & Yilmaz, this volume, for related discussion). Given that implicit learning, statistical learning, and procedural memory are all claimed to be broad, domain-general constructs and are often assessed with the same cognitive task, e.g., the Serial Reaction Time Task, there is likely a substantial amount of overlap among the constructs. This may be especially true for implicit learning and procedural memory, since both systems are understood to be implicit memory systems. However, comparing the contributions of these systems may reveal some intriguing differences. Clearly delineating the relationships among these constructs will add to our understanding of the neurocognitive mechanisms underlying L2 acquisition and will undoubtedly generate important questions for future research.

While research on the contributions of declarative and procedural memory to L2 acquisition is just beginning to emerge, the early findings show that declarative/procedural theories of L2 acquisition can explain a number of L2 acquisition phenomena, and work in this area is inviting and leading to research on important theoretical questions regarding the component mechanisms underlying the ability to learn languages. Finally, to the extent that L2 aptitude is composed of cognitive abilities that together could serve as a "composite measure regarded as the general capacity to master a foreign language" (Wen et al., 2017), we posit that declarative and procedural memory, as domain-general, cognitive, long-term memory constructs should potentially be considered a part of L2 aptitude.

Acknowledgement

We would like to thank Robert DeKeyser for comments on an earlier version of this chapter. We also thank attendees of the 2017 International Round Table Forum on Language Aptitude at the Macao Polytechnic Institute and members of the Cognition of Second Language Acquisition Laboratory at the University of Illinois at Chicago for helpful discussions related to this chapter.

Notes

1 Ettlinger et al. (2014) use 'simple' and 'complex' rules to refer to the simple pattern rule and the complex analogistic rule, respectively. Because of the opacity of the terms

'simple' and 'complex,' we will refer to the two types of rules as 'pattern' and 'analogistic,' respectively, as we believe these terms are more descriptive and clearer.

2 Participants completed either the Serial Reaction Time Task or the Alternating Serial Reaction Task. It seems that the reason for including two different tasks was that the Alternating Serial Reaction Task could not be run in the UK for technical reasons, and so the Serial Reaction Time Tasks was used as a substitute (around half of participants were run in the UK and half in the United States).

3 Coefficient of variance is the standard deviation divided by the mean ($s/\bar{x}$). In this study, the coefficient of variance was indexed by dividing the standard deviation of reaction time by the mean reaction time. The authors refer the reader to Segalowitz and Segalowitz (1993) for the rationale of using the coefficient of variance to index automatization.

References

Anderson, J. R. (1996). ACT: A simple theory of complex cognition. *American Psychologist*, *51*(4), 355–365. doi:10.1037/0003-066X.51.4.355

Antoniou, M., Ettlinger, M., & Wong, P. C. M. (2016). Complexity, training paradigm design, and the contribution of memory subsystems to grammar learning. *PLoS One*, *11*(7), e0158812. doi:10.1371/journal.pone.0158812

Ashby, F. G., Turner, B. O., & Horvitz, J. C. (2010). Cortical and basal ganglia contributions to habit learning and automaticity. *Trends in Cognitive Sciences*, *14*(5), 208–215. doi:10.1016/j.tics.2010.02.001

Brill-Schuetz, K. A., & Morgan-Short, K. (2014). The role of procedural memory in adult second language acquisition. *Proceedings of the 36th Annual Conference of the Cognitive Science Society*, 260–265.

Buffington, J., & Morgan-Short, K. (2018). Construct validity of procedural memory tasks used in adult-learned language. In C. Kalish, M. Rau, J. Zhu, and T. T. Rogers (Eds.), *Proceedings of the 40th Annual Conference of the Cognitive Science Society* (pp. 1420–1425). Madison, Wisconsin: Cognitive Science Society.

Cabeza, R., & Moscovitch, M. (2013). Memory systems, processing modes, and components: Functional neuroimaging evidence. *Perspectives on Psychological Science*, *8*(1), 49–55. doi:10.1177/1745691612469033

Carroll, J. B., & Sapon, S. M. (1959). *Modern language aptitude test*. San Antonio, TX: Psychological Corporation.

Cohen, N. J., & Squire, L. R. (1980). Preserved learning and retention of pattern-analyzing skill in amnesia: Dissociation of knowing how and knowing that. *Science*, *210*(4466), 207–210. doi:10.1126/science.7414331

DeKeyser, R. M. (2000). The robustness of critical period effects in second language acquisition. *Studies in Second Language Acquisition*, *22*(4), 499–533.

DeKeyser, R. M. (2007). Study abroad as Foreign language practice. In R. M. DeKeyser (Ed.), *Practice in a second language: Perspectives from applied linguistics and cognitive psychology* (pp. 208–226). New York, NY: Cambridge University Press.

DeKeyser, R. M. (2010). Monitoring processes in Spanish as a second language during a study abroad program. *Foreign Language Annals*, *43*(1), 80–92. doi:10.1111/j.1944-9720.2010.01061.x

DeKeyser, R. M. (2012a). Age effects in second language learning. In S. M. Gass & A. Mackey (Eds.), *The Routledge handbook of second language acquisition* (pp. 442–460). New York, NY: Taylor & Francis.

DeKeyser, R. M. (2012b). Individual differences in native language attainment and their implications for research on second language acquisition. *Linguistic Approaches to Bilingualism, 2*(3), 260–263. doi:10.1075/lab.2.3.03dek

DeKeyser, R. M. (2015). Skill acquisition theory. In B.VanPatten & J.Williams (Eds.), *Theories in second language acquisition: An introduction* (2nd ed., pp. 94–112). Mahwah, NJ: Lawrence Erlbaum Associates, Inc.

DeKeyser, R. M., Alfi-Shabtay, I., & Ravid, D. (2010). Cross-linguistic evidence for the nature of age effects in second language acquisition. *Applied Psycholinguistics, 31*(3), 413–438. doi:10.1017/S0142716410000056

DiGiulio, D.V., Seidenberg, M., Oleary, D. S., & Raz, N. (1994). Procedural and declarative memory: A developmental study. *Brain and Cognition, 25*(1), 79–91. doi:10.1006/brcg.1994.1024

Eichenbaum, H. (2011). *The cognitive neuroscience of memory: An introduction.* New York, NY: Oxford University Press.

Eichenbaum, H., & Cohen, N. J. (2001). *From conditioning to conscious recollection: Memory systems of the brain.* New York, NY: Oxford University Press.

Ettlinger, M., Bradlow, A. R., & Wong, P. C. M. (2014). Variability in the learning of complex morphophonology. *Applied Psycholinguistics, 35*(4), 807–831. doi:10.1017/S0142716412000586

Faretta-Stutenberg, M., & Morgan-Short, K. (2018). The interplay of individual differences and context of learning in behavioral and neurocognitive second language development [special issue on neurolinguistics]. *Second Language Research, 34,* 67–101. doi:10.1177/0267658316684903

Foerde, K., Knowlton, B. J., & Poldrack, R. A. (2006). Modulation of competing memory systems by distraction. *Proceedings of the National Academy of Sciences of the United States of America, 103*(31), 11778–11783. doi:10.1073/pnas.0602659103

Friederici, A. D., Steinhauer, K., & Pfeifer, E. (2002). Brain signatures of artificial language processing: Evidence challenging the critical period hypothesis. *Proceedings of the National Academy of Sciences of the United States of America, 99*(1), 529–534. doi:10.1073/pnas.012611199

Frost, R., Siegelman, N., Narkiss, A., & Afek, L. (2013). What predicts successful literacy acquisition in a second language? *Psychological Science, 24*(7), 1243–1252. doi:10.1177/0956797612472207

Granena, G. (2013). Individual differences in sequence learning ability and second language acquisition in early childhood and adulthood. *Language Learning, 63*(4), 665–703. doi:10.1111/lang.12018

Hamrick, P. (2013). *Development of conscious knowledge during early incidental learning of L2 syntax* (Doctoral dissertation, Georgetown University). Retrieved from PsycINFO. (2014–99031–236).

Hamrick, P. (2015). Declarative and procedural memory abilities as individual differences in incidental language learning. *Learning and Individual Differences, 44,* 9–15. doi:10.1016/j.lindif.2015.10.003

Henke, K. (2010). A model for memory systems based on processing modes rather than consciousness. *Nature Reviews Neuroscience, 11*(7), 523–532. doi:10.1038/nrn2850

Howard, J. H., & Howard, D.V. (1997). Age differences in implicit learning of higher order dependencies in serial patterns. *Psychology and Aging, 12*(4), 634–656. doi:10.1037/0882-7974.12.4.634

Kaller, C. P., Unterrainer, J. M., & Stahl, C. (2012). Assessing planning ability with the Tower of London task: Psychometric properties of a structurally balanced problem set. *Psychological Assessment*, *24*(1), 46–53. doi:10.1037/a0025174

Knowlton, B. J., Mangels, J. A., & Squire, L. R. (1996). A neostriatal habit learning system in humans. *Science*, *273*(5280), 1399–1402. doi:10.1126/science.273.5280.1399

Knowlton, B. J., Squire, L. R., & Gluck, M. A. (1994). Probabilistic classification learning in amnesia. *Learning & Memory*, *1*(2), 106–120. doi:10.1101/lm.1.2.106

Linck, J. A., Hughes, M. M., Campbell, S. G., Silbert, N. H., Tare, M., Jackson, S. R., . . . Doughty, C. J. (2013). Hi-LAB: A new measure of aptitude for high-level language proficiency. *Language Learning*, *63*(3), 530–566. doi:10.1111/lang.12011

Lum, J. A. G., & Kidd, E. (2012). An examination of the associations among multiple memory systems, past tense, and vocabulary in typically developing 5-year-old children. *Journal of Speech, Language, and Hearing Research*, *55*(4), 989–1006. doi:10.1044/1092-4388(2011/10-0137)

Lum, J. A. G., Kidd, E., Davis, S., & Conti-Ramsden, G. (2010). Longitudinal study of declarative and procedural memory in primary school-aged children. *Australian Journal of Psychology*, *62*(3), 139–148. doi:10.1080/00049530903150547

McDonald, R. J., & White, N. M. (1993). A triple dissociation of memory systems: Hippocampus, amygdala, and dorsal striatum. *Behavioral Neuroscience*, *107*(1), 3–22. doi:10.1037/0735-7044.107.1.3

Meara, P. (2005). *LLAMA language aptitude tests*. Swansea, UK: Lognostics.

Morgan-Short, K. (2013a). Declarative memory and knowledge. In P. Robinson (Ed.), *The Routledge encyclopedia of second language acquisition* (pp. 157–160). New York, NY and London: Routledge.

Morgan-Short, K. (2013b). Procedural memory and knowledge. In P. Robinson (Ed.), *The Routledge encyclopedia of second language acquisition* (pp. 509–512). New York, NY and London: Routledge.

Morgan-Short, K., Deng, Z., Brill-Schuetz, K. A., Faretta-Stutenberg, M., Wong, P. C. M., & Wong, F. (2015). A view of the neural representation of second language syntax through artificial language learning under implicit contexts of exposure. *Studies in Second Language Acquisition*, *37*(2), 383–419. doi:10.1017/S0272263115000030

Morgan-Short, K., Faretta-Stutenberg, M., Brill-Schuetz, K., Carpenter, H., & Wong, P. C. M. (2014). Declarative and procedural memory as individual differences in second language acquisition. *Bilingualism: Language and Cognition*, *17*(1), 56–72. doi:10.1017/S1366728912000715

Morgan-Short, K., Finger, I., Grey, S., & Ullman, M. T. (2012). Second language processing shows increased native-like neural responses after months of no exposure. *PLoS One*, *7*(3), e32974. doi:10.1371/journal.pone.0032974

Morgan-Short, K., Sanz, C., Steinhauer, K., & Ullman, M. T. (2010). Second language acquisition of gender agreement in explicit and implicit training conditions: An event-related potential study. *Language Learning*, *60*(1), 154–193. doi:10.1111/j.1467-9922.2009.00554.x

Morgan-Short, K., Steinhauer, K., Sanz, C., & Ullman, M. T. (2012). Explicit and implicit second language training differentially affect the achievement of native-like brain activation patterns. *Journal of Cognitive Neuroscience*, *24*(4), 933–947. doi:10.1162/jocn_a_00119

Nilsson, L. (2003). Memory function in normal aging. *Acta Neurologica Scandinavica*, *107*(s179), 7–13. doi:10.1034/j.1600-0404.107.s179.5.x

Packard, M. G., & McGaugh, J. L. (1996). Inactivation of hippocampus or caudate nucleus with lidocaine differentially affects expression of place and response learning. *Neurobiology of Learning and Memory, 65*(1), 65–72. doi:10.1006/nlme.1996.0007

Paradis, M. (2009). *Declarative and procedural determinants of second languages.* Philadelphia, PA: John Benjamins Publishing Company.

Robinson, P. (2007). Aptitudes, abilities, contexts, and practice. In R. M. DeKeyser (Ed.), *Practice in a second language: Perspectives from applied linguistics and cognitive psychology* (pp. 256–286). Cambridge: Cambridge University Press. doi:10.1017/CBO9780511667275.015

Rönnlund, M., Nyberg, L., Bäckman, L., & Nilsson, L. (2005). Stability, growth, and decline in adult life span development of declarative memory: Cross-sectional and longitudinal data from a population-based study. *Psychology and Aging, 20*(1), 3–18. doi:10.1037/0882-7974.20.1.3

Scoville, W. B., & Milner, B. (1957). Loss of recent memory after bilateral hippocampal lesions. *Journal of Neurology, Neurosurgery, and Psychiatry, 20*(1), 11–21.

Segalowitz, N. S., & Segalowitz, S. J. (1993). Skilled performance, practice, and the differentiation of speed-up from automatization effects: Evidence from second language word recognition. *Applied Psycholinguistics, 14*(3), 369–385. doi:10.1017/S0142716400010845

Skehan, P. (2016). Foreign language aptitude, acquisitional sequences, and psycholinguistic processes. In G. Granena, D. O. Jackson, & Y. Yilmaz (Eds.), *Cognitive individual differences in second language processing and acquisition* (pp. 17–50). Amsterdam, The Netherlands: John Benjamins Publishing Company. doi:10.1075/bpa.3.02ske

Squire, L. R., & Dede, A. J. O. (2015). Conscious and unconscious memory systems. *Cold Spring Harbor Perspectives in Biology, 7*(a021667). doi:10.1101/cshperspect.a021667

Squire, L. R., & Wixted, J. T. (2011). The cognitive neuroscience of human memory since HM. *Annual Review of Neuroscience, 34.* doi:10.1146/annurev-neuro-061010-113720

Squire, L. R., & Zola-Morgan, S. (1991). The medial temporal lobe memory system. *Science, 253*(5026), 1380–1386.

Squire, L. R., & Zola, S. M. (1996). Structure and function of declarative and nondeclarative memory systems. *Proceedings of the National Academy of Sciences of the United States of America, 93*(24), 13515–13522.

Suzuki, Y. (2017). The role of procedural learning ability in automatization of L2 morphology under different learning schedules [First view online publication]. *Studies in Second Language Acquisition, 1–15.* doi:10.1017/S0272263117000249

Tagarelli, K. M., Ruiz, S., Vega, J. L. M., & Rebuschat, P. (2016). Variability in second language learning: The roles of individual differences, learning conditions, and linguistic complexity. *Studies in Second Language Acquisition, 38*(Special Issue 2), 293–316. doi:10.1017/S0272263116000036

Trahan, D. E., & Larrabee, G. J. (1988). *Continuous visual memory test.* Odessa, FL: Psychological Assessment Resources.

Tulving, E. (1985). How many memory systems are there? *American Psychologist, 40*(4), 385–398. doi:10.1037/0003-066X.40.4.385

Ullman, M. T. (2004). Contributions of memory circuits to language: The declarative/procedural model. *Cognition, 92,* 231–270. doi:10.1016/j.cognition.2003.10.008

Ullman, M. T. (2015). The declarative/procedural model: A neurobiologically-motivated theory of first and second language. In B. VanPatten & J. Williams (Eds.), *Theories of second language acquisition: An introduction* (2nd ed., pp. 135–158). Mahwah: NJ: Lawrence Erlbaum Associates, Inc.

Ullman, M. T. (2016). The declarative/procedural model: A neurobiological model of language learning, knowledge and use. In G. Hickok & S. A. Small (Eds.), *The neurobiology of language* (pp. 953–968). Oxford: Academic Press. doi.org/10.1016/B978-0-12-407794-2.00092-4

Unterrainer, J., Rahm, B., Leonhart, R., Ruff, C., & Halsband, U. (2003). The Tower of London: The impact of instructions, cueing, and learning on planning abilities. *Cognitive Brain Research, 17*(3), 675–683. doi:10.1016/S0926-6410(03)00191-5

Wen, Z. E., Biedroń, A., & Skehan, P. (2017). Foreign language aptitude theory: Yesterday, today and tomorrow. *Language Teaching, 50*(1), 1–31. doi:10.1017/S0261444816000276

Woodcock, R. W., Mather, N., & McGrew, K. S. (2001). *Woodcock-Johnson III tests of cognitive abilities examiner's manual.* Itasca, IL: Riverside Pub.

12

COGNITIVE APTITUDES FOR EXPLICIT AND IMPLICIT LEARNING

Gisela Granena and Yucel Yilmaz

Explicit and Implicit Language Aptitude: ELA and ILA

The belief that some individuals have a remarkable talent for picking up languages, or are simply 'good at languages,' is one regularly encountered among language learners, teachers, and researchers. Such 'talent' is referred to as 'second language learning aptitude' and defined as a combination of cognitive and perceptual abilities that predispose individuals to learn well or rapidly (Carroll, 1981). Carroll's work using the Modern Language Aptitude Test Battery (MLAT; Carroll & Sapon, 1959) showed the power of aptitude as a predictor of course grades with correlations in the range of .4 to .6 (Carroll, 1966). Similar predictive validity coefficients were reported for other aptitude test batteries such as the Pimsleur Language Aptitude Test Battery (PLAB; Pimsleur, 1966) and the Defense Language Aptitude Battery (DLAB; Peterson & Al-Haik, 1976). Ehrman and Oxford (1995) also found that aptitude was the strongest predictor of language proficiency (with correlations up to .51), and almost the same magnitude (.49) was reported in a more recent meta-analysis examining the construct validity of aptitude (Li, 2016). Aptitude can explain approximately 25% of the variance in L2 learning when operationalized as learners' course grades or standardized language test scores. When the role of aptitude is examined in L2 grammar acquisition, the overall effect size becomes medium, with correlations around .3, approximately accounting for 10% of the total variance (Li, 2015). This is still an impressive proportion if we consider the predictive power of other factors (biographical, affective, linguistic, and contextual) that influence language learning.

Aptitude has been related to success in both naturalistic (informal) and instructed (formal) language learning contexts. All other things being equal, a language learner with high language aptitude will reach higher levels of linguistic competence in the long term when immersed in the L2-speaking environment (Abrahamsson & Hyltenstam, 2008; DeKeyser, 2000; Granena & Long, 2013). The mean effect size of aptitude as a predictor in this learning context was reported as being between small and medium and significant (Li, 2015). A language learner with high language aptitude will also be faster to learn and will enjoy higher overall learning success in an instructed learning environment under a variety of learning conditions and instructional methods, from more form focused to more meaning oriented (De Graaff, 1997; Robinson, 2002; Sheen, 2007). In this type of learning context, the mean effect size of aptitude as a predictor was reported as being medium and therefore greater than in the case of naturalistic learning (Li, 2015). It is precisely in these instructional contexts where aptitude has a lengthy track record as a reliable predictor of L2 learning outcomes (for review, see Dornyei & Skehan, 2003; for findings from both experimental and nonexperimental research, see De Graaff, 1997; Ehrman & Oxford, 1995; Harley & Hart, 1997; Robinson, 1997; Williams, 1999).

Because the vast majority of teaching approaches and commercially published materials for the last 60 years have focused on forms (Long, 2015), research on aptitude has been weighted heavily in favor of cognitive abilities that allow for explicit language learning, such as language analytic ability. After all, it is cognitive abilities in the explicit domain that can predict learning outcomes in classrooms with synthetic, focus-on-forms approaches, syllabi, and tests best.

The major standardized aptitude measures, such as the Modern Language Aptitude Test (MLAT; Carroll & Sapon, 1959) and the Pimsleur Language Aptitude Battery (PLAB; Pimsleur, 1966), were created at a time when the audio-lingual method was the prevailing teaching methodology and loaded heavily on the same explicit and metalinguistic abilities favored by traditional teaching approaches, with an emphasis on attention to linguistic code features. As an example, the strongest correlation reported by Carroll's (1958) factor analysis was between an explicit associative memory factor composed of paired associates and a number learning task and the criterion variable (L2 Chinese course grades). The other two strongest correlations corresponded to linguistic interest, as measured by tests such as the Turse spelling, and explicit inductive learning, as measured by an artificial language test with linguistic forms prompting the learner to arrive at grammatical rules for himself or herself. These results are not surprising considering the audio-lingual methodology at the time, which exposed learners to target structures via drills and written exercises.

This bias toward components of aptitude in the domain of explicit cognition spread to aptitude research exploring the potential of aptitude in naturalistic contexts, despite the crucial differences that, in many cases, can be found between both. DeKeyser (2000) operationalized language aptitude as verbal aptitude and more specifically verbal analytical ability as measured by a Hungarian version of MLAT IV ("Words in Sentences"), the subtest measuring the ability to understand the function of words and phrases in L1 sentence structure.

DeKeyser (2000) claimed that language analytic ability was a necessary condition for adult learners to reach high levels of ultimate attainment, due to the explicit learning mechanisms they are hypothesized to rely on. According to Bley-Vroman's (1990) Fundamental Difference Hypothesis, adults can no longer rely on the innate mechanisms for implicit language acquisition and must therefore rely on alternative problem-solving mechanisms for explicit language learning. Since verbal analytical ability allows for explicit learning, DeKeyser argued, and adults rely on explicit mechanisms in L2 learning, it follows that those adults who are successful in L2 learning should also have high analytical ability.

However, the capacity for implicit learning, defined as learning in the absence of intention to learn and awareness of the fact that we are learning, but in the presence of selective attention (Jimenez, 2002) does not disappear in adulthood; it just deteriorates in efficiency (Janacsek, Fiser, & Nemeth, 2012; Kalra, 2015). This runs contrary to Reber's (1993) claim that implicit learning is developmentally invariant because it reflects a primitive cognitive system and points instead toward the existence of individual differences in the domain of implicit cognition. In educational psychology, recent views (e.g., Woltz, 2003) have, in fact, proposed the general domain of implicit cognitive processes (implicit memory, implicit learning, and procedural knowledge) as a fruitful area in which to investigate new aptitude constructs. This domain involves cognitive processes labeled in the literature as automatic, associative, nonconscious, and unintentional. Woltz's research (e.g, 1988, 1990a, 1990b, 1999) showed that priming, the extent to which performance is facilitated by a prior processing event, varies across individuals. His studies looked specifically at repetition priming and demonstrated measurable individual differences with acceptable reliability estimates, one of the challenges of implicit measures, which tend to rely on change scores (not overall performance) and place fewer constraints on performance processes than their explicit counterparts.[1]

In addition to priming, meaningful individual differences have been reported in other implicit cognitive abilities such as implicit inductive learning. Using a probabilistic serial reaction time task, Kaufman et al. (2010) found meaningful variation in the extent to which individuals automatically detect complex and noisy regularities in a set of probabilistic stimuli. In a probabilistic serial reaction time task, participants have to track a stimulus that can appear at one of four locations. The stimulus follows a repeating sequence 85% of the time only (15% of the time the stimulus follows an alternative control sequence). Kaufman et al. found significant learning scores on the task by comparing the mean reaction time for trials following the target sequence with the mean reaction time for trials following the alternative sequence. They further reported evidence in support of a dissociation between cognitive abilities in the explicit and implicit domains. Implicit learning was unrelated to working memory and explicit associative learning. It was also more weakly related to psychometric intelligence than explicit learning.

Kaufman et al's (2010) sample included 153 participants ages 16 to 18. Studies with older populations have found similar results. A dissertation at Harvard (Kalra, 2015) compared performance across a series of implicit learning tasks between a group of children (mean age 10 years) and adults (mean age 23 years). Tasks included artificial grammar learning, probabilistic classification task, serial response task, implicit category learning, rotary pursuit, and mirror tracing. Kalra's results provided evidence of qualitative differences in implicit learning between the two age groups. Similar to Kaufman et al. (2010), psychometric intelligence and working memory were not correlated with implicit learning performance. Kalra further showed reliable individual differences in implicit learning via a test-retest study with parallel forms.

One of the advantages of these new constructs in the domain of implicit cognition is that they have minimal overlap with existing ones in the domain of explicit cognition, as suggested by the weak-to-zero correlations between cognitive abilities that rely on executive processing resources such as working memory and psychometric intelligence as measured by conventional IQ tests and implicit memory measures of priming or implicit induction (Engle, Tuholski, Laughlin, & Conway, 1999; Kaufman et al., 2010; Kyllonen, 1996; Kyllonen & Christal, 1990; Woltz, 1999). The implication to bear in mind of such a proposal distinguishing between implicit and explicit abilities is that it supports dual system models in cognitive psychology. These models, which date back to the 1960s and 1970s (Reber, 1967; Schneider & Shiffrin, 1977; Evans, 2008), pose that there are two largely distinct processing modes or systems of learning: one that is fast, automatic, and nonconscious and another that is slow, controlled, and conscious, each of which is related to other cognitive behaviors. Alternative single-system models have also been proposed, which are more aligned with current connectionist accounts (e.g., Cleeremans & Jimenez, 2002) and which defend that cognitive processes only enter awareness under certain conditions, thus accounting for both implicit and explicit learning. These models stand in opposition to skill acquisition theory, which defends that learning draws on explicit processes in the initial stages (Ackerman, 1988; Anderson, 1993).

Such considerations have led to a re-examination and reconceptualization of language aptitude, informed by the past 40 years of research findings in cognitive science, and to a departure from some of the constructs and kinds of measures employed in the first aptitude test batteries. This can be seen in the two most recent batteries, the LLAMA (Meara, 2005) and the Hi-LAB (Linck et al., 2013). The LLAMA is a freely available computer-based aptitude test battery that grew out of a series of projects by students at the University of Wales. Although largely based on the MLAT, the LLAMA departs from the MLAT in two main ways. First, the tests are language independent and therefore suitable for speakers of any L1 with a Roman alphabet. Second, the battery includes a sound recognition test that is not present in the MLAT. The test, which measures the ability to recognize patterns in spoken language, allows no time to study and plays test items only once. Immediately after listening to the items, test-takers complete a recognition test. Based on the features of the test and on the results of a factor analysis showing that LLAMA D loaded separately from the other LLAMA subtests, Granena (2013a) argued that the learning conditions created by the test were closer to implicit induction (i.e., acquiring patterns unintentionally through exposure) than explicit induction (i.e., figuring out rules and relations) and that, therefore, LLAMA D could be measuring a cognitive ability involving more implicit cognitive processes than LLAMA B, E, and F. In view of these findings, Granena (2013a) proposed a distinction between *explicit language aptitude* (ELA) and *implicit language aptitude* (ILA). Whereas ELA would be tapping cognitive aptitudes that are more relevant for explicit language learning and processing and that depend on executive attention, such as explicit inductive learning and rote memory, ILA would be tapping cognitive aptitudes that are more relevant for implicit language learning, such as implicit inductive learning and implicit memory. These cognitive abilities rely on selective attention but do not engage central executive resources like explicit abilities. Subsequent research by Granena (2013b, 2016) further supported the two-way aptitude distinction by showing that LLAMA D loaded on the same factor as a probabilistic serial reaction time task measuring implicit inductive learning and was related to an experiential-intuitive cognitive approach to information processing, whereas LLAMA B, E, and F loaded on the same factor as a psychometric intelligence test and were related to a rational-analytic cognitive approach to information processing.

The Hi-LAB (Linck et al., 2013) was created in order to predict high-level L2 attainment. The battery measures a set of 11 cognitive and auditory perceptual abilities hypothesized to have the potential to make up for the expected deterioration in L2 learning capacity in adult learners. The measures are grouped into six different constructs, several of which were not present in the MLAT or in any of the first aptitude test batteries. Two of these constructs, long-term memory retrieval and implicit learning, rely on abilities in the domain of implicit cognitive processes. Long-term memory retrieval is measured by a semantic priming task that shows the extent to which memory contents that are not in the focus of attention have heightened availability for processing, whereas implicit learning is measured by a serial reaction time task. Except for processing speed, all the other constructs in the battery (working memory, explicit associative memory, and perceptual acuity) fall well under abilities that engage explicit, attention-driven cognitive processes.

The proposals reviewed earlier show that the current understanding of aptitude is that of a multicomponential construct encompassing abilities from both the implicit and explicit cognitive domains, which may be differentially related to L2 outcomes in different learning contexts and/or instructed conditions. In the following section, we will focus on a widely researched area of instructed SLA, i.e., corrective feedback (CF), to illustrate the extent to which factors representing each of the mentioned aptitude domains (ILA and ELA) have featured in previous research. As mentioned earlier, we expect ILA and ELA to be differentially related to L2 acquisition under explicit and implicit instructed conditions. Since CF has been operationalized into explicit and implicit types, reviewing this literature will allow us to evaluate the extent to which this hypothesis is supported by the results of CF research. It is important to note that our review is not exhaustive, but rather it aims to be broadly representative of the literature.

Corrective Feedback and Aptitude

Research on CF occupies a central role in instructed SLA. Studies synthesizing the research on the topic (Goo, Granena, Yilmaz, & Novella, 2015; Li, 2010; Long, 2007; Lyster, Saito, & Sato, 2013; Mackey & Goo, 2007; Nassaji, 2015; Sheen & Ellis, 2011; Yilmaz, 2016) have demonstrated the benefits of receiving CF for L2 acquisition. Research on CF has been motivated primarily by two related theoretical proposals, the interaction hypothesis (Long, 1996) and the focus-on-form perspective (Long, 1991; Long & Robinson, 1998), both influenced by the work done in the role of attention and awareness in L2 acquisition (Robinson, 1995; Schmidt, 2001; Tomlin & Villa, 1994). Researchers who have contributed to the literature on the role of attention agree that focal attention on linguistic properties is necessary in order for those properties to be acquired, but they disagree on whether learners should be consciously aware of the forms to be learned. Both Schmidt (2001) and Robinson (1995) hold that some form of awareness of the forms is necessary, whereas Tomlin and Villa (1994) do not consider awareness a necessary feature. Schmidt (2001) also makes a distinction about the content of this awareness. What he considers necessary is the awareness at the level of instantiations of the forms (awareness at the level of noticing), not awareness at the level of understanding the rules of the language (awareness at the level of understanding). Recognizing the essential role of attention for L2 acquisition, the interaction hypothesis (Long, 1996) postulates that conversational interaction, especially when it involves CF, facilitates L2 acquisition by drawing learners' attention to L2 forms. The focus-on-form perspective (Long, 1991; Long & Robinson, 1998) argues that L2 acquisition is most effective when learners' attention is briefly drawn to formal elements of language when the need arises during a communicative or meaning-based activity (Long, 1991; Long & Robinson, 1998). The provision of CF has been viewed as one of the major ways of implementing focus on form.

Although there are different ways of classifying feedback types, a widely accepted classification scheme in the literature (e.g., Li, 2010) involves determining where along an explicit/implicit continuum feedback types fall. Explicit feedback refers to linguistic code features by providing either one or both of the following: (a) metalinguistic information in the form of clues or rules and (b) information indicating that the learner's production is not targetlike. Feedback types lacking both (a) and (b) have been considered implicit. According to this distinction, explicit correction (i.e., explicit rejection of learners' production, followed by the provision of the targetlike form) and metalinguistic feedback (i.e., comments about the accuracy of learners' non-targetlike production, including the provision of metalinguistic terminology, clues or rules) are typically classified as explicit. Recasts (i.e., targetlike reformulations of learners' non-targetlike productions) constitute one type of feedback that is considered implicit. It is important to note that the explicit or implicit label as applied to CF qualifies the information provided via the feedback, not the type of processing the feedback engages the learner in. In theory at least, either feedback type could lead to explicit or implicit processing. As Long (2017) wrote, "the learners' use of this or that cognitive process can be intended by the instructional designer, but cannot be stipulated or guaranteed." It may sound counterintuitive to some to expect CF, the goal of which is to draw learners' attention to language forms, to lead to a type of cognitive processing that involves no conscious awareness. Current theories, however, leave room for this possibility. As discussed earlier, Tomlin and Villa's (1994) theoretical position permits learning through attended input without being consciously aware of target linguistic forms. In addition, the content of awareness might matter in determining whether learning through feedback can take place without awareness. Schmidt (2001) considers awareness at the level of instances of language a necessary component, but not awareness at the level of understanding the rules. In theory then, in cases where the learning target is governed by a rule, implicit processing can happen for learning the rule even if the learner becomes aware of the feedback and its linguistic target as an instance.

Recently, a growing number of studies have examined the role of cognitive factors in the rate of L2 development due to CF. The goal of this research has been to determine which cognitive individual differences might constitute an aptitude for learning through different CF types. Most of the studies contributing to this line of research have focused on two variables: *language analytic ability* (LAA) (Arroyo & Yilmaz, in press; Li, 2013; Sheen, 2007; Trofimovich, Ammar, & Gatbonton, 2007; Yilmaz, 2013) and *working memory capacity* (WMC) (Goo, 2012, 2016; Li, 2013; Révész, 2012; Trofimovich et al., 2007; Yilmaz, 2013). Other variables, such as attention control (Trofimovich et al., 2007), phonological short-term memory (Mackey, Philp, Egi, Fujii, & Tatsumi, 2002; Révész, 2012), phonetic coding ability (Yilmaz & Koylu, 2016), and explicit language aptitude (e.g., Yilmaz & Granena, 2016) have also been investigated but much less intensively. In addition, some of these studies have focused either only on implicit feedback (e.g., Arroyo & Yilmaz, in press; Révész, 2012; Trofimovich et al., 2007) or only on explicit feedback (Yilmaz & Koylu, 2016), and thus, they are not ideal to determine the differential relationship between cognitive factors and the effectiveness of feedback under explicit and implicit conditions. Later, we will review those studies that included both implicit and explicit feedback conditions.

Skehan (1998) has considered LAA a component of his language aptitude model, along with phonemic coding ability and memory, and defined it as "the capacity to infer rules of language and make linguistic generalizations or extrapolations" (Skehan, 1998, p. 204). Skehan has claimed that language analytic ability is related to discovering patterns in the language to which learners are exposed. Three studies (Li, 2013; Sheen, 2007; Yilmaz, 2013) have investigated the relationship between LAA and learning under implicit and explicit feedback conditions. The feedback types compared were explicit correction and recasts in Yilmaz (2013) and metalinguistic feedback (reformulation plus metalinguistic rule) and recasts in both Sheen (2007) and Li (2013). Conflicting findings have been reported in these studies. Li (2013) reported that LAA predicted learners' pretest-delayed posttest gain scores under the implicit feedback condition, whereas Sheen (2007) and Yilmaz (2013) reported no significant correlations between LAA and language outcomes under the implicit feedback condition. Regarding LAA's role in learning under explicit feedback conditions, Sheen (2007) and Yilmaz (2013) showed a significant relationship between learning and LAA under explicit feedback conditions, whereas Li (2013) did not.

CF researchers have also showed a considerable amount of interest in the role of WMC in feedback effectiveness. WMC has been defined by Kane, Conway, Hambrick, and Engle (2007) as "attentional processes that allow for goal-directed behavior by maintaining relevant information in an active, easily accessible state outside of conscious focus, or to retrieve that information from an inactive memory, under conditions of interference, distraction or conflict" (p. 23). Goo (2012, 2016), in addition to Li (2013) and Yilmaz (2013), which were briefly discussed earlier, investigated the differential relationship between WMC and learning outcomes under implicit and explicit feedback conditions. Goo (2012, 2016) operationalized implicit feedback as recasts and explicit feedback as metalinguistic feedback as in Li (2013). Unlike in Li (2013), the metalinguistic feedback in Goo did not provide the reformulation of the learner's error. The results were mixed. Li (2013) and Yilmaz (2013) found a statistical relationship between WMC and the learning outcomes in explicit conditions, whereas Goo (2012, 2016) did not find such a relationship. As for implicit feedback, Goo (2012) reported a statistical link between WMC and learning outcomes under recast conditions; however, such a link was not found by Goo (2016), Li (2013), or Yilmaz (2013).

As mentioned earlier, there are studies that investigated the role of cognitive variables other than LAA and WMC in feedback effectiveness, but most of these studies focused on either implicit feedback or explicit feedback. The only study that included both implicit (i.e., explicit correction) and explicit feedback (i.e., recasts) types was Yilmaz and Granena (2016), which investigated *explicit language aptitude* (ELA). The difference between Yilmaz and Granena (2016) and the studies reviewed earlier is that Yilmaz and Granena used three LLAMA subtests (LLAMA F, E, and B) to measure a broader type of cognitive aptitude, ELA, hypothesized to be related to learning under explicit conditions (Granena, 2013a). ELA, it is argued, captures various explicit cognitive abilities, including explicit inductive learning ability, explicit associative learning, and rote memory ability. The results showed that ELA was predictive of performance in the explicit group, suggesting that explicit feedback engaged explicit cognitive processes and that such feedback differentially affected learners' acquisition, depending on ELA. ELA did not predict the implicit group's performance, indicating that implicit feedback did not engage the type of explicit cognitive processes captured by ELA.

As shown by this short review on the relationship between cognitive variables and the amount of L2 development due to implicit or explicit feedback, previous research is characterized by mixed findings. Trying to determine what accounts for these mixed findings is beyond the scope of this study, let alone the fact that the methodological differences across the studies might render such an effort an exercise of pure speculation. For example, although implicit feedback has been operationalized exclusively through recasts, the way recasts were provided differed across studies. In the Goo (2012, 2016) studies, the learner's full utterance was reformulated, whereas in the other studies (Li, 2013; Sheen, 2007; Yilmaz, 2013; Yilmaz & Granena, 2016), only the non-targetlike portion of the learner's utterance was reformulated. Explicit feedback has also been operationalized in many different ways. Some of the studies (Yilmaz, 2013; Yilmaz & Granena, 2016) operationalized explicit feedback through explicit correction, whereas other studies operationalized it through metalinguistic feedback with (Li, 2013; Sheen, 2007) or without (Goo, 2012, 2016) the reformulation of the learner's non-targetlike utterance. Methodological differences were not limited to the way feedback was operationalized. Target structure, method of feedback delivery, and instruments used to measure cognitive variables (see Table 12.1 for these differences) also showed considerable variability.

This review shows that previous research has focused exclusively on cognitive abilities that can be readily identified as belonging to the domain of explicit cognitive processes. LAA, for example, has been measured either with the Words in Sentences (Part IV) subtest of the MLAT (Carroll & Sapon, 1959), which measures learners' awareness of grammatical structure, or LLAMA F, a subtest of the LLAMA Aptitude tests (Meara, 2005), which explicitly asks learners to work out the rules of a language by studying a corpus. In both of these tests, learners can be expected to engage in conscious and intentional cognitive processes because they are encouraged to approach the task with the intention to reflect on the functions or rules of the language. The other frequently investigated cognitive factor, WMC, has been measured with complex span tasks such as the operation span task (Goo, 2012, 2016; Yilmaz, 2013) and the reading span task (Goo, 2012; Li, 2013), which require learners to remember target stimuli (e.g., words, letters) while comprehending sentences in their L1 or verifying simple arithmetic equations. Working memory and the executive functions of attention it depends on have been associated with conscious, intentional, and reflective learning processes (Barrett, Tugade, & Engle, 2004). Although not everyone agrees that working

TABLE 12.1 Studies investigating the interaction between cognitive variables and CF

Study	Participants	Language Feature	Feedback modality	Cognitive Variable	Cognitive Measure	Outcome Measure
Goo (2012)	54 L1 Korean	the English *that*-trace	oral	WMC	OSPAN RSPAN	grammaticality judgment written production
Goo (2016)	83 L1 Korean	the English *that*-trace	oral	WMC	OSPAN	grammaticality judgment oral production
Li (2013)	72 mixed-L1	Chinese classifiers	oral	LAA WMC	MLAT Part IV LSPAN	grammaticality judgment elicited imitation
Sheen (2007)	80 mixed-L1	English articles	oral	LAA	Otto test	speeded dictation written production error correction
Yilmaz (2013)	48 L1 English	Turkish plural and locative morphemes	text-based SCMC or oral	LAA WMC	LLAMA F OSPAN	oral production comprehension recognition

Note. LAA = *Language analytic ability*, WMC = *Working memory capacity*, LSPAN = *Listening span task*, MLAT = *Modern Language Aptitude Test*, RSPAN = *Reading span task*, OSPAN = *Operation span task*, SCMC = *Synchronous computer-mediated communication*.

memory involves conscious awareness (see, for example, Bergström & Eriksson, 2014, 2015), the most commonly accepted view is that working memory is engaged under explicit learning instructions in order to guide the focus of attention (Kaufman et al., 2010).

Although the mixed findings and methodological diversity of the studies reviewed does not permit a straightforward conclusion to be drawn, there seems to be an emerging pattern. Of eight cases, from six studies reviewed earlier, where an association between a cognitive variable and learning under each of the conditions was sought, only in two of them was the cognitive variable significantly associated with learning outcomes in the implicit condition, whereas in five of them the cognitive variable was significantly associated with learning outcomes in the explicit condition. Although a conclusion based on a vote-count approach such as this is admittedly simplistic (Norris & Ortega, 2000), the fact that similar conclusions were reached by other research syntheses (Li, 2015; Skehan, 2015) adds validity to it. Skehan's (2015) review included all the feedback studies, regardless of whether they included both implicit and explicit feedback conditions, and concluded that "as a generalization, then, it seems that participants with higher aptitude are more likely to draw on this in the explicit condition" (Skehan, 2015, p. 376). Similarly, Li's (2015) meta-analysis, which synthesized the results of 16 studies that examined how aptitude moderates the effects of implicit and explicit instructional treatments (including feedback), found that language aptitude was more likely to be drawn upon in explicit than implicit instruction. The studies reviewed in both Skehan (2015) and Li (2015) focused on cognitive variables that can be considered as belonging to the domain of explicit cognitive processes. In sum, the conclusion that cognitive variables that might be considered part of explicit language aptitude is broadly in line with the prediction that ELA would be more relevant for feedback conditions that favor explicit processes. The prediction, however, that ILA would be more relevant for learning under implicit learning conditions still needs empirical confirmation.

Avenues for Future Research on Language Aptitude

Given the relatively recent proposals putting forward an aptitude for implicit learning, much work remains to be done. In our view, there are two main avenues for future research where work is clearly needed:

1. Research on the reliability and construct validity of implicit measures: implicit learning and memory tasks
2. Research on the relative effects of types of instruction as a function of explicit and implicit language aptitude: ATI designs

The implicit cognitive domain is a complex one, with constructs that do not necessarily overlap. A main distinction to make is between implicit learning and implicit memory. When researchers study implicit learning, they typically focus on encoding, the first stage of memory where information is acquired and consolidated. Implicit memory, on the other hand, refers to the retrieval stage, the process of recalling stored information. Both implicit learning and implicit memory can be measured with different tasks, and the jury is still out on whether each is a single construct measured by several tasks or several constructs. Implicit learning can be measured by tasks such as serial response learning, artificial grammar learning, probabilistic classification, and prototype-distortion category learning. Kalra et al. (2014) ran a factor analysis with four implicit learning tasks which showed that the tasks did not correlate with one another as expected, even though a one-factor model could not be rejected. The probabilistic classification task displayed the strongest loading, followed by moderate loadings by artificial grammar learning and category learning. The serial reaction time task, however, correlated poorly with the other tasks. Implicit memory, on the other hand, has been typically measured by means of priming tasks. However, it can take different forms, and some researchers in SLA (e.g., Brill-Schuetz & Morgan-Short, 2014; Morgan-Short, Faretta-Stutenberg, Brill-Schuetz, Carpenter, & Wong, 2014; Faretta-Stutenberg & Morgan-Short, 2017) have focused on individual differences in procedural memory, a subset of implicit memory in charge of sensory-motor habits or automatic skills, using tasks such as the Tower of London (Unterrainer et al., 2003) and the Weather Prediction Task (Knowlton, Squire, & Gluck, 1994). Although these procedural memory tasks are different from implicit memory tasks measuring priming, it is not clear the extent to which they differ from implicit learning tasks such as the serial reaction time task. Therefore, research is needed that investigates the construct validity of implicit learning aptitude by means of factor analyses and/or structural equation models that test the underlying structure of a variety of implicit learning and implicit memory tasks. Research is also needed that investigates the reliability of implicit learning and memory tasks. As discussed in endnote 1, implicit tasks tend to be noisier than their explicit counterparts. However, not all implicit tasks have low reliability estimates. Research should identify the most reliable tasks and find ways to increase the reliability of assessment for the construct.

The second avenue for future research is *aptitude-treatment interaction* (ATI) studies. The ATI paradigm aims to examine how learning outcomes depend on a match or mismatch between learners' specific cognitive individual differences and the treatments they receive. ATI research serves two purposes. First, the relationship between cognitive individual differences and L2 instruction could be used to gain maximum benefit from instructional practices by determining the best instructional option(s) for learners with particular cognitive profiles. When multiple instructional options are available, it is not enough to know "which treatment is the best." One also needs to answer the question "best or better for whom?" Second, the investigation of the relationship between cognitive individual differences and treatments could provide indirect evidence regarding how learning under different instructional conditions takes place. A positive association between a cognitive ID and learning outcomes under a specific condition would mean that the cognitive processes that are engaged by the instructional condition are facilitated by the specific cognitive ID. This second use of ATI research offers potential to determine the extent to which ELA and ILA play a role in explicit and implicit instructional treatments. Researchers intending to contribute to this line of research can start by measuring one of the aptitude types (ELA or ILA) or both using the tests mentioned previously and then assign learners randomly to treatment groups representing the implicit and explicit options of their chosen instructional feature, corrective feedback, for example; next, measure learning outcomes using at least two tests, each creating favorable conditions to tap onto one type of L2 knowledge (implicit or explicit); and, finally, determine the differential relationship between the aptitude and learning outcomes under each of the conditions. If learning outcomes under the explicit condition are associated with learners' ELA but not ILA, this finding would be consistent with the claim that explicit learning took place in the explicit condition. This design, however, would not be sufficient to eliminate alternative explanations for the observed relationship. For example, it would be possible that learners might have become aware of the learning target during the assessment stage, even though they had not been aware of it during the treatment. In order to have greater confidence that this finding indicates that explicit learning took place during the treatment, one should collect data on learners' awareness of the learning target through introspective measures and cross-validate the nature of the learning process.

Cognitive variables by their nature do not lend themselves to experimental manipulations like CF or other instructional variables because one cannot deliberately vary cognitive variables. Therefore, it is difficult to establish a causal relationship between ILA and ELA and learning outcomes. Despite this general limitation, researchers can do their best to eliminate possible alternative explanations for the relationship observed. One such frequently mentioned alternative explanation is whether aptitude is the effect of the language learning experience. For example, although this is intuitively unlikely, learners' aptitude scores might be the result of their participation in the experiment. It is easy to eliminate this possibility by providing the aptitude tests before the treatment. It is also possible that learners' previous language learning experience, such as the languages they studied, their proficiency level, or the number of years they studied those languages, might constitute plausible explanations for the degree of their aptitude. Researchers can eliminate these possible explanations by controlling learners' language learning background. Another alternative explanation to the presence or absence of a relationship between aptitudes and learning outcomes is the varying amount of learning under different treatment conditions. That is, differential relationships between aptitudes and learning under different conditions can arise because learners in one of the conditions could not reach a threshold level of learning beyond which learners start drawing upon a specific aptitude. This can easily be controlled for if researchers control for the amount of learning by establishing a criterion level of learning, requiring all learners to reach this criterion, and letting time to criterion vary, instead of the more common method in instructional SLA studies where time or task is controlled for and the amount of learning is varied.

In this chapter, we have tried to put a spotlight on a long-standing bias in previous aptitude research toward including cognitive aptitudes that belong to the domain of explicit, attention-driven cognitive processes. We have illustrated this bias in the context of CF research and called for more attention to implicit cognitive processes by proposing two avenues of future research that will help determine the reliability and construct validity of measures that can be used to operationalize ILA, as well as the predictive validity of ILA and ELA in the context of instructional conditions.

Note

1 Compared to explicit cognitive measures, implicit measures face the problem of reliability. On the one hand, standard internal-consistency approaches are not appropriate for some types of implicit learning tasks. On the other hand, reliability indices are not as high as those reported for explicit learning tasks. Granena (2013a) reported a reliability of .44 for a probabilistic serial reaction time task, using split-halves with Spearman-Brown correction. Kaufman et al. (2010) also reported a reliability of .44 and considered it standard for probabilistic SRT tasks on the basis of the reliability of implicit learning in the literature (Dienes, 1992; Reber, Walkenfeld, & Hernstadt, 1991; Robinson, 1997). Reber et al. (1991), and Robinson's (1997) replication study reported split-half reliabilities of .51 and .52, respectively, also using the Spearman-Brown correction. While low reliability indices are a cause for concern, not all implicit measures have low reliability. Kalra (2015), for instance, reported moderate test-retest reliability indices for a serial reaction time task, a category learning task, and a probabilistic classification task. Also, as explained by Woltz (2003), imposing greater processing constraints on a task will increase reliability. For example, one option is to set specific performance goals and avoid multiple solutions for an item, since these can involve different cognitive processes.

References

Abrahamsson, N., & Hyltenstam, K. (2008). The robustness of aptitude effects in near-native second language acquisition. *Studies in Second Language Acquisition, 30*, 481–509.

Ackerman, P. L. (1988). Determinants of individual differences during skill acquisition: Cognitive abilities and information processing. *Journal of Experimental Psychology: General, 117*, 288–318.

Anderson, J. R. (1993). *Rules of the mind*. Hillsdale, NJ: Lawrence Erlbaum Associates, Inc.

Arroyo, D., & Yilmaz, Y. (in press). The role of language analytic ability in the effectiveness of different feedback timing conditions. In L. Gurzynski-Weiss (Ed.), *Expanding individual difference research in the interaction approach: Investigating learners, instructors, and other interlocutors*. Amsterdam, The Netherlands: John Benjamins Publishing Company.

Barrett, L. F., Tugade, M. M., & Engle, R. W. (2004). Individual differences in working memory capacity and dual-process theories of the mind. *Psychological Bulletin, 130,* 553–573.

Bergstrom, F., & Eriksson, J. (2014). Maintenance of non-consciously presented information engages the prefrontal cortex. *Frontiers in Human Neuroscience, 8.* https://doi.org/10.3389/fnhum.2014.00938

Bergstrom, F., & Eriksson, J. (2015). The conjunction of non-consciously perceived object identity and spatial position can be retained during a visual short-term memory task. *Frontiers in Psychology, 6.* https://doi.org/10.3389/fpsyg.2015.01470

Bley-Vroman, R. (1990). The logical problem of Foreign language learning. *Linguistic Analysis, 20,* 3–49.

Brill-Schuetz, K. A., & Morgan-Short, K. (2014). The role of procedural memory in adult second language acquisition. In P. Bello, M. Guarini, M. McShane, & B. Scassellati (Eds.), *Proceedings of the 36th annual conference of the cognitive science society* (pp. 260–265). Quebec City: Cognitive Science Society.

Carroll, J. B. (1958). A factor analysis of two Foreign language aptitude batteries. *Journal of General Psychology, 59,* 3–19.

Carroll, J. B. (1966). A parametric study of language training in the Peace Corps. Cambridge, MA: Laboratory for Research in Instruction, Graduate School of Education, Harvard University Press.

Carroll, J. B. (1981). Twenty-five years of research in Foreign language aptitude. In K. Diller (Ed.), *Individual differences and universals in language learning aptitude* (pp. 83–118). Rowley, MA: Newbury House.

Carroll, J. B., & Sapon, S. (1959). *Modern language aptitude test: Form a.* New York, NY: Psychological Corporation.

Cleeremans, A., & Jimenez, L. (2002). Implicit learning and consciousness: A graded, dynamic perspective. In R. M. French & A. Cleeremans (Eds.), *Implicit learning and consciousness: An empirical, computational and philosophical consensus in the making?* (pp. 1–40). Hove, UK: Psychology Press.

De Graaff, R. (1997). The Esperanto experiment: Effects of explicit instruction on second language acquisition. *Studies in Second Language Acquisition, 19,* 249–276.

DeKeyser, R. (2000). The robustness of critical period effects in second language acquisition. *Studies in Second Language Acquisition, 22,* 499–533.

Dienes, Z. (1992). Connectionist and memory-array models of artificial grammar learning. *Cognitive Science, 16,* 41–79.

Dornyei, Z., & Skehan, P. (2003). Individual differences in second language learning. In C. J. Doughty & M. H. Long (Eds.), *The handbook of second language acquisition* (pp. 589–630). Oxford: Blackwell Publishing.

Ehrman, M., & Oxford, R. (1995). Cognition plus: Correlates of language learning success. *Modern Language Journal, 79,* 67–89.

Engle, R. W., Tuholski, S. W., Laughlin, J. E., & Conway, A. R. A. (1999). Working memory, short-term memory, and general fluid intelligence: A latent-variable approach. *Journal of Experimental Psychology: General, 128,* 309–331.

Evans, J. S. B. T. (2008). Dual-processing accounts of reasoning, judgment, and social cognition. *Annual Review of Psychology, 59,* 255–278.

Faretta-Stutenberg, M., & Morgan-Short, K. (2017). The interplay of individual differences and context of learning in behavioral and neurocognitive second language development. *Second Language Research,* 1–35.

Goo, J. (2012). Corrective feedback and working memory capacity in interaction-driven L2 learning. *Studies in Second Language Acquisition, 34,* 445–474.

Goo, J. (2016). Corrective feedback and working memory capacity: A replication. In G. Granena, D. O. Jackson, & Y. Yilmaz (Eds.), *Cognitive individual differences in second language processing and acquisition* (pp. 279–302). Amsterdam, The Netherlands: John Benjamins Publishing Company.

Goo, J., Granena, G., Yilmaz, Y., & Novella, M. (2015). Implicit and explicit instruction in L2 learning. In P. Rebuschat (Ed.), *Implicit and explicit learning of languages* (pp. 443–482). Amsterdam, The Netherlands: John Benjamins Publishing Company.

Granena, G. (2013a). Cognitive aptitudes for second language learning and the LLAMA language aptitude test. In G. Granena & M. H. Long (Eds.), *Sensitive periods, language aptitude, and ultimate L2 attainment* (pp. 105–129). Amsterdam, The Netherlands: John Benjamins Publishing Company.

Granena, G. (2013b). Individual differences in sequence learning ability and SLA in early childhood and adulthood. *Language Learning, 63,* 665–703.

Granena, G. (2016). Cognitive aptitudes for implicit and explicit learning and information-processing styles: An individual differences study. *Applied Psycholinguistics, 37,* 577–600.

Granena, G., & Long, M. H. (2013). Age of onset, length of residence, aptitude and ultimate L2 attainment in three linguistic domains. *Second Language Research, 29,* 311–343.

Harley, B., & Hart, D. (1997). Language aptitude and second language proficiency in classroom learners of different starting ages. *Studies in Second Language Acquisition, 19,* 379–400.

Janacsek, K., Fiser, J., & Nemeth, D. (2012). The best time to acquire new skills: Age-related differences in implicit sequence learning across the human lifespan. *Developmental Science, 15,* 496–505.

Jimenez, L. (2002). Attention in probabilistic sequence learning. In L. Jimenez (Ed.), *Attention and implicit learning* (pp. 43–67). Amsterdam, The Netherlands: John Benjamins Publishing Company.

Kalra, P. (2015). *Implicit learning: Development, individual differences, and educational implications* (Unpublished doctoral dissertation), Harvard University.

Kalra, P., Finn, A., & Gabrieli, J. D. E. (2014). *Construct validity of implicit learning: Agreement across tasks.* Poster presented at the Association for Psychological Science Annual Convention San Francisco, CA.

Kane, M. J., Conway, A. R. A., Hambrick, D. Z., & Engle, R. W. (2007). Variation in working memory capacity as variation in executive attention and control. In A. R. A. Conway, C. Jarrold, M. J. Kane, A. Miyake, & J. N. Towse (Eds.), *Variation in working memory* (pp. 21–48). New York, NY: Oxford University Press.

Kaufman, S., DeYoung, C., Gray, J., Jimenez, L., Brown, J., & Mackintosh, N. (2010). Implicit learning as an ability. *Cognition, 116,* 321–340.

Knowlton, B., Squire, L. R., & Gluck, M. A. (1994). Probabilistic classification in amnesia. *Learning and Memory, 1,* 106–120.

Kyllonen, P. C. (1996). Is working memory capacity Spearman's g? In I. Dennis & P. Tapsfield (Eds.), *Human abilities: Their nature and measurement* (pp. 49–75). Hillsdale, NJ: Lawrence Erlbaum Associates, Inc.

Kyllonen, P. C., & Christal, R. E. (1990). Reasoning ability is (little more than) working-memory capacity? *Intelligence, 14,* 389–433.

Li, S. (2010). The effectiveness of corrective feedback in SLA: A meta-analysis. *Language Learning, 60,* 309–365.

Li, S. (2013). The interactions between the effects of implicit and explicit feedback and individual differences in language analytic ability and working memory. *The Modern Language Journal, 97*, 634–654.

Li, S. (2015). The associations between language aptitude and second language grammar acquisition: A meta-analytic review of five decades of research. *Applied Linguistics, 36*, 385–408.

Li, S. (2016). The construct validity of language aptitude. A meta-analysis. *Studies in Second Language Acquisition, 38*, 801–842.

Linck, J. A., Hughes, M. M., Campbell, S. G., Silbert, N. H., Tare, M., Jackson, S. R., Smith, B. K., Bunting, M. F., Doughty, C. J. (2013). Hi-LAB: A new measure of aptitude for high-level language proficiency. *Language Learning, 63*, 530–566.

Long, M. H. (1991). Focus on form: A design feature in language teaching methodology. In K. de Bot, R. B. Ginsberg, & C. Kramsch (Eds.), *Foreign language research in cross-cultural perspective* (Vol. 2, pp. 39–52). Philadelphia, PA: John Benjamins Publishing Company.

Long, M. H. (1996). The role of the linguistic environment in second language acquisition. In W. Ritchie & T. K. Bhatia (Eds.), *Handbook of second language acquisition* (pp. 413–468). New York, NY: Academic Press.

Long, M. H. (2007). *Problems in SLA.* Mahwah, NJ: Lawrence Erlbaum Associates, Inc.

Long, M. H. (2015). *Second language acquisition and task-based language teaching.* Malden, MA: Wiley-Blackwell.

Long, M. H. (2017). Instructed Second Language Acquisition (ISLA): Geopolitics, methodological issues, and some major research questions. *Instructed Second Language Acquisition, 1*, 7–44.

Long, M. H., & Robinson, P. (1998). *Focus on form in classroom second language acquisition.* New York, NY: Cambridge University Press.

Lyster, R., Saito, K., & Sato, M. (2013). Oral corrective feedback in second language classrooms. *Language Teaching, 46*, 1–40.

Mackey, A., & Goo, J. (2007). Interaction research in SLA: A meta-analysis and research synthesis. In A. Mackey (Ed.), *Conversational interaction in SLA: A collection of empirical studies* (pp. 408–452). New York, NY: Oxford University Press.

Mackey, A., Philp, J., Egi, T., Fujii, A., & Tatsumi, T. (2002). Individual differences in working memory, noticing of interactional feedback and L2 development. In P. Robinson (Ed.), *Individual differences and instructed language learning.* Philadelphia, PA: John Benjamins Publishing Company.

Meara, P. (2005). *LLAMA language aptitude tests.* Swansea, UK: Lognostics.

Morgan-Short, K., Faretta-Stutenberg, M., Brill-Schuetz, K., Carpenter, H., & Wong, P. C. M. (2014). Declarative and procedural memory as individual differences in second language acquisition. *Bilingualism: Language and Cognition, 17*, 56–72.

Nassaji, H. (2015). *The interactional feedback dimension in instructed second language learning: Linking Theory, Research and Practice.* New York, NY: Bloomsbury Publishing.

Norris, J. M., & Ortega, L. (2000). Effectiveness of L2 instruction: A research synthesis and quantitative meta-analysis. *Language Learning, 50*, 417–528.

Peterson, C. R., Al-Haik, A. R. (1976). The development of the Defense Language Aptitude Battery DLAB. *Educational and Psychological Measurement, 36*, 369–380.

Pimsleur, P. (1966). *Pimsleur Language Aptitude Battery (PLAB).* New York, NY: Psychological Corporation.

Reber, A. S. (1967). Implicit learning of artificial grammars. *Journal of Verbal Learning and Verbal Behavior, 6*, 317–327.

Reber, A. S. (1993). *Implicit learning and tacit knowledge: An essay on the cognitive unconscious.* London: Oxford University Press.

Reber, A. S., Walkenfeld, F., & Hernstadt, R. (1991). Implicit and explicit learning: Individual differences and IQ. *Journal of Experimental Psychology: Learning, Memory, and Cognition, 17,* 888–896.

Révész, A. (2012). Working memory and the observed effectiveness of recasts on different l2 outcome measures. *Language Learning, 62,* 93–132.

Robinson, P. (1995). Attention, memory, and the "noticing" hypothesis. *Language Learning, 45,* 283–331.

Robinson, P. (1997). Individual differences and the fundamental similarity of implicit and explicit adult second language learning. *Language Learning, 47,* 45–99.

Robinson, P. (2002). Individual differences in intelligence, aptitude and working memory during adult incidental second language learning: A replication and extension of Reber, Walkenfeld, and Hernstadt (1991). In P. Robinson (Ed.), *Individual differences and instructed language learning* (pp. 211–266). Amsterdam, The Netherlands: John Benjamins Publishing Company.

Schmidt, R. (2001). Attention. In P. Robinson (Ed.), *Cognition and second language instruction* (pp. 3–32). Cambridge, UK: Cambridge University Press.

Schneider, W., & Shiffrin, R. M. (1977). Controlled and automatic human information processing: I. Detection, search and attention. *Psychological Review, 84,* 1–66.

Sheen, Y. (2007). The effect of focused written corrective feedback and language aptitude on ESL learners' acquisition of articles. *TESOL Quarterly, 41,* 255–283.

Sheen, Y., & Ellis, R. (2011). Corrective feedback in L2 teaching. In E. Hinkel (Ed.), *Handbook of research in second language teaching and learning* (pp. 593–610). New York, NY: Routledge.

Skehan, P. (1998). *A cognitive approach to language learning.* Oxford, UK: Oxford University Press.

Skehan, P. (2015). Foreign language aptitude and its relationship with grammar: A critical overview. *Applied Linguistics, 36,* 367–384.

Tomlin, R., & Villa, V. (1994). Attention in cognitive science and second language acquisition. *Studies in Second Language Acquisition, 16,* 183–204.

Trofimovich, P., Ammar, A., & Gatbonton, E. (2007). How effective are recasts? The role of attention, memory, and analytical ability. In A. Mackey (Ed.), *Conversational interaction in second language acquisition* (pp. 144–171). Oxford: Oxford University Press.

Unterrainer, J. M., Rahm, B., Leonhart, R., Ruff, C. C., & Halsband, U. (2003). The Tower of London: The impact of instructions, cueing, and learning on planning abilities. *Cognitive Brain Research, 17,* 675–683.

Williams, J. (1999). Memory, attention, and inductive learning. *Studies in Second Language Acquisition, 21,* 1–48.

Woltz, D. J. (1988). An investigation of the role of working memory in procedural skill acquisition. *Journal of Experimental Psychology: General, 117,* 319–331.

Woltz, D. J. (1990a). Decay of repetition priming effects and its relation to retention from text processing: A study of forgetting. *Learning and Individual Differences, 2,* 241–261.

Woltz, D. J. (1990b). Repetition of semantic comparisons: Temporary and persistent priming effects. *Journal of Experimental Psychology: Learning, Memory, and Cognition, 16,* 392–403.

Woltz, D. J. (1999). Individual differences in priming: The roles of implicit facilitation from prior processing. In P. L. Ackerman, P. C. Kyllonen, & R. D. Roberts (Eds.), *Learning and individual differences: Process, trait, and content determinants* (pp. 135–156). Washington, DC: American Psychological Association.

Woltz, D. (2003). Implicit cognitive processes as aptitudes for learning. *Educational Psychologist, 38,* 95–104.

Yilmaz, Y. (2013). Relative effects of explicit and implicit feedback: The role of working memory capacity and language analytic ability. *Applied Linguistics, 34,* 344–368.

Yilmaz, Y. (2016). The linguistic environment, interaction and negative feedback. *Brill Research Perspectives in Multilingualism and Second Language Acquisition, 1,* 45–86.

Yilmaz, Y., & Granena, G. (2016). The role of cognitive aptitudes for explicit language learning in the relative effects of explicit and implicit feedback. *Bilingualism: Language and Cognition, 19,* 147–161.

Yilmaz, Y., & Koylu, Y. (2016). The interaction between feedback exposure condition and phonetic coding ability. In G. Granena, D. O. Jackson, & Y. Yilmaz (Eds.), *Cognitive individual differences in second language processing and acquisition* (pp. 303–326). Amsterdam, The Netherlands: John Benjamins Publishing Company.

PART IV

Perspectives From Cognitive Neuroscience

13

NEUROPHYSIOLOGICAL INDICATORS OF THE LINGUISTIC COMPONENTS OF LANGUAGE APTITUDE

Jinxing Yue

Introduction

Language learning is highly complex and needs most components of the cognitive and the sensory-motor systems. As a result, aptitude for learning a language has been treated as a componential concept, covering those most important abilities that are decisive to the outcome of learning (Carroll, 1981; Skehan, 1998; Sparks, Patton, Ganschow, & Humbach, 2011; Wen, Biedroń, & Skehan, 2017). These abilities can be roughly divided into two categories, linguistic and general cognitive abilities, as reflected in most aptitude-assessing instruments (e.g., the Modern Language Aptitude Test [MLAT], Carroll & Sapon, 1959; the Pimsleur Language Aptitude Battery [PLAB], Pimsleur, 1966; the High-level Language Aptitude Battery [Hi-LAB], Linck et al., 2013). The linguistic category usually consists of phonological/phonetic, semantic, and (morpho-)syntactic components, whereas the general cognitive category may include several types of memory (working memory, long-term memory, rote memorization, associative memory), executive functioning, and sequence learning.

While growing attention has been placed on the role of general cognition, how to assess the linguistic components of language aptitude, "linguistic aptitude" for short, remains underdeveloped. The linguistic aptitude we propose here refers to the talent of acquiring a language at three fundamental levels, namely phonological, semantic, and (morpho-)syntactic levels. Our proposal of linguistic aptitude is based on the assumption of language autonomy, meaning that language rules and knowledge are an autonomous "cognitive organ", which is independent from other cognitive systems in the human brain (Chomsky, 2005; Epstein, 2007). That is to say, one's talent for learning a language can, to some extent, be decided by the condition of his or her *pure* linguistic brain function, conceptualized as linguistic aptitude.

However, it might be enormously difficult if one wants to assess linguistic aptitude without involving any general cognition. The reasons are twofold. First, the tasks in existing aptitude tests, even those claimed to design for testing linguistic abilities (e.g., MLAT and PLAB), are bound to induce high cognitive complexity beyond linguistic dimensions, given their paper-and-pencil or computer-based testing formats. In order to display good performance in choosing a correct answer from alternatives, participants must try to make use of not only their linguistic abilities but also other cognitive abilities such as short-term memory and executive functioning. Second, since language learning is very complex in nature, the *pure* linguistic abilities are subjected to be mixed with general cognition during communication, especially when they are judged by referring to the results of language-learning or language-related tasks.

Thanks to the development of noninvasive neural technologies, researchers can monitor real-time neural activities in cognitive processing by using proper experimental methods and neurophysiological indicators. Therefore, this chapter aims to address how to test linguistic aptitude from a neurophysiological perspective and present our evaluation of the applicability of three event-related brain responses for assessing linguistic aptitude.

A Neurophysiological Perspective of Linguistic Aptitude

Our focus on the linguistic components of language-learning aptitude is not only derived from linguistic theories but also corroborated by accumulating evidence. Specifically, the processing of language is not merely the summation of processing of physical cues comprising linguistic input, but rather demonstrates high linguistic specificity in terms of phonology (Sharma, Kraus, McGee, Carrell, & Nicol, 1993; Tervaniemi & Hugdahl, 2003; Zatorre & Gandour, 2008), semantics (Kutas & Hillyard, 1980, 1984), and syntax (Friederici, 2011; Makuuchi, Bahlmann, Anwander, & Friederici, 2009). Thus, the human brain can develop high-order mental/neural representations encoding linguistic information above the basic sensory, episodic, and hierarchical representation levels. As a result, language input can directly activate these experience-based representations at a remarkable speed to achieve communication. Therefore, it is reasonable to propose that the linguistic abilities, regardless of their related behavioral phenotypes, are decided by the specific brain function for representing and processing linguistic input. Moreover, by forging a link between the behavioral changes induced by learning and the neural changes correspondingly, we propose that one's linguistic components of language aptitude, the *pure* linguistic aptitude, is decided by the individual's neural plasticity of related neural networks. Following this idea, linguistic aptitude can be quantified by measuring the neuronal changes induced by novel linguistic input.

Is there such a method allowing us to access the neural features underlying the alleged *pure* linguistic abilities? The advancement of noninvasive neurophysiological recording techniques for humans may provide some possible solutions to this issue. Two widely used techniques are electroencephalography (EEG) and magnetoencephalography (MEG), both of which record the electrical and corresponding magnetic reflections of neural activities instantly. Taking EEG as an example, electrical signals are collected with highly sensitive sensors placed over the scalp. After being amplified, the analogue signals are transformed into digital data for further analysis.

Since far-field signals are inevitably confounded with noise, how to extract the indication of brain waves is a key to understanding human neurocognition. A classic method used in cognitive research for this purpose is called event-related potential (ERP, Luck, 2005). To obtain meaningful ERPs, the onset of events must be marked in the first place. Then, continuous EEG before and after the onset marker is segmented according to a fixed time epoch. By averaging the segmentation of the same type of cognitive events, relatively stable brain potential patterns will emerge. ERP effects related to certain cognitive processing are reflected by comparing the potential differences between two conditions, which differ only in such assumed cognitive processing. With this technique, a large body of literature has documented the association between linguistic processes and neurophysiological responses (see Kaan, 2007 for a general overview of ERP studies). Thus far, the most robust neural indicators of language processes include but are not limited to auditory evoked potentials for phonological processing (e.g., P1-N1-P2 complex in Tremblay, Kraus, McGee, Ponton, & Otis, 2001; N1 in Yue, Alter, Howard, & Bastiaanse, 2017); mismatch negativity for phonological, semantic, and syntactic processes (MMN, Shtyrov & Pulvermüller, 2007); early left anterior negativity for revising anomalous local phrasal structure (ELAN, Friederici, Pfeifer, & Hahne, 1993); left anterior negativity for processing morphosyntactic errors (Neville, Nicol, Barss, Forster, & Garrett, 1991); N400 for semantic-related processing (Kutas & Hillyard, 1980, 1984); and P600 for syntactic-related processing (Osterhout & Holcomb, 1992). These fundamental processes provide a pool of linguistic-related neurophysiological effects that may be developed for use in assessing linguistic aptitude.

Another merit of neurophysiology is its high temporal resolution, allowing researchers to capture simultaneous neural activities related to cognitive analysis at a millisecond level. Furthermore, such neural responses tend to reflect more automatic (and less strategic) cognitive processes than behavioral responses, as neurophysiological data are usually gleaned in a strictly controlled experimental context in which participants are often asked to perform some simple tasks and thus are exempt from doing traditional aptitude tests in a pencil-and-paper style. Moreover, a number of studies have shown that linguistic processing could begin even in the pre-attentive processing stage, as indicated by obligatory evoked brain responses obtained without any overt tasks (e.g., Hanna, Shtyrov, Williams, & Pulvermüller, 2016; Näätänen et al., 1997; Luo et al., 2006; Pulvermüller et al., 2001; Shtyrov, Kimppa, Pulvermüller, & Kujala, 2011; Yue et al., 2017). This means that neurophysiology may offer a peculiar perspective for testing one's biological foundation of linguistic aptitude before confounding cognitive factors set in, without using complicated tests. In order to choose the most applicable neurophysiological indicators for measuring linguistic aptitude, we first tentatively discuss the criteria that a qualified indicator should meet. Then, we evaluate three candidates: N400, P600, and MMN, by referring to the criteria.

Possible Criteria for Measuring Linguistic Aptitude Neurophysiologically

As mentioned earlier, language-related processes have been linked with many types of brain responses, electrical and magnetic. However, there is no guarantee that all these effects are suitable to be used as neurophysiological indictors for language aptitude. Here, we tentatively propose five criteria for a further survey: 1) being sensitive to (psycho)linguistic manipulations, 2) showing sensitivity toward native and foreign/second language speakers, 3) being modulatable by language learning, 4) showing sensitivity to individual differences, and 5) being elicitable without complex tasks.

Criterion 1: Being Sensitive to (Psycho)Linguistic Manipulations

Linguistic processes involve many aspects such as phonology, semantics, and (morpho-)syntax. Psycholinguistic studies have also revealed systemic variations of some neurophysiological responses with different manipulations in terms of phonetic features, word frequency, or syntactic complexity (Friederici, 1997; Friederici & Singer, 2015; Shtyrov & Pulvermüller, 2007). Therefore, a neurophysiological measure can be potentially applicable for assessing linguistic aptitude only when it can be sensitive to manipulations in one of these aspects as an indication of its linguistic specificity.

Criterion 2: Sensitivity in Native and Foreign/Second Language Processing

Although the processing of similar linguistic features in native and non-native languages is not required to follow the same routine (e.g., Osterhout et al., 2008), we still take the sensitivity of a neurophysiological response to native and L2 (including foreign languages) into consideration. The rationale is that only when a neurophysiological response could present itself in processing both native and non-native languages could we generate a reasonable interpretation for the lack of native-like brain responses in, for example, L2 language processing, and establish associations between various response patterns with linguistic aptitude further.

Criterion 3: Being Modulatable by Language Learning

As proposed in an earlier section, we hold that the linguistic ability of learning a language is decided by an individual's neural plasticity. Changes in the neurophysiological responses have been widely used to indicate neural plasticity of language function (e.g., Shtyrov, 2011; Shtyrov, Nikulin, & Pulvermüller, 2010; Yue, Bastiaanse, & Alter, 2014). Therefore, if a linguistically specific neurophysiological response can vary with language learning, it is very likely to become an indicator of one's neurobiological plasticity in response to linguistic input.

Criterion 4: Sensitivity to Individual Difference

This criterion is very important for an indicator to become an assessment tool to quantify linguistic aptitude. However, as most neurophysiological studies are designed based on group comparison, our understanding about the individual difference of ERP and ERF effects is still limited. As a result, there should be a less restricted version of this criterion as well in which we expect a neurophysiology response to be able to reflect group characteristics in terms of linguistic aptitude.

Criterion 5: Being Elicitable Without Complex Tasks

As mentioned earlier, one of the most valuable merits for the neurophysiological method is its independence from complicated procedures while measuring language aptitude. Ideally, if a neural response can be obtained without overt tasks, such a response is very likely to reflect autonomous and automatic linguistic mechanisms with minimal interaction with the general cognition.

Evaluation of Neurophysiological Effects: N400, P600, and MMN

In this section, we chose three language-related neurophysiological responses, namely N400, P600, and MMN, to be the candidates for a further survey. N400 and P600 are discussed together, considering their similarity in elicitation conditions.

N400 and P600

N400 and P600 may be the most well-known neurophysiological indices for linguistic processes. Although the functional correlates of the N400 and P600 are still far from conclusive, a dichotomy of semantics and syntax, as indicated by the two ERPs, has been widely accepted (for N400 see, Kutas & Federmeier, 2011; for P600 see, Kaan, Harris, Gibson, & Holcomb, 2000).

The N400 is a negative-going deflection, peaking around 400 ms after the onset of a stimulus, with a typical scalp distribution around the centroparietal region. It was first reported by Kutas and Hillyard (1980) when they recorded the ERPs to words triggering semantic incongruity during sentence reading (e.g., *He spread the warm cream on his SOCKS★*). Nowadays, greater N400 amplitude is generally related to semantic processing/accessing difficulties.

The P600, on the other hand, is related to syntactic processing. This late component is a slow positivity, being prominent around 600 ms after stimulus onset, typically distributed in the centroparietal scalp region. It was first reported in Osterhout and Holcomb (1992) by using garden-path sentences in which the sentence comprehension system has to revise its original parsing in order to correctly interpret a sentence when receiving the input of a critical word (e.g., *The broker persuaded TO sell the stock was tall*). The capitalized TO is the critical word leading to correction of the original parsing. The P600 has also been found when participants comprehend sentences containing grammatical errors, including tense, gender, case, and wh-dependency (Gouvea, Phillips, Kazanina, & Poeppel, 2009; Hagoort, Brown, & Groothusen, 1993; Kaan et al., 2000). To be brief, although P600 can be elicited in various conditions, it is clear that it is closely related to syntactic processes.

Moreover, the two ERPs have not only been discovered in the processing of native languages but have also been found elicitable in L2 language processing (Hahne, 2001; Kaan, 2007; Xue et al., 2013; Qi et al., 2017), suggesting some general linguistic processing mechanisms (e.g., semantics and syntax) are shared by native and non-native languages. For example, in a seminal study, Hahne (2001) found that the N400 responses to L2 words showed decreased amplitude and prolonged latency relative to the N400 features to words in L1. L2 speakers with high grammatical proficiency could also demonstrate native-like P600 effects (McLaughlin et al., 2010) even under a classroom instructional context (Osterhout et al., 2008). In sum, the N400 and P600 have distinctive sensitivity to linguistic processes in both native and non-native languages and thus meet Criteria 1 and 2.

N400 and P600 have been found to reflect the neural changes induced by some aspects of language learning (Criterion 3). Word learning usually leads to attenuated N400 responses to novel lexical items (Bakker, Takashima, Hell, Janzen, & McQueen, 2015; Batterink & Neville, 2011; Borovsky, Kutas, & Elman, 2010; McLaughlin, Osterhout, & Kim, 2004; Mestres-Missé, Rodriguez-Fornells, & Münte, 2007) or enhanced N400 effects when trained lexical units induce semantic anomalies (Angwin, Phua, & Copland, 2014). For example, Mestres-Missé and colleagues (Mestres-Missé et al., 2007) monitored the changes of N400 responses in healthy adults while they were exposed to novel word-forms embedded in different contexts. Novel words refer to pseudowords that are created by following the phonotactic rules of the participants' native language. In their study, after being exposed to novel Spanish words (e.g., *★anclana*, the asterisk indicates a meaningless word-form) three times while reading sentences in silence, participants showed decreased, real-word-like N400 to novel words only when contexts encouraged meaning derivation but no prominent changes in semantically confusing contexts. Furthermore, the learning effect could also be observed in the semantic processes of trained novel words when presented in isolation. This study contributed reliable evidence that the N400 dynamics are related to semantic learning in one's native language.

The P600 has been used as a neural indicator for grammar learning (Bowden, Steinhauer, Sanz, & Ullman, 2013; Sabourin & Stowe, 2008; White, Genesee, & Steinhauer, 2012). For example, White et al. (2012) examined the brain responses in late L2 learners during reading English before and after an intensive training program. The participants had different L1 backgrounds. They found no P600 responses in both Korean and Chinese L1 participants, even though Korean also has regular morphological inflections to express past tense as in English. (There is no such grammatical rule in Chinese.) After the nine-week intensive learning session, significant P600 effects were identified in both L1 groups. Furthermore, the neurophysiological changes were accompanied by enhanced behavioral performance in grammaticality judgment, indicating a very close relationship between the P600 and syntactic learning.

More interestingly, the N400 and P600 can reflect individual difference of the ability to learn words and grammar (Criterion 4). According to a very recent study, the researchers (Qi et al., 2017) first established participants' N400 and P600 profiles during auditory sentence comprehension. Then they put subjects in a four-day artificial language training. The mastery of vocabulary and novel syntactic rules was tested after the training. The results revealed that the size of people's N400 could predict their performance in both vocabulary and syntactic learning, whereas the P600 could predict the outcome of syntactic learning only. However, this study did not measure language-learning aptitude with standardized aptitude batteries, but the results still suggest that N400 and P600 can capture individual traits of language learning and may be possible tools for measuring the aptitude of storing novel semantic and syntactic input.

However, in terms of individual differences, great care must be taken, especially when testing for language-learning aptitude with non-native materials, because linguistic processes in a non-native language may present qualitatively different patterns from those in a native language. The reasons are as follows. First, even for the same grammatical devices, non-native speakers may rely on distinctive mechanisms in different stages of learning (Bowden et al., 2013; McLaughlin et al., 2010; Osterhout et al., 2008; Tanner et al., 2013; van Hell & Tokowicz, 2010). For example, Osterhout and colleagues (Osterhout et al., 2008) found that a grammatical anomaly (missing phonological cues in verbal person spelling) in French elicited an N400 effect in early L2 learners. In contrast, the same anomalies triggered a P600 effect in the later phase of L2 learning. In another study, Tanner and colleagues (Tanner et al., 2013) recruited English L1 students studying German as a foreign language in first-year and third-year courses. They found that only the third-grade students exhibited native-like P600 to violated subject–verb agreement during sentence reading. Faced with the same grammatical violation, only some of the first-year students showed P600 responses, whereas others showed N400 effects.

Second, linguistic processing may have varied sensitivity to different grammatical rules in a non-native language (Foucart & Frenck-Mestre, 2012; Sabourin & Stowe, 2008). For example, Foucart and Frenck-Mestre (2012) tested late L2 French learners whose L1 was English. They found similar P600 effects in both L1 and L2 French speakers when reading gender agreement violations between a noun and a postposed adjective, which is the canonical word order. However, when the violation is between a preposed adjective and noun, a less frequent but correct word order in French, a P600 effect was found in native speakers but an N400 effect was identified in L2 French learners. Such variation in grammatical sensitivity may be caused by the changing similarities between those grammatical rules in L1 and L2 (Sabourin & Stowe, 2008; Foucart & Frenck-Mestre, 2012). That is, only grammatical rules in L2 that are similar to those in L1 can be fully acquired and thus be indicated by the P600 (but see Meulman, Stowe, Sprenger, Bresser, & Schmid, 2014 for data showing no role of grammatical similarity in modulating the P600 sensitivity).

Moreover, even though the two ERP responses meet Criteria 1 to 4, the N400 and P600 have a methodological limitation for revealing the *pure* linguistic aptitude, which is supposedly independent from the other general cognitive functions as mentioned in Criterion 5. First, the cognitive processes in the typical time windows (300–700 ms) of the two ERPs are generally considered to be more controlled by awareness rather than more automatic in nature (Batterink, Karns, Yamada, & Neville, 2010; Hahne & Friederici, 1999). Therefore, the linguistic processes related to the N400 and P600 are unlikely to be based solely on the linguistic module of cognition. Second, both N400 and P600 are reliably observed when participants are asked to perform some overt tasks with full attention paid to lexical or sentential stimuli (for N400 see Coulson & Brang, 2010; for P600 see related Batterink & Neville, 2013; Gunter & Friederici, 1999; Hahne & Friederici, 2002). In order to complete a task, one has to make use of attention, memory retrieval, executive function, and other brain capacities apart from linguistic cognition. Consequently, it is difficult to decide whether the N400 and P600 represent semantic and syntactic processes or reflect a mixture of various cognitive functions.

This methodological concern is of highly practical interest because studies have shown that the magnitude of N400 and P600 are indeed influenced by the degree of attention (Holcomb, 1988). Therefore, although the two ERPs may be very powerful tools used to reveal some neural correlates of overall language learning, they may not be perfect neurophysiological indicators for linguistic aptitude, as the two candidates do not meet Criterion 5.

Mismatch Negativity (MMN)

As discussed in the previous section, although N400 and P600 seem to be very promising neural markers for predicting achievement in learning a new language, they are not ideal tools for assessing linguistic aptitude because they are thought to reflect postlexical processes based on the interaction of many components of cognition. In this section, our discussion is centered around another classic neurophysiological effect, MMN, which has the potential to overcome the limitations of N400 and P600.

The MMN is a time-locked electrical or magnetic response[1] elicited by rare events (the 'deviant' stimuli) amid a repetitive sequence of another more frequently presented stimuli (the 'standard' stimuli). This is called an 'oddball paradigm'. The MMN is mainly used to study auditory processing and has been reliably elicited in visual modality as well, called vMMN (Czigler, Balázs, & Winkler, 2002; Stagg, Hindley, Tales, & Butler, 2004). Considering its elicitation conditions, the MMN has been primarily associated with change detection and auditory discrimination at a sensory level (Näätänen, Gaillard, & Mäntysalo, 1978). MMN waves are negative-going deflections, peaking between 100 ms and 250 ms time-locked to the point when an infrequent event differs physically from the frequent event (Näätänen, 1995). MMNs can be elicited when subjects' attention is distracted by performing some irrelevant tasks (Näätänen, 1995), or even when subjects are coma patients (Fischer, Morlet, Bouchet, Luaute, Jourdan, & Salord, 1999; Fischer, Morlet, & Giard, 2000). Together with its early time window, the MMN has been widely considered to reflect automatic and pre-attentive cognitive processing mechanisms. This feature makes the MMN meet Criterion 5, and is an essential advantage compared with the N400 and P600, whose full elicitation depends on the involvement of attention.

There is a vast literature showing that MMN responses can reflect cognitive processes with linguistic specificity, which is beyond the sensory processing (for reviews, see Kraus McGee, Sharma, Carrell, & Nicol, 1992; Pulvermüller & Shtyrov, 2006; Shtyrov & Pulvermüller, 2007). Researchers first established the association between MMNs to speech sounds and specific memory traces for phonemes in one's native language (Dehaene-Lambertz, 1997; Näätänen et al., 1997). For example, Näätänen and associates found that for Finnish speakers, the MMN response to the deviant Finnish vowel /e/ was significantly stronger than that to the Estonian vowel /ô/, even if the two vowels share many common acoustic features. In contrast, native Estonian speakers had enhanced MMNs to /ô/ relative to /e/, which is a prototype vowel in Finnish. Moreover, the MMN can also reflect how the neural bases for the processing segmental cues differ from those for suprasegmental cues (e.g., consonant/vowel vs. lexical tones in Chinese, Luo et al., 2006).

Aside from the phonemic and phonetic processing, a rich body of literature has also documented that the MMN is sensitive to higher-level linguistic processes, such as the access of whole-word phonology (Pulvermüller et al., 2001), lexical semantic category (Shtyrov, Hauk, & Pulvermüller, 2004; Pulvermüller, 2005), lexical frequency (Alexandrov, Boricheva, Pulvermüller, & Shtyrov, 2011 in Russian; Shtyrov et al., 2011 in English), and syntax (e.g., Pulvermüller, Shtyrov, Hasting, & Carlyon, 2008 in English; Shtyrov, Pulvermüller, Näätänen, &

Ilmoniemi, 2003 in Finnish; Herrmann, Maess, Hasting, & Friederici, 2009 in German; Hanna, & Pulvermüller, 2014 in French). To summarize, the MMN is a neurophysiological indicator that has complete sensitivity to linguistic manipulations and thus meets Criterion 1 for measuring linguistic aptitude.

Considerable evidence has demonstrated that the MMN responses can reflect the cortical plasticity induced by language learning (Menning, Imaizumi, Zwitserlood, & Pantev, 2002; Shtyrov et al., 2010; Shtyrov, 2011; Tremblay, Kraus, Carrell, & McGee, 1997; Yue et al., 2014; Zhang et al., 2009). This feature makes the MMN consistent with Criterion 3. For example, Trembley and colleagues (Tremblay et al., 1997) trained a group of native English speakers with a prevoiced labial stop sound not used phonemically in English. They found enhanced MMNs to this sound after training accompanied by improved group performance in discrimination and identification. In a more recent MEG study, Zhang and colleagues (Zhang et al., 2009) found similar enhanced MMN responses over the left hemispheric sensors after Japanese speakers were trained to discriminate between /l/ and /r/, which are not distinctive phonemes in the participants' native language.

At a lexical level, a study of our own showed that perceptual training of a novel tonal word form (a nonlexical combination of a lexical segment and a lexical tone) in native Mandarin speakers can lead to word-like MMNs after only 14 mins of exposure (Yue et al., 2014). Since the MMN elicited by words, under strict control of acoustic factors, has been associated with the cortical memory traces for lexical items (Pulvermüller et al., 2001), our finding suggests that the MMN can be an indicator for measuring one's cortical plasticity, which is induced specifically by not only features at a phonemic level but also lexical input as a whole unit.

Moreover, many studies have shown that the MMN is capable of distinguishing between successful and unsuccessful learners of languages, suggesting its potential diagnostic usage to reveal the individual difference, or even deficit, in learning a language, which is the requirement of Criterion 4. For L1 development, the MMN has drawn great attention because of its correlation with reading disorders (e.g., dyslexia) (Baldeweg, Richardson, Watkins, Foale, & Gruzilier, 1999; Schulte-Korne, Deimel, Bartling, & Remschmidt, 1998; for reviews see Näätänen, 2003; Bishop, 2006; Gabrieli, 2009). The MMN elicited by L1 materials reflects personal speech/phonological perception capability, which, in essence, determines how well a person's reading capability could develop.

More interestingly, the MMN to stimuli of non-native languages has also been investigated. Some studies have found that the MMN response to L2 stimuli differs between subjects with good or poor performance in L2 learning tasks (Diaz, Baus, Escera, Costa, & Sebastián-Gallés, 2008; Diaz, Mitterer, Broersma, & Sebastián-Gallés, 2012, 2016; Jakoby, Goldstein, & Faust, 2011). For example, in a study by Diaz and colleagues (Diaz et al., 2012), the researchers compared the MMNs in tonal contrasts, native vowel contrasts, and L2 vowel contrasts. They found decrement of MMN amplitude to L2 deviants in poor perceivers relative to good perceivers of L2 phonological contrasts as defined by their performance in a discrimination task. Moreover, attenuated MMN responses to L2 phonemic contrasts were identified in both early (Diaz et al., 2008) and late L2 learners (Diaz et al., 2016), suggesting that the individual difference in L2 phonemic processing may be a constant nature of a learner, shaping one's ability to attain speech-specific features from non-native linguistic input. In another study, Jakoby et al. (2011) found that in discriminating between foreign vowels that are phonetically contrasted, successful L2 learners showed shorter MMN latencies than unsuccessful L2 learners. Together, these studies showed that both amplitude and latency of the MMN may be indicators of linguistic aptitude.

The MMN in non-native languages also varies with a speaker's fluency or proficiency. Using acoustically similar vowel contrasts in Finnish, Winkler et al. (1999) found MMNs only in fluent Finnish speakers as a foreign language but not in those without knowledge about Finnish. Recently, Hanna and colleagues (Hanna et al., 2016) examined the brain magnetic responses to local agreement violation in English with a multifeature MMN paradigm design in which they repeatedly presented agreement-correct and -incorrect sentences as the deviant stimuli (low recurrence probability) with grammatical sentences as the standards (high recurrence probability). All stimulus sentences differed only at the sentences' final phonemes (e.g., standard: "We tick"; ungrammatical deviant: "We ticks"; grammatical deviant: "We ticked"). Control sentences were also applied to rule out the potential acoustic effect on the MMN responses. They found MMN in both native and highly proficient English learners but not in English learners with low proficiency. Moreover, the source strength of the MMN localized in the superior temporal gyrus, which is the primary auditory cortex, was found to be correlated with an individual's grammatical proficiency.

In summary, these studies have shown that the MMN can reflect linguistically specific brain mechanisms that may be used to process language input automatically even before selective attention begins to influence cognitive processing. Furthermore, the MMN is able to reflect various facets of linguistic processes according to different experimental designs. The MMN can also be modulated by language learning suggesting language-related cortical plasticity. Moreover, the MMN has shown to be a potential neurophysiological marker for native language-learning disorders and its particular sensitivity to some aspects of L2 learning. Considering all these features, the MMN meets all five criteria that we proposed in the early part of this chapter. Although the relationship between the MMN and L1 and L2 language learning is still in need of more studies, existing literature has suggested that the MMN could be a unique neurophysiological indicator of linguistic aptitude, which is the core of language-learning aptitude, given our assumption of language specificity in the human brain.

Concluding Remarks

Supported by emerging experimental evidence that the brain may realize its high efficiency in language processing by hosting some linguistic-specific representations and mechanisms, we argue that an individual's difference in learning or acquiring languages might be caused by the distinctions of the linguistic neurophysiology. Based on this idea, testing the linguistic components of language-learning aptitude is to examine the neural plasticity induced by linguistic inputs, which is supposedly independent from other modules of general cognition. However, the assessment of linguistic aptitude can be very difficult, in that traditional methods are subject to mixing both linguistic and other general cognitive components. Taking advantage of noninvasive, neurophysiological methods offering super-high-temporal resolution, we try to examine the most promising neural indicators to quantify linguistic aptitude by following five criteria. We found that the N400, P600, and MMN all have the potential to become such indicators. N400 and P600 have relatively clear interpretations of their related linguistic functions. However, a limitation is that in order to fully elicit the two neurophysiological responses, participants must be attentive and perform some tasks. Consequently, interactions between the linguistic and other general cognitive modules are inevitable.

In contrast the MMN, primarily used to study auditory function and closely related to language processing, is highly automatic and is known for representing cognitive processes before attention is activated. Therefore, the MMN has unique values for studying *pure* linguistic talents and has already been used as a measure of cortical plasticity induced by language learning. However, more studies are needed to investigate the linkage between the MMN and various aspects of language learning because current research is mainly in the auditory mode, primarily focusing on phonemes and word-form training with a few studies on syntactic learning. Our survey also shows that the three ERPs could predict some domains of language learning, but in different ways. The N400 and P600 in one's native language seem to be powerful enough to predict one's achievement in learning a new language. On the other hand, the MMN is more sensitive to the learning ability within the language by which it is elicited.

Admittedly, these ERPs are not only elicitable by linguistic stimuli but are also elicitable by nonlinguistic stimuli. For example, the MMN was originally observed by using pure tones (Näätänen et al., 1978). Although the N400 is a typical electrical response to written and spoken words presented in either an isolated or a sentential context, it can also be evoked by any potentially meaningful materials such as faces, pictures, and environmental sounds (Federmeier, Kutas, & Dickson, 2016). However, it must be noted that by setting proper experimental conditions, the ERP effects (instead of the responses themselves) can demonstrate sensitivity to psycholinguistic manipulations. Moreover, by including carefully designed control conditions, the possibility that an ERP effect merely reflects brain activities at a sensory level can be minimized.

To conclude, the existent research has provided a pool of potentially useful neural responses indicating linguistic aptitude. In order to develop these neural measures into neurophysiological indicators that examine individual linguistic aptitude, future studies should focus on the correlation between linguistic-related ERPs and the aptitude as reflected by traditional assessment tools. Then experimental protocols that can reliably elicit neural indicators for linguistic aptitude should be established and optimized for shorter duration and simpler operation continuously to enhance their practicality.

Acknowledgements

The author would like to thank Richard L. Sparks for his revision of an earlier version of this chapter and also thank David Anthony for help in proofreading. This study was financially supported by the Grant for Junior Researchers from National Social Science Fund of China [16CYY024], the Fundamental Research Funds for the Central Universities, and the Grant for Junior Researchers from Funds for Humanities and Social Sciences by Ministry of Education of P. R. China [12YJCZH262].

Note

1 The magnetic analogue of MMN is usually termed mismatch field (MMF). In this chapter we use MMN in an inclusive way to refer to both electrophysiological and magentophysiological mismatch responses.

References

Alexandrov, A. A., Boricheva, D. O., Pulvermüller, F., & Shtyrov, Y. (2011). Strength of word-specific neural memory traces assessed electrophysiologically. *PLoS One, 6*, e22999.

Angwin, A. J., Phua, B., & Copland, D. A. (2014). Using semantics to enhance new word learning: An ERP investigation. *Neuropsychologia, 59*, 169–178.

Bakker, I., Takashima, A., Hell, J. G. V., Janzen, G., & McQueen, J. M. (2015). Tracking lexical consolidation with ERPs: Lexical and semantic-priming effects on N400 and LPC responses to newly-learned words. *Neuropsychologia, 79*, 33–41.

Baldeweg, T., Richardson, A., Watkins, S., Foale, C., & Gruzilier, J. (1999). Impaired auditory frequency discrimination in dyslexia detected with mismatch evoked potentials. *Annals of Neurology, 45*, 495–503.

Batterink, L., Karns, C. M., Yamada, Y., & Neville, H. J. (2010). The role of awareness in semantic and syntactic processing: An ERP attentional blink study. *Journal of Cognitive Neuroscience, 22*, 2514–2529.

Batterink, L., & Neville, H. (2011). Implicit and explicit mechanisms of word learning in a narrative context: An event-related potential study. *Journal of Cognitive Neuroscience, 23*, 3181–3196.

Batterink, L., & Neville, H. J. (2013). The human brain processes syntax in the absence of conscious awareness. *Journal of Neuroscience, 33*, 8528–8533.

Bishop, D. V. (2006). Dyslexia: What's the problem? *Developmental Science, 9*, 256–257.

Borovsky, A., Kutas, M., & Elman, J. (2010). Learning to use words: Event related potentials index single-shot contextual word learning. *Cognition, 116*, 289–296.

Bowden, H. W., Steinhauer, K., Sanz, C., & Ullman, M. T. (2013). Native-like brain process-ing of syntax can be attained by university Foreign language learners. *Neuropsychologia*, *51*, 2492–2511.

Carroll, J. B. (1981). Twenty-five years of research on Foreign language aptitude. In K. C. Diller (Ed.), *Individual differences and universals in language learning aptitude*. Rowley, MA: Newbury House.

Carroll, J. B., & Sapon, S. (1959). *Modern language aptitude test: Form a*. New York, NY: The Psychological Corporation.

Chomsky, N. (2005). Three factors in language design. *Linguistic Inquiry*, *36*, 1–22.

Coulson, S., & Brang, D. (2010). Sentence context affects the brain response to masked words. *Brain and Language*, *113*, 149–155.

Czigler, I., Balázs, L., & Winkler, I. (2002). Memory-based detection of task-irrelevant visual changes. *Psychophysiology*, *39*, 869–873.

Dehaene-Lambertz, G. (1997). Electrophysiological correlates of categorical phoneme per-ception in adults. *Neuroreport*, *8*, 919–924.

Diaz, B., Baus, C., Escera, C., Costa, A., & Sebastián-Gallés, N. (2008). Brain potentials to native phoneme discrimination reveal the origin of individual differences in learning the sounds of a second language. *Proceedings of the National Academy of Sciences of the United States of America*, *105*, 16083–16088.

Díaz, B., Mitterer, H., Broersma, M., Escera, C., & Sebastián-Gallés, N. (2016). Variability in L2 phonemic learning originates from speech-specific capabilities: An MMN study on late bilinguals. *Bilingualism Language and Cognition*, *19*, 955–970.

Diaz, B., Mitterer, H., Broersma, M., & Sebastián-Gallés, N. (2012). Individual differences in late bilinguals' L2 phonological processes: From acoustic-phonetic analysis to lexical access. *Learning and Individual Differences*, *22*, 680–689.

Epstein, S. D. (2007). Physiological Linguistics, and some implications regarding discipli-nary autonomy and unification. *Mind & Language*, *22*, 44–67.

Federmeier, K. D., Kutas, M., & Dickson, D. S. (2016). A common neural progression to meaning in about a third of a second. In G. Hickok & S. Small (Eds.), *Neurobiology of language* (pp. 557–567). Cambridge: Academic Press.

Fischer, C., Morlet, D., Bouchet, P., Luaute, J., Jourdan, C., & Salord, F. (1999). Mismatch negativity and late auditory evoked potentials in comatose patients. *Clinical Neurophysi-ology*, *110*, 1601–1610.

Fischer, C., Morlet, D., & Giard, M. H. (2000). Mismatch negativity and N100 in comatose patients. *Audiology and Neurotology*, *5*, 192–197.

Foucart, A., & Frenck-Mestre, C. (2012). Can late L2 learners acquire new grammatical features? Evidence from ERPs and eye-tracking. *Journal of Memory & Language*, *66*, 226–248.

Friederici, A. D. (1997). Neurophysiological aspects of language processing. *Clinical Neu-roscience*, *4*, 64–72.

Friederici, A. D. (2011). The brain basis of language processing: From structure to function. *Physiological Reviews*, *91*, 1357–1392.

Friederici, A. D., Pfeifer, E., & Hahne, A. (1993). Event-related brain potentials during natural speech processing: Effects of semantic, morphological and syntactic violations. *Brain Research*, *1*, 183–192.

Friederici, A. D., & Singer, W. (2015). Grounding language processing on basic neurophysi-ological principles. *Trends in Cognitive Sciences*, *19*, 329–338.

Gabrieli, J. D. (2009). Dyslexia: A new synergy between education and cognitive neurosci-ence. *Science*, *325*, 280–283.

Gouvea, A., Phillips, C., Kazanina, N., & Poeppel, D. (2009). The linguistic processes underlying the P600. *Language and Cognitive Processes, 25,* 149–188.

Gunter, T. C., & Friederici, A. D. (1999). Concerning the automaticity of syntactic processing. *Psychophysiology, 36,* 126–137.

Hagoort, P., & Brown, C. M., & Groothusen, J. (1993). The syntactic positive shift as an ERP measure of syntactic processing. *Language and Cognitive Processes, 8,* 439–483.

Hahne, A. (2001). What's different in second-language processing? Evidence from event-related brain potentials. *Journal of Psycholinguistic Research, 30,* 251–266.

Hahne, A., & Friederici, A. D. (1999). Electrophysiological evidence for two steps in syntactic analysis: Early automatic and late controlled processes. *Journal of Cognitive Neuroscience, 11,* 194–205.

Hahne, A., & Friederici, A. D. (2002). Differential task effects on semantic and syntactic processes as revealed by ERPs. *Cognitive Brain Research, 13,* 339–356.

Hanna, J., & Pulvermüller, F. (2014). Neurophysiological evidence for whole form retrieval of complex derived words: A mismatch negativity study. *Frontiers in Human Neuroscience, 8,* 886.

Hanna, J. H., Shtyrov, Y., Williams, J., & Pulvermüller, F. (2016). Early neurophysiological indices of second language morphosyntax learning. *Neuropsychologia, 82,* 18–30.

Hell, J. G. V., & Tokowicz, N. (2010). Event-related brain potentials and second language learning: Syntactic processing in late L2 learners at different L2 proficiency levels. *Second Language Research, 26,* 43–74.

Herrmann, B., Maess, B., Hasting, A. S., & Friederici, A. D. (2009). Localization of the syntactic mismatch negativity in the temporal cortex: An MEG study. *NeuroImage, 48,* 590–600.

Holcomb, P. J. (1988). Automatic and attentional processing: An event-related brain potential analysis of semantic priming. *Brain and Language, 35,* 66–85.

Jakoby, H., Goldstein, A., & Faust, M. (2011). Electrophysiological correlates of speech perception mechanisms and individual differences in second language attainment. *Psychophysiology, 48,* 1517–1531.

Kaan, E. (2007). Event-related potentials and language processing: A brief overview. *Language and Linguistics Compass, 1,* 571–591.

Kaan, E., Harris, A., Gibson, E., & Holcomb, P. J. (2000). The P600 as an index of syntactic integration difficulty. *Language and Cognitive Processes, 15,* 159–201.

Kraus, N., McGee, T., Sharma, A., Carrell, T., & Nicol, T. (1992). Mismatch negativity event-related potential elicited by speech stimuli. *Ear and Hearing, 13,* 158–164.

Kutas, M., & Federmeier, K. D. (2011). Thirty years and counting: Finding meaning in the n400 component of the Event-Related Brain Potential (ERP). *Annual Review of Psychology, 62,* 621–647.

Kutas, M., & Hillyard, S. A. (1980). Reading senseless sentences: Brain potentials reflect semantic incongruity. *Science, 207,* 203–208.

Kutas, M., & Hillyard, S. A. (1984). Brain potentials during reading reflect word expectancy and semantic association. *Nature, 307,* 161–163.

Linck, J. A., Hughes, M. M., Campbell, S. G., Silbert, N. H., Tare, M., Jackson, S. R., . . . Doughty, C. J. (2013). Hi-LAB: A new measure of aptitude for high-level language proficiency. *Language Learning, 63,* 530–566.

Luck, S. J. (2005). *An introduction to the event-related potential technique.* Cambridge: MIT Press.

Luo, H., Ni, J. T., Li, Z. H., Li, X. O., Zhang, D. R., Zeng, F. G., & Chen, L. (2006). Opposite patterns of hemisphere dominance for early auditory processing of lexical tones and consonants. *Proceedings of the National Academy of Sciences of the United States of America, 103,* 19558–19563.

Makuuchi, M., Bahlmann, J., Anwander, A., & Friederici, A. D. (2009). Segregating the core computational faculty of human language from working memory. *Proceedings of the National Academy of Sciences of the United States of America, 106,* 8362–8367.

McLaughlin, J., Osterhout, L., & Kim, A. (2004). Neural correlates of second-language word learning: Minimal instruction produces rapid change. *Nature Neuroscience, 7,* 703–704.

McLaughlin, J., Tanner, D. S., Pitkanen, I., Frenckmestre, C., Inoue, K., Valentine, G., & Osterhout, L. (2010). Brain potentials reveal discrete stages of L2 grammatical learning. *Language Learning, 60,* 123–150.

Menning, H., Imaizumi, S., Zwitserlood, P., & Pantev, C. (2002). Plasticity of the human auditory cortex induced by discrimination learning of non-native, mora-timed contrasts of the Japanese language. *Learning and Memory, 9,* 253–267.

Mestres-Missé, A., Rodriguez-Fornells, A., & Münte, T. F. (2007). Watching the brain during meaning acquisition. *Cerebral Cortex, 17,* 1858–1866.

Meulman, N., Stowe, L. A., Sprenger, S., Bresser, M., & Schmid, M. S. (2014). An ERP study on L2 syntax processing: When do learners fail? *Frontiers in Psychology, 5,* 1072.

Näätänen, R. (1995). The mismatch negativity: A powerful tool for cognitive neuroscience. *Ear and Hearing, 16,* 6–18.

Näätänen, R. (2003). Mismatch negativity: Clinical research and possible applications. *International Journal of Psychophysiology, 48,* 179–188.

Näätänen, R., Gaillard, A. W., & Mäntysalo, S. (1978). Early selective-attention effect on evoked potential reinterpreted. *Acta Psychologica, 42,* 313–329.

Näätänen, R., Lehtokoski, A., Lennes, M., Cheour, M., Houtilainen, M., Livonen, A., . . . Alho, K. (1997). Language-specific phoneme representations revealed by electric and magnetic brain responses. *Nature, 385,* 432–434.

Neville, H. J., Nicol, J. L., Barss, A., Forster, K. I., & Garrett, M. F. (1991). Syntactically based processing classes: Evidence from event-related potentials. *Journal of Cognitive Neuroscience, 3,* 151–165.

Osterhout, L., & Holcomb, P. J. (1992). Event-related potentials elicited by syntactic anomaly. *Journal of Memory and Language, 31,* 785–806.

Osterhout, L., Poliakov, A. V., Inoue, K., McLaughlin, J., Valentine, G., Pitkanen, I., . . . Hirschensohn, J. (2008). Second-language learning and changes in the brain. *Journal of Neurolinguistics, 21,* 509–521.

Pimsleur, P. (1966). *Pimsleur Language Aptitude Battery (PLAB).* New York, NY: The Psychological Corporation.

Pulvermüller, F. (2005). Brain mechanisms linking language and action. *Nature Reviews Neuroscience, 6,* 576–582.

Pulvermüller, F., Kujala, T., Shtyrov, Y., Simola, J., Tiitinen, H., Alku, P., . . . Näätänen, R. (2001). Memory traces for words as revealed by the mismatch negativity. *NeuroImage, 14,* 607–616.

Pulvermüller, F., & Shtyrov, Y. (2006). Language outside the focus of attention: The mismatch negativity as a tool for studying higher cognitive processes. *Progress in Neurobiology, 79,* 49–71.

Pulvermüller, F., Shtyrov, Y., Hasting, A. S., & Carlyon, R. P. (2008). Syntax as a reflex: Neurophysiological evidence for early automaticity of grammatical processing. *Brain and Language, 104,* 244–253.

Qi, Z., Beach, S. D., Finn, A. S., Minas, J., Goetz, C., Chan, B., & Gabrieli, J. D. (2017). Native-language N400 and P600 predict dissociable language-learning abilities in adults. *Neuropsychologia, 98,* 177–191.

Sabourin, L., & Stowe, L. A. (2008). Second language processing: When are first and second languages processed similarly? *Second Language Research, 24*, 397–430.

Schulte-Korne, G., Deimel, W., Bartling, J., & Remschmidt, H. (1998). Auditory processing and dyslexia: Evidence for a specific speech processing deficit. *Neuroreport, 9*, 337–340.

Sharma, A., Kraus, N., McGee, T., Carrell, T., & Nicol, T. (1993). Acoustic versus phonetic representation of speech as reflected by the mismatch negativity event-related potential. *Electroencephalography and Clinical Neurophysiology, 88*, 64–71.

Shtyrov, Y. (2011). Fast mapping of novel word forms traced neurophysiologically. *Frontiers in Psychology, 2*, 340.

Shtyrov, Y., Hauk, O., & Pulvermüller, F. (2004). Distributed neuronal networks for encoding category-specific semantic information: The mismatch negativity to action words. *European Journal of Neuroscience, 19*, 1083–1092.

Shtyrov, Y., Kimppa, L., Pulvermüller, F., & Kujala, T. (2011). Event-related potentials reflecting the frequency of unattended spoken words: A neuronal index of connection strength in lexical memory circuits? *NeuroImage, 55*, 658–668.

Shtyrov, Y., Nikulin, V. V., & Pulvermüller, F. (2010). Rapid cortical plasticity underlying novel word learning. *The Journal of Neuroscience, 30*, 16864–16867.

Shtyrov, Y., & Pulvermüller, F. (2007). Language in the passive auditory oddball: Motivations, benefits and prospectives. *Journal of Psychophysiology, 21*, 176–186.

Shtyrov, Y., Pulvermüller, F., Näätänen, R., & Ilmoniemi, R. J. (2003). Grammar processing outside the focus of attention: An MEG study. *Journal of Cognitive Neuroscience, 15*, 1195–1206.

Skehan, P. (1998). *A cognitive approach to language learning*. Oxford: Oxford University Press.

Sparks, R., Patton, J., Ganschow, L., & Humbach, N. (2011). Subcomponents of second-language aptitude and second-language proficiency. *The Modern Language Journal, 95*, 253–273.

Stagg, C. J., Hindley, P., Tales, A., & Butler, S. M. (2004). Visual mismatch negativity: The detection of stimulus change. *Neuroreport, 15*, 659–663.

Tanner, D., Mclaughlin, J., Herschensohn, J., & Osterhout, L. (2013). Individual differences reveal stages of l2 grammatical acquisition: ERP evidence. *Bilingualism Language & Cognition, 16*, 367–382.

Tervaniemi, M., & Hugdahl, K. (2003). Lateralization of auditory-cortex functions. *Brain Research Reviews, 43*, 231–246.

Tremblay, K., Kraus, N., Carrell, T., & McGee, T. (1997). Central auditory system plasticity: Generalization to novel stimuli following listening training. *The Journal of Acoustic Society of America, 102*, 3762–3773.

Tremblay, K., Kraus, N., McGee, T., Ponton, C. W., & Otis, B. (2001). Central auditory plasticity: Changes in the N1-P2 complex after speech-sound training. *Ear and Hearing, 22*, 79–90.

Wen, Z., Biedroń, A., & Skehan, P. (2017). Foreign language aptitude theory: Yesterday, today and tomorrow. *Language Teaching, 50*, 1–31.

White, E. J., Genesee, F., & Steinhauer, K. (2012). Brain responses before and after intensive second language learning: Proficiency based changes and first language background effects in adult learners. *PLoS One, 7*, e52318.

Winkler, I., Kujala, T., Tiitinen, H., Sivonen, P., Alku, P., Lehtokoski, A., . . . Näätänen, R. (1999). Brain responses reveal the learning of Foreign language phonemes. *Psychophysiology, 36*, 638–642.

Xue, J., Yang, J., Zhang, J., Qi, Z., Bai, C., & Qiu, Y. (2013). An ERP study on Chinese natives' second language syntactic grammaticalization. *Neuroscience Letters, 534*, 258–263.

Yue, J., Bastiaanse, R., & Alter, K. (2014). Cortical plasticity induced by rapid Hebbian learning of novel tonal wordforms: Evidence from mismatch negativity. *Brain and Language, 139,* 10–22.

Yue, J., Kai, A., Howard, D., & Bastiaanse, R. (2017). Early access to lexical-level phonological representations of mandarin word-forms: Evidence from auditory N1 habituation. *Language Cognition and Neuroscience, 32,* 1148–1163.

Zatorre, R. J., & Gandour, J. T. (2008). Neural specializations for speech and pitch: Moving beyond the dichotomies. *Philosophical Transactions of the Royal Society B, 363,* 1087–1104.

Zhang, Y., Kuhl, P. K., Imada, T., Iverson, P., Pruitt, J., Stevens, E. B., . . . Nemoto, I. (2009). Neural signatures of phonetic learning in adulthood: A magnetoencephalography study. *NeuroImage, 46,* 226–240.

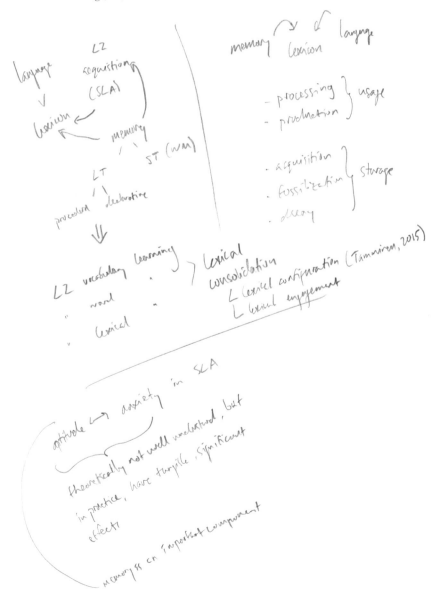

14

NEURO-PSYCHO-COGNITIVE MARKERS FOR PRONUNCIATION/ SPEECH IMITATION AS LANGUAGE APTITUDE

Susanne Maria Reiterer

Language Aptitude Research as an Interdisciplinary Inquiry

Language behaviour comprises many different aspects of our lives: emotional, intellectual-cognitive, physical-motion/motoric, biochemical (neurotransmitters, hormones), social-interactional, socio-cultural, psychological, expressive and the like. Even individual differences in ultimate attainment or proficiency level at a given point in a second or foreign language depends on many factors. Within the sphere of biological factors acting upon our language learning capacities, I would like to mention *genes*, DNA (Fisher, 2017), including *epigenetics* (Markman et al., 2011) and *gene-by-treatment interactions* (Plomin, DeFries, Knopik, & Neiderhieser, 2014; Plomin, DeFries, Knopik, & Neiderhieser, 2016), *neuro-transmitters* (dopamine (Ripolles et al., 2014) and glutamate), *hormones*, *sex/gender* and *brain structure and function*.

The "Polyglot" Advantage

Other actors in our language abilities are environmental or social factors, like *attitudes* towards or *status* of languages, *input* or teaching/acquiring methods, *exposure* times and bilingual or *multilingual settings* or contact opportunities. As an example, a bilingual or multilingual, in comparison to a polyglot, would be someone who happens to grow up in a multilingual home environment without purposefully forcing this environment to be around them. Thus, mere multilingualism should not be confounded or equated with language aptitude. Polyglots, or even hyper-polyglots, on the other hand, are self-chosen and actively seek out opportunities to indulge in multiple language learning because of a noticed inner need to do so (intrinsic motivation).

One can sometimes hear the opinion that multilinguals or bilinguals are more apt for language learning, but scientific evidence does not point in this direction. We investigated this hypothesis by using language aptitude tests (Meara, 2005; Carroll & Sapon, 2002) on groups of 30 bilinguals/multilinguals versus monolinguals (Hörder, 2018) and 14 clear polyglots speaking more than five languages versus 14 typical language learners (Auer, 2017) and found that bilinguals/multilinguals do not show any significant differences in language aptitude tests to monolinguals, but clear and proficient polyglots have almost double the scores on language aptitude measures (e.g. mean of 86.07 (SD = +/-9.4) points versus 44.29 (SD = +/-12); p = .000 (t-test), LLAMA F (grammar aptitude).

This was a first, but impressive, result from investigations into the differences between multiple language learning by intrinsic (polyglots) versus extrinsic (multilingualism) motivation. Motivation, or "curiosity about speech and language", pivotal to language aptitude, is one of the middle factors (cognitive or psychological) in my tripartite schema because it falls neither clearly within the biological nor in the social/environmental domain. In this third category (psycho-cognitive domain), one could list variables which typically are investigated in the field of psychology of language learning, i.e.: personality, empathy, anxiety, memory, executive functions, intelligence and musicality. We have investigated many of those factors of the third category (mostly in relation to phonetic aptitude) with the exception of anxiety. Details will be reported in the results section later.

On Speaker Variation: Basic Theoretical Considerations

All these diverse dimensions, which create our communicative behaviour (and ultimately our language or languages as a system), show a lot of individual variation, giving rise to individual language learner and speaker profiles. This variation is seen when speaking and acquiring mother tongues, dialects and foreign languages alike. Even in their first languages, people are so different in their communicative behavior, which can range from mutism to logorrhoea, from poor expressive abilities to outstanding rhetoric orator gifts, from dyslexia and agrammatism to eloquent genius in literature, from unclear speech in articulation difficulties (e.g. developmental apraxia of speech) to hyperarticulation capacities in comedians, parodists and impersonators, or even singers, as well as from autism to high pragmatic ability in communication talent. Speaker-based individual differences in speech, language and communication behaviour are enormous and all too often forgotten in scientific models.

The models or theories try to capture the reality of speech and language behaviour mostly through written language sources, are simplified, assume averaged or ideal speakers' behaviour and often use a binary logic of truth (absence or presence of something, true or false, normal or abnormal). One example is the often-quoted question related to variation in pronunciation performance of early versus later foreign language learners (sensitive period theory). Can a speaker with a late onset of L2 ever achieve native-like proficiency in pronunciation? The answer given or expected is either yes or no. This also accounts for the often-posed question: Is it nature or nurture? The answer should rather start with: it depends on the distribution of the phenomenon. In our case, language aptitude (like aptitudes in other domains) has long been known to be normally distributed in populations (Gaussian distribution, Neufeld, 1979; Plomin et al., 2014).

A solution to under-realistic or dichotomous theories is to model language aptitude by a Gaussian distribution continuously and predict theoretical outcomes in terms of percentages. According to this model around 5% to 15% of individuals (very roughly speaking, every tenth person) can attain phonetic native speaker pronunciation, based on their aptitude profiles and time resources.[1] Seventy per cent of individuals will arrive at an average pronunciation proficiency in a later learned second language; however, those 70% (and not 100%) are the ones for whom most models and theories have been developed. Those are the so-called "norm". For yet another 5% to 15%, it might be enormously difficult to learn foreign languages in general or the pronunciation of it, if we stick to the earlier example, and yet for another 2% (or, every fiftieth person) the ability barriers might make it even almost impossible or just utterly difficult. However, if we leave out 30% of the whole population, we can no longer talk about inclusivity or the phenomenon as a whole. Exception and rule ("abnormal" and normal) should both be included and accommodated in the models and theories to arrive at a description of 100% of all individuals—the whole continuum.

In the present chapter and in our own previous research about the impact of different neuro-cognitive factors on language aptitude for speech imitation (phonetic aptitude), we could repeatedly and clearly demonstrate that all aspects of language aptitude we investigated so far (e.g. aptitude for pronunciation, vocabulary learning and associative memory, syntactic sensitivity, even pragmatic or singing ability) are always normally distributed (Reiterer, 2018; Reiterer et al., 2011; Reiterer, Hu, Sumathi, & Singh, 2013; Dogil & Reiterer, 2009; Hu et al., 2013; Christiner & Reiterer, 2013, 2015; Wucherer & Reiterer, 2018; Marusakova, 2015; Zapcevic, 2017).

Where Individual Differences Meet Universal Laws

Considering all the inter-individual and intra-individual variation in behaviour alongside distributions, I would like to suggest a more variable, "distributional" view of language aptitude. Since it is difficult to explain all individual behaviour by one law (e.g. language aptitude being either static or dynamic, genetically driven or not, or to a certain percentage), categorical generalizations like this may simply not hold for all individuals. Rather, we might start thinking of "grouped, variable or distributional laws", in the sense that environmental (training) or genetic impact might be subject to individual variation, with some individuals having higher and others lower shares of those influences.

Thus, language aptitudes might be more stable and trait-like in some individuals and more dynamic in others. A very simplified analogy to the field of medicine could be drawn by using the metaphor of the different blood groups or metabolism types. Such a conceptualization is less universal and more individual on a group level and might reduce theoretical unfulfilling controversies, which are ubiquitous in this field.

Biological Markers of Individual Differences in Language Aptitude

The normal distribution of a phenomenon (be it aptitude, body weight, body size, etc.) also points at a potential underlying biological system. However, there is still rare, though increasing, research (e.g. Fisher, 2017) into the biological, biochemical or genetic roots of language aptitude apart from very recent growing interest into the genetic foundations and hereditability of second language learning/acquisition (as opposed to first language acquisition) and language abilities in general and the individual differences thereof (for examples see: Dale, Harlaar, Haworth, & Plomin, 2010; Hayiou, Dale, & Plomin, 2012; Dediu, 2008; Dediu & Ladd, 2007; Plomin et al., 2014; Fisher, 2017).

Still in its beginnings and complex to investigate, it seems that second language acquisition (and hence what we can observe as adult second language learning aptitude) is subserved to a higher degree by hereditable factors than first language acquisition (Dale et al., 2010; Plomin et al., 2014, 2016). Trying to explain this interesting pattern of observation, I would interpret that this is due to the fact that massive exposure time and experience with native languages overrides genetic influences and "levels them out". Differences are more evident in the classical case of a late second/foreign language learner. This might be one of the reasons why language aptitude is a prominent achievement factor in second language acquisition.

Another similar and seemingly paradoxical observation in genetic studies of the heritability of cognitive traits is an intra-individual difference of the amount of heritability, observed with IQ increasing over the life span, called "genetic amplification" (Plomin et al., 2016). Likewise, intra-individual variation in hereditability (of a motor learning skill) has been observed to also increase as a function of training, from 55% to 70%, suggesting not only inter-individual differences but also intra-individual differences in abilities or skill acquisition. This gene interaction with training gives rise to speculations and potentially could underpin (1) the "dynamic" concept of language aptitude and (2) would underscore the importance of "aptitude treatment interaction research" (DeKeyser, 2012).

The Current Research Project: Different Layers of Language Aptitude—From Behaviour to Brain

Language aptitude has many faces, and I think it is as difficult as defining what "language" is if you want to define "language aptitude or aptitudes". Is language more speech, more communicative behaviour or more structure? What we can safely say is that its definitions depend on the point of view of what we understand as "language" and that the phenomenon is complex. So is aptitude for this complex system or set of subsystems, be it more the communicative, physical side of it (acoustic, motor, somatosensory, olfactory and gustatory—hearing, seeing, smelling, and feeling communication in "articulated" or "gesticulated" speech, the *word turned into flesh and blood* figuratively and at the same time biochemically spoken) or more the "cognitive" side of it, represented by semantic, syntactic, pragmatic systems and underlying structures. Universal or not, the phenomena here turn into a more remote cognitive sphere, which we tend to see as less sensory and biochemical.

In language aptitude research so far, the question often arises as to whether the phenomenon should be seen more in a strictly linguistic (domain specific) or in a more domain-general light (general cognitive processes) or as a mixture of all of them. Additionally, and still in the linguistic sphere, I would even further separate rhetoric and pragmatic abilities (usually, unfortunately, not tested in available aptitude test batteries).[2] New research on the theories underlying language aptitudes are currently and recently undertaken, but the issue is far from being settled (Biedroń, 2015; Granena & Long, 2013; Hu & Reiterer, 2009; Linck et al., 2013; Rota & Reiterer, 2009; Safronova & Mora, 2012; Wen et al., 2017). The way we conceptualized language aptitude at the outset of our research was that it is a multi-componential phenomenon, and we based it on a heuristic approach and partly used very classical approaches with testing for the standard subcomponents, like "phonetics", "grammar" (morphology/syntax, syntactic sensitivity) and "vocabulary learning, associative memory". Complementarily, we also know that many factors influence language learning, and general cognitive processes interfere with language aptitude.

Here, we also tested for as many cognitive processes as possible, with one of the central components being the auditory working memory. We focused primarily on phonetic aptitude, or speech imitation/pronunciation ability as a subcomponent, because of various reasons. First and pragmatically, one cannot afford to test all possible components, including brain functions, due to time and financial reasons. The choice fell on speech production and phonetic ability, since it is a completely under-investigated component within language aptitude research, is not represented in any of the available testing batteries and is highly interesting as a candidate for large-scale reinvestigation because pronunciation and speech imitation are often claimed to be the subcomponent which is subject to a putative critical period.

282 Susanne Maria Reiterer

Methods: The Research Project "Tübingen talent corpus"

We pre-tested approximately 200 adult German native speakers for their pronunciation skills, suitability and availability for the research purpose. Out of this
pool of academically educated speakers, 138 (aged 20–40 years, mean = 25.9,
SD = +/-5.2; age of onset of learning first L2 English at 10 years, late learners, no
early and "true" bilinguals) were tested with a battery of linguistic tests and questionnaires (language learning history, max. 10 languages acquired), validated language aptitude measures (short form of MLAT, parts 3–5, Carroll & Sapon, 2002)
and our own tests about pronunciation ability, speech production and speech
perception measurements. Our measures of speech production and perception
ability are described in detail in Jilka, 2009; Reiterer et al., 2011; Hu et al., 2013
and comprise mainly sound-booth recordings of direct and delayed speech imitations in L1 German, L2 English and L0 Hindi.

The speech production and imitation material varied from free speech, the
retelling of cartoons and faking foreign accents in L1 to sentence and word imitation, including prosody imitations. Here I tried out for the first time Hindi
sentences and words as stimulus material (Reiterer et al., 2011) as a completely
unknown language to be imitated without any contamination of prior training, as
typically used in language aptitude test batteries. I decided on Hindi as an example because none of our informants had any knowledge of Hindi before testing
and because it is a typologically relatively distant language to German and English.
Thus the "Hindi" task was developed and used to detect pure speech imitation
ability, whereas English was just measured as a kind of control condition for foreign language pronunciation ability, including different levels of prior training
and proficiency. L1 was measured mainly by prosody realizations and imitations
of mother tongue sentences. Speech perception measures centred around foreign
accent identification tasks and detecting prosody differences in paired statements
(for further details see Jilka, 2009).

The two tasks which were subjected to large-scale international native speaker
evaluations finally were the Hindi task (originally comprising four Hindi words
[3 to 6 syllables] and four Hindi sentences [7, 8, 9 and 11 syllables]) and the global
English pronunciation fit of the spoken text "The Northwind and the Sun".
Both recordings of all participants were evaluated on different Internet sites by
30 blind native speakers each, 50% females, within India by Indian natives, mostly
Hindi (see Reiterer et al., 2011). Within the realm of English-speaking countries,
we asked 30 natives from many different English-speaking corners of the world
(United States, Great Britain and Ireland, Australia, New Zealand, South Africa
and Singapore) to evaluate the native speaker qualities of the recordings on a scale
from 0 to 10 (max) by giving a quick intuitive overall judgement on a continuous
Likert scale. Inter-rater reliability in both cases was close to perfect, between 0.96
and 0.90 (probably due to the many raters).

The first interesting global result was that the ability scores followed a normal distribution and thus typically reflected the individual differences of language aptitude expected in a given population (see Figure 14.1). Even L1 measures (prosody production) followed this pattern (Coumel, 2017). The results of the English pronunciation ranged from 1.52 to 9.69, mean = 5.84, SD± 1.69, ranking 8% of German speakers within 8 to 10 points, which I call the "native speaker range" (because all natives rated by blind other natives fall into this range).

Thus, we could show that 8% of German native speakers, late learners of L2 English, could cheat the native ears and were taken as natives themselves despite their late learning onset. This figure conforms well to the literature and is already known. We would not call those people "exceptions", but rather higher than average phonetically talented. With Hindi as an unknown language, however, none of the participants made it into the "native range", because scores ranged from 2.42 to 7.74, mean = 4.62, SD±0.99; the Hindi natives ranged within 8 to 10 points, mean = 9.5, SD ±0.6.

This task, to imitate an exotic language from scratch, was rather difficult and would require more exceptional "phonetic talent", which was not represented in our sample, simply because finding those cases needs a nation-wide search. However, it was interesting to see already at this point that the completely different Hindi score (different in task design and language) significantly correlated with the English score

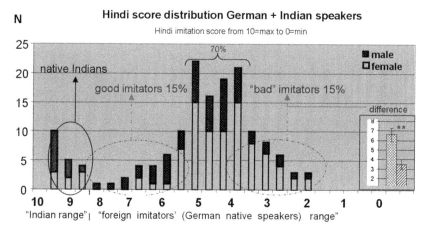

FIGURE 14.1 Legend: Hindi score normal distribution: speech imitation score reflecting the degree of native speaker likeness and distribution (as rated by blind Indian native judges), including the scores for the native Hindi speakers immersed in the German subject pool. $N = 138$; immersed Indian natives $N = 18$; overall $N = 156$. Maximum score for sounding "native-like" Indian = 10; minimum = 0. 30 The 18 Indian natives scored highest (between 8 and 10).

($r = 0.3$) and the English score significantly correlated with an L1 score ($r = 0.49$) evaluated by blind German native listeners (a third online evaluation database) about the prosodic and segmental well-formedness of the German sentences (Coumel, 2017; Coumel, Christiner, & Reiterer, 2016). The Hindi score even showed a significant moderate correlation ($r = 0.34$) with the MLAT aptitude test battery, and the English score an even higher one ($r = 0.6$) with the MLAT total score. The subscore "phonetic coding ability", part 3, showed the highest subcorrelations in both cases, followed by grammatical sensitivity and last by vocabulary learning.

This shows two interesting things. First, we could observe an underlying phenomenon, namely that of *basic phonetic sensitivity*, because pronunciation/imitation measures across the board (validated well-established and own measures) and across languages and designs (Hindi, English, L1 German) were significantly and moderately correlated, meaning that there is some relationship between those skills; however, they are not the same. Second, the validation with an existing test was provided (parallel forms reliability).

From those earlier-mentioned 138 subjects who underwent the linguistic testing, we further examined $N = 116$ by psychological and cognitive tests:

- auditory working memory (WAIS digit span forward+backward, non-word repetition according to German phonotactic rules)
- empathy test (Baron-Cohen & Wheelwright, 2004)
- two personality questionnaires (the BIS/BAS [behavioural inhibition system/behavioural activation system] (Carver & White, 1994) and the NEO-FFI, Borkenau & Ostendorf, 1993)
- a non-verbal IQ test (RAVEN advanced matrixes, Raven, Raven, & Court, 1998) and a verbal IQ (Lehrl, Triebig, & Fischer, 1995)
- a musicality test (AMMA, Gordon, 1989)
- mental flexibility (as measured by an adapted version of the SIMON task)
- a reading speed test (Salzbuger Lesegeschwindigkeitstest, Landerl, Wimmer, Moser, 1997).

A further 70 subjects, who did all of the testing so far, additionally were scanned by a 1.5T SIEMENS VISION MR scanner for functional and structural magnetic resonance images. Anatomical images included a diffusion tensor imaging (DTI) sequence measurement, visualizing white matter fibre connections. Having completed all test batteries, our participants had spent about 10 hours in testing.

Results of the Brain Imaging (Neuroscientific Markers)

fMRI (Functional Magnetic Resonance Imaging)

Slowly, steadily and only recently, there is a growing number of brain imaging and cognitive neuroscientific studies investigating individual differences in language aptitude at a general or sub-ability level (e.g., grammar, phonetic) with diverse neurofunctional and neuroanatomical methods (Chai et al., 2016; Golestani & Pallier, 2007; Golestani & Zatorre, 2004; Kepinska, de Rover, Caspers, & Schiller, 2017a, 2017b; Miro-Padilla, Bueichekú, Ventura-Campos, Palomar-García, & Ávila, 2017; Prat, Yamasaki, Kluender, & Stocco, 2016).

The first analyses were based on extreme group comparisons reflecting the scoring for the Hindi imitation ($N = 9$ high phonetic vs. 9 low phonetic ability). According to the global main effects for each group during sentence production (L1 and L2 mixed), a large bilateral speech-language network is activated in both groups comprising the auditory cortices (superior temporal gyri, Wernicke's area), the inferior parietal areas, the post-central "somatosensory" cortices, the motor and pre-motor areas surrounding the representation for the "mouth" area, including Broca's area BA44 and 45 as well as portions of the middle frontal gyri and insular cortex, the supplementary motor areas, the basal ganglia system (globus pallidus, putamen and caudates), thalamus, the upper part of the cerebellar cortices and parts of the visual cortex. One can already see by visual inspection (see Figure 14.2) that the two groups do not differ so much in localization,

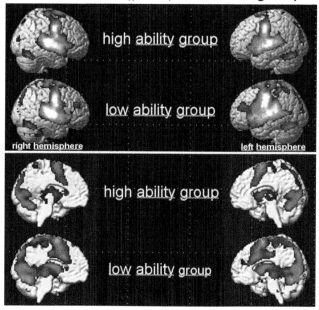

FIGURE 14.2 Legend: fMRI main effects for groups (Hindi score based) during L1 and L2 sentence production (repetition) against baseline: high-ability group always in the higher panel, versus low-ability group in the lower panel; the upper picture shows peak activations bilaterally and cortically, with a focus over the perisylvian language network. The lower picture shows subcortical counterparts, comprising thalamic and cerebellar activations. The low-ability group generally shows more extended activation.

but in the extent of activation, with the low-(diffusion tensor imaging)ability imitation group showing more extended activation clusters, especially in the left hemisphere.

The effect is known as "cortical efficiency theory", and it clearly was found in all the subtasks and conditions (word production in Tamil and English as L0, L2; as well as sentence production in L1 and L2) at the cortical as well as the sub-cortical level bilaterally, but with significant left lateralized focus, with the peak activated voxel cluster being in the left supramarginal gyrus in combination with the pre-motor cortex adjacent to Broca 44. Thus, the higher-ability participants activated fewer cortical and subcortical resources in typical speech motor– and working memory–related areas and the difference was most pronounced for the left hemisphere (see also Reiterer et al., 2011).

In a second line of analyses (Hu et al., 2013), now based on the individual differences from the English imitation ability, we observed higher levels of hemodynamic responses for the high-aptitude group at the whole speech-motor network, including regions for speech-motor preparation/planning as well as speech-motor execution and parts of the auditory-perceptual network. This fMRI result indicated that these components crucially contribute to the excellence of L2 pronunciation aptitude in advanced learners. In line with the behavioural results, the vital region for the phonological storage component was not involved in this network. It is different from the early-stage learning (based on the Hindi imitation), for which the phonological working memory (as we will see later) plays a more important role. We deduced that the acquisition of L2 pronunciation aptitude is a dynamic process, requiring different neural resources for different stages for languages at different proficiency levels.

Structural Magnetic Resonance Imaging

For visualizing the structure and brain anatomy in relation to the behavioural performance of our participants, we performed three different kinds of analyses. The first two volumetric approaches made use of the high-resolution anatomical MR images (MDEFT sequence, TR = 12 min) and are called (1) whole-brain "voxel-based-analysis" (VBM) and (2) individual volumetric measurements of a special structure of the brain important for language, namely the primary auditory cortex, or "Heschl's gyrus". In the first case, we could identify that higher imitation scores (Hindi) correlated with increased grey matter volume in the left inferior parietal cortex (supramarginal gyrus), but only in the subgroup of the male subjects ($N = 20$). For the female subgroup, or at the level of the whole group, we could not detect any significant volumetric correlations with our pronunciation measures (Reiterer et al., 2011).

In the second case of the volumetric individual measurements, we analysed 30 subjects (17 females) with a segmentation analysis developed by Peter Schneider at the university clinic in Heidelberg (Schneider et al., 2002) detecting gyrification and found that those with higher scores in Hindi imitation ability showed different morphology and neuro-anatomical shape in their auditory cortex as compared to the ones with lower scores. Remarkably, adults with very high scores in the Hindi testing (and the perceptive musicality test) had significantly more complete posterior duplications of Heschl's gyrus, especially in the right hemisphere, but also in the left (Turker, Reiterer, Seither-Preisler, & Schneider, 2017). This may remind us of the discussion of the importance of the right hemisphere for language processing, especially when linked to common resources sharing or the inter-dependency between phonetic and musical aptitude.

In the third line of anatomical analyses, we made use of the DTI MR images and analysed by a time-consuming manual segmentation procedure (Vaquero, Rodriguez-Fornells, & Reiterer, 2017) 52 of our participants' arcuate fasciculi (bilateral white matter tracts connecting the most important language networks/hubs in the brain) and correlated the characteristic DTI tractographical parameters with the behavioural performance of the Hindi task. We found that a larger lateralization of the volume of the arcuate fascicle toward the left hemisphere predicted the performance of our participants in the imitation task, meaning the better the scores, the higher the volumes of this structure in the left hemisphere and the smaller in the right hemisphere. Thus, we found a lateralization advantage towards the left hemisphere, reflected in the white matter structure of the arcuate fascicle connectivity and diffusivity. Thus, we could find various neuro-anatomical and neuro-functional markers for phonetic speech imitation aptitude mainly concerning the left hemisphere.

Results of the Behavioural Tests (Cognitive and Psychological Markers)

First of all, one has to mention eye-catching gender differences, which were not expected but are plausible, if one comes to think of the rare research and what is known from the literature about hyperpolyglots (extremely gifted and motivated language learners), namely that they are preponderantly males (Erard, 2012; Hyltenstam, 2016). In the first instance of analysing the behavioural data ($N = 138$), we found a significant gender difference for both the Hindi and a special case of the English imitation scores. Both times the males had higher scores: Hindi mean (males): 4.9 (SD±1.0); mean (females): 4.4 (SD±0.9), significant difference, $p = .005$); English pronunciation mean (males): 6.1 (SD±1.8); mean (females) 5.6 (SD±1.8) (non sig. difference), but in the subscores of the ratings by the American raters only (male and female American raters, $N = 7$), the difference was significant.

This result seemed shocking at first glance: two different task designs, direct speech imitation and pronunciation and a different global context with different native speaker evaluators (America, India, both gender-balanced) but similar outcomes. In a "gender streamlined" world, one does not like to hear about either such topics or such results. However, dealing with those differences, it became obvious that other behavioural measures in the psycho-motoric or psychological domain also were subject to gender biases. For example, in the score "behavioral inhibition" as measured by the BIS/BAS biologically motivated personality test measuring inhibition/withdrawal versus drive tendencies in persons, we found females to be significantly more inhibited (mean score females: 7) than males (mean males: 5.6), $p = .000\star\star$. Furthermore, females had extremely significantly higher empathy scores (Baron-Cohen empathy quotient); higher neuroticism, agreeableness and conscientiousness scores (according to the NEO-FFI personality questionnaire); and last but not least a striking difference was found for one of the questions for their musical hobbies, with females like "dancing" strikingly more than males. Such gender differences in the psychological sphere are not particularly upsetting since they are already well known—only the results for pronunciation skills give some food for thought; thus, we replicated them in another experiment with completely new participants in a different country (Austria instead of Germany).

The replication study (Wucherer & Reiterer, 2018) investigated 64 age- (19–29 yrs, 50% females), education- and gender-matched participants in roughly the same dimensions (e.g. Hindi task, English task, MLAT 3–5, LLAMA tests (Meara, 2005), Raven non-verbal IQ, verbal IQ, personality by NEO-FFI). The study could replicate the gender differences for the Hindi task (again, males significantly outperformed females in Hindi direct speech imitation); however, here females outperformed males significantly on a test for grammatical sensitivity (grammar aptitude, MLAT IV, motivation). There were no other significant gender differences in the performance of the other tests and questionnaires, like non-verbal and verbal IQ (equal results) or personality (trend results of differences).

Overall, we can say two factors emerged from all the collateral psychological and cognitive tests and questionnaires we performed to correlate most (repeatedly and independently in different studies) with our variable of interest: phonetic ability. Those were working memory and musicality. These two cognitive abilities, musical aptitude and auditory working memory, seem to play an important role in the pronunciation and speech imitation ability of foreign languages, especially in the initial stages. Thus, those participants from our large study who had high scores on the Hindi imitation ability also had high scores on auditory working memory ($r = 0.37, p < .0001$); high scores on the overall MLAT test battery ($r = 0.34, p < .0001$); could sing better ($r = 0.3, p < .001$); were more fun-seeking according to the subscale of the BIS/BAS test ($r = 0.22, p < .01$) and were less conscientious ($r = 0.28, p < .01$). Non-verbal and verbal IQ, the Simon task (executive functions) or reading speed do not correlate significantly ($r = 0.15$, $r = 0.1, r = 0.1, r = 0.04$, respectively) as other variables which had been measured.

In a multiple regression model ($N = 113$, dependent variable Hindi imitation score; independent variables: verbal and non-verbal IQ, auditory working memory plus non-word repetition, MLAT 3 [phonetic coding ability], musicality

[AMMA], singing ability self-rated, neuroticism, extraversion, openness to new experience, agreeableness, conscientiousness and empathy) 45% of the variance was explained by auditory working memory (digit span plus non-word repetition) plus "singing ability". Thus, the Hindi imitation score was predicted by working memory together with the self-rated singing ability (a component of musicality).

These were the main results for the prediction of the pronunciation aptitude as measured by an unknown language (Hindi). A slightly, but not completely, different picture emerged for the results of the English pronunciation ability score, a language our participants already had years of experience with. Those who had better scores on English pronunciation as rated by the independent native raters also high scores on the American MLAT test ($r = 0.6, p < .0001$), liked "acting" more ($r = 0.36, p < .0001$), had higher scores on "openness to new experience" ($r = 0.33, p < .0001$), had spent more time abroad in an English-speaking country ($r = 0.33, p < .0001$), had more school years in English ($r = 0.33, p < .0001$), spoke more dialects in their L1 German ($r = 0.3, p < .001$), had higher scores on the AMMA musicality test ($r = 0.3, p < .001$), had higher singing ability ($r = 0.28, p < .01$) and had higher empathy ($r = 0.28, p < .01$).

Other results were insignificant, for example, verbal IQ, non-verbal IQ, mental flexibility (or executive functions as measured by the Simon task) and reading speed ($r = 0.15, 0.15, 0.14$ and 0.06, respectively). In a multiple regression model ($N = 113$, dependent variable English pronunciation score as rated by blind native speakers, independent variables as given earlier in the Hindi regression model), 35% of the variance was explained by "phonetic coding ability" (MLAT3) together with empathy and singing ability. One has to mention, of course, that the finding that the subtest 3 of the MLAT series, which measures phonetic coding ability in English, a construct similar to ours, tested in the same language of interest is a good result for validating the results, but it is rather intuitive because both tests should test similar things.

What is new in this model is that empathy and singing ability predict the pronunciation aptitude of a well-trained L2, like English. Singing ability as vocal musicality we already observed with the Hindi imitations, but empathy is an interesting result here. It conforms to well-established, classical psycho-SLA literature, where a decrease of ego boundaries (and thus increase in social and emotional empathy with the surroundings, called ego-permeability or flow) resulted in better foreign language pronunciation (Guira et al., 1972). This also shows that someone with elevated levels of empathy is more phonetically sensitive towards their own proprioceptive speech production. It would remain to be shown whether this is also the case for speech perception.

Musical Aptitude and Language Aptitude

Since we found strong evidence (Nardo & Reiterer, 2009) that musicality, and within that, singing, other than working memory, was a very good predictor for foreign/second language pronunciation and phonetic ability, regardless of the language investigated or the level of proficiency and experience with that language, we further investigated singing and musical aptitude in more detail. What followed was a replication study to see whether we could replicate the strong correlations between phonetic aptitude and singing in a different setting and a series of further experiments (Christiner & Reiterer, 2013, 2015, 2016, 2017, 2018; Christiner, Rüdegger, & Reiterer, 2018) about musical factors with different age groups of participants other than adults (school children and kindergarten children to compare the developmental trajectory) and various different exotic languages other than Hindi.

In the first replication study, we examined 44 mixed educational background adult advanced amateur (hobby) singers of varying degrees of singing ability and proficiency in Vienna in relation to their general perceptive musicality (AMMA musicality test), auditory working memory and phonetic abilities (Hindi task, English task [Northwind]). To investigate their singing skills, a song was composed by Markus Christiner which they had to imitate and sing while they were recorded, in addition to the well-known "happy birthday song". Seven naïve and experienced singing teacher raters evaluated their singing profiles (0–10 score) considering the following parameters: pitch (melody), rhythm, quality of voice and creativity.

Indeed we found very high correlations again between singing ability, working memory and phonetic abilities. If Hindi and English were taken together as general L2 pronunciation ability, it correlated $r = 0.68, p < .001$ with working memory digit span and $r = 0.58, p < .001$ with a compound score of general singing ability (all parameters together), followed by the single singing parameters. The English pronunciation ability score alone correlated highest with the compound singing ability score $r = 0.52, p < .001$, followed by a high correlation to the imitation of Hindi (the other phonetic aptitude score) $r = 0.51, p < .001$. Digit span, AMMA musicality test, educational level and a number of dialects also were correlated but to a lesser degree. The Hindi score, on the other hand, correlated most prominently with working memory (digit span, $r = 0.63, p < .001$) and the singing parameter "rhythm" ($r = 0.53, p < .001$), closely followed by the parameter of "melody", non-word repetition, educational background and the parameter "voice quality". The perceptive musicality test was correlated still ($r = 0.28, p < .05$) but to a trend level only (like in the case with the English score), considering the multiple testing situations.

In a multiple regression model trying to predict the Hindi score, we found that working memory (digit span forward and backward) together with singing ability (rhythm and quality of voice) and educational background could explain 66% of the variance. Resuming these findings, we could observe that first, we were able to replicate the strong connection between singing behaviour and pronunciation ability, and within singing ability, there seems to be no strong position of uniqueness for one singing parameter, because three seemed to be equally important:

rhythm, pitch and quality of voice. Only of less importance was creativity in singing, which correlated only with "singing lessons in years". It was interesting to see that voice quality correlated with "singing in childhood". Singing, in general had more predictive power for phonetic ability than general perceptive musicality as measured by a standardized test, and instrument playing as a hobby was not correlating at all (Christiner & Reiterer, 2013).

This finding is important insofar as many researchers in the SLA field, or in general, when performing a study on language learning in relation to musicality often ask for instrumental playing as an indicator for a person's musicality (instead of performing detailed musicality or singing tests). However, one should consider that in this respect and with regard to at least pronunciation, instrument playing does not play an important role, and instrument playing (or the number of instruments only) is a poor indicator of someone's level and composition of musicality. To validate this argument further, we performed a small meta-analysis of our data and investigated a pooled sample of $N = 96$, separated into three groups: explicit singers, explicit instrumentalists and non-singers/non-musicians (Christiner & Reiterer, 2015).

The results were very clear about the supremacy of singers when it comes to the imitation of foreign language speech and accents. Statistical contrasts (ANOVA) revealed that vocalists are significantly better speech imitators compared to instrumentalists ($t(93) = 6.58$, $p < 0.01$), and to non-musicians/non-singers ($t(93) = 9.54$, $p < 0.01$), although their perceptive musicality is almost uniform (no significant difference between singers and instrumentalists). Further contrasts indicated that instrumentalists are also significantly better speech imitators compared to non-musicians/non-singers ($t(93) = 2.32$, $p < 0.05$; see Figure 14.3). The emerging picture shows that Pavarottis (explicit singers) are different still from instrumentalists or theoretical musicians (Mozarts) who perform well on perception musicality tests, when it comes to speech imitation, probably due to shared neural and anatomical bodily resources (somatosensory and proprioceptive cortex, voice box, larynx, pharynx), and it is important to distinguish them.

We did many studies in adults, but if some traits or skills correlate in adulthood, we still do not know how they developed and whether they co-exist by then because of a special experience or because of a pre-existing aptitude. Thus, in this area of research, the question always arises whether language aptitude in general or a subaptitude in particular is either more stable and pre-existing either at birth or at a very early stage in life, or whether the whole phenomenon is just subject to training and anyone can acquire aptitude for languages over a lifetime. To better understand the developmental trajectory and a possible influence of training, we initiated new and replication studies in younger children, school children of about 8 to 10 years of age and kindergarten children of about 4 to 6 years of age.

In a rather large study investigating the reciprocal relationship between musicality and language learning in the other direction, namely investigating the impact of linguistic training (bilingual upbringing) onto musicality, we tested

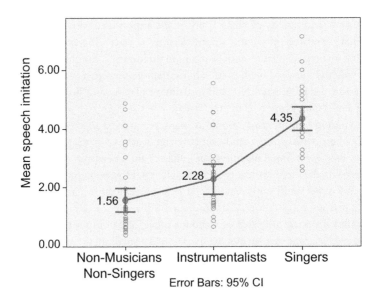

FIGURE 14.3   Legend: ANOVA Hindi speech imitation. This figure shows the differences in the performance of Hindi of non-musicians/non-singers, instrumentalists and vocalists (singers). Instrumentalists were significantly better than non-musicians/non-singers, but singers were significantly better compared to both non-musicians/non-singers and instrumentalists.

about 125 school children between 8 and 11 years (mean age 9.4 years) in Germany who were monolingually (German) and bilingually raised in either English-German, French-German, Turkish-German or other languages (mixed global L1 background)-German (Hörl, 2019). The children performed various tests (musicality, PROMS: melody, pitch, tuning, rhythm, tempo, timbre; musical skills questionnaire; working memory; IQ; language performance skills for grammar and vocabulary). The assumption that bilingual language training could impact on their musicality could not be corroborated. All children had equal musicality scores, and neither a bilingual subgroup nor all the bilinguals together scored higher on musicality than the monolinguals. Thus, such a "big" transfer effect from one domain to the other (language to music) was not observable.

What we found, however, were within-domain transfers or inter-relations. Those who played an instrument got significantly higher scores on the musicality test ($t(103) = 4.47, p < .001$). This does not prove automatically that initial training on a musical instrument for a few years or even less makes you more musical. The effect can be due to a self-selection mechanism, meaning that those who were already more musical beforehand were more prone to take musical instrument lessons (Hörl & Reiterer, 2017; Hörl, 2019). As Seither-Preisler and Schneider (Seither-Preisler et al., 2014) in their big longitudinal study investigating musicality in children could observe, it is those children with elevated musicality scores at start of investigation (prior to testing and intervention) who more voluntarily take an opportunity to learn an instrument if offered as a school (or research intervention) programme. Based on this research, they conceived a theoretical model of musical aptitude and performance ("neurocognitive model of competence development") where the biological pathway, as one part, based on anatomical predispositions enacts upon motivation to learn through "intrinsic" motivation, and this intrinsic motivation again works as modifier variable in the interplay between experiential, interventional variables of training and neurogenetic variables.

Thus, in our study, bilingualism per se did not influence musical aptitude. A different picture emerged when investigating deliberately and more focally language aptitude and musical aptitude in children—here kindergarten children between ages 5 and 6. Thirty-six Austrian preschool children performed similarly to the earlier-mentioned tests of phonetic speech imitation of exotic foreign languages they had never heard before: Hindi, Turkish, Russian, Tagalog and Chinese. Other tests included an abbreviated auditory working memory task, the children's version ("PMMA") of the earlier-mentioned AMMA musicality test and caretaker questions about musical behaviour. Results revealed that the participants who scored higher on the musicality tests also scored higher on the speech imitation tasks and had better developed working memory (Christiner & Reiterer, 2018; Christiner, 2018). The results are very similar to the results in adults, where phonetic aptitude is highly related to musical aptitude and working memory capacities—only the kindergarten children showed a preference for pitch discrimination over rhythm discrimination, i.e. they were better in pitch discrimination. Thus, musicality and speech imitation ability are also already linked to 5- to 6-year-old children without a noteworthy instrument or musical training or special linguistic training except for what they experience in their home environments. This leads to the suggestion that excluding a massive training effect, inherent factors might be at play, which predetermines musical aptitude (Oikkonen et al., 2015).

In another study (Christiner, Rüdegger, & Reiterer, 2018) investigating 9- to 10-year-old school children ($N = 30$) with a similar paradigm (speech imitation: Tagalog, Chinese; auditory working memory, non-verbal IQ, musicality [IMMA], LLAMA B,F), we found similar results, only we now could for the first time also discriminate the type of musicality interacting with specific phonetic language characteristics. Generally speaking, we found that the tonal dimension of musicality was especially important in Chinese imitation and the rhythm component of musicality for imitating Tagalog. Forty-three per cent of the variance in Chinese imitation was predicted by tonal musicality (IMMA) together with working memory and singing ability, and 38% of the variance in Tagalog imitation can be explained by IMMA rhythm together with WM. For IQ, there were no significant correlations to working memory, speech imitation or musicality, and no noticeable correlations could be detected for the LLAMA subtests B and F, except for a correlation between LLAMA B and the education of the parents and to a lesser degree with Chinese imitation. Thus, again, at an early stage in life, in 9- to 10-year-old children without massive exposure to instrumental musical training, musicality and singing behaviour seems to be intrinsically interwoven with phonetic speech imitation capacities and acoustic working memory, with specific musical aspects impacting on specific languages' phonotactic profiles, especially when tone and non-tone languages are involved.

This first finding into a more specific aptitude from one domain (e.g. tonal musicality) being related to another domain (e.g. phonetic level of language), for example, specific language classes, gives rise to both new and old anecdotal speculations, according to which some individuals might be more apt to learn specific foreign languages because the phonotactic or more general linguistic nature of this language fits their individual musicality and language talent profile—in short, their "ear" for languages. To follow up on this line of thinking, and not solely because of this reason but because of the lack of language aptitude tests in general, we started to develop a new battery of phonetic aptitude tests for perception (and later production) based on multiple foreign exotic languages for acoustic discrimination and imitation. The tests will have different duration and phonetic specificity (e.g. predict tone language aptitude); will comprise sound chunks from languages from tone-based, stress-based, syllable-based and mora-based language families (Chinese, Thai, Russian, Farsi, Hindi, Tagalog, Tamil and Japanese); and are currently being investigated, evaluated and validated (MULT/AP multilingual aptitude test; Christiner & Reiterer, 2017).

Conclusion

In our own research we focussed on phonetic and speech imitation aptitude, but apart from brain markers (i.e. individual differences in pronunciation/ speech imitation capacities as reflected by brain structure or different activation patterns, as in Reiterer et al., 2011; Hu et al., 2013; Vaquero et al., 2017; Turker et al., 2017), we also found markers in other psycho-cognitive domains. Higher speech imitation aptitude in adults, as well as young children, was accompanied, first and foremost, by higher singing abilities but also higher general musicality and auditory working memory (Christiner & Reiterer, 2013, 2015, 2016) and increased openness to new experience and empathy as personality markers; also it and differed between the sexes, with males showing elevated speech imitation skills and females showing superiority in grammar and vocabulary learning aptitude. As a phonetic marker of pronunciation aptitude for English as a second language, we could repeatedly isolate the initial schwa sound as a good predictor of overall pronunciation ability in L2 but also acoustic-articulatory predictors reflected in characteristic "articulation space" patterns, which were larger for the high- versus low-aptitude individuals, as analysed by modulation spectrum analysis (e.g. Reiterer et al., 2013). Minor markers were found in the knowledge of multiple L1 dialects and increased speech imitation ability in L2; finally, we found very low to no correlations between L2 phonetic imitation aptitude and general non-verbal IQ, reading speed and executive functions. We also found no transfer effects from bilingualism on musical or linguistic aptitude.

Notes

1 I speculate that there are even more, given enough time, motivation and exposure opportunities. Adults usually do not have the same time and quality of exposure to a language children typically have when growing up in a surrounding language community. This is probably due to the necessity of pursuing a job for financial reasons.
2 As for the initial tests on pragmatic ability that we did, we could find that pragmatic ability is normally distributed and is significantly correlated to empathy (Reiterer & Marusakova; 2015; Marusakova, 2015) and that empathy and pragmatic ability are expressed differently in males and females (Zapcevic, 2017).

References

Auer, S. (2017). *Language learning aptitude and polyglottism* (Bachelor Thesis), University of Vienna, Vienna, Austria.

Baron-Cohen, S., & Wheelwright, S. (2004). The empathy quotient: An investigation of adults with Asperger syndrome or high functioning autism, and normal sex differences. *Journal of Autism and Developmental Disorders, 34,* 163–175.

Biedroń, A. (2015). Neurology of Foreign language aptitude. *Studies in Second Language Learning and Teaching, 5*(1), 13–40.

Borkenau, P., & Ostendorf, F. (1993). *NEO-Fünf-Faktoren Inventar (NEO-FFI) nach Costa und McCrae: Handanweisung.* Göttingen: Hogrefe.

Carroll, J. B., & Sapon, S. (2002). *Modern language aptitude test.* Bethesda, MD: Second Language Testing, Inc.

Carver, C. S., & White, T. L. (1994). Behavioral inhibition, behavioral activation, and affective responses to impending reward and punishment: TheBIS/BAS scales. *Journal of Personality and Social Psychology, 67,* 319–333.

Chai, X. J., Berken, J. A., Barbeau, E., Soles, J., Callahan, M., Chen, J. K., & Klein, D. (2016). Intrinsic functional connectivity in the adult brain and success in second-language learning. *Journal of Neuroscience, 36*(3), 755–761.

Christiner, M. (2018). Let the music speak: Examining the relationship between music and language aptitude in pre-school children. In S. M. Reiterer (Ed.), *Exploring language aptitude: Views from psychology, the language sciences, and cognitive neuroscience.* Heidelberg: Springer-Nature.

Christiner, M., & Reiterer, S. M. (2018). Early influence of musical abilities and working memory on speech imitation abilities: Study with pre-school children. *Brain Sciences, 8*(9), 169.

Christiner, M., & Reiterer, S. M. (2017). *MULT/AP Multilingual aptitude test.* Vienna: Christiner Questionnaires. Retrieved from www.multap.net

Christiner, M., & Reiterer, S. M. (2016). Music, song and speech: A closer look at the interfaces between musicality, singing and individual differences in phonetic language aptitude. In G. Granena, D. O. Jackson, & Y. Yilmaz (Eds.), *Cognitive individual differences in second language processing and acquisition* (pp. 131–156). Amsterdam, The Netherlands: John Benjamins Publishing Company. doi:10.1075/bpa.3.07chr

Christiner, M., & Reiterer, S. M. (2015). A mozart in not a pavarotti: Singers outperform instrumentalists on Foreign accent imitation. *Frontiers in Human Neuroscience, 9*, Article 482. doi:10.3389/fnhum.2015.00482

Christiner, M., & Reiterer, S. M. (2013). Song and speech: Examining the link between singing talent and speech imitation ability. *Frontiers in Psychology, 4*, Article 874. doi:10.3389/fpsyg.2013.00874

Christiner, M., Rüdegger, S. M., & Reiterer, S. (2018). Sing Chinese and tap Tagalog? Predicting individual differences in musical and phonetic aptitude using language families differing by sound-typology. *International Journal of Multilingualism, 15*(4), 455–471.

Coumel, M. (2017). *Talent for accent: Is there a correlation between phonetic native and foreign language aptitude?* (Master Thesis in Cognitive Science), University of Vienna, Austria.

Coumel, M., Christiner, M., & Reiterer, S. (2016, November 20). *A talent for accent versus a talent for prosody? Trying to link individual differences in foreign accent imitation ability to prosodic imitation ability in L1.* Poster presented at the 2nd Workshop on Second Language Prosody (SLaP), University of Graz, Graz, Austria.

Dale, P. S., Harlaar, N., Haworth, C., & Plomin, R. (2010). Two by two: A twin study of second language acquisition. *Psychological Science, 21*(5), 635–640.

Dediu, D. (2008). The role of genetic biases in shaping the correlations between languages and genes. *Journal of Theoretical Biology, 254*(2), 400–407.

Dediu, D., & Ladd, R. (2007). Linguistic tone is related to the population frequency of the adaptive haplogroups of two brain size genes, ASPM and Microcephalin. *PNAS, 104*, 10944–10949.

DeKeyser, R. (2012). Interactions between individual differences, treatments, and structures in SLA. *Language Learning, 62*, 189–200.

Dogil, G., & Reiterer, S. (2009). *Language talent and brain activity.* Berlin: Mouton De Gruyter.

Erard, M. (2012). *Babel no more: The search for the world's most extraordinary language learners.* New York, NY: Free Press.

Fisher, S. (2017). Evolution of language: Lessons from the genome. *Psychonomic Bulletin and Review, 24*(1), 34–40.

Golestani, N., & Pallier, C. (2007). Anatomical correlates of Foreign speech sound production. *Cerebral Cortex, 17*(4), 929–934.

Golestani, N., & Zatorre, R. J. (2004). Learning new sounds of speech: Reallocation of neural substrates. *NeuroImage, 21*(2), 494–506.

Gordon, E. E. (1989). *Advanced measures of music audiation.* Chicago: GIA Publications.

Granena, G., & Long, M. (Eds.). (2013). *Sensitive periods, language aptitude, and ultimate L2 attainment.* Amsterdam, The Netherlands: John Benjamins Publishing Company.

Guira, A., Brannon, R., & Dull, C. (1972). Empathy and second language learning. *Language Learning, 22*, 111–130.

Hayiou, T., Dale, P. S., & Plomin, R. (2012). The etiology of variation in language skills changes with development: A longitudinal twin study of language from 2 to 12 years. *Developmental Science, 15*(2), 233–249.

Hörder, S. (2018). The correlation of early multilingualism and language aptitude. In S. M. Reiterer (Ed.), *Exploring language aptitude: Views from psychology, the language sciences, and cognitive neuroscience.* Heidelberg: Springer-Nature.

Hörl, M. (2019). *The impact of bilingualism on musical abilities* (Dissertation in English Linguistics), University of Mannheim, Germany.

Hörl, M., & Reiterer, S. (2017). *The impact of bilingualism on musical abilities.* Paper presented at the 11th International Symposium on Bilingualism (ISB11), University of Limerick, Ireland, June 12–15, 2017.

Hu, X., Ackermann, H., Martin, J. A., Erb, M., Winkler, S., & Reiterer, S. (2013). Language aptitude for pronunciation in advanced second language (L2) learners: Behavioural predictors and neural substrates. *Brain & Language, 127,* 366–376.

Hu, X., & Reiterer, S. (2009). Personality and pronunciation talent. In G. Dogil & S. M. Reiterer (Eds.), *Language talent and brain activity* (pp. 97–129). Berlin: Mouton de Gruyter.

Hyltenstam, K. (Ed.). (2016). *Advanced proficiency and exceptional ability in second languages.* Series: Studies on Second Language Acquisition 51. Berlin and New York, NY: De Gruyter.

Jilka, M. (2009). Assessment of phonetic ability. In G. Dogil & S. M. Reiterer (Eds.), *Language talent and brain activity* (pp. 17–66). Berlin: Mouton de Gruyter.

Kepinska, O., de Rover, M., Caspers, J., & Schiller, N. O. (2017a). Whole-brain functional connectivity during acquisition of novel grammar: Distinct functional networks depend on language learning abilities. *Behav Brain Res, 320,* 333–346. doi:10.1016/j.bbr

Kepinska, O., de Rover, M., Caspers, J., & Schiller, N. O. (2017b). On neural correlates of individual differences in novel grammar learning: An fMRI study. *Neuropsychologia, 98,* 156–168. doi:10.1016/j

Landerl, K., Wimmer, H., & Moser, E. (1997). *Salzburger Lese-und Rechtschreibtest (SLT) [Salzburg reading and spelling test (SLT)].* Bern, Switzerland: Huber.

Lehrl, S., Triebig, G., & Fischer, B. (1995). Multiple choice vocabulary test MWT as a valid and short test to estimate premorbid intelligence. *Acta Neurologica Scandinavica, 91,* 335–345.

Linck, J., Hughes, M., Campbell, S., Silbert, N., Tare, M., Jackson, S., . . . Doughty, C. (2013). Hi-LAB: A new measure of aptitude for high-level language proficiency. *Language Learning, 63,* 530–566.

Markman, T., Quittner, A., Eisenberg, L., Tobey, E., Thal, D., Niparko, J., Wang, N. Y., The CDaCI Investigative Team. (2011). Language development after cochlear implantation: An epigenetic model. *Journal of Neurodevelopmental Disorders, 3*(4), 388–404.

Marusakova, M. (2015). *Pragmatics and empathy in second language aptitude.* Master Thesis in Cognitive Science), University of Vienna, Vienna, Austria.

Meara, P. (2005). *Llama language aptitude tests.* Retrieved June, 2017, from www.lognostics.co.uk/tools/llama/

Miro-Padilla, A., Bueichekú, E., Ventura-Campos, N., Palomar-García, M. Á, & Ávila, C. (2017). Functional connectivity in resting state as a phonemic fluency ability measure. *Neuropsychologia, 97,* 98–103. doi:10.1016/j.neuropsychologia.2017.02.009

Nardo, D., & Reiterer, S. (2009). Musicality and phonetic language aptitude. In G. Dogil & S. M. Reiterer (Eds.), *Language talent and brain activity* (pp. 213–256). Berlin: Mouton de Gruyter.

Neufeld, G. (1979). Towards a theory of language learning ability. *Language Learning, 29*(2), 227–241.

Oikkonen, J., Huang, Y., Onkamo, P., Ukkola-Vuoti, L., Raijas, P., Karma, K., . . . Järvelä, I. (2015). A genome-wide linkage and association study of musical aptitude identifies loci containing genes related to inner ear development and neurocognitive functions. *Molecular Psychiatry, 20*(2), 275–282. doi:10.1038/mp.2014.8

Oikkonen, J., & Järvelä, I. (2015). Genomics approaches to study musical aptitude. *Bioessays, 36*(11), 1102–1108. doi:10.1002/bies.201400081

Plomin, R., DeFries, J., Knopik, V. S., & Neiderhieser, J. (2016). Top 10 replicated findings from behavioral genetics. *Perspectives in Psychological Science, 11*(1), 3–23.

Plomin, R. Shakeshaft, N., McMillan, A., & Trzaskowski, M. (2014). Nature, nurture and expertise. *Intelligence, 45*, 46–59.

Prat, C. S., Yamasaki, B. L., Kluender, R. A., & Stocco, A. (2016). Resting-state qEEG predicts rate of second language learning in adults. *Brain and Language, 157–158*, 44–50. doi:10.1016/j.bandl.2016.04.007

Raven, J., Raven, J. C., & Court, J. H. (1998). *Manual for raven's advanced progressive matrices.* Oxford: Psychologists Press.

Reiterer, S. M. (2018). *Exploring language aptitude: Views from psychology, the language sciences, and cognitive neuroscience.* Heidelberg: Springer-Nature.

Reiterer, S. M., Hu, X., Erb, M., Rota, G., Nardo, D., Grodd, W., . . . Ackermann, H. (2011). Individual differences in audio-vocal speech imitation aptitude in late bilinguals: Functional neuroimaging and brain morphology. *Frontiers in Psychology, 2*(271), 1–12.

Reiterer, S. M., Hu, X., Sumathi, T. A., & Singh, N. C. (2013). Are you a good mimic? Neuro-acoustic signatures for speech imitation ability. *Frontiers in Psychology, 4*, 782.

Reiterer, S. M., & Marusakova, M. (2015, September 17–19). *Pragmatic ability, the forgotten factor in language aptitude research: Exploring its relationship to empathy in L2.* Paper presented at the international conference "The Self in Language Learning (SiLL)", Çağ University, Turkey.

Ripolles, P., Marco-Pallares, J., Hielscher, U., Mestres-Misse, A., Tempelmann, C., Heinze, H. J., . . . Noesselt, T. (2014). The role of reward in word learning and its implications for language acquisition. *Current Biology, 24*(21), 2606–2611.

Rota, G., & Reiterer, S. (2009). Cognitive aspects of pronunciation talent: How empathy, mental flexibility, working memory and intelligence interact with phonetic talent. In G. Dogil & S. Reiterer (Eds.), *Language talent and brain activity* (pp. 67–96). Berlin: Mouton de Gruyter.

Safronova, E., & Mora, J. C. (2012). Acoustic and phonological memory in L2 vowel perception. *Proceedings of 22nd EUROSLA*, 384–390.

Schneider, P., Scherg, M., Dosch, H. G., Specht, H. J., Gutschalk, A., & Rupp, A. (2002). Morphology of Heschl's gyrus reflects enhanced activation in the auditory cortex of musicians. *Nature Neuroscience, 5*(7), 688–694.

Seither-Preisler, A., Parnkutt, R., & Schneider, P. (2014). Size and synchronization of auditory cortex promotes musical, literacy, and attentional skills in children. *Journal of Neuroscience, 34*(33), 10937–10949. doi:10.1523/JNEUROSCI.5315-13.2014

Turker, S., Reiterer, S. M., Seither-Preisler, A., & Schneider, P. (2017). "When music speaks": Auditory cortex morphology as a neuroanatomical marker of language aptitude. *Frontiers in Psychology, 8*, 2096. doi:10.3389/fpsyg.2017.02096

Vaquero, L., Rodriguez-Fornells, A., & Reiterer, S. M. (2017). The left, the better: White-matter brain integrity predicts Foreign language imitation ability. *Cerebral Cortex, 27*(8), 3906–3917. doi:10.1093/cercor/bhw199

Wen, Z. E., Biedroń, A., & Skehan, P. (2017). Foreign language aptitude theory: Yesterday, today and tomorrow. *Language Teaching* (CUP), *50*(1), 1–31.

Wucherer, B., & Reiterer, S. M. (2018). Language is a girlie thing, isn't it? A psycholinguistic exploration of the L2 gender gap. *International Journal of Bilingual Education and Bilingualism, 19*, 1–17.

Zapcevic, E. (2017). *Individual differences in L2 pragmatics: Relation between empathy, gender, and the sociopragmatic competence* (Master Thesis in English Linguistics), University of Vienna, Austria.

15

IN SEARCH OF A COGNITIVE MODEL FOR INTERPRETING EXPERTISE

Minhua Liu

Introduction

Interpreter aptitude has been a popular topic in the field of interpreting. Studies have approached the topic from different perspectives, such as language abilities (e.g., Gerver, Longley, Long, & Lambert, 1989), personality traits (e.g., Schweda-Nicholson, 2005), cognitive abilities (e.g., Macnamara, Moore, Kegl, & Conway, 2011), learner characteristics (e.g., Bontempo & Napier, 2011; Timarová & Salaets, 2011), and the ability to deal with stress (e.g., Rosiers, Eyckmans, & Bauwens, 2011), many of which are discussed in the context of aptitude testing. However, we still do not have clear evidence for what an interpreter aptitude may be composed of. To a large extent, this lack of knowledge on interpreter aptitude has to do with a lack of a true understanding of the competence that learners need to attain to become an expert in interpreting.

Shreve, Angelone, and Lacruz (2018) discuss how competence has been studied in the field of translation and advocate grounding the discussion on competence in psychological realities and adopting the concept and the term of 'expertise' to describe these realities. This is what this chapter aims to achieve—to describe what we have so far as evidence for the cognitive realities of interpreting expertise and the development of such abilities that may result from practice and experience in interpreting. It is hoped that a clearer picture of the cognitive realities of interpreting expertise and its development can better inform us of the cognitive potentials, i.e., the aptitude, that one may need to possess to make the development and the attainment of such expertise possible.

Understandably, what constitutes the aptitude for bilinguals or multilinguals can be considered part of the interpreter aptitude. It is fair to say, though, that interpreter aptitude is more than the traits or abilities that categorize interpreters as highly advanced bilinguals or multilinguals. This is mainly because what inter-preters do professionally—the way they process information, particularly in the mode of simultaneous interpreting—is not what noninterpreter bilinguals nor-mally do. This can explain why among the different perspectives taken to address the topic of interpreter aptitude, studies on the interpreter's cognitive abilities as a bilingual have gained increasing traction in research. This is in part due to the recent proliferation of articles on the cognitive characteristics, specifically the executive functions, of bilinguals and multilinguals in the field of bilingualism. This chapter will focus on this aspect of the interpreter's cognitive abilities and specifically on the executive functions of interpreters. Working memory will also be discussed with its connection to the executive functions.

The central questions behind much of the research on executive functions are whether frequent use results in improvements and whether the effect of training executive functions transfers to other tasks. The assumption underlying the second question is that executive functions are domain-general abilities that are used in many cognitive tasks, including bilingual language control. Another critical ques-tion is "Which executive functions are involved in bilingual language control?" Answers to or assumptions made about these three questions are critical to our discussion on the interpreter's cognitive abilities and, potentially, the interpreter's cognitive aptitude. Specifically, if being bilingual benefits the executive functions, do interpreters enjoy even more enhanced benefits in this regard as advanced bilinguals? Or rather, do interpreters develop abilities specific to their practice in simultaneous interpreting that go beyond the bilingual benefits observed in noninterpreter bilinguals?

Executive Functions and Potential Interpreter Benefits

 The executive functions are known to be a multicomponent attentional or con-trol mechanism that monitors and coordinates our cognitive behaviors. The three most frequently studied executive functions are response inhibition, working memory updating, and task shifting (or shifting), based on the model of Miyake and colleagues (Miyake et al., 2000).

There has been ample evidence showing that both language sets of a bilingual are simultaneously activated—phonologically and semantically—even if only one language is being used (e.g., Hoshino & Kroll, 2008; Kroll & Bialystok, 2013; Kroll, Bobb, & Wodniecka, 2006; Wu & Thierry, 2011). The two co-activated lan-guages constantly compete for cognitive resources, and there is a need to select one language but at the same time inhibit the other (Kroll, Bobb, Misra, & Guo, 2008). This interplay is considered to contribute to enhanced language control abilities in bilinguals (e.g., Green, 1998; Kroll, Dussias, Bice, & Perrotti, 2015). Compared to monolinguals, bilinguals perform better on various tasks that engage conflict resolution, an executive function that involves inhibition (e.g., Blumenfeld & Marian, 2011; Costa, Hernández, & Sebastián-Gallés, 2008). This suggests that the benefits bilinguals gain in the executive functions are not limited to language-related activities. Similar bilingual benefits have also been observed in updating and shifting (e.g., Morales, Calvo, & Bialystok, 2013; Prior & Macwhinney, 2010). However, there are also counter-evidence and arguments that do not support the existence of bilingual benefits (e.g., de Bruin, Treccani, & Sala, 2015; Kousaie, Sheppard, Lemieux, Monetta, & Taler, 2014; Paap, Johnson, & Sawi, 2015; Paap & Sawi, 2014). It is argued, though, that the lack of evidence may be a result of the lower bilingual management demands of the tasks on which participants were observed (Macnamara & Conway, 2016).

How about interpreters? To start with, interpreters who practice simultaneous interpreting professionally are highly advanced bilinguals who use both their languages intensively, often in highly challenging situations. Research has shown that bilinguals who often switch languages outperform bilinguals who do not switch languages as frequently in shifting tasks (Prior & Gollan, 2011). In this sense, if bilingual advantages exist, professional interpreters should show even more enhanced advantages in executive functions as a result of an extension of bilingualism. However, interpreters are more than advanced bilinguals. The way they use their two languages while interpreting is different from how the two languages are normally used. In simultaneous interpreting, not only are the interpreters' two languages simultaneously activated and constantly competing but the two languages also have to be maintained, not inhibited, so that comprehending in one language and concurrently producing a matching output in another language can be facilitated. All the while, the production of one language continues to interfere with the reception of the other language. Simultaneous interpreting can be considered an extreme case of language management (Babcock & Vallesi, 2017). It is unlikely that what makes professional interpreters highly functional in what they do is only due to enhanced domain-general cognitive functions. Is it the case that the interpreter's expertise is a result of the development of skills that are specific to the domain of simultaneous interpreting? A further question is: will these highly practiced domain-specific cognitive skills affect the domain-general abilities such as the executive functions?

This chapter aims to find answers to these questions by looking for evidence in the literature. In the next section, research on interpreters that involves each of the three executive functions, i.e., inhibition, updating, and shifting, will be discussed.

Inhibition

Inhibition (aka, inhibitory control or conflict resolution) is the ability to block unwanted responses in a cognitive task (Miyake et al., 2000). This executive function is usually studied in tasks such as Stroop, Simon, flanker, ANT, etc. Bilingual benefits in inhibition have been observed in various studies (e.g., Bialystok, 2006; Costa et al., 2008).

Research on the ability of inhibition in interpreters has not shown that experience or expertise in interpreting confers further advantages on interpreters
beyond what is observed as bilingual benefits (Babcock & Vallesi, 2017; Dong &
Xie, 2014; Köpke & Nespoulous, 2006; Morales, Padilla, Gómez-Ariza, & Bajo,
2015; Yudes, Macizo, & Bajo, 2011). Since both languages have to be kept active
all the time during simultaneous interpreting, a lack of interpreter advantage in
this aspect is not surprising. It is possible that instead of showing an advantage in
inhibition, skilled interpreters may have an advantage in keeping both languages
active. This is exactly what was found in a study comparing interpreters with noninterpreter bilinguals where they had to read and repeat sentences in Spanish and
English (Ibáñez, Macizo, & Bajo, 2010). The sentences included both cognate and
matched control words. Whereas noninterpreter bilinguals showed no difference
in the speed of processing cognate and control words, interpreters were faster in
processing cognate words in both English and Spanish. It is commonly understood that simultaneous activation of two languages facilitates faster processing of
cognates (Babcock & Vallesi, 2015).

The interpreters' better ability to maintain more than one task is also observed
in nonlinguistic tasks in a study where professional interpreters were compared
with matched multilinguals (Babcock & Vallesi, 2017) in sustained (or global)
control and transient (or local) control. Although the two groups showed no difference in transient control, the interpreters showed greater sustained control.
This discrepancy demonstrates a unique interpreter advantage, according to the
authors, because of the need for interpreters to maintain multiple task sets (i.e.,
both language sets) during simultaneous interpreting instead of shifting between
task sets, characterized by transient control.

Updating

Updating is the function to continuously monitor incoming information against
information held in working memory and to rapidly delete from or add to memory content, with a goal to completing the task concerned (Miyake et al., 2000).
Updating is considered important in allowing the retrieval of knowledge from
long-term memory to be more efficient (Babcock & Vallesi, 2017). Updating is
usually measured through a dual *n*-back task.

Morales and colleagues (2013) observed a bilingual advantage in updating,
and Morales et al. (2015) showed that interpreters doing various updating tasks
showed that interpreters also excelled in updating in various tasks.

Shifting

Shifting is the ability to flexibly switch between different tasks or mental sets
(Miyake et al., 2000). Research has shown that task shifting exacts a cost on the
functions of working memory (Liefooghe, Barrouillet, Vandierendonck, & Camos,

2008). Task shifting is conventionally measured in 'shifting cost'—the toll that the act of shifting may cause. A bilingual advantage in shifting has been observed in research (Prior & MacWhinney, 2010).

There is evidence showing that task-shifting speed is part of a group of predictors that differentiates high-performing and low-performing sign language interpreters (Macnamara et al., 2011). Shifting ability has also been observed to improve after students receive training in interpreting—consecutive interpreting in this case—but not in translation (Dong & Liu, 2016). However, as mentioned previously, Babcock and Vallesi (2017), in their study comparing a group of professional interpreters with matched multilinguals on tests of memory and executive control, found no interpreter advantages in shifting cost. Nevertheless, they found an advantage in the mixing cost in the task-shifting paradigm that seems to be specific to interpreting. Babcock and Vallesi (2017) concluded that interpreters do not experience further bilingual benefits beyond those they already had, but they do appear to possess benefits specific to their experience in simultaneous interpretation.

In Search of a Cognitive Model for Interpreting Expertise

Our discussion so far has not yielded a clear answer as to whether interpreters have more enhanced executive functions as advanced bilinguals. However, research indicates that interpreters may develop interpreting-specific advantages that are not simply due to a bilingual advantage, but rather are the result of their practice in interpreting. In this section, we will discuss the possible sources for such advantages.

Verbal Working Memory and the Role of the Phonological Loop

Among the various cognitive abilities of interpreters, verbal working memory capacity may have been the most studied. It has been shown that professional interpreters have larger verbal working memory and short-term memory spans than various control groups (Babcock & Vallesi, 2015; Bajo, Padilla, & Padilla, 2000; Christoffels, de Groot, & Kroll, 2006; Padilla, Bajo, Cañas, & Padilla, 1995; Stavrakaki, Megari, Kosmidis, Apostolidou, & Takou, 2012; Yudes et al., 2011, 2012; but see Liu, Schallert, & Carroll, 2004; Köpke & Nespoulous, 2006). One factor that may contribute to the mixed results is the use of different combinations of participants, i.e., the use of professionals and bilingual controls in some studies, professionals and student interpreters in others, and student interpreters and bilingual controls in yet other studies.

While it is still unclear if professional interpreters have a larger verbal working memory capacity, evidence has shown that the way interpreters process verbal information may be different from the way it is normally processed. We may be able to get a clue from the function of the phonological loop. The phonological loop in Baddeley's working memory model (Hitch & Baddeley, 1976) is responsible for maintaining verbal information in its temporal order and in the form of verbatim auditory memory before it disappears or passes on to long-term memory. The auditory memory traces decay rapidly if they are not maintained. The phonological loop is also conceptualized to prevent these memory traces from decaying by rehearsing them subvocally in the articulatory loop. When the rehearsal mechanism is blocked under the condition of articulatory suppression—for example, by repeating some irrelevant sound aloud while listening to and trying to memorize some verbal information—participants' recall of the verbal information is impaired.

In simultaneous interpreting, not only are the interpreters' two languages constantly activated but concurrent speaking also continues to interfere with the function of the phonological loop to rehearse the other language. Expert interpreters have been shown to be less affected in the condition of articulatory suppression, and in some cases, they demonstrate near-equivalent recall, as in the condition of no articulatory suppression (Bajo et al., 2000; Padilla et al., 1995; Yudes et al., 2012; but see Köpke & Nespoulous, 2006). This suggests that the phonological interference caused by producing output in one language does not greatly affect the processing of the input in the other language for professional interpreters during simultaneous interpreting.

It is possible that interpreters learn to bypass the need to rehearse the speech they hear in their phonological loop or employ some nonverbal strategies to keep the information alive for that very short period before they utter the information in another language. It is also possible that interpreters resort to a nonverbatim processing pattern and rely on processing the input information semantically when verbally producing the interpretation output. Semantic processing will be discussed in a later section of this chapter.

The Connection Between Updating and Shifting

The different components of the executive functions are usually studied separately through different measures designed specifically for examining a particular task. However, these different components have also been shown to be connected, and the effect of one component may carry over to other components in executive functioning (Prior & Gollan, 2011; Verreyt, Woumans, Vandelanotte, Szmalec, & Duyck, 2016).

The connection among different components of the executive functions has also been demonstrated in studies involving interpreters. In interpreting, the ability to quickly update information in working memory may be shown in the length of ear-voice-span (EVS), the time between the moment a segment is heard in the source language and the moment when it is expressed in the target language. Research has found that a shorter EVS is associated with either interpreting experience or better performance in simultaneous interpreting (Timarová, Cenkova, Meylaerts, Hertog, Szmalec, & Duyck, 2014). Interpreters who kept a shorter EVS were found to be better at the shifting task, as measured by the number-letter task (Timarová et al., 2014). The same study also showed that updating and shifting were moderately but significantly related. The authors suggested that these two executive functions may be jointly responsible for executing the task of simultaneous interpreting more effectively.

Though the length of EVS differs in individual interpreters and oftentimes depends on factors such as the source text and the languages involved, the average EVS as found in studies on professional interpreters is between two and four seconds (Pio, 2003; Timarová et al., 2014). It has been shown that memory traces decay in two seconds if the content of the memory is not rehearsed (Baddeley, 1986). The shorter EVS adopted by interpreters who are either more experienced or who produce more accurate output may be using a task-specific strategy to bypass the need to rehearse the content temporarily kept in the phonological loop.

The fact that high performers may depend less on the phonological loop is also evidenced in other fields. Otsuka and Osaka (2015) studied high and low performers of complex mental arithmetic under different conditions where load was imposed on the central executive, phonological loop, and visuo-spatial sketchpad. Whereas the errors of low performers increased in both the conditions where the central executive and the phonological loop were burdened, high performers had more errors only under the condition where the central executive was loaded. According to the authors, the results indicate that high performers might rely less on the phonological loop and that they might have used strategies that allowed them to use less working memory capacity.

This observation may also explain why high-performing interpreters seem to be less affected by articulatory suppression. What possible strategies may interpreters employ to allow this to happen? We have three hypotheses: efficient access to the mental lexicon, semantic processing, and the use of nonverbal working memory.

Access to Mental Lexicon

It is part of a professional interpreter's life to learn and use words and terms in many different fields. Naturally, having a wide range of vocabulary is essential for a successful interpreting career. Does this mean that interpreters have a larger vocabulary than noninterpreter bilinguals? Do higher-performing interpreters use a wider variety of words than lower-performing interpreters when they interpret? What role does access to the interpreters' mental lexicon play in their expertise in interpreting? Though we do not have enough evidence to fully answer these questions, we may be able to gain a partial picture on how professional interpreters' mental lexicon works from the literature.

Research evidence shows that, compared with noninterpreter bilinguals, professional interpreters are faster at making lexical decisions on nonwords (Bajo et al., 2000), categorizing nontypical exemplars (Bajo et al., 2000), naming pictures in both languages (Christoffels et al., 2006), and translating words in both directions (Christoffels et al., 2006). Interpreters may not necessarily be more accurate in their use of words, but they have been shown to be more efficient (i.e., faster) at such tasks. These studies suggest that, rather than the size of the mental lexicon or the accuracy of lexical use, it may be the speed (i.e., efficiency) of accessing the mental lexicon that differentiates professional interpreters from noninterpreter bilinguals.

Since the speed of choosing words from the mental lexicon is thought to relate to how fast memory is updated (Timarová et al., 2014), this may explain the association of a shorter EVS and better interpreting performance and the connection between the performance in shifting and updating, as observed in the study of Timarová et al. (2014). It is possible that interpreters adopt specific strategies to speed up the process of accessing the mental lexicon, thus allowing lexical retrieval to become more efficient. Two observed strategies that interpreters use may explain this phenomenon.

To allow a more automatic lexical retrieval to happen, interpreters may need to resort to a more direct route to finding the equivalent in the target language. Paradis (1994) proposed a translation strategy that involves transcoding a term in the source language directly to its equivalent in the target language, as opposed to the concept-mediated strategy, where a shared memory representation is first accessed before the target language output is produced. This may allow the process of lexical retrieval to become more automatic. Automaticity is generally considered central to the development of expertise (Ericsson, 2008). What can potentially contribute to the quick updating of working memory may be the automaticity or near automaticity of word retrieval. Paradis (1994) assumed that more experienced interpreters take advantage of this more direct route when necessary, and there is empirical evidence for the strategy of transcoding in simultaneous interpreting (de Groot & Christoffels, 2006).

It is also possible that interpreters use a strategy of economy during the interpreting task. Timarová et al. (2014) have shown that interpreters who updated their memory more efficiently tended to use a less extensive vocabulary. This finding cannot be interpreted to indicate that interpreters have a less extensive vocabulary, though. It is more of a strategy that interpreters adopt when performing simultaneous interpreting. The speed and efficiency that interpreters demonstrate in lexical retrieval may be specific to the type of training or experience they have. For example, Elmer, Meyer, and Jäncke (2010) have observed that interpreters only showed distinct neurophysiological modulations for word pairs presented in the professionally trained direction during semantic decision.

Semantic Processing

Automaticity or a close-to-automatic processing strategy in the access of the mental lexicon may not fully explain why interpreters are generally less affected by the condition of articulatory suppression. The content that is temporarily stored in the phonological loop must be understood in the first place. While the interpreters' concurrent speech suppresses the subvocal rehearsal necessary to process incoming information in a verbatim manner, it is possible that interpreters resort to a processing strategy that is more semantic in nature. Evidence for this hypothesis can be found in neuroscience. For example, studies conducted by Elmer and his colleagues show that training in simultaneous interpreting has an effect on the regions responsible for top-down processing of auditory functions (cited in Injoque-Ricle, Barreyro, Formoso, & Jaichenco, 2015).

Studies comparing simultaneous interpreting with shadowing show that the two tasks are similar in their linguistic and executive demands. However, although all the regions involved in shadowing are also involved in simultaneous interpreting, two left inferior frontal gyrus regions—pars triangularis and pars orbitalis—are also recruited during simultaneous interpreting (Hervais-Adelman, Moser-Mercer, & Golestani, 2015). Pars triangularis is known for its role in semantic processing (Bookheimer, 2002; Dapretto & Bookheimer, 1999 cited in Hervais-Adelman et al. 2015), and pars orbitalis for semantic memory and the cognitive control of memory (Badre & Wagner 2007; cited in Hervais-Adelman et al., 2015).

What can be considered a manifestation of interpreters' semantic processing is the high-performing interpreters' ability to select the more important information over the less important when full interpretation of both is not feasible (Liu et al., 2004). Studies on noninterpreter bilinguals also showed that bilinguals are better at selectively attending to the more important elements of a stimulus (Bialystok & Martin, 2004; Kroll et al., 2008).

Spatial Working Memory and the Role of the Episodic Buffer

In Baddeley's working memory model, there are two more slave systems other than the phonological loop—the visuo-spatial sketchpad and the episodic buffer (Baddeley, 1986, 2000). While the phonological loop is responsible for storing and processing verbal information, the visuospatial sketchpad does the same for visual and spatial information (Baddeley, 1986). The mechanism of the episodic buffer seems to be more holistic. Not only is it assumed to access semantic meaning and to provide links to long-term memory, it is also believed to combine sources across domains to form information that is at the same time visual, spatial, and verbal (Baddeley, 2000).

Babcock and Vallesi (2017) show that interpreters have larger spatial memory spans. Interpreters have also been observed to consistently make use of visual cues during an Attention Networks Test for Interaction-Vigilance (ANTI-V), while noninterpreter bilinguals could only do this when an alerting tone was present (Morales et al., 2015). No research has focused on the use of the epidemic buffer in interpreting, but it is possible that interpreters learn to take advantage of all possible information available to them during simultaneous interpreting and rely on the epidemic buffer for this strategy.

From what we have discussed so far, it seems that "[i]nterpreters do not continue to garner benefits from bilingualism, but they do appear to possess benefits specific to their experience with simultaneous interpretation" (Babcock & Vallesi, 2017, p. 403). The next question is whether these domain-specific benefits are a result of training or professional experience, or both.

The Effect of Training and Experience

When we search for a neurocognitive model for interpreting expertise, we first look for abilities that can be improved through training or expertise that can be gained from experience. When evidence is lacking for the effect of training or the benefit of experience, we hope that effective screening mechanisms can be developed to help trainers or their institutions find candidates who have the right aptitude.

Research on bilinguals has shown that training in shifting and updating can lead to cognitive changes (e.g., Strobach, Becker, Schubert, & Kühn, 2015). As mentioned before, interpreters seem to enjoy an advantage in shifting and updating, or the combined effect of the two. Our next question is: how much does this advantage come from training in interpreting or from experience in practicing interpreting as a profession?

To observe the effect of training or experience, it is common to study the effect in a longitudinal study or in a cross-sectional study that compares participants with different levels of expertise. Both approaches have been adopted in studies on interpreters, though longitudinal studies are comparatively fewer than cross-sectional studies.

Studies on interpreters' performance under the condition of articulatory suppression are good examples for demonstrating the effect of interpreting experience on improving cognitive functions. In a cross-sectional study, professional interpreters were compared with two groups of interpretation students (before and after their training in simultaneous interpreting) and a group of noninterpreter controls (Padilla et al., 1995). The professional interpreters not only outperformed the other three groups on verbal short-term and working memory but they were also not affected by articulatory suppression in a verbal recall task, unlike the other three groups. In a similar study, professional interpreters' recall under articulatory suppression was only hindered in the most difficult of the four conditions. In comparison, student interpreters' performance was affected in two of the conditions, and monolingual controls in all four conditions (Yudes et al., 2012). This shows that the advantages that interpreters gain in their cognitive functions are not inherent, but are the result of their experience in practicing simultaneous interpreting (Babcock & Vallesi, 2015).

What has been observed in the effect of experience in studies comparing professional interpreters and less skilled interpreters and noninterpreters has also been found in studies targeting the benefits gained from training. In the experiment of Dong and Xie (2014), students with three years of training in interpreting completed more categories in the Wisconsin Card Sorting Task (WCST) than students with only one year of training, who in turn outperformed noninterpreting students.

Several longitudinal studies also provide evidence for the training and experience effect. In a longitudinal study using functional magnetic resonance imaging (fMRI), it was found that student interpreters' caudate nucleus, a brain region that supports executive functions, became less activated—meaning more efficient—during interpreting after they received more training (Hervais-Adelman et al., 2015). In another study on interpreting students, these researchers observed through fMRI an increase in cortical thickness of the regions involved in executive control and attention (Hervais-Adelman, Moser-Mercer, Murray, & Golestani, 2017).

Among translator and interpreter training schools in the world, it is very common that students who receive training in interpreting also train in translation, albeit for a shorter period or only in the first part of their training in some cases. It is not clear if changes in student interpreters' cognitive skills result from training in translating between two languages, be it in the written or the oral form, or both. Dong and Liu (2016) conducted a longitudinal study where they investigated whether experiences in written translation or consecutive interpreting would have different effects on the cognitive control abilities in bilinguals. Three groups of Chinese-English young adult bilinguals were tested twice on the number Stroop (for inhibition), shifting color-shape (for shifting), and N-back (for updating) tasks after they received general L2 written translation and consecutive interpreting training, respectively, for a half-year. The results showed that although students showed marginally significant improvements in updating after training in translation, the interpreting experience produced significant cognitive advantages in both shifting and updating. Though language shifting is involved in both translation and interpreting tasks, the authors concluded that it may be the experience of language shifting under higher processing demands that brings more domain-general advantages.

This view of high-demand–induced cognitive changes found evidence in a longitudinal study on interpreting students of American Sign Language (ASL) and English. Macnamara and Conway (2014) measured various cognitive abilities and simultaneous interpreting performance at four different time points during the two years when students received interpreting training. Students improved in almost all cognitive measures, showing the benefits from training. These results are significant in light of the findings from a study (Emmorey, Luk, Pyers, & Bialystok, 2008) involving bilinguals of ASL and English in which no bilingual advantage was found in the ASL and English bilingual group, compared with bilinguals of English and three other spoken languages. Emmorey and colleagues explained the results in terms of the lower-level demands on conflict resolution for bimodal bilinguals (i.e., of a signed language and a spoken language) than unimodal bilinguals (i.e., having two spoken languages in their language combination). The fact that bimodal bilinguals can concurrently express themselves in both languages and do not need to actively suppress one language in order to activate the other may not challenge their ability in conflict resolution as much as in the case of unimodal bilinguals. Macnamara and Conway (2014) explained their different results in terms of the more intense demands from the task of simultaneous interpreting.

Conclusion

Bilingualism is a necessary but not a sufficient condition for becoming an interpreter (de Groot, 2011). Though it is safe to say that most bilinguals have the ability to translate between their two languages (Harris & Sherwood, 1978), to practice interpreting professionally is different. Professional interpreting may demand further cognitive adaptations that natural translators may not have developed (Muñoz Martín, 2015).

In this chapter, we reviewed the literature and tried to find out if further cognitive adaptations may develop with experience and/or training in performing the task of interpreting and how such skills develop. We were particularly interested in the existence of an interpreter advantage in the executive functions, as many studies in bilingualism have suggested a bilingual advantage in these cognitive functions.

We know from research that interpreters, and particularly high-performing ones, seem to have an advantage in the executive function of shifting. As the task-shifting ability has been observed in connection with updating, it is possible that the two executive functions work together to make simultaneous interpreting more efficient or even possible.

The interpreter advantage shown in shifting and updating does not seem to derive from the fact that interpreters are a group of advanced bilinguals who actively use both their languages in their trade. That is, if there is such a thing as a bilingual advantage, interpreters do not seem to garner further benefits beyond being bilinguals. Instead, interpreters seem to have developed domain-specific strategies that they use when performing the task of interpreting, particularly simultaneous interpreting—the interpreting mode most studied in research.

There is also evidence showing that interpreters only use these domain-specific strategies in the tasks they are trained for or have experience in.

The interpreting-specific strategies that have been observed in research include making lexical retrieval more efficient by taking a more direct route for translation, processing information semantically, shortening the EVS, and pulling information of different natures—verbal, visual, spatial—from different sources to form a more integrated unit of information.

Research has also shown that these advantages or use of strategies is not part of what interpreters bring with them before training or before gaining experience in interpreting. Longitudinal studies following student interpreters from several months to two years show that the gains in any cognitive functions or interpreting skills come from the demands of their training and the "extreme bilingual language management" (Babcock & Vallesi, 2017, p. 403) tasks they learn to perform. In other words, simultaneous interpreting is a learned ability.

Though we are still uncertain if constant practice or training in the domain-specific skills of interpreting benefits domain-general cognitive functions, it is quite clear that experience in interpreting has consequences for the brain. In this sense, studying interpreters as a unique group of bilinguals can potentially inform our understanding of people speaking more than two languages and of their cognitive abilities. Whyatt (2010) argues that bilingual language control should not be only studied in bilinguals performing monolingual tasks, but that it also needs to be studied when bilinguals are engaged in tasks where both language systems are simultaneously activated. Though research on simultaneous interpreting was not a part of the mainstream psycholinguistic work on bilingual language control 10 years ago (De Groot & Christoffels, 2006), it seems the interest in studying interpreters has picked up speed in recent years. This is a welcome trend, as findings from such research can potentially inform research not only on a bilingual advantage but also on expertise development and individual differences.

References

Babcock, L., & Vallesi, A. (2015). Language control is not a one-size-fits-all languages process: Evidence from simultaneous interpretation students and the n-2 repetition cost. *Frontiers in Psychology, 6*(1622).

Babcock, L., & Vallesi, A. (2017). Are simultaneous interpreters expert bilinguals, unique bilinguals, or both? *Bilingualism: Language and Cognition, 20*(2), 403–417.

Baddeley, A. (1986). *Working memory*. Oxford: Clarendon Press.

Baddeley, A. (2000). The episodic buffer: A new component of working memory? *Trends in Cognitive Sciences, 4*(11), 417–423.

Bajo, M. T., Padilla, F., & Padilla, P. (2000). Comprehension processes in simultaneous interpreting. In A. Chesterman, N. Gallardo San Salvador, & Y. Gambier (Eds.), *Translation in context* (pp. 127–142). Amsterdam, The Netherlands: John Benjamins Publishing Company.

Bialystok, E. (2006). Effect of bilingualism and computer video game experience on the Simon task. *Canadian Journal of Experimental Psychology, 60*(1), 68–79.

Bialystok, E., & Martin, M. M. (2004). Attention and inhibition in bilingual children: Evidence from the dimensional change card sort task. *Developmental Science, 7*(3), 325–339.

Blumenfeld, H. K., & Marian, V. (2011). Bilingualism influences inhibitory control in auditory comprehension. *Cognition, 118*(2), 245–257.

Bontempo, K., & Napier, J. (2011). Evaluating emotional stability as a predictor of interpreter competence and aptitude for interpreting. *Interpreting, 13*(1), 85–105.

Christoffels, I. K., de Groot, A. M. B., & Kroll, J. F. (2006). Memory and language skills in simultaneous interpreters: The role of expertise and language proficiency. *Journal of Memory and Language, 54*(3), 324–345.

Costa, A., Hernández, M., & Sebastián-Gallés, N. (2008). Bilingualism aids conflict resolution: Evidence from the ANT task. *Cognition, 106*(1), 59–86.

de Bruin, A., Treccani, B., & Sala, S. D. (2015). Cognitive advantage in bilingualism: An example of publication bias? *Psychological Science, 26*(1), 99–107.

de Groot, A. M. (2011). *Language and cognition in bilinguals and multilinguals: An introduction.* New York, NY: Psychological Press.

de Groot, A. M., & Christoffels, I. K. (2006). Language control in bilinguals: Monolingual tasks and simultaneous interpreting. *Bilingualism: Language and Cognition, 9*(2), 189–201.

Dong, Y., & Liu, Y. (2016). Classes in translating and interpreting produce differential gains in switching and updating. *Frontiers in Psychology, 7*, 1297.

Dong, Y., & Xie, Z. L. (2014). Contributions of second language proficiency and interpreting experience to cognitive control differences among young adult bilinguals. *Journal of Cognitive Psychology, 26*(5), 506–519.

Elmer, S., Meyer, M., & Jäncke, L. (2010). Simultaneous interpreters as a model for neuronal adaptation in the domain of language processing. *Brain Research, 1317*, 147–156.

Emmorey, K., Luk, G., Pyers, J. E., & Bialystok, E. (2008). The source of enhanced cognitive control in bilinguals. *Psychological Science, 19*(12), 1201–1206.

Ericsson, K. A. (2008). Deliberate practice and acquisition of expert performance: A general overview. *Academic Emergency Medicine, 15*(11), 988–994.

Gerver, D., Longley, P., Long, J., & Lambert, S. (1989). Selection tests for trainee conference interpreters. *Meta, 34*(4), 724–735.

Green, D. W. (1998). Mental control of the bilingual lexico-semantic system. *Bilingualism: Language and Cognition, 1*(2), 67–81.

Harris, B., & Sherwood, B. (1978). Translating as an innate skill. In D. Gerver & W. H. Sinaiko (Eds.), *Language interpretation and communication* (pp. 155 170). New York, NY: Plenum.

Hervais-Adelman, A., Moser-Mercer, B., & Golestani, N. (2015). Brain functional plasticity associated with the emergence of expertise in extreme language control. *Neuroimage, 114*, 264–274.

Hervais-Adelman, A., Moser-Mercer, B., Murray, M. M., & Golestani, N. (2017). Cortical thickness increases after simultaneous interpretation training. *Neuropsychologia, 98*, 212–219.

Hitch, G. J., & Baddeley, A. D. (1976). Verbal reasoning and working memory. *Quarterly Journal of Experimental Psychology, 28*, 603–621.

Hoshino, N., & Kroll, J. F. (2008). Cognate effects in picture naming: Does cross-language activation survive a change of script? *Cognition, 106*(1), 501–511.

Ibáñez, A. J., Macizo, P., & Bajo, M. T. (2010). Language access and language selection in professional translators. *Acta Psychologica, 135*(2), 257–266.

Injoque-Ricle, I., Barreyro, J. P., Formoso, J., & Jaichenco, V. I. (2015). Expertise, working memory and articulatory suppression effect: Their relation with simultaneous interpreting performance. *Advances in Cognitive Psychology, 11*(2), 56–63.

Köpke, B., & Nespoulous, J. L. (2006). Working memory performance in expert and novice interpreters. *Interpreting, 8*(1), 1–23.

Kousaie, S., Sheppard, C., Lemieux, M., Monetta, L., & Taler, V. (2014). Executive function and bilingualism in young and older adults. *Frontiers in Behavioral Neuroscience, 8*, 250. Retrieved August 4, 2017, from http://journal.frontiersin.org/article/10.3389/fnbeh.2014.00250/full

Kroll, J. F., & Bialystok, E. (2013). Understanding the consequences of bilingualism for language processing and cognition. *Journal of Cognitive Psychology, 25*(5), 497–514.

Kroll, J. F., Bobb, S. C., Misra, M., & Guo, T. (2008). Language selection in bilingual speech: Evidence for inhibitory processes. *Acta Psychologica, 128*(3), 416–430.

Kroll, J. F., Bobb, S. C., & Wodniecka, Z. (2006). Language selectivity is the exception, not the rule: Arguments against a fixed locus of language selection in bilingual speech. *Bilingualism: Language and Cognition, 9*, 119–135.

Kroll, J. F., Dussias, P. E., Bice, K., & Perrotti, L. (2015). Bilingualism, mind, and brain. *Annual Review of Linguistics, 1*(1), 377–394.

Liefooghe, B., Barrouillet, P., Vandierendonck, A., & Camos, V. (2008). Working memory costs of task switching. *Journal of Experimental Psychology: Learning, Memory, and Cognition, 34*(3), 478–494.

Liu, M., Schallert, D. L., & Carroll, P. J. (2004). Working memory and expertise in simultaneous interpreting. *Interpreting, 6*(1), 19–42.

Macnamara, B. N., & Conway, A. R. A. (2014). Novel evidence in support of the bilingual advantage: Influences of task demands and experience on cognitive control and working memory. *Psychonomic Bulletin & Review, 21*, 520–525.

Macnamara, B. N., & Conway, A. R. A. (2016). Working memory capacity as a predictor of simultaneous language interpreting performance. *Journal of Applied Research in Memory and Cognition, 5*(4), 434–444.

Macnamara, B. N., Moore, A. B., Kegl, J. A., & Conway, A. R. A. (2011). Domain-general cognitive abilities and simultaneous interpreting skill. *Interpreting, 13*(1), 121–142.

Miyake, A., Friedman, N. P., Emerson, M. J., Witzki, A. H., Howerter, A., & Wager, T. D. (2000). The unity and diversity of executive functions and their contributions to complex 'frontal lobe' tasks: A latent variable analysis. *Cognitive Psychology, 41*(1), 49–100.

Morales, J., Calvo, A., & Bialystok, E. (2013). Working memory development in monolingual and bilingual children. *Journal of Experimental Child Psychology, 114*(2), 187–202.

Morales, J., Padilla, F., Gómez-Ariza, C. J., & Bajo, M. T. (2015). Simultaneous interpretation selectively influences working memory and attentional networks. *Acta Psychologica, 155*, 82–91.

Muñoz Martín, R. (2015). Natural translation/interpreting. In F. Pöchhacker (Ed.), *Routledge encyclopedia of interpreting* (pp. 269). New York, NY: Routledge.

Otsuka, Y., & Osaka, N. (2015). High-performers use the phonological loop less to process mental arithmetic during working memory tasks. *The Quarterly Journal of Experimental Psychology, 68*(5), 878–886.

Paap, K. R., Johnson, H. A., & Sawi, O. (2015). Bilingual advantages in executive functioning either do not exist or are restricted to very specific and undetermined circumstances. *Cortex, 69*, 265–278.

Paap, K. R., & Sawi, O. (2014). Bilingual advantages in executive functioning: Problems in convergent validity, discriminant validity, and the identification of the theoretical constructs. *Frontiers in Behavioral Neuroscience, 5*, 962.

Padilla, P., Bajo, M. T., Cañas, J. J., & Padilla, F. (1995). Cognitive processes of memory in simultaneous interpretation. In J.Tommola (Ed.), *Topics in interpreting research* (pp. 61–71). Turku, Finland: University of Turku.

Paradis, M. (1994).Toward a neurolinguistic theory of simultaneous translation:The framework. *International Journal of Psycholinguistics, 10*(3), 319–335.

Pio, S. (2003).The relation between ST delivery rate and quality in simultaneous interpretation. *The Interpreters' Newsletter, 12*, 69–100.

Prior, A., & Gollan, T. H. (2011). Good language-switchers are good task-switchers: Evidence from Spanish—English and Mandarin—English bilinguals. *Journal of the International Neuropsychological Society, 17*(4), 682–691.

Prior, A., & MacWhinney, B. (2010). A bilingual advantage in task switching. *Bilingualism: Language & Cognition, 13*(2), 253–262.

Rosiers, A., Eyckmans, J., & Bauwens, D. (2011). A story of attitudes and aptitudes? Investigating individual differencevariables within the context of interpreting. *Interpreting, 13*(1), 53–69.

Schweda-Nicholson, N. (2005). Personality characteristics of interpreter trainees: The Myers-Briggs type indicator (MBTI). *The Interpreters' Newsletter, 13*(13), 109–142.

Shreve, G. M.,Angelone, E., & Lacruz, I. (2018).Are expertise and translation competence the same? Psychological reality and the theoretical status of competence. In I. Lacruz & R. Jääskeläinen (Eds.), *Innovation and expansion in translation process research* (pp. 37–54). Amsterdam,The Netherlands: John Benjamins Publishing Company.

Stavrakaki, S., Megari, K., Kosmidis, M. H.,Apostolidou, M., & Takou, E. (2012).Working memory and verbal fluency in simultaneous interpreters. *Journal of Clinical and Experimental Neuropsychology, 34*(6), 624–633.

Strobach, T., Becker, M., Schubert, T., & Kühn, S. (2015). Better dual-task processing in simultaneous interpreters. *Frontiers in Psychology, 6*, 1590.

Timarová, S., Čeňkova, I., Meylaerts, R., Hertog, E., Szmalec, A., & Duyck, W. (2014). Simultaneous interpreting and working memory executive control. *Interpreting, 16*(2), 139–168.

Timarová, S., & Salaets, H. (2011). Learning styles, motivation and cognitive flexibility in interpreter training Self-selection and aptitude. *Interpreting, 13*(1), 31–52.

Verreyt, N.,Woumans, E.,Vandelanotte, D., Szmalec,A., & Duyck,W. (2016).The influence of language-switching experience on the bilingual executive control advantage. *Bilingualism: Language and Cognition, 19*(1), 181–190.

Whyatt, B. (2010). Bilingual language control in translation tasks: A TAP study into mental effort management by inexperienced translators. In J. Arabski & A. Wojtaszek (Eds.), *Neurolinguistic and psycholinguistic perspectives on SLA* (pp. 79–92). Bristol, UK: Multilingual Matters.

Wu,Y. J., & Thierry, G. (2011). Event-related brain potential investigation of preparation for speech production in late bilinguals. *Frontiers in Psychology, 2*, 114.

Yudes, C., Macizo, P., & Bajo,T. (2011).The influence of expertise in simultaneous interpreting on non-verbal executive processes. *Frontiers in Psychology, 2*, 309. Retrieved August 4, 2017, from www.ncbi.nlm.nih.gov/pmc/articles/PMC3203554/

Yudes, C., Macizo, P., & Bajo,T. (2012). Coordinating comprehension and production in simultaneous interpreters: Evidence from the articulatory suppression effect. *Bilingualism: Language and Cognition, 15*(2), 329–339.

PART V

Research Agenda and Future Directions

16

THE FUTURE OF LANGUAGE APTITUDE RESEARCH

Robert DeKeyser

Introduction

As many contributors to this volume show, aptitude research has come a long way in the new millennium after decades of neglect. Several factors contributed to making the very concept of aptitude for foreign language learning unpopular for an entire generation before that. The reasons for that were many, from factors internal to the field of applied linguistics, such as perceived immutability of aptitude and the belief that it was only relevant in the context of outdated teaching methodologies (Skehan, 2002; Wen, Biedroń, & Skehan, 2017), to broader educational and sociopolitical concerns, such as the difficulties in applying aptitude–treatment interaction research and the perception that aptitude research was not politically correct and could even lead to some form of educational apartheid.

The climate has changed now, and aptitude research is blossoming. We have moved from aptitude testing with mere predictive validity to at least somewhat theoretically motivated measures. At the same time, we have moved from trying to predict global proficiency after a long period of instruction to learning at specific points in time, i.e., at certain stages of the learning process, at certain levels of proficiency, or from specific learning pedagogical tasks or forms of feedback. After several calls for more aptitude-treatment interaction (ATI) research over the previous decades (e.g., McLaughlin, 1980; Robinson, 2002; Skehan, 1989), we now have a rapidly increasing number of ATI studies, and even researchers whose primary interest is not in aptitude are beginning to use aptitude measures in order to avoid overgeneralizations or inconclusive or contradictory results. At the same time, learning outcome measures have been developed that provide more valid and reliable assessment of more specific and theoretically motivated aspects of knowledge and skill.

In spite of all these advances, the field of aptitude research has a long way to go. In what follows, I will list outstanding questions and provide suggestions for future research in seven areas: work on the independent variable, work on the dependent variable, the research designs to link the two, the advantages of micro and macro studies, contributions to theory, practical applications, and public perceptions of aptitude.

The Independent Variable: Aptitudes

Aptitude researchers have come to agree that there is no such thing as one unitary aptitude for foreign language learning. While we continue to use the word 'aptitude' for convenience and as an encompassing term, we have gone beyond using one test that turns out to load on various factors, such as the MLAT (Carroll & Sapon, 1959) or the PLAB (Pimsleur, 1966), and have at least one aptitude *test battery* now, Hi-LAB, consisting of a set of measures of separate, theoretically motivated constructs (Linck et al., 2013).

Nobody would claim, however, that we know exactly how many of those aptitudes there are, or even how fine-grained our measures should be, whether it be for research purposes or for practical applications such as learner selection or adaptation of instruction. This is, of course, an important theoretical issue, but when it comes to empirical research, it is even more important. Few studies use multiple measures of the same construct (e.g. phonological short-term memory, PSTM, or complex working memory, WM), and when they do, these measures often do not correlate (well) with each other and can correlate significantly with different outcome measures (e.g. Liu, this volume). The extent to which these measures are predictive can even depend on different scoring methods used for the same measure (Leeser & Sunderman, 2016).

For the time being, therefore, we need to use multiple measures of each construct if we are going to have any generalizability of findings across studies, or at the very least only use established measures of very fine-grained constructs, e.g., attention, inhibition, mixing, switching, and updating, instead of simply working memory. As classroom research, especially longitudinal classroom research, has increasingly been replaced (in the second language acquisition field in general and to some extent also in the study of aptitude more specifically) by narrowly focused and strictly controlled learning experiments (e.g. Brooks & Kempe, 2013; Brooks, Kempe, & Sionov, 2006; Brooks, Kwoka, & Kempe, 2017; Yilmaz, 2012; Yilmaz, 2013; Yilmaz & Granena, 2016), we can no longer blame participant attrition, imperfect control over the treatment, and other external factors for inconsistent results, and the measures themselves are facing increased scrutiny (and not only those for the independent variables but also those used to measure learning outcome, as we will see in the next section).

Another interesting development is that of adapting predictors to the outcome measures, e.g., by including both L1 and L2 phonology-orthography decoding skills in the aptitude tests (e.g., Chan, Skehan, & Gong, 2011; Sparks & Ganschow, 2001). This, of course, may level the playing field for learners of different L1/L2 backgrounds and may increase predictive validity in specific contexts, but on the other hand may make generalizability across studies also more difficult.

In the same vein, the concept of aptitude complexes (Robinson, 2005; Snow, 1987) seems like a mixed blessing to me. It stands to reason that aptitudes interact with each other, just like they may interact with treatments, and that particular combinations of aptitudes are of particular importance under certain learning conditions or for certain stages of the learning process. Research on aptitude complexes is tempting, therefore, but the potential combinations of aptitudes and their second-order interaction with (aspects of) treatments is endless, which does not bode well for generalizability of results and even less for educational practice. It is a painful paradox that as we get closer to the truth by finding how it is the interaction of variables rather than individual variables that determines the outcome and therefore should be more generalizable, the chances of actually replicating, let alone implementing, such findings is even smaller than it already is for simpler designs and main effects. Cronbach's (1975) "hall of mirrors" is not an attractive prospect.

More promising, it seems to me, would be the development of a good test for implicit language learning aptitude. Even though many, myself included, have argued that the ability to learn all aspects of a language fully through implicit mechanisms is seriously diminished in adult learners, nobody would deny that even adults have some capacity for implicit language learning. At the same time, however, although cognitive psychologists, psycholinguistics, and second language acquisition researchers have shown a great interest in implicit learning processes (for summaries, see esp. DeKeyser, 2003; Perruchet & Poulin-Charronnat, 2015; Williams, 2009), interest in testing aptitude for implicit language learning is very recent. It has shown some promise (e.g., Granena, 2013a; Suzuki & DeKeyser, 2015, 2017), but the predictive validity of the tests used is probably limited to some extent because of their nonlinguistic nature: the serial reaction time (SRT) task works with sequential positions of a nonverbal stimulus (Nissen & Bullemer, 1987; Kaufman et al., 2010), and even the artificial grammar learning tasks used as measures of implicit learning by Misyak and Christiansen (2012) are not really linguistic in nature ('grammar' here is used in the sense of an allowable sequences of letters; there is no form–meaning mapping as in a natural language). The only test using verbal material that may potentially measure implicit learning abilities is part D of Meara's (2005) LLAMA test: Granena (2013b) provides some evidence that, unlike the other components of the LLAMA test, part D may be implicit in nature, but these findings remain to be replicated, and the test (component) certainly was not *designed* to measure aptitude for implicit learning. Aptitude for implicit learning and its measurement are definitely areas in need of a concentrated research effort.

At the same time, we also need to consider the requirement for tests that are adequate for different populations. A great many L2 learners have little schooling, and the existing tests probably do not have the same validity for them as for other populations. All the tests we have were developed with mostly college-age students in mind, in other words, people with at least a high school education. People with little experience with test-taking in general, or focusing on the form of decontextualized language in particular, risk doing poorly because of the testing format. This is not only a problem of underserving a large segment of our target population but also limits our ability to incorporate a meaningful aptitude component in studies of SLA in that population, which constitutes a large segment of the total number of L2 learners in at least some countries, especially countries with a high ratio of immigrants to foreign language learners like the United States or Britain.

This may be the most obvious example of not taking the learner's background into account for aptitude testing, but to some extent it also affects both research and applications of research with more highly educated populations, especially at the other end of the scale, i.e., people with not only a high level of education in general but also many years of instruction in various foreign languages, perhaps followed by many years of using those languages. In particular, when it comes to predicting actual communicative proficiency, a standard aptitude test is likely to underestimate these learners' potential for accurate and fluent use of complex language. A broad conceptualization of aptitude (e.g., Cronbach & Snow, 1977) already includes previous knowledge and learning experience, of course, but even when we are mostly interested in aptitude in a more narrow sense, we ignore these other variables at our peril.

The Dependent Variable: Learning Outcomes

On the side of learning outcomes as well, the implicit end of the spectrum has been and still is vastly underrepresented. This is very problematic, because any serious work in the area of aptitude test development requires that we know what knowledge/skill we want to predict. Implicit knowledge, in the strict sense of knowledge the test-taker is not aware of, is very hard to measure. Taking all focus on form out of a language test is not easy to do, but progress has been made in this area. Word monitoring, self-paced reading, and the visual world paradigm (VWP) are all useful for measuring implicit knowledge, but the complicated setup for the VWP makes it hard to use to assess outcomes for more than a few structures. Elicited imitation has also been suggested as a possible measure of implicit knowledge, but several studies have cast doubt on that recently (e.g., Spada, Shiu, & Tomita, 2015; Suzuki & DeKeyser, 2015). That essentially leaves us with word monitoring and self-paced reading, which also have some limitations (see, e.g., Jiang, 2012).

Even the very concepts of implicit knowledge (and of aptitude for acquiring it) are somewhat problematic, in the sense that different measures tend not to correlate well (see esp. Suzuki & DeKeyser, 2017), which casts doubt on the validity of the construct itself. It may very well be that there are different forms of implicit learning and implicit knowledge, just as there are various kinds of declarative or nondeclarative knowledge (e.g., Henke, 2010).

On the other hand, the problem is not as daunting as it may seem, because the ability that most end users of aptitude tests are interested in predicting is not implicit knowledge in the strict sense, but rather automatized explicit knowledge. The criteria for such knowledge are easier to meet. A strict definition of automatization may be hard to adhere to and is not fully agreed upon (DeKeyser & Criado-Sánchez, 2012; Hulstijn, van Gelderen, & Schoonen, 2009; Lim & Godfroid, 2015; Segalowitz, 2010; Segalowitz & Segalowitz, 1993), but as long as the focus is not on the automatization process per se, but simply on knowledge that can be used with a high degree of accuracy and fluency at the same time, valid and reliable testing can be conducted in various ways, from oral proficiency interviews to more focused and controlled tests such as timed grammaticality judgments. This is, from my point of view, one of the highest priorities for language learning aptitude at this point: making the research more practically meaningful by assessing how well (specific kinds of) aptitude tests predict real communication skills.

Meanwhile, from a more theoretical perspective, in the sense of trying to understand the process of second language acquisition, it is important that we take Skehan's (1998, 2016) suggestion seriously to relate specific aptitudes to specific stages of the learning process such as input processing, noticing, pattern identification, or automatization. Serafini and Sanz (2016) have done something similar from a bird's-eye view, showing that working memory becomes a less important predictor as proficiency increases, perhaps even within a one-semester course. We have to be careful, of course, not to confuse stages of learning with proficiency levels or course levels. Moreover, an individual learner is at different stages of learning for different structures (some are already being automatized when others have not even been noticed or identified). It seems to me, therefore, that for a more fine-grained look at aptitude and learning processes, specific aptitude tests designed to focus on particular aspects of language at a particular point in time for a particular individual are necessary, which means there are enough possibilities here to inspire many dissertations.

Designs to Link Dependent and Independent Variables

These issues of linking specific aptitudes to specific learning outcomes lead us to various broad considerations for research design. As mentioned earlier in the introduction, a strong tendency in terms of a design for aptitude research in SLA has been a turn from broad pre-post designs looking at progress over a semester or more to much more narrowly focused experiments documenting how aptitude predicts learning from a specific learning task or treatment such as corrective feedback (e.g., Goo, 2012, 2016; Mackey, Philp, Egi, Fujii, & Tatsumi, 2002; Trofimovich,

Ammar, & Gatbonton, 2007). This is a fortunate development, because it helps us to take more of a process perspective: What is it that people with certain aptitudes do in very specific learning situations that makes them learn more?

In the same vein, ATI research, which finally seems to have taken off in applied linguistics, can contribute to such a focus on process even more. As I argued in DeKeyser (2012), ATI research not only helps us determine which treatment or which aptitude or which combination of aptitude and treatment is most helpful, but the interaction between an aptitude and a treatment shows why a treatment may be helpful (but not always), i.e., because it allows for a specific aptitude to do its work, and why an aptitude may be helpful (but not always), i.e., because it provides the learner with what is needed for learning with the specific treatment that is available. Such understanding of why something succeeds or doesn't under a given constellation of factors is absolutely necessary before we can generalize and predict, i.e., before we can recommend educational practices on the basis of ATI research without taking big, perhaps unethical, risks. A particularly interesting example of how ATI effects seem to reveal different learning processes is Brooks et al. (2006), showing how higher-IQ students tended to rely more on analysis of exemplars in the input, and therefore did better with a wider variety of exemplars, whereas lower-IQ students relied more on memorization, and therefore did worse when the variety in the input increased. Other interesting examples are to be found in studies of corrective feedback, such as Li (2013), showing that working memory predicted learning from explicit feedback and analytic ability from implicit feedback, and Yilmaz's work on ATI in error correction, showing that explicit feedback was better than implicit feedback but only for learners with a high aptitude for explicit learning (Yilmaz, 2013) and, reversely, that explicit aptitude was only predictive of learning under explicit feedback conditions (Yilmaz & Granena, 2016).

So far ATI research has been a bit haphazard, looking at a variety of combinations of aptitudes and treatments with little attempt to replicate a specific interaction. When ATI studies do ask very much the same questions, they sometimes come to rather different conclusions, as in the just mentioned studies of Li (2013) vs. Yilmaz (2013), and even when a researcher has made the laudable effort to replicate his own work, the results have not necessarily been replicated. Goo (2012), e.g., found that WM (operation span) was predictive of the effect of recasts but not of metalinguistic feedback, whereas Goo (2016) did not find WM to be predictive in either (even though the structure used, the treatments, and the outcome measures were the same).

In my opinion, then, there is a great need for ATI research in SLA, both for theoretical and practical reasons (the latter perhaps indirectly through better understanding of learning processes than directly in terms of concrete evidence for matching learners and treatments). A great many different questions can be explored in this framework, but in this area, perhaps even more than in other areas of SLA (see e.g. Mackey, 2012), we need more replication. Replicating an ATI study seems like a good topic, if not for a dissertation, then at least for a master's thesis or a PhD-qualifying paper.   *grammatical*

Besides aptitude–treatment interactions, various researchers have also documented aptitude–structure interactions and aptitude–age interactions. Recent examples of the former are Kempe, Brooks, and Kharkhurin (2010), showing that a culture-fair intelligent test predicted learning the gender of transparent nouns and a reading span test that of nontransparent nouns; and Brooks and Kempe (2013) as well as Brooks et al. (2017), showing that nonverbal intelligence predicted learning and generalization of case marking, while an artificial grammar aptitude test predicted only learning but not generalization. Another interesting example is Antoniou, Ettlinger, and Wong (2016) showing that procedural memory predicted learning of simple rules and declarative memory that of complex rules.

Examples of aptitude–age interaction are DeKeyser (2000) and DeKeyser, Alfi-Shabtay, and Ravid (2010), showing that aptitude (for explicit learning) was a predictor of ultimate attainment for adult learners but not for child learners, and Abrahamsson and Hyltenstam (2008), who replicated DeKeyser's finding that among postpuberty learners only those with high (explicit) aptitude did well. Granena (2013a), on the other hand, provides a somewhat different picture, showing that aptitude for implicit learning was predictive of ultimate attainment for both child learners and adults.

These aptitude–structure and aptitude–age interactions are equally as interesting from a theoretical point of view as aptitude–treatment interactions, and their practical implications are perhaps more important. While it is very difficult for various reasons to provide different instruction to different children or different adults, there are no social or logistic reasons why it should be a problem to teach different structures differently or to provide children and adults with different forms of instruction. Research on the interaction of aptitude with treatment, structure, and age, therefore, should be a high priority, but again with the caveat that replication should precede application.

The Need for Longitudinal Perspectives

So far I have stressed the micro perspective, digging ever deeper into the role aptitude plays in particular learning tasks, for particular structures, and so on, but at the same time it is important to keep a longitudinal perspective. Language learning is a long-term endeavor, and if we zero in on a particular point in time, we are likely to miss most of the picture. As mentioned earlier, Peter Skehan in particular has drawn attention to the likelihood that different aptitudes play a role at different stages in the learning process, and at least a few studies provide empirical evidence of the changing role of aptitude over time. Morgan-Short, Faretta-Stutenberg, Bill-Schuetz, Carpenter, and Wong (2014) showed how declarative memory played a stronger role early on and procedural memory later on in the learning of a miniature linguistic system. Serafini and Sanz (2016) also provide evidence for the changing role of time, in this case, for the diminishing role of WM and PSTM as proficiency increases. Similar changes over time have been documented for other forms of skill acquisition; Neçka (1999), for instance, showed that the influence of intelligence decreased during the skill acquisition process, presumably because of increased automatization. We need a lot more work along these lines, integrating the micro perspective looking at different stages in the acquisition of specific structures with the macro perspective of, e.g., a multiyear sequence. Presumably, as more and more structures move through the various stages over time, the changes in the roles of aptitudes that we find for specific structures over a relatively short period should also be reflected in the predictive value of these aptitudes for a broad selection of structures over longer periods. If a truly longitudinal study is not feasible, a pseudo-longitudinal, cross-sectional design may also be possible, of course, assuming that the participants in the various time slices are highly comparable.

The Need for Theoretical Integration

As I hinted at when dealing with aptitude–treatment interaction, research on aptitude is not just about aptitude. It can help with understanding the broader picture and with building more realistic and complete theories of SLA, but on this point in particular we have done a poor job so far. The vast majority of studies on aptitude content themselves with establishing that a given aptitude predicts or does not predict a particular outcome, and often that is not particularly interesting by itself. Some studies have tried to approach some big theoretical issues in the field by documenting the role of aptitudes, e.g., Abrahamsson and Hyltenstam (2008), DeKeyser (2000), DeKeyser et al. (2010), Granena (2013a), and Granena and Long (2013) for the nature of the critical period, or Suzuki and DeKeyser (2017) for the interface hypothesis, but they are all in need of extensive replication, in particular, of replications that keep the same theoretical relevance in mind.

The theoretical relevance of aptitude will not be fully realized until we see many aptitude studies as contributing to a very large but structured puzzle. By documenting the different roles of various aptitudes for acquiring different domains of language, for acquiring different structures within the same domain, for different stages in learning the same structure, and for learning under different conditions of practice or feedback and by doing this systematically, we can perhaps shed more light than any other approach can on what various aspects of second language acquisition have in common and what sets them apart.

Practical Applications

From a more immediate practical point of view, caution is required. While existing aptitude tests or test batteries are a fairly reliable tool for selecting learners who are likely to succeed, most educational systems have little use for them because they cannot afford selection; they are expected to provide second (and sometimes third or fourth) language teaching to all students at a certain grade level and in a certain track. This is where findings from ATI research should, in principle, be able to provide guidance for matching learners with treatments on the basis of their aptitude profiles. As argued earlier, however, ATI findings that have been duly replicated are almost nonexistent at this point, which makes assigning students to different treatments on the basis of ATI research a risky and potentially unethical undertaking for the time being. Duly replicated findings with explanatory adequacy, however, could indeed provide much-needed guidance for educational practice and be very helpful in those contexts where differential treatments are logistically and socially possible.

For this last problem, however, help may be on the way. On the one hand, serious adaptation to a student's aptitude profile (and ideally also current knowledge and skill) is impossible in a classroom context; at most, some adaptation to group differences is possible. Constant adaptation to an individual student seems to require an amount of information processing that only a computer can do. On the other hand, computer-assisted language learning has so far failed to live up to one of its most important promises: that of individualizing instruction; at most, it tends to offer variation in speed of presentation or amount of practice, or perhaps some choice at the level of the whole curriculum. In a sense, then, one problem is the solution to the other: effective ATI is impossible without computer-assisted language learning (CALL), and CALL does not have one of the most important advantages it could have if it could incorporate sophisticated ATI.

Fortunately, several developments at this point in time make such a rapprochement more likely. One is the proliferation of curricula that are to a large extent computer based, whether they are called computer assisted, computer guided, computer mediated, or blended. That means that at least the logistic and social context for serious individualization is impossible. The computers are available, and the student, working individually, perhaps even at home, does not have to be puzzled or embarrassed by receiving a treatment that is different from what other students are experiencing. The other one is the promise of the particular kind of artificial intelligence that is called student modeling (e.g., Koedinger & Corbett, 2006; Nakic, Granic, & Glavinic, 2015). To the best of my knowledge, there are no examples of that in second language teaching yet, but in areas such as algebra and physics there are systems already that include aptitude information about the individual student and that constantly update the student profile with information about the student's knowledge of or skill with various elements to be mastered, that know how to provide the ideal immediate follow-up activities, given the assessment of current knowledge and skill as well as the aptitude profile, provide that treatment, update the profile, and so on. What we are waiting for in the meantime is replicated, consistent ATI findings.

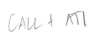

CALL + ATI

Reaching a Wider Audience

Finally, I would like to stress the importance of communicating our work better to language teaching professionals and the public at large. On many occasions when giving a lecture here or there to teachers or teacher trainees, I realize that virtually nobody in the audience has ever heard of aptitude tests and that they only have a vague idea of what aptitude might mean. These people would be the first-line consumers of our research or our tests, so obviously we have a lot of work to do to try to get our ideas across via popularizing articles, the media, teacher conferences, and so on. The public at large may even doubt there is such a thing as an aptitude or "talent" for language learning, or conversely, may think that's what language learning is all about. Yet although there is much we don't know and much we may disagree on among ourselves, I think it would be good if in our contacts with the media, we could make it clear that 1) yes, there is such a thing as aptitude for learning a second language, and yes, it is important; 2) it is not everything, i.e., quantity and quality of practice, for instance, are also very important factors; 3) different aptitudes play a different role for different elements of language under different circumstances and at different stages; 4) aptitude plays a big role during communicative practice, for monitoring output, for learning from producing 'comprehensible output'; and, of course, for making the correct inferences from comprehensible input.

Conclusion

In conclusion, then, from my perspective I see five priorities for aptitude research: further test development for specialized aptitudes and special populations; longitudinal research; research on aptitude in interaction with age, linguistic structure, educational treatment or context; much more replication; and broader dissemination. The future for aptitude research looks promising, and some particular areas, like aptitude by age interaction and aptitude by structure interaction research, may very well produce important implications for practice within a reasonable time frame.

References

Abrahamsson, N., & Hyltenstam, K. (2008). The robustness of aptitude effects in near-native second language acquisition. *Studies in Second Language Acquisition, 30*(4), 481–509.

Antoniou, M., Ettlinger, M., & Wong, P. C. M. (2016). Complexity, training paradigm design, and the contribution of memory subsystems to grammar learning. *PLoS One, 11*(7), 1–20.

Brooks, P. J., & Kempe, V. (2013). Individual differences in adult Foreign language learning: The mediating effect of metalinguistic awareness. *Memory and Cognition, 41*(2), 281–296.

Brooks, P. J., Kempe, V., & Sionov, A. (2006). The role of learner and input variables in learning inflectional morphology. *Applied Psycholinguistics, 27*(2), 185–209.

Brooks, P. J., Kwoka, N., & Kempe, V. (2017). Distributional effects and individual differences in L2 morphology learning. *Language Learning, 67*(1), 171–207.

Carroll, J. B., & Sapon, S. (1959). *Modern language aptitude test: Form a.* New York, NY: The Psychological Corporation.

Chan, E., Skehan, P., & Gong, G. (2011). Working memory, phonemic coding ability and Foreign language aptitude: Potential for construction of specific language aptitude tests—the case of Cantonese. *Ilha do Desterro: A Journal of English Language, Literatures and Cultural Studies, 60*, 45–73.

Cronbach, L. J. (1975). Beyond the two disciplines of scientific psychology. *American Psychologist, 30*, 116–127.

Cronbach, L. J., & Snow, R. E. (1977). *Aptitudes and instructional methods: A handbook for research on interactions.* New York, NY: Irvington.

DeKeyser, R. M. (2000). The robustness of critical period effects in second language acquisition. *Studies in Second Language Acquisition, 22*(4), 499–533.

DeKeyser, R. M. (2003). Implicit and explicit learning. In C. Doughty & M. Long (Eds.), *Handbook of second language acquisition* (pp. 313–348). Oxford, UK: Blackwell Publishing.

DeKeyser, R. M. (2012). Interactions between individual differences, treatments, and structures in SLA. *Language Learning, 62*(Suppl. 2), 189–200.

DeKeyser, R. M., Alfi-Shabtay, I., & Ravid, D. (2010). Cross-linguistic evidence for the nature of age effects in second language acquisition. *Applied Psycholinguistics, 31*(3), 413–438.

DeKeyser, R. M., & Criado-Sánchez, R. (2012). Automatization, skill acquisition, and practice in second language acquisition. In C. A. Chapelle (Ed.), *The encyclopedia of applied linguistics* (pp. 323–331). Oxford, UK: Wiley-Blackwell.

Goo, J. (2012). Corrective feedback and working memory capacity in interaction-driven L2 learning. *Studies in Second Language Acquisition, 34*(3), 445–474.

Goo, J. (2016). Corrective feedback and working memory capacity. A replication. In G. Granena, D. O. Jackson, & Y. Yilmaz (Eds.), *Cognitive individual differences in second language processing and acquisition* (pp. 279–302). Amsterdam, The Netherlands: John Benjamins Publishing Company.

Granena, G. (2013a). Individual differences in sequence learning ability and second language acquisition in early childhood and adulthood. *Language Learning, 63*(4), 665–703.

Granena, G. (2013b). Cognitive aptitudes for second language learning and the LLAMA language aptitude test. In G. Granena & M. H. Long (Eds.), *Sensitive periods, language aptitude, and ultimate L2 attainment* (pp. 105–129). Amsterdam, The Netherlands: John Benjamins Publishing Company.

Granena, G., & Long, M. (2013). Age of onset, length of residence, language aptitude, and ultimate L2 attainment in three linguistic domains. *Second Language Research, 29*(3), 311–343.

Henke, K. (2010). A model for memory systems based on processing modes rather than consciousness. *Nature Reviews Neuroscience, 11*, 523–532.

Hulstijn, J. H., van Gelderen, A., & Schoonen, R. (2009). Automatization in second language acquisition: What does the coefficient of variation tell us? *Applied Psycholinguistics, 30*(4), 555–582.

Jiang, N. (2012). *Conducting reaction time research in second language studies.* London: Routledge.

Kaufman, S. B., DeYoung, C. G., Gray, J. R., Jiménez, L., Brown, J., & Mackintosh, N. (2010). Implicit learning as an ability. *Cognition, 116*, 321–340.

Kempe, V., Brooks, P. J., & Kharkhurin, A. (2010). Cognitive predictors of generalization of Russian grammatical gender categories. *Language Learning, 60*(1), 127–153.

Koedinger, K. R., & Corbett, A. (2006). Cognitive tutors: Technology bringing learning sciences to the classroom. In R. K. Sawyer (Ed.), *The Cambridge handbook of the learning sciences* (pp. 61–77). New York, NY: Cambridge University Press.

Leeser, M., & Sunderman, G. (2016). Methodological implications of working memory tasks for L2 processing research. In G. Granena, D. O. Jackson, & Y. Yilmaz (Eds.), *Cognitive individual differences in second language processing and acquisition* (pp. 89–104). Amsterdam, The Netherlands: John Benjamins Publishing Company.

Li, S. (2013). The interactions between the effects of implicit and explicit feedback and individual differences in language analytic ability and working memory. *The Modern Language Journal, 97*(3), 634–654.

Lim, H., & Godfroid, A. (2015). Automatization in second language sentence processing: A partial, conceptual replication of Hulstijn, Van Gelderen, and Schoonen's 2009 study. *Applied Psycholinguistics, 36*(5), 1247–1282. doi:10.1017/S0142716414000137

Linck, J. A., Hughes, M. M., Campbell, S. G., Silbert, N. H., Tare, M., Jackson, S. R., . . . Doughty, C. J. (2013). Hi-LAB: A new measure of aptitude for high-level language proficiency. *Language Learning, 63*(3), 530–566.

Liu, M. (this volume). In search of a cognitive aptitude model for interpreting. In Z. Wen, P. Skehan, A. Biedroń, S. Li, & R. L. Sparks (Eds.), *Rethinking language aptitude: Contemporary insights and emerging trends*. London: Routledge.

Mackey, A. (2012). Why (or why not), when and how to replicate research. In G. K. Porte (Ed.), *Replication research in applied linguistics* (pp. 21–34). Cambridge, UK: Cambridge University Press.

Mackey, A., Philp, J., Egi, T., Fujii, A., & Tatsumi, T. (2002). Individual differences in working memory, noticing of interactional feedback and L2 development. In P. Robinson (Ed.), *Individual differences and instructed language learning* (pp. 181–209). Amsterdam; Philadelphia: Benjamins.

McLaughlin, B. (1980). Theory and research in second-language learning: An emerging paradigm. *Language Learning, 30*, 331–350.

Meara, P. (2005). *LLAMA language aptitude tests: The manual*. Swansea, UK: University of Wales.

Misyak, J. B., & Christiansen, M. H. (2012). Statistical learning and language: An individual differences study. *Language Learning, 62*(1), 302–331.

Morgan-Short, K., Faretta-Stutenberg, M., Bill-Schuetz, K. A., Carpenter, H., & Wong, P. C. M. (2014). Declarative and procedural memory as individual differences in second language acquisition. *Bilingualism: Language and Cognition, 17*(1), 56–72.

Nakic, J., Granic, A., & Glavinic, V. (2015). Anatomy of student models in adaptive learning systems: A systematic literature review of individual differences from 2001 to 2013. *Journal of Educational Computing Research, 51*(4), 459–489.

Nećka, E. (1999). Learning, automaticity, and attention: An individual-differences approach. In P. L. Ackerman, P. C. Kyllonen, & R. D. Roberts (Eds.), *Learning and individual differences: Process, trait, and content determinants* (pp. 161–184). Washington, DC: American Psychological Association.

Nissen, M. J., & Bullemer, P. (1987). Attentional requirements of learning: Evidence from performance measures. *Cognitive Psychology, 19*(1), 1–32.

Perruchet, P., & Poulin-Charronnat, B. (2015). The learnability of language: Insights from the implicit learning literature. In P. Rebuschat (Ed.), *Implicit and explicit learning of languages* (pp. 139–165). Amsterdam, The Netherlands: John Benjamins Publishing Company.

Pimsleur, P. (1966). *Pimsleur Language Aptitude Battery (PLAB)*. New York, NY: The Psychological Corporation.

Robinson, P. (2002). Learning conditions, aptitude complexes, and SLA. In P. Robinson (Ed.), *Individual differences and instructed language learning* (pp. 113–133). Amsterdam, The Netherlands: John Benjamins Publishing Company.

Robinson, P. (2005). Aptitude and second language acquisition. *Annual Review of Applied Linguistics, 25*, 46–73.

Segalowitz, N. (2010). *Cognitive bases of second language fluency.* London: Routledge.

Segalowitz, N. S., & Segalowitz, S. J. (1993). Skilled performance, practice, and the differentiation of speed-up from automatization effects: Evidence from second language word recognition. *Applied Psycholinguistics, 14*, 369–385.

Serafini, E. J., & Sanz, C. (2016). Evidence for the decreasing impact of cognitive ability on second language development as proficiency increases. *Studies in Second Language Acquisition, 38*, 607–646.

Skehan, P. (1989). *Individual differences in second language learning.* London: Edward Arnold.

Skehan, P. (1998). *A cognitive approach to language learning.* Oxford, UK: Oxford University Press.

Skehan, P. (2002). Theorising and updating aptitude. In P. Robinson (Ed.), *Individual differences and instructed language learning* (pp. 69–93). Amsterdam, The Netherlands: John Benjamins Publishing Company.

Skehan, P. (2016). Foreign language aptitude, acquisitional sequences, and psycholinguistic processes. In G. Granena, D. O. Jackson, & Y. Yilmaz (Eds.), *Cognitive individual differences in second language processing and acquisition* (pp. 17–40). Amsterdam, The Netherlands: John Benjamins Publishing Company.

Snow, R. E. (1987). Aptitude complexes. In R. E. Snow & M. J. Farr (Eds.), *Aptitude, learning, and instruction* (pp. 13–59). Hillsdale, NJ: LEA.

Spada, N., Shiu, J. L. J., & Tomita, Y. (2015). Validating an elicited imitation task as a measure of implicit knowledge: Comparisons with other validation studies. *Language Learning, 65*(3), 723–751.

Sparks, R., & Ganschow, L. (2001). Aptitude for learning a Foreign language. *Annual Review of Applied Linguistics, 21*, 90–111.

Suzuki, Y., & DeKeyser, R. (2015). Does elicited imitation measure implicit knowledge? Evidence from the word-monitoring task. *Language Learning, 65*(4), 860–895. doi:10.1111/lang.12138

Suzuki, Y., & DeKeyser, R. (2017). The interface of explicit and implicit knowledge in a second language. *Language Learning, 67*(4), 747–797. doi:10.1111/lang.12241

Trofimovich, P., Ammar, A., & Gatbonton, E. (2007). How effective are recasts? The role of attention, memory, and analytical ability. In A. Mackey (Ed.), *Conversational interaction in second language acquisition* (pp. 171–195). New York, NY: Oxford University Press.

Wen, Z., Biedroń, A., & Skehan, P. (2017). Foreign language aptitude theory: Yesterday, today and tomorrow. *Language Teaching, 50*(1), 1–31.

Williams, J. (2009). Implicit learning in second language acquisition. In T. Bhatia & W. Ritchie (Eds.), *The new handbook of second language acquisition* (pp. 319–353). Bingley, UK: Emerald.

Yilmaz, Y. (2012). The relative effects of explicit correction and recasts on two target structures via two communication modes. *Language Learning, 62*(4), 1134–1169.

Yilmaz, Y. (2013). Relative effects of explicit and implicit feedback: The role of working memory capacity and language analytic ability. *Applied Linguistics, 34*(3), 344–368.

Yilmaz, Y., & Granena, G. (2016). The role of cognitive aptitudes for explicit language learning in the relative effects of explicit and implicit feedback. *Bilingualism: Language and Cognition, 19*(1), 147–161.

17

FROM INDIVIDUAL DIFFERENCES IN LANGUAGE APTITUDE TO PERSONALIZED LEARNING

Loan C. Vuong and Patrick C. M. Wong

Language Aptitude

A query on 'language aptitude' in the PubMed database shows a surge in language aptitude research, which started in the mid-2000s (see Figure 17.1). The collection of chapters in this volume present some of the latest developments on the topic. Following a historical account and an update to the pioneering work behind the Modern Language Aptitude Test (Stansfield and Reed), a series of recent studies offer empirical findings about language aptitude across diverse populations, including native speakers of Chinese who learn English as a foreign language (Li and Luo), primary school children (Lambelet and Berthele), high school students (Sparks), interpreters (Liu), and exceptional learners (chapters by Biedroń and by Erard). As empirical work accumulates, quantitative meta-analyses have been performed with new lessons learned (Li).

Conceptually, complementary aspects of memory and cognition are proposed to be distinct constituents of language aptitude. They include executive and phonological components of working memory (Wen), implicit and explicit learning (Granena and Yilmaz), and declarative and procedural long-term memory (Buffington and Morgan-Short). Skehan reviews the literature and suggests that both language-specific factors and general cognition constitute essential components of foreign language aptitude. Finally, technological advances have allowed brain activities to be measured in different states, while participants are exposed to linguistic materials, when they perform specific tasks and during resting states. Multiple brain indexes may serve as markers of language aptitude (chapters by Yue, by Reiterer, and by Buffington and Morgan-Short).

As we gain better and better understanding of the components of foreign language aptitude, i.e., factors that predict individual differences in foreign language

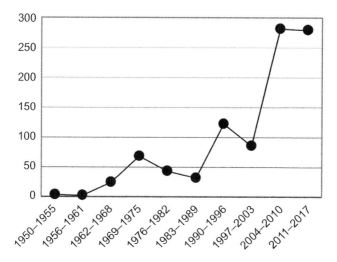

FIGURE 17.1   The number of publications from 1950 to 2017 with "language aptitude" entered as the search term in the PubMed database (January 2018)

attainment, to where may the advances lead? We propose that the time is ripe for Personalized Learning, a program of research where genetic, neural, and behavioral (e.g., perceptual/cognitive) predictors can be used to customize learning paradigms at the individual level (see also Wong, Vuong, & Liu, 2017). The goal of this research is not to find predictors that identify "good learners," regardless of the type of learning. Rather, this research stresses the importance of considering *what* is being learned and *how* learning occurs. To illustrate, assume we know that certain cognitive indexes, such as higher working memory, tend to predict good learning. How can this information be used toward designing optimal training for each learner, especially those with lower working memory? We will argue that finding predictors of individual differences *under a particular learning paradigm*, combined with careful consideration of the aspects and stages of learning that have and have not yet been reached, is key. In the rest of this epilogue, we will outline the framework for Personalized Learning, consider whether it may be applicable to language learning, and discuss some of the issues and challenges for implementing Personalized Learning in practice.

Personalized Learning

The Framework. Personalized Learning depends on three conditions: (1) finding individual differences in learning, that not everyone learns optimally under the same training paradigm; (2) finding that individual differences in learning can be predicted by genotypic, neural, and/or behavioral factors; and (3) using predictors to place learners into the most optimal learning conditions, individualized to their specific learning needs. For Personalized Learning to be applicable to any domain, several core questions need to be answered: Do individual differences exist in this domain of learning? To what extent can these individual differences be predicted? Can predictors be used to modify approaches to individual learning?

Individual Differences in Language Learning

Research has shown widespread differences in language learning across individuals. Individual differences exist in how fast children normally acquire their native language (Bates, Dale, & Thal, 1995) and in how well adult native speakers utilize complex grammatical structures (Dabrowska, 2012). Compared to first language acquisition, the variability in second language acquisition may be even greater. Whereas young immersed learners exhibit a smaller and native-like range of grammatical performance, evidence suggests that grammatical variability becomes increasingly large in later immersion (see Figure 17.2; Flege, Yeni-Komshian, & Liu, 1999). Studies that examine adult language learning in laboratory environments have likewise reported considerable individual differences in the learning of phonology (Golestani & Zatorre, 2009), vocabulary (Brooks & Kempe, 2012), and grammar (Brooks & Kempe, 2012; Ettlinger, Bradlow, & Wong, 2012).

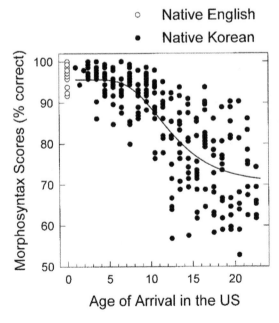

FIGURE 17.2   Grammaticality judgment by native English and Korean participants. Reprinted from "Age Constraints in Second Language Acquisition," by J. E. Flege et al., 1999, *Journal of Memory and Language*, 41, p. 85, copyright 1999, with permission from Elsevier.

The identification of individual differences in learning outcomes is not the sole focus of Personalized Learning, as these individual differences alone give us little information as to why some learners do not succeed. It is information about predictors that could ultimately be used to modify training approaches.

Predictors of Individual Differences in Language Learning

As reviewed in the preceding chapters of this volume, individual differences in language learning can be predicted from a number of cognitive factors, including aspects of working memory, aspects of long-term memory, and simple associative and sequencing abilities. Here we focus on two sets of factors that are relevant to our discussion in the following sections, namely working memory and perceptual aptitude.

Laboratory studies have shown that learners with greater phonological working memory take fewer trials to learn foreign language vocabulary (Cheung, 1996). Given the same exposure, they learn more words (Speciale, Ellis, & Bywater, 2004) and have greater success in learning new grammatical patterns (Martin & Ellis, 2012). Outside the lab, it appears that working memory can predict longitudinal gains in an academic term in receptive proficiency (Linck & Weiss, 2015; Sagarra, 2017) and spoken fluency (O'Brien, Segalowitz, Freed, & Collentine, 2007). Phonological working memory is supported by a set of anterior and posterior regions in the brain (Paulesu, Frith, & Frackowiak, 1993). Individual differences in memory-related activity within an anterior node of this network, the left insula, correlate significantly with individual differences in second language attainment (Chee, Soon, Lee, & Pallier, 2004), thus raising the possibility that part(s) of this network may serve as a marker for language talent (Perani, 2005). Evidence from animal and human studies suggests that the neurotransmitter dopamine plays an important role in working memory and executive functions (Nieoullon, 2002). Individual differences in working memory have been linked to genetic variants of dopamine-related genes (Egan et al., 2001; Rybakowski et al., 2005).

Many languages in the world, including those in East Asia, Southeast Asia, and Africa, use pitch patterns to mark word meanings (Yip, 2002). Pitch is a perceptual quality that reflects the highness or lowness of a sound. For example, the syllable / ma/ can have four different lexical meanings in Mandarin Chinese depending on the pitch. It means 'mother' when the pitch starts high and stays level for the duration of the syllable, 'scold' when started high then fallen low, 'hemp' when started middle then risen high, and 'horse' when started low and fallen lower before rising up. Two acoustic cues are important to the perception of these tones: pitch height (high, middle, low) and pitch direction (rising, falling). Native speakers of tone languages tend to weigh pitch direction more heavily than pitch height (Gandour, 1983). In our own work, we have found that native speakers of English who were naïve to lexical tones varied in how they weighed the two cues (Chandrasekaran, Sampath, & Wong, 2010). We and others have also found considerable individual differences in the learning of lexical tone vocabulary (Asaridou, Takashima, Dediu, Hagoort, & McQueen, 2016; Wong & Perrachione, 2007).

To identify predictors of individual differences in lexical tone vocabulary acquisition, we focused on *pretraining* variables that distinguished successful from less successful learners. Behavioral studies found that successful learners were better at identifying pitch patterns in a pitch pattern perception test administered before training (Wong & Perrachione, 2007). These learners also paid more attention to pitch direction, whereas less successful learners showed less marked difference in the relative weighting of pitch direction and pitch height (Chandrasekaran et al., 2010). Brain imaging studies found that successful learners had greater gray matter volume in the left Heschl's gyrus (Wong et al., 2008) and they activated the bilateral auditory cortex more than less successful learners (Wong, Perrachione, & Parrish, 2007). When we considered the three predictors, pitch pattern perception, bilateral auditory cortex activation, and left Heschl's gyrus volume—all measured before training was carried out—over half of the variance in vocabulary attainment was explained (61%; Wong et al., 2008). Removing each of these predictors from the regression model significantly affected the amount of variance explained, suggesting the importance of each. In a recent study, we further observed a significant association between pitch pattern perception and variants of a gene important for brain growth, the abnormal spindle-like microcephaly-associated (ASPM) gene, making *ASPM* a potential genetic marker for language acquisition involving pitch (Wong, Chandrasekaran, & Zheng, 2012; see also Dediu & Ladd, 2007).

Using Predictors to Optimize Language Learning

In a first step toward finding optimal training for individual learners, we compared the efficacy of two vocabulary training paradigms for learners with stronger and weaker perceptual aptitude (Perrachione, Lee, Ha, & Wong, 2011). Before training, we divided participants into two groups based on their pitch pattern perception performance: those with stronger perceptual aptitude (good perceivers) and those with weaker perceptual aptitude (poor perceivers). Members of each group were randomly assigned to either a low-variability or a high-variability training paradigm. In the low-variability condition, the words to be learned were spoken by a single talker. In the high-variability condition, the words to be learned were spoken by four different talkers whose tokens were intermixed within each training block. Partially consistent with previous findings, we found that high-variability training resulted in better vocabulary learning, but this was true only for good perceivers. In contrast, poor perceivers showed worse learning with high variability and superior learning when variability was limited (see Figure 17.3, left panel). Thus, as a predictor, pitch pattern perception can be used for placing tone language learners into more optimal training conditions.

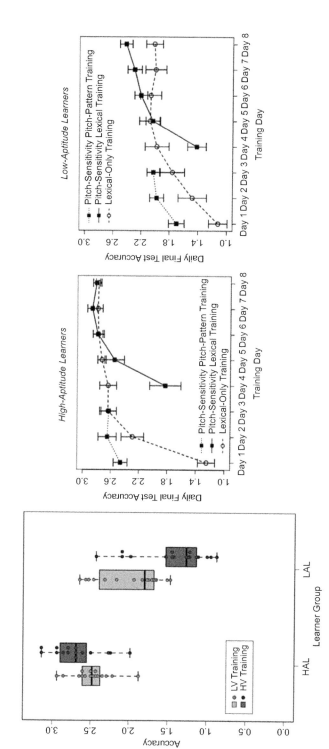

FIGURE 17.3 Reprinted with permission from "Learning a novel phonological contrast depends on interactions between individual differences and training paradigm design," by Perrachione et al., 2011, *The Journal of the Acoustical Society of America*, 130, p. 85, copyright 2011, Acoustic Society of America; and republished with permission of American Speech-Language-Hearing Association, from "Poorer phonetic perceivers show greater benefit in phonetic phonological speech learning," by Ingvalson, Barr, & Wong, 2013, *Journal of Speech, Language, and Hearing Research*, 56, p. 1047, copyright 2013; permission conveyed through Copyright Clearance Center, Inc.

These findings suggest that poor perceivers benefit from learning in an environment with lower perceptual demand. Are there other ways to help improve learning outcomes for poor perceivers? We reasoned that if suboptimal vocabulary acquisition was partly due to lower perceptual readiness for pitch patterns, then alleviating the perceptual demand by training learners to discriminate pitch patterns *before* lexical training might also help, even if lexical training then involved high variability. We thus focused on high-variability vocabulary training but compared the efficacy of lexical training alone to a staged training procedure—pitch training followed by lexical training (Ingvalson et al., 2013). The entire training took place over eight days for both groups. Both better and poorer perceivers in the latter group received pitch training on the first three days and lexical training on the last five days. Lexical-only groups received lexical training on all eight days. As Figure 17.3 (right panel) shows, staged training resulted in better vocabulary learning outcomes than lexical training alone for the learners with weaker perceptual aptitude. The benefit of receiving pitch training prior to lexical training was evident in daily training outcomes, as well as in a final generalization test. Learners with stronger perceptual aptitude performed well under both training conditions.

The interaction between "aptitudes and treatments" (DeKeyser, 2012) is not restricted to phonetic and vocabulary learning. Brooks, Kempe, and Sionov (2006) found significant relationships between working memory/fluid intelligence and the learning of Russian inflectional morphology only in the group receiving a large training vocabulary. Suzuki and DeKeyser (2017) found correlations between working memory and the learning of Japanese present progressive form in massed practice but not in distributed practice. Similarly, Yilmaz (2013) found that in learning Turkish locative and plural structures, how much and what type of feedback learners could benefit from depended on their working memory and language analytic ability. Moreover, interactions may also involve age and the linguistic structures to be learned (see DeKeyser, this volume). Therefore, in order for Personalized Learning to be fully realized, interactions among these factors must also be considered.

In the education field, the concept of learning style has received a lot of interest, although a review found that high-quality evidence for learning styles is virtually nonexistent (Pashler, Mcdaniel, Rohrer, & Bjork, 2008). This is primarily because the research reviewed failed to find a learner-by-instruction interaction. As an example, Massa and Mayer (2006) used numerous measures to classify participants according to the verbalizer-visualizer dimension. Measures included tests of spatial ability, learning preference, and cognitive style such as the Cognitive Style Analysis (Riding, 1991). Participants were randomly assigned to online science lessons differing in instruction format—instruction that used text definitions, presumably better suited for verbal learners, or instruction that used picture illustrations, presumably better suited for visual learners. Across three experiments with college students as well as nonstudent participants the authors found little evidence showing significant learning style × treatment interaction effects on learning results. By grounding our framework in biological and cognitive predictors and by aspiring to use the appropriate experimental methodology to demonstrate learner-by-instruction interaction under clear and uniform outcome measures, it is hoped that Personalized Learning will produce high-quality evidence that is directly applicable to teaching and education.

Issues and Challenges

The examples cited earlier provide some evidence for Personalized Learning as a concept, but extensive testing in both laboratory and authentic learning settings remains to be completed. Here we highlight some of the issues and challenges that need to be considered in implementing Personalized Learning.

Finding Predictors Across Multiple Sources

Personalized Learning requires identification of predictors that are both efficient and objective measures. While earlier studies have identified cognitive predictors, other objective measurements such as genetic testing remain to be explored. Clearly, one single-nucleotide polymorphism alone cannot be perfectly mapped onto behaviors. The genetic basis of complex traits, including learning and cognition, is widely recognized as multifaceted. The emphasis for future research is on identifying genotypic information from multiple sources along with neural and behavioral factors for predicting success in learning. Recent advances in the genetic basis of higher-order behaviors show great promise in helping to identify genetic pathways and environmental factors that shape human learning. The development of newer technologies such as whole-genome sequencing (Lupski et al., 2010) and analytic techniques (HYPERLINK "15031-2596-FullBook. docx" \l "Ref_1074_FILE150312596PV017" \o "(AutoLink):Manolio, T.A., Collins, F.S., Cox, N.J., Goldstein, D.B., Hindorff, L.A., Hunter, D.J., McCarthy, M.I., Ramos, E.M., Cardon, L.R., Chakravarti, A., Cho, J.H., Guttmacher, A.E., Kong, A., Kruglyak, L., Mardis, E., Rotimi, C.N., Slatkin, M., Valle, D., Whittemore, A.S., Boehnke, M., Clark, A.G., Eichler, E.E., Gibson, G., Haines, J.L., Mackay, T.F., McCarroll, S.A., & Visscher, P.M. (2009. Finding the missing heritability of complex diseases. Nature, 461, 747–753. UserName - DateTime: mbl-1/24/2019 11:22:36 PM" Manolio et al., 2009) will hopefully assist in finding the best predictors for Personalized Learning, as they can likely increase the sensitivity and specificity of the investigation.

Dynamics of Learning

In finding predictors, it is important to consider the dynamics of learning. The acquisition of a cognitive skill may proceed through a series of transitions, such as from declarative to procedural stages (Anderson, 1982). Language acquisition is an extraordinary feat that requires successful acquisition of multiple interrelated aspects—how words sound, what they mean, and how they can be combined into meaningful utterances. Each aspect may in turn involve a complex process of learning and consolidation. As each aspect develops, predictors of learning may change. For example, early stages of learning may place high demand on general cognitive abilities, as these abilities are required for understanding and performing the novel task. General cognitive factors may be highly predictive of individual differences in early learning. However, as cognitive demand decreases with task practice, the predictive power of general cognitive factors may decline (Ackerman, 1988). It is important to keep in mind the dynamics of learning in evaluating predictors of individual differences in learning.

Pathways to Optimization

Once predictors have been identified, how can they be used to place learners into the most optimal learning conditions? More concretely, once we have established that higher working memory (or stronger perceptual aptitude) predicts superior learning, what can we do to help improve learning outcomes among those with lower working memory (or those with weaker perceptual aptitude)? There are two broad ways by which optimization can be pursued: modify the training regimen or improve the underlying ability predictive of learning. In the first approach, training is changed so as to fit the learner's existing characteristics. Potential changes include reducing the perceptual/memory demand of the current training procedure or switching to a different training paradigm if viable aptitude × treatment interactions have been established (see also DeKeyser, this volume). In the second approach, the focus is on the learner. This approach seeks to help improve a learner's underlying ability as indexed by the relevant predictor. Evidence suggests that musical training may help sharpen basic perceptual sensitivities, which are beneficial to speech and language (Patel, 2011; Wong, Skoe, Russo, Dees, & Kraus, 2007). It also appears that targeted verbal working memory training may help improve verbal working memory performance to some degree (Holmes, Gathercole, & Dunning, 2009; Ingvalson, Dhar, Wong, & Liu, 2015).

Ecological Validity

As the vast majority of the studies cited are from laboratory studies, the ecological validity of the concept remains to be established. Although linking basic genetic information to authentic learning environments might seem far-fetched, one study has already demonstrated the increasing need of appropriate educational reading programs for children who are genetically predisposed to having reading problems (Taylor, Roehrig, Hensler, Connor, & Schatschneider, 2010). Taylor and colleagues examined oral reading fluency in monozygotic and dizygotic twin pairs in the Florida Twin Project on Reading. They found an interesting interaction between estimates of genetic variance and teaching quality in predicting reading achievement such that when teacher quality is higher, the genetic variance associated with reading increases. Thus, measurably, high-quality teaching is needed for learners to achieve their full genetic potential, at least as far as reading in authentic learning environments is concerned.

Ethical Considerations

Most critically, as in all research and practice concerning genetics and human performance, ethical considerations are paramount. The question addressed by Personalized Learning is not one that concerns who *can* or *cannot* learn, but rather one that seeks to determine how each and every individual can be provided with an optimal learning environment. It is worth mentioning the possibility that better cognitive abilities alone do not guarantee successful learning in all learning situations (Beilock & Carr, 2005; Decaro, Thomas, & Beilock, 2008). Individuals with higher working memory were found to require more trials to learn information-integration category structures compared to individuals with lower working memory; thus, higher working memory may sometimes result in less efficient learning (Decaro et al., 2008). This highlights the need to ascertain how training can be tailored to individuals in particular learning situations and domains. To achieve optimal learning for each learner, effective teaching could include a combination of common classroom learning, where all learners receive a set of core skills; smaller tutorial sessions for subgroups of learners with different learning needs; and an adaptive e-learning platform for personalizing additional learning, practice, and review. Thus, we do not advocate "segregation" of learners based on predictors of learning, but rather a form of inclusive learning that also recognizes the possibility that individual learners indeed learn differently and can benefit from different forms of learning support.

Conclusions

Research on second language acquisition has long observed individual differences in language learning success. As attested by the current volume, language aptitude research has provided an impressive wealth of empirical findings on predictors of individual differences. Central to Personalized Learning, and in accordance with the spirit of language aptitude research, we argue that it is critical for us to attend to individual differences in learning, to identify efficient and objective predictors of individual differences, and to use predictors to help design training paradigms that enable more effective learning at the individual level. In the end, we hope that this program of research will allow for better and more efficient learning for all learners.

Acknowledgments

We thank Robert DeKeyser, Peter Skehan, and Edward Wen for valuable comments. We also thank the Language Learning Small Grants Research Program (USA), National Institutes of Health (USA), National Science Foundation (USA), Research Grants Council (Hong Kong), Health and Medical Research Fund (Hong Kong), Global Parent Child Resource Centre Limited, and the Dr. Stanley Ho Medical Development Foundation for supporting our research over the years.

References

Ackerman, P. L. (1988). Determinants of individual differences during skill acquisition: Cognitive abilities and information processing. *Journal of Experimental Psychology General, 117,* 288–318.

Anderson, J. R. (1982). Acquisition of cognitive skill. *Psychological Review, 89,* 369–406.

Asaridou, S. S., Takashima, A., Dediu, D., Hagoort, P., & McQueen, J. M. (2016). Repetition suppression in the left inferior frontal gyrus predicts tone learning performance. *Cerebral Cortex, 26,* 2728–2742.

Bates, E., Dale, P., & Thal, D. (1995). Individual differences and their implications for theories of language development. In P. Fletcher & B. MacWhinney (Eds.), *The handbook of child language* (pp. 96–151). Oxford: Basil Blackwell.

Beilock, S. L., & Carr, T. H. (2005). When high-powered people fail: Working memory and "choking under pressure" in math. *Psychological Science, 16,* 101–105.

Brooks, P. J., & Kempe, V. (2012). Individual differences in adult Foreign language learning: The mediating effect of metalinguistic awareness. *Memory & Cognition, 41,* 281–296.

Brooks, P. J., Kempe, V., & Sionov, A. (2006). The role of learner and input variables in learning inflectional morphology. *Applied Psycholinguistics, 27,* 185–209.

Chandrasekaran, B., Sampath, P. D., & Wong, P. C. M. (2010). Individual variability in cue-weighting and lexical tone learning. *The Journal of the Acoustical Society of America, 128,* 456–565.

Chee, M. W. L, Soon, C. S., Lee, H. L., & Pallier, C. (2004). Left insula activation: A marker for language attainment in bilinguals. *Proceedings of the National Academy of Sciences, 101,* 15265–15270.

Cheung, H. (1996). Nonword span as a unique predictor of second-language vocabulary language. *Developmental Psychology, 32,* 867–873.

Dąbrowska, E. (2012). Different speakers, different grammars. *Linguistic Approaches to Bilingualism, 2,* 219–253.

Decaro, M. S., Thomas, R. D., & Beilock, S. L. (2008). Individual differences in category learning: Sometimes less working memory capacity is better than more. *Cognition, 107,* 284–294.

Dediu, D., & Ladd, D. R. (2007). Linguistic tone is related to the population frequency of the adaptive haplogroups of two brain size genes, ASPM and Microcephalin. *Proceedings of the National Academy of Sciences, 104,* 10944–10949.

DeKeyser, R. (2012). Interactions between individual differences, treatments, and structures in SLA. *Language Learning, 62,* 189–200.

Egan, M. F., Goldberg, T. E., Kolachana, B. S., Callicott, J. H., Mazzanti, C. M., Straub, R. E., . . . Weinberger, D. R. (2001). Effect of COMT Val108/158 Met genotype on frontal lobe function and risk for schizophrenia. *Proceedings of the National Academy of Sciences, 98,* 6917–6922.

Ettlinger, M., Bradlow, A. R., & Wong, P. C. M. (2012). Variability in the learning of complex morphophonology. *Applied Psycholinguistics, 35,* 807–831.

Flege, J. E., Yeni-Komshian, G. H., & Liu, S. (1999). Age constraints on second-language acquisition. *Journal of Memory and Language, 41,* 78–104.

Gandour, J. (1983). Tone perception in Far Eastern languages. *Journal of Phonetics, 11,* 149–175.

Golestani N., & Zatorre R. J. (2009). Individual differences in the acquisition of second language phonology. *Brain and Language, 109,* 55–67.

Holmes, J., Gathercole, S. E., & Dunning, D. L. (2009). Adaptive training leads to sustained enhancement of poor working memory in children. *Developmental Science, 12,* F9–F15.

Ingvalson, E. M., Barr, A. M., & Wong, P. C. M. (2013). Poorer phonetic perceivers show greater benefit in phonetic-phonological speech learning. *Journal of Speech, Language, and Hearing Research, 56,* 1045–1050.

Ingvalson, E. M., Dhar, S., Wong, P. C. M., & Liu, H. (2015). Working memory training to improve speech perception in noise across languages. *The Journal of the Acoustical Society of America, 137,* 3477–3486.

Linck, J. A., & Weiss, D. J. (2015). Can working memory and inhibitory control predict second language learning in the classroom? *Sage Open, 5,* 1–11.

Lupski, J. R., Reid, J. G., Gonzaga-Jauregui, C., Rio Deiros, D., Chen, D. C., Nazareth, L., . . . Gibbs, R. A. (2010). Whole-genome sequencing in a patient with Charcot-Marie-Tooth neuropathy. *The New England Journal of Medicine, 362,* 1181–1191.

Manolio, T. A., Collins, F. S., Cox, N. J., Goldstein, D. B., Hindorff, L. A., Hunter, D. J., . . . Visscher, P. M. (2009. Finding the missing heritability of complex diseases. *Nature, 461,* 747–753.

Martin, K. I., & Ellis, N. C. (2012). The roles of phonological short-term memory and working memory in L2 grammar and vocabulary learning. *Studies in Second Language Acquisition, 34,* 379–413.

Massa, L. J., & Mayer, R. E. (2006). Testing the ATI hypothesis: Should multimedia instruction accommodate verbalizer-visualizer cognitive style? *Learning and Individual Differences, 16,* 321–336.

Nieoullon, A. (2002). Dopamine and the regulation of cognition and attention. *Progress in Neurobiology, 67,* 53–83.

O'Brien, I., Segalowitz, N., Freed, B., & Collentine, J. (2007). Phonological memory predicts second language oral fluency gains in adults. *Studies in Second Language Acquisition, 29,* 557–582.

Pashler, H., Mcdaniel, M., Rohrer, D., & Bjork, R. (2008). Learning styles: Concepts and evidence. *Psychological Science, 9,* 105–119.

Patel, A. D. (2011). Why would musical training benefit the neural encoding of speech? The OPERA hypothesis. *Frontiers in Psychology, 2,* 142. doi:10.3389/fpsyg.2011.00142

Paulesu, E., Frith, C. D., & Frackowiak, R. S. (1993). The neural correlates of the verbal component of working memory. *Nature, 362,* 342–345.

Perani, D. (2005). The neural basis of language talent in bilinguals. *Trends in Cognitive Sciences, 9,* 211–213.

Perrachione, T. K., Lee, J., Ha, L. Y., & Wong, P. C. (2011). Learning a novel phonological contrast depends on interactions between individual differences and training paradigm design. *The Journal of the Acoustical Society of America, 130,* 461–472.

Riding, R. J. (1991). *Cognitive styles analysis*. Birmingham, UK: Learning and Training Technology.

Rybakowski, J. K., Borkowska, A., Czerski, P. M., Kapelski, P., Dmitrzak-Weglarz, M., & Hauser, J. (2005). An association study of dopamine receptors polymorphisms and the Wisconsin card sorting test in schizophrenia. *Journal of Neural Transmission, 112,* 1575–1582.

Sagarra, N. (2017). Longitudinal effects of working memory on L2 grammar and reading abilities. *Second Language Research, 33,* 341–363.

Speciale, G., Ellis, N., & Bywater, T. (2004). Phonological sequence learning and short-term store capacity determine second language vocabulary acquisition. *Applied Psycholinguistics, 25,* 293–321.

Suzuki, Y., & DeKeyser, R. (2017). Exploratory research on second language practice distribution: An Aptitude × Treatment interaction. *Applied Psycholinguistics, 38,* 27–56.

Taylor, J., Roehrig, A. D., Hensler, S. B., Connor, C. M., & Schatschneider, C. (2010). Teacher quality moderates the genetic effects on early reading. *Science, 328,* 512–514.

Wong, P. C. M., Chandrasekaran, B., & Zheng, J. (2012). The derived allele of ASPM is associated with lexical tone perception. *PloS One, 7,* e34243.

Wong, P. C. M., & Perrachione, T. K. (2007). Learning pitch patterns in lexical identification by native English-speaking adults. *Applied Psycholinguistics, 28,* 565–585.

Wong, P. C. M., Perrachione, T. K., & Parrish, T. B. (2007). Neural characteristics of successful and less successful speech and word learning in adults. *Human Brain Mapping, 28,* 995–1006.

Wong, P. C. M., Skoe, E., Russo, N. M., Dees, T., & Kraus, N. (2007). Musical experience shapes human brainstem encoding of linguistic pitch patterns. *Nature Neuroscience, 10,* 420–422.

Wong, P. C. M., Vuong, L. C., & Liu, K. (2017). Personalized learning: From neurogenetics of behaviors to designing optimal language training. *Neuropsychologia, 98,* 192–200.

Wong, P. C. M., Warrier, C. M., Penhune, V. B., Roy, A. K., Sadehh, A., Parrish, T. B., & Zatorre, R. J. (2008). Volume of left Heschl's gyrus and linguistic pitch learning. *Cerebral Cortex, 18,* 828–836.

Yilmaz, Y. (2013). Relative effects of explicit and implicit feedback: The role of working memory capacity and language analytic ability. *Applied Linguistics, 34,* 344–368.

Yip, M. (2002). *Tone*. Cambridge, MA: Cambridge University Press.

INDEX